The Last of the Gnostic Masters

A Novel

By *Thomas Sawyer Spivey*

This book is an open challenge
to Christianity.

PUBLISHED AND DISTRIBUTED
— BY —
THOMAS SAWYER SPIVEY
BEVERLY HILLS, CALIFORNIA

Price $2.50 the Copy.

Dedicated to

The great masses of humanity chained to the wheels of eternal physical drudgery; dragging the chariots of the godly great, and too weary in body and soul to delve into the world of books and the realms of individual thought for the knowledge so essential to give them a true understanding of the purposes of human existence.

We especially seek to give vision and understanding to those who, "seeing they do not perceive; and hearing they do not understand."

—Mark 4:11-12.

OTHER BOOKS

— BY —

THOMAS SAWYER SPIVEY

INDEX TO CHAPTERS

PREFACE

In publishing this book we are challenging the forces which have set all the precedents for modern human governments, therefore we are opening wide the door for that rampant "righteous indignation" which assails him who has the courage to demand a show-down in the business of governing the world, and an explanation of the horrible conditions which beset men under our ruling systems, after two thousand years of promises.

Why should one man point to the earth and say to another, "Kneel in my presence, I am divinely appointed your master?"

Because, in an age of ignorance, humanity was taught by vain, conceited hypocrites, that some men are gods and others their slaves.

This theory insults nature and cheats mankind. The world is enslaved to an invisible power which may, not be reached by ordinary processes—Ecclesiasticism is its name, Christianity its shield, and weak governments its working machinery.

How many persons know the origin of the word ecclesia? What has it to do with Christianity? This was the original, concealed priesthood which conceived a theocratic form of government, to be made universal, and to rule and exploit humanity for profit and self-glorification.

The word *Ecclesia* is from the Greek, signifying the legislative body which ruled ancient Athens.

Catholic means *universal.*

The word *bishop* belonged to the Athenian ecclesia, meaning a *ward inspector.*

"That which is of the church is holy" has been hammered into humanity with every stroke of the bigoted power which riveted the irons of slavery upon men.

"The church is firmly established by divine power, and endowed with the godly authority," is the answer to every inquiry regarding its legal status.   What folly!

Could any one reasonably expect to hold a logical discussion with fanatics?

When the word fanatic is applied to a pious fakir, his upraised hands drop to the attitude of a pugilist, for no man likes to be charged with being in some degree an imbecile.   But, when the facts and palpable results of fanaticism are thrust under his nose, he pauses.   What is the difference between a fanatic on a given subject, and vainly advocating the dogmas of known fanatics?

We say a vast difference!

One need not be a fanatic to advocate the cause of fanatics; he may be a knave.

We shall not give any one an opportunity to say we are fanatical.   We are not exploiting any new form of religion; we are not forwarding any propaganda; we are not advocating any other cause than natural human rights, and we are not imbued with an ambition to shine either as a hero or a martyr.   Moreover, we view any form of *vicarious sacrifice* as a species of insanity. *Altruism* is a political snare, and maintains an endless number of parasitic bodies.

Chauvinism is but an hysterical outburst of fanatical or false patriotism to conceal ulterior fear of the powers which inspire the intolerant mob. Hypocrisy, greed, vanity, selfishness and hatred conceal themselves behind all such specious and unnatural sentimentality. Ecclesiasticism lives, thrives and fattens upon such stuff.

Sophistry is more potent and pliable than intrigue, when dealing with ignorant masses, therefore, when we find sophistry conspicuous in the defense of a cause, we may at once know that duplicity lurks in the background. Credulous humanity is the victim of sophistry. As long as physical slavery and "self-sacrifice" are preached as the saviors of mankind, duplicity will thrive. Human energy, and what it creates, are the sole objects of all selfish institutions dispensing this "sob stuff" to its own hysterical weaklings.

Humanity has been driven as "sheep" and herded as "cattle" long enough. The gaping crowd should be told that "sheep" mean disciples, and *"cattle"* mean *capital,* in the ecclesiastical code.

Moreover, the masses of ignorant, credulous people, who have no time or opportunity to themselves learn the truth, should be told the truth.

Jesus is the Greek form of *Joshua.*

Joseph means *increase.*

Sephar means *numbers.*

Jo is an abbreviation of *Joseph.*

Shua means *wealth.*

Jo-Shua means *increased wealth,* the *savior* and *salvation* of ecclesiasticism and Christianity.

We shall enlarge upon this throughout our story.

There must be a motive for writing a book of this character. Let us be frank. We have found Christianity a snare, and a tremendous failure, as an ethical force. Its own eternal accusation against mankind proves this.

Proof? Why ask for proof, with the visible evidence everywhere, every day, and indisputable? After two thousand years of church fanaticism we find ourselves smothered in all that makes life a burden. The world is in a state of turmoil; war stalks mankind on every turn; crime, imbecility and groveling ignorance are everywhere; they cannot be escaped. Our courts are overcrowded, our prisons are overflowing, yet the mills of the gods go grinding merrily on, smothering humanity in statutory, criminal laws, adding new classes to the already endless variety of criminals.

Who are clamoring for more laws to crush humanity down into abject terrorism? The clergy! The church! The Sunday blue laws are infamous crimes in themselves.

There must also be a motive for this drastic chastisement of men. What is it?

Did it ever occur to you, reader, that it was Christianity which introduced evil into the world? That damnable doctrine of "original sin" must be vindicated, else the church stands convicted. It was aware of this originally. It must break humanity, bring all men under sin, and choke off resentment by bringing them under the law which forbids free speech. The constant grind of statutory criminal laws is the process.

"Now we know that what things soever the law saith, it saith to them who are under the law: that *every mouth may be stopped, and all the world may become guilty.*" (Rom. 3:19.)

"Because the law worketh wrath: for where no law is, there is no transgression." (Rom. 4:15.)

Without crime and sin the church could not exist. It has amassed wealth to the extent of billions of dollars, upon which it pays no taxation. Today it is competing with honest labor by conducting secret manufacturing institutions on a tremendous scale. If not checked it will absorb the wealth of the world. Why should struggling humanity have to compete with a great, non-taxed monopoly?

We are particularly interested in conditions in the United States, for here is where the culmination is to occur; here is the Babylon of the world system where all nations assemble under one government.

Babylon means *mixture* and *confusion.*

This is the concealing cloud behind which ecclesiasticism hides.

Pause a moment, reader, and think of the shame of it; two thousand years after the introduction of Christianity, accident of war revealed that twenty per cent of the adult population of the United States are in a state of abject ignorance.

The world stands aghast to hear broadcasted over the radio the yawping evangelist, gleefully declaring that there are but five thousand recognized scientists in the whole world of more than two billion human beings.

Directly preceding Christianity the most brilliant scientific and philosophic schools thrived. Christianity suppressed all this and began burning at the stake those who advocated the higher education and the enlightenment of the masses of humanity.

This is authentic, historical fact.

For a thousand years (486 to 1495) the world was smothered in ignorance.

There was a motive for this drastic debasement of mankind. It was to bring all men down to a common level, to be worked into a plastic mass. The unit man had to be suppressed, that all original thought should arise in the priesthood.

Ecclesiasticism seized control of the temporal power over European monarchs, through a control over their peoples, and maintained this supremacy for nearly five centuries.

The salvation of Christianity was the discovery of the Western Hemisphere, where it has builded a power which no man can measure.

England, the strongest nation in Europe, drove out Catholicism. Nearly every nation in Europe expelled the Catholic, secret service system, Jesuitry. Both came to America, where they have developed a secret empire amidst a conglomerate mass of nationalities; made a working alliance with Protestantism; formed a strong alliance with predatory commercial forces, and have intruded their influences into the national politics to such an extent that they boast of influencing the most vital legislation of the country.

Result: Europe is writhing in the agonies of dissolution and the United States is smothered in crime, ignorance, imbecility and taxation.

We are going to deal with the most prolific period in the development of this all devouring power. We are lending romance to our story to relieve our readers of dry, monotonous routine. There is plenty of good material, and we shall follow the facts woven together by appropriate fiction to give it spice.

We have made a technical analysis of the history of the period treated, and a translation of the Bible by the ecclesiastical code, as our foundation. We have had at our disposal endless commentaries, codes, dictionaries and vocabularies. This will be a revelation to those who have given no thought to so vital a subject.

Gnosticism was the cumulative, scientific and philosophic learning up to the time of the introduction of Chritsianity.

Gnosis means *to know, knowledge.*

Christianity means *to believe, ignorance.*

It required five hundred years for Christianity to suppress gnosticism.

THE AUTHOR.

CHAPTER I
SATAN LOOSED

THE HAND OF USURPATION KNOWS NEITHER HONOR
NOR MERCY.

DOUBTLESS nature intended that the evolution of human enlightenment like the evolution of all living systems, should follow the line of least resistance in the acquirement of sustaining food; providing the best protection against dangers to the physical body, and the safeguarding of the broadest individual liberty in the pursuit of knowledge, peace, comfort, happiness and general prosperity, for the aggregate body. It is a self-evident fact, that, without such cumulative mental advantage, man could not have risen above the unthinking reptile or beast; hence, he could not have evoluted to the higher state—a natural promotion.

Memory is the tabulated record of cumulative facts, gathered by the external sense organs, and stored in the brain and body for future reference in physical progression, the record of experiences —this is traditional education.

This proves, beyond dispute, that, nature intended to develop a visible evolution by a unit system, first subject to the survival of the physically fittest, and rising to the mentally fittest, which is man, the super being, capable of individual, initiative thought, reason, judgment and self-support. If this were not true, each individual would not be independently endowed with identical, like organs. Knowledge and understanding are food for the process of mentation as much as material substances are food for physical upkeep and development; therefore, to deprive mankind of his natural individual powers to acquire knowledge and understanding, by initiative methods, is to imprison his mind, and subject him to the will and judgment of external minds seeking to bend his physical development to their purposes at the expense of mental or intellectual evolution.

This is why Christianity is so radically opposed to evolution. Its own God is derived from a process of elimination, exactly corresponding to the system of animal evolution. By elimination, the survival of the fittest establishes the fittest as the highest production of the system up to the *Jehovah*, the self-sustaining man.

Let us apply this to the development of the Christian God. To say he existed before the advent of Christianity and did not make himself manifest to humanity, would be too preposterous for belief, for that would condemn untold millions of mankind who did not know God. For only through Christ could God "reconcile mankind to himself." (11 Cor. 5:21.)

Hence, the Christian God must be an evoluted thing.

The Bible very plainly gives us that evolution. The worship of the *sun*. (Ps. 19:4.)

The worship of *fire*.   (Heb. 12:29.)

The worship of *light*.   (Jno. 8:12.)

The worship of God through Christ as *personified human intellect*.

"Christ is the wisdom of God."   (1 Cor. 1:24.)

And, to clinch this, and eliminate all other forms of God, Christ is worshiped by the modern Christians as God upon earth, as embodied, and personified, in the head of the church—contrary to their own teachings.

If Christ is the head of the Church (Col. 1:18), it is evident that the head of the Church is Christ.

This was all worked out by a process of elimination and the survival of the intellectually fittest in mankind, contrary to the intent of nature to culminate her work in equal human units.

This very clearly explains why these selfish brutes desired to deprive humanity at large of the higher education; they could no longer pose as all-knowing gods. Every man would become a Christ were all men equally wise. "Behold the man is become as one of us." (Gen. 3:22.)   This was uttered by the head of the priesthood.

This same evolution is specifically found where any form of progression is necessary in the system.

Prophecy is especially subject to a progressive personification of church attitudes and forces.

The line of major prophets and their functions:

        Isaiah = the salvation of the Lord.

        Jeremiah = the grandeur of the Lord.

        Ezekiel = the strength of the Lord.

        Daniel = the judgment of the Lord.

Hosea = the help of the Lord.

Joel = the will of the Lord.

Obadiah = the servant of the Lord.

This foretells a state of servitude for the masses in the support of the system.

The major prophets symbolize the direct attributes and agents of the Lord—the master of the order; the loaf warden; the high priest, and head of the church.

The suffix *iah*, terminating several of these names, signifies *light* or *fire*. The suffix *el* means *power*. This signifies the combined power of intellect and judgment.

The minor prophets mean quite a different thing, symbolizing action:

Jonah = he that oppresses.

Micah = he that humbles.

Nahum = he that comforts.

Habakkuk = he that persuades.

Zaphaniah = he who discovers secrets (confessional).

Haggi = he who gives impressiveness.

Zechariah = he who remembers.

Malachi = God's messenger.

Palpably, this line of so-called prophets conceals a premeditated scheme of propaganda and procedure as the priestly instructions for the inner circle.

This is sufficient, here, to reveal the nature of our interpretations which will be found throughout our story.

That mankind has been shamefully deceived, and debased, there can be no shadow of a doubt. He has been treated as a beast of burden, and made the *footstool* of a mean, hypocritical, designing institution.

The first ten words in the bible prove that it was premeditated.

"In the beginning God created the heaven and the earth." (Gen. 1:1.)

Christianity is founded upon an elaborate system of personification, to conceal its true character and purposes. It is convicted by its own code. *Heaven* means an *ecclesiastical government. Earth* means *producing humanity. God* is the *head of the church,* and he proposes to place all humanity "beneath his feet." It goes without argument that, if God has feet he is human, or else a lower animal.

"The earth is the Lord's." (Ex. 9:29.)

"As for the earth, out of it cometh bread." (Job 28:5.)

"Then shall the earth yield her increase." (Ps. 67:6.)

"Behold the Lord maketh the earth empty." (Is. 24:1.)

This specifically refers to the condition of ignorance which befell the people for a thousand years after the introduction of Christianity.

"The earth is utterly broken down." (Isa. 24:19.)

"The earth shall reel to and fro like a drunkard." (Isa. 24:20.)

"The Lord shall punish the kings of the earth." (Isa. 24:21.)

It is evident that the earth here signifies the people ruled by kings, called *beasts.*"

"And the tree of the field shall yield its fruit, and the earth shall yield her increase, and they shall be safe in their land, and shall know that I am the Lord when I have broken their yoke." (Eze. 34:27.)

This clearly identifies the *earth* as the people, for *trees* mean the *great nobles, land* means a *state or condition.*

"The first man is of the earth earthy; the second man is the Lord from heaven." (I Cor. 15:47.)

"Thus saith the Lord, the heaven (ecclesiastical government), is my throne, and the earth (producing humanity), is my footstool." (Isa. 66:1.)

We challenge the defenders of Christianity to refute what we have here revealed.

This attitude toward humanity was diametrically opposed to the intent and purpose of nature, and it explains why Christianity opposes the theory of consecutive animal evolution.

Man, the highest type of animal creation, was endowed by nature with reason of a higher degree than that possessed by the lower animals. Must we ignore this truth? No!

Reasoning man is the crowning act in a natural and well-defined evolution. Only by reason could the natural animal instincts be eradicated from man to promote him to a higher and nobler purpose. Deprive mankind of individual thought and reason, and he quickly reverts to the original animalism.

It was originally intended that thought and reason should supercede the mechanical, animal instinct, and sagacity should take the place of savage brute force. This was the one great desideratum of nature, to establish a state of harmonious balance among living beings, *reason being the only means for averting com-*

petition and antagonism, as between like units, and establishing peace.

To the contrary, these contrasts were actually set up and cultivated, encouraged and applauded among men, to create a state of confusion behind which predatory forces might conceal themselves, bending from one side to the other, as a balancing power in the affairs of mankind. Therefore, the church is as much an enemy to *reason* as it is to *evolution;* moreover, it has always inspired warfare.

That it was a premeditated intent and purpose to make discontent, and conflict among men, allies to the ecclesiastic enterprise, is made plain by their own confession regarding future conditions.

"And ye shall hear of wars and rumors of wars, for all these things must come to pass.

"For nation shall rise against nation, and kingdom against kingdom." (Matt. 24:6, 7.)

There has not been one single day of peace upon earth since the introduction of Christianity—it was not intended there should be. This is definitely declared by words placed in the mouth of the figurative Christ himself:

"Think not that I am come to send peace on earth: I come not to send peace, but a sword.

"For I am come to set a man at variance with his father, and the daughter against her mother." (Matt. 10:34, 35.)

He was not the savior of souls; he employed his followers as snares.

"Come ye after me, and I will make you to become fishers of men." (Mark 1:17.)

"Prince of peace!" Bah! What rot! After two thousand years of this, the world lies in ruins. Christ has kept his faith; the most sacred ties of blood kin have been ruthlessly torn asunder, and children scoff at their own parents as they drink of cultivated and inspired crime, to vindicate the doctrine of "original sin," to save the face of the church.

Humanity is shriveling up under the withering fires of the Christian hell.

It does not reflect to the credit of mankind that it has tamely submitted to being brought under abject brute control, and ignoble servitude, through its own credulity. A superstitious fear of an unknown authority, having the power to kill, has done its deadly work. Physical coercion, and mental terrorism, are the inherited foundation stones of all human government, and these are the breeders of moral cowardice and all the evils which beset mankind.

"But I will forewarn you whom ye shall fear: Fear him which after he hath killed hath power to cast into hell; yea, I say unto you, Fear him." (Luke 12:5.)

This is the baleful stuff which has deprived humanity of its reason.

Hell means *death* and the *grave*. Death is called the *destroyer*.

Paul originally was named *Saul*, meaning the *destroyer* and the *grave*.

Paul means *the church worker;* hence, the fear of death and the grave becomes a church agent, and a foundation stone in the church.

Yet, in the same breath, while teaching this doctrine, Christ warns against hypocrisy.

Under this vile influence is it any wonder that the present theory of human control is proven a fallacy and a failure?

Personal restraint begets mental fear and uncertainty, leading to many forms of insanity.

Vengeance, merely to vindicate the law, is a horrible error, and leads to major crime and contempt for law. Morality has never been legislated into men, but universal crime has been made by a multitude of criminal statutes, only too often placed upon the books for the profit they yield. There is no difference between the *sale of criminal indulgences* and a *system of fines and licenses,* both set a price, upon classified crime.

Terrorism does not beget respect, it inspires soul destroying fear, and nourishes secret hatred and evil.

Nature provides one avenue of relief for men hampered, restrained, irritated, persecuted and insulted by bigoted powers of control, based upon divine authority; they can think in secrecy; they may curse their persecutors with full assurance that no one can punish them as long as their thoughts are unspoken—provided they are not Hittites.

Hundreds of millions of innocent human beings have been wantonly tortured and murdered, and untold millions of property and treasure confiscated, in a bitter determination to erect a super-power to control and exploit mankind for the vital energy which may be coaxed, coerced and tortured out of him.

During the fifteenth, sixteenth and seventeenth centuries an orgy of bloodshed and terrorism swept Europe, blackened ruins dotting the lands once covered by happy, peace-abiding communities.

During many gloomy centuries, Europe actually ate the fruits of her soil, fertilized with the blood of her own people. Blood-spattered trails led directly to the doors of the perpetrators of these crimes of arson, plunder and wanton murder.

It is of that fanatical period we shall write, portraying the horrors of Christian hysteria inspired by besotted fiends, drunken with the frenzy of a blood-lust to kill all who would not worship Satan disguised beneath a lamb's skin.

Back of it sat that coterie of bigoted, hellish ghouls whose history is too vile to be printed, softly purring their instructions to the leaders of the hysterical mob.

Our descriptions of this awful period are composite pictures, greatly modifying the truths and facts of history, because they are too horrible to relate. It would be impossible to exaggerate the fiendish butcheries of the periods of the crusades and the Inquisition. No authority attempts to deny that popery was responsible for these ungodly things. The history of the popes specifically records their responsibility, under their blasphemous cry:

"It is the will of God."

Humanity should rise as one man and curse such an unnatural and preposterous God of hate and bloodshed.

CHAPTER II

THE RAPE OF PAMPERO

Hell Hath No Wrath Like a Strong Man's Grief

THE happy and peaceful little community of Pampero, situated in northern Spain, was snugly tucked away in a sun-kissed valley at the juncture of a tumbling little mountain stream with the more imposing river Ebro. Its rich soil was under a high state of cultivation, producing the necessities and good things of life sufficient to maintain the people, and provide a surplus to send to outside markets to be bartered for other needful commodities. Rich pastures provided for their flocks, and well kept vineyards and orchards covered the available hillsides.

Here was as nearly a replica of the original idea of the Garden of Eden as could be found in treacherous Europe. The people were happy, prosperous and progressive; a worthy example to the nations. Its mode of life was exemplary; it had no crime, no poverty and no ignorance, thanks to its noble founder and patron, for he had, from the beginning, implanted in the colony a desire for education, art and music, which raised them far above the average peoples of other places at this generally benighted period, when the rising sun of intelligence was struggling to pierce through the clouds of superstition and bigoted intolerance.

Pampero, especially, was not cursed by any form of religion, the government assuming all moral and ethical responsibility in the conduct of the people. Few laws, and much liberty ruled and harmony prevailed.

No God in heaven or earth could find a reasonable excuse for criticising this delightful people.

By some miracle it had been overlooked by the ghouls of Rome; at least, it had escaped the ravages of the plundering crusaders scouring Europe— a system of licensed brigandage.

The founder and Patriarch of Pampero was the good, sturdy, fatherly Don Alvard de Balde, whose sister was the wife of the very Catholic Count Bertram, Lord of Ognez, in the province of Guipuscoa.

Don Alvard had spent much of his early life in travel, consequently he had not become identified with, or involved in, the poisonous religio-political intrigues which were bent on leveling Europe in a sea of corruption and dishonor. He had not attached himself to the fanatical religious movements which gripped the civilized world, and throttled human progress.

Being most happily married, he was determined to live a life of peace and joy, therefore he avoided entanglements and disagreements with his zealous brother-in-law, by gathering together a few close and trusted friends and retiring to this secluded valley. Here they planted the colony of Pampero, which rapidly developed into a prosperous and happy community.

Don Alvard had a devoted and accomplished wife, a beautiful daughter, and a splendid son just budding into manhood.

God himself would have been guilty of a wilful crime, had he been the one who destroyed this perfect family and meddled with this peaceful and contented commununity.

No complaints concerning Pampero had reached Rome, doubtless because of its obscurity, therefore, the people dwelt in apparent safety.

Sad to relate, however, in those evil times which tried the souls of men, the reward for deeds done in the name of blood-thirsty institutions was rapine and pillage, hence the most trivial incidence brought unexpected disaster.

No communiuty, family nor individual, was immune against the ravages of the savage bands of irresponsible criminals, prowling over southern Europe under the name of crusaders, and garbed in the vestures of the pontifical troops. Never, in all the history of the world was a more irresponsible horde of vampires and bandits turned loose to plunder helpless humanity, and this in the name of Christ and his holy church.

It was licensed brigandage, with no semblance of legality or justice back of it, other than the will of the Pope. Moreover, sovereigns dared not raise a voice of protest, such was the pontifical prestige.

Don Alvard's son, also named Alvard, had been carefully trained by his father and mother, who were both persons of culture, and he was a bright and promising youth, full of life, keen of intellect, and, withal, an extraordinary athlete,

At the age of twenty, young Alvard was a tall, angular, big-boned lad, bidding fair to develop into a giant; he was the pride of his parents and the favorite of Pampero. The time of all times in the life of young men was at hand, the turning point between adolescence and sedate manhood; the point where ambition ceases, or looks far into the distance with eager anticipation.

Alvard was already a well educated young man. His father had taken him into his confidence and had warned him of the dangers of the religious frenzy which was entangling nations, and submerging the unthinking masses in the fanaticism of a woefully erroneous system which dared not confess its mistakes. There was but one formula for the church— *rule or ruin*. It could not compromise without confessing error, and this the proud and arrogant men, posing as Gods, at Rome, would never do. The future held no promise of better conditions for the people.

After a period of preparation, the father personally took the son to friends in Barcelona, and entered him in the great University located at this historic old city, where Ferdinand and Isabella greeted Columbus upon his return from his first expedition to America.

By a prudent understanding Alvard was to privately take a course in theology, that he might be able to understand the burning question of the period when he had completed his course and taken his place in the world.

He stood manfully up to all of his proud father's expectations, and was preparing for his return to his home, when he received the sad news of his father's death. He had been four years at college, which time had made a tremendous change in him; he was no longer a youth, but a strong, resolute, self-reliant man.

To the amazement of Pampero, a giant arrived in their midst—they could scarcely believe their own eyes. The big, growing boy had flowered into a splendid man, seven feet tall, and large of body in proportion; broad of shoulders, deep chested, and possessed of superhuman, physical strength, withal, a courage and mental strength which presaged some extraordinary future. A clean-souled, brave-hearted, courageous man had stepped into the worthy boots of his sire, and Pampero was proud of him.

He soon dispelled the gloom which had settled over the community because of the death of the Patriarch, and had even brought cheerfulness back into the sad hearts of his own household, at once becoming the successor of his beloved father as the advisor of the community. In Barcelona he had been named the giant philosopher, and the most dangerous swordsman in all Europe, even at his youthful age.

After the first grief and mourning, at the loss of the good husband, kind father, and wise coun-

selor, had subsided, Alvard settled to the task of
caring for his mother and sister, not neglecting to
spend a goodly portion each day, in research and
study, in the splendid library left him by his father.
His broader glimpse of the world had changed his
views regarding the future. He had seen a pall of
gloom settling over Europe which boded evil to mankind. It was a curious fact, that, it threatened all
alike, Christian and heathen; the Godly hordes were
no respecter of persons. Christianity had apparently
attempted to culminate its enterprise and reap its
harvest, by loosing Satan in the world. He feared
for Pampero, but kept his fears well guarded.

Ominous reports were drifting into Pampero,
of persecution and massacres sweeping Europe. To
this innocent hearted people it was all a mystery.
They could not understand such wickedness, and
Alvard thought it best not to enlighten them. They
did not dream that, they, too, might fall victims
to this hellish stream of hate, they not being attached to any religious system.

It is from a clear sky the unexpected lightning
comes.

Don Alvard kept to himself the well grounded
fears which beset his own heart; he knew that the license granted to the murderous bands gave them the
privilege to kill Christians and non-believers alike,
under the Satanic cry placed in their mouths by the
Pope himself, "God will save his own." He also
knew that the chief-devil at Rome had absolved
these criminal marauders in advance, for any crimes

committed in the name of Christ and the church. The vatican soldiers had for ages been the collected scum of the earth. During the tenth and eleventh centuries the popes had openly advertised, that, those who joined in the crusades would have all their crimes forgiven and cancelled. This emptied all the prisons of Europe, and forbid the apprehension of the most vicious of criminals, allegedly on their way to join the crusades. The result was, that, Europe was flooded with the vilest types of men, brazenly taking advantage of papal dispensation.

It grieved Alvard's heart to know this, why grieve others?

Robbery and outrage were rampant and uncontrolled. The paid and licensed mob-at-arms had taken the place of the inspired, local mobs, because the latter too willingly fell into line in self-defense, leaving fewer to be plundered.

Might had succeeded cunning and intrigue, and brazen impudence had taken the place of ironical politeness. The church had cast off its mask and stood armed and prepared; the troops of Gad had crossed the Jordan to challenge humanity at large. Secretly, all the rulers in Europe had alligned themselves with the church and stood watching the scourge, if not openly aiding and abetting it.

This attitude of rulers was due to a fear of the deadly edicts of the popes, the excommunication releasing the people from their oath of allegiance to their rulers, and setting free the ravenous mob.

A knowledge of these dreadful things, and the possibility of Pampero coming under the baleful eye, greatly worried Don Alvard. He was to be vindicated in the most cruel manner, proving to him conclusively, that, there was no Christian God protecting the good and the innocent. The most vicious scoundrels in all the world were reveling in the blood of the good and virtuous.

It was two years after his return to his home that a little band of half-crazed refugees staggered into Pampero—starved and in tatters. They were a pitiable sight. Mothers fell prone upon the ground clinging to their famished babes, and men succumbed to utter exhaustion.

The scared people of Pampero sent for Don Alvard. Arriving, he looked upon the pathetic scene, raised his hands high and said in his great, trumpet-like voice:

"If God himself commanded us to refuse succor to these victims of bigotry, I would feed and comfort them," and the people of Pampero did so.

The refugees were well provided for and sent on their way rejoicing that there still remained in the world people with humane instincts. Filled with gratitude and new hopes, they knelt and blessed their benefactors, then passed out of the village singing joyous songs. With pitying eyes the people watched them trudge away.

Ah! here was the entering wedge, with fear and trepidation they pondered the consequences. Their own safety was imperiled did this act of charity become known, for the church edicts reached all alike, whether under the church jurisdiction or not. The edicts of the popes superceded the civil laws in all matters pertaining to the church.

Satan chuckled as he watched all this. It was a rare opportunity. A short distance away from Pampero, the refugees encountered a roving band of crusaders. They were cruelly tortured to compel them to betray those who had given them succor. Upon learning the truth, all were massacred, because, the purpose of exile was to turn defenseless people out to die of starvation and privation, the excommunication forbidding all persons to give succor or relief even to dying persons.

The soldiers now had a holy duty to perform in the cause of Christ and the church. Pampero must be chastised as an example to other communities.

Young Don Alvard was at work in the harvest field, when he sensed unusual commotion toward his home.

With his pitchfork over his sturdy shoulder he hurriedly walked homeward. What he saw upon reaching there almost paralyzed his senses. Some twenty soldiers, headed by a priest in the garb of a traveling cardinal, were pillaging the place.

As he plunged into their midst he beheld with horror the upturned face of his beloved mother— dead from a gaping saber-wound in her neck.

His beautiful sister was being tossed from soldier to soldier, and the house was in flames. These

fiends in human form were shouting and laughing
as though it were great sport. Each had been absolved in advance, in anticipation of just such acts,
upon starting upon their mission of vengeance in
the name of God and the church. With each death
stroke the murderers acquitted their conscience with
the formula put in their mouths by the pope: "God
wills it."

Before the plunderers could fully realize his
presence, Alvard, with the roar of a lion, bounded
into their midst, plunging his deadly hay-fork right
and left, each thrust reaching the vitals of a soldier.
He had placed half of them, writhing in the throes
of death upon the ground, before his terrible hand
could be stayed.

The priest confronted the giant with hand aloft,
in which he held a cross.

Looking Alvard over impudently, he said: "It
would be a pity to kill so fine a young man."

Alvard, recovering from the diverting survey of
the pompous priest, made a menacing motion toward him with his deadly weapon.

The priest quickly crossed himself and roared
the usual Catholic formula to inspire fear.

"What! would you assault a priest of God?"

Alvard raised his weapon exclaiming, "To hell
with you! You murderous dog! The lives of ten
thousand vultures like you will not atone for the
murder of my good mother, who never in her whole
life harmed a living creature. I shall spend the
balance of my life killing priests. I hope I may be

spared until I have wiped the contemptible pests from the face of the earth."

Taking cowardly advantage of Alvard's overwhelming, grief inspired rage, the priest quickly stepped aside, leaving the way clear for a soldier, almost as large as Don Alvard, to make a deadly lunge, in the belief that Alvard could be taken off his guard. Striking the pitchfork upward he made a stroke at Alvard which was intended to finish him. How could he know that he was challenging the greatest master-at-arms in all Europe?

With a dexterous motion of the butt of the fork Alvard parried the thrust and instantly delivered a counter stroke which buried the fork deep in the vitals of the soldier, adding one more to the number upon the ground.

The cowardly priest and the balance of his followers had wasted no time in mounting their horses, no doubt guessing what their fate would be did they remain to parley with this wrathful avenger.

They dashed madly away, thankful that they, too, were not wallowing in their own gore.

Alvard, believing they would return with other soldiers, hastily turned to the sad task of secreting the bodies of his dear mother and sister.

The mother lay upon the earth, with clenched hands, and horror depicted upon her face, her head being half severed from her body.

The rage of the brother knew no bounds upon discovering that the fiends had cast his innocent sister's body into the flames while she was yet alive.

She had attempted to save herself by crawling through an open casement, and her charred and mutilated body was now hanging from the window, quite dead.

As Alvard looked down upon this sacrifice to Moloch, he wept bitterly, at the same time surcharging his outraged soul with the wrath which would avenge the crime.

Raising his hand he swore to avenge them as no vengeance ever before had been executed. He thanked his creator for having given him a great and powerful body and for having spared him to dedicate it to the duty before him. He believed that some just power knew his grievance and would be his willing ally.

Carrying the precious forms to a secret place, he buried them, marking the spot with stones.

Returning to where the dead soldiers lay, he stripped the clothing from the giant and placed them upon himself. Buckling on the soldier's sword he surveyed the smoldering ruins of his happy, peaceful home with a grievous heart, and, for a moment only, gave way to grief.

He looked every inch a cavalier in the uniform, which consisted of a new form of hauberk, or crusader's coat, reaching below the hips, open on the sides, and made of strips of bright metal woven in slashes in heavy, coarse cloth. It was sleeveless, permitting a free use of the arms. The balance of the outfit was in keeping—breeches, helmet and buskins. Examining the sword he grunted:

"Huh! A good fighting iron, but I'll extend it a couple of feet."

Observing the dead soldiers lying about, he laughed like a madman. seizing them, one by one, he cast them through the window and into the seething flames, exclaiming:

"You made your own hell, roast in it! Satan will not receive your poisonous souls."

Pounding himself upon the chest, he roared:

"But this hell, which you have kindled, I reserve for priests!"

Selecting one of the horses left behind by the fleeing soldiers he rode away. At the top of the hill he paused for a moment to look back upon the paradise out of which fate had thrust him.

"But I am no Cain," he muttered. "I go now of my own will. From this day forward no man is my master. I am that I am."

He saw a blue pillar of smoke arising from the smouldering ruins of his home. A new sensation aroused him as he beheld the burning homes of the good people of Pampero, and could discover mounted soldiers riding wildly about, doubting not they were wantonly massacreing the innocent people. He could with difficulty restrain a desire to rush back into the village and do what he could to prevent this awful catastrophe, but he had an urgent duty before him. Over the ridge dwelt a neighbor; he must hasten to warn this household of the impending evil which was flaying the community alive.

As he turned about he saw, down in the plain,

a body of horsemen riding toward the ruins of his own home. Well did he know that his surmise was correct; the priest had returned with reenforcements.

Hastening to the home of his neighbor he was contemplating the idea of himself carrying to safety the daughter of that house, the only woman to whom he had ever paid serious attention—the beloved friend of his sister.

Upon reaching the place he was shocked to find that the family already had been murdered, and the house pillaged and burned. In a pile of straw he found the mutilated body of his sweetheart. He turned old in that moment, and holding his sword above the body he swore to avenge her. Then drawing the straw over the poor broken form he mounted and dashed back towards Pampero, muttering:

"My work begins now; my cause is just; I shall be the judge as to what extent my vengeance shall reach; my conscience has departed; the pain in my heart shall be my guide, and mercy shall be my last resort."

A great resolve had seized him and he chuckled as he galloped, so eager was he to begin. Again he paused at the top of the ridge, and made a careful survey. Alert discretion to insure his own personal safety was now one of his precautions.

He watched a score of soldiers prowling about the ruins of his home. Soon they mounted and rode away taking a highway leading from Pampero.

Down in the village he could see soldiers riding

wildly through the streets and reveling in their bloody orgie.

Looking over himself he laughed.

"Ha! Ha! I am one of them, I will add zest to their hellish frolic," and he dashed across the fields and entered the village like a cyclone.

The soldiers were roistering and looting. Riding wildly about they were killing the people as they were driven out of their homes by fire and smoke, cutting and slashing every living thing, even the pigs and dogs.

Joining the bloody revel Alvard drew his sword and began slashing right and left, cleaving the head or neck of a soldier with every swing of his blade. He filled the streets with carcasses till there remained no more to kill, but it was too late; he was the only living thing remaining in the town, which now resembled a shambles.

With great and gloomy sadness he looked down upon the horrible scene; soldiers and citizens mingled in safety. "Death levels all classes to a common equality." The Don grunted:

"A good beginning. God help the priest, or soldier of the holy see, coming within reach of my blade."

Then, this man, who was nature's model, sent into the world to set good examples for other men, equipped to do great things for the betterment of humanity, but now converted into a brooding nemesis by Satan's emissaries, started out into the world, without any particular objective point, but having a well defined purpose. Keen of instinct, strong of body, and absolutely sure of the justice of his cause, he feared neither God, devil nor man.

He just kept on riding until he met some travelers who, out of holy fear of his occoutrement, gave him all the information they could. He especially sought knowledge of the whereabouts of the priest who had caused the destruction of his home and the murder of his loved ones.

Pampero now seemed far away, the farther he traveled the lighter seemed his worldly responsibilities, his whole thought being his specific task, acknowledging no master, and no restraining hand, his mind was his own, he was a free lance.

Later, he came upon the train of a *legate* on his way to the Duchy of Sevoe. Being clad in the uniform of a soldier of the Holy see, he was confidentially informed that his excellency, Sanatos, was proceeding to Savoe to carry forward the instructions to the faithful concerning the extension of the correction of the protestants. This was at the request of the defender of the faith, the very Catholic Duke of Savoe, himself a blood-thirsty ally of Rome.

A great light was shed in the heart of Don Alvard; he would broaden his opportunities for vengeance by temporarily sparing the life of this agent of Satan whom fate had cast under the shadow of his eager sword. Diplomacy would become his first recruit to his deadly campaign. He would kill with his sword as occasion required. A wide field of operation opened up before him.

Mentioning, that, at the time, he was detached, he offered his services to his excellency the *legate*. Which offer was quickly accepted because of his imposing personality, and he was at once assigned to duty as one of the legate's body guards.

He introduced himself by his correct name, Don Alvard de Balde.

"Then you must know Count Bertram, Lord of Ognez," said the legate.

"He is my uncle; his wife is my father's sister, Mary Saez de Balde," replied Alvard.

"And your father and mother, where do they reside?" inquired the legate.

"I recently suffered the misfortune of losing both; that is the reason why I am become a soldier," sadly responded the Don, bowing his head.

The *legate* little knew that he was at that moment near unto death for having recalled to Alvard's mental vision the horrid picture of the tragedy at Pampero.

"Ah! but the life of a soldier in the cause of Christ soon makes us all forget our own personal sorrows for those of suffering humanity. In your ardent devotion to the cause, your own griefs will fall like a mantle and new joys in the field of action will be a happy diversion," murmured the hypocritical *legate*. "I am proud indeed to enroll you as one of my body guard. Your illustrious uncle is one of the staunch defenders of the faith. Did not Christ say: 'He that loveth father or mother more than me is not worthy of me'?"

Thus began the active life of adventure of the

greatest soldier of fortune of the sixteenth century, who had secretly pledged his soul and body, and dedicated his life to the business of avenging the ungodly murder of his mother and sister, and the blighting of the splendid community of Pampero. Had the whole world consisted of priests he felt justified in killing all.

This nemesis put back the culmination of the Christian exploitation of humanity three hundred years, making it possible to eradicate from its blood the poisonous germs of bigotry, intolerance and fanaticism had humanity not been so ignorant.

Don Alvard had formed no definite plans of operation, but he had an abiding faith in a kindly fate to guide and call him at the proper hour of execution for those who ripened for the plucking. His was to be a "rich harvest" and an "abundant crop," to be garnered before the wicked, ecclesiastical system could reach its final goal—the abject enslavement of mankind to its narrow, selfish will, and the control of all legislation for smothering humanity in sin and evil by law to vindicate its damnable doctrine of "original sin," a doctrine which insults our mothers, sisters and wives and defames all men alike.

"What is man, that he should be clean? and he which is born of a woman, that he should be righteous?" (Job 15:14)

Thus they unblushingly defame their own Christ born of a woman.

Alvard's theological education had revealed to

him many such inconsistencies and he and his father had long discussed them.

He remained nearly three years as *attache* to Sanatos, *legate* to Savoe. In so far as all outward relations revealed, the secret of his experiences at Pampero remained unknown to the *legate*. Nevertheless, he was wise to the deep cunning of these princes of the church and was ever on the alert for treachery.

During his sojourn in Savoe, he had saved thousands of lives by giving secret warnings of contemplated raids and massacres.

His vision broadened with each new day's experience, and he believed an invisible power was preparing him for higher work than he himself had contemplated. He would add to his scheme of vengeance a diplomacy and refinement which would keep him wholly within the working code of the Christian enterprise, which he no longer considered from the standpoint of religion.

He longed for action, and some opportunity which might bring him closer to the origin of systematized evil, and under the sinister shadow of the papal throne.

That longed for chance came unexpectedly, and while it seemed an answer to his desires, the surrounding circumstances seemed to reveal the hand of fate taking advantage of the intrigues of his enemies.

He was called into the august presence of the pompous *legate* and questioned regarding the conveyance to Rome of urgent and important messages.

CHAPTER III

THE MISSION TO ROME

THE BEST REWARD OF TREACHERY IS DISCOVERY

DON ALVARD was elated at the turn in his fortune, be it good or bad, for it promised action. He had about reached the limit of endurance waiting for something to turn up, and, now, that for which he had most yearned had occurred. He more than ever believed that fate was playing a friendly game in his favor, and his courage and self reliance increased in proportion.

His sojourn in Savoe had been like a post-graduate course to him, bringing him in close contact with the church intrigues and propaganda, causing him to marvel at the audacity of the ecclesiastical pretensions. Religion was the least important element in a vast enterprise, involving all that the world stood for. Through that horrible weapon of the church, the deadly excommunication, civil rulers had been brought groveling about the feet of the Roman Catholic popes, and the masses had been subjected to a state of superstitious fear akin to idiocy. The church was so strongly entrenched, it seemed impossible to stay its progress toward absolutism. Alvard's knowledge of the basis for this usurpation, caused him to wonder if humanity had really risen from the brute animalism. His wits were on edge to take due advantage of the turn in his affairs, but, at the same time, he was on the alert for treachery. Any snare that caught him must indeed be well set. His suspicions did not begin with menials, he could take care of them with his trusty, five-foot blade. It was Sanatos he eagerly watched. His own education served him well, giving him a more definite understanding of the subtlety of the ecclesiastical system.

He had observed with deep concern, that, during the early part of his stay in Savoe, the *legate* treated him with some cordiality, but, gradually, this merged into a palpable patronizing politeness, and then to an austere frigidity wholly inconsistent with his original attitude—this meant something.

Patience was a virtue with Dan Alvard; he could wait, therefore, when the *legate* summoned him, he was prepared for surprises.

Sanatos called him into his august presence, in his own private apartment, his fawning attitude betraying to Alvard the treachery which he suspected. The change in his manner was too conspicuous to be mistaken. There was some mystery here, and he was not to be caught napping.

He was handed the official portfolio—usually called a *gipciere*—allegedly containing messages to be transmitted to the Holy See, and he was informed that he was a duly authorized *curiall* of the papal court until he had discharged this mission.

By this procedure Don Alvard realized the vast power of pomp and ceremony in church formality. This external austerity was one of the most awe inspiring attitudes of church officials, bringing the ignorant to their knees, and inspiring fear in the "wise hearted."

As the smug prelate, in black satin *rochet*, sat in his throne chair—a pompous dignity affected by all *legates* — he deceitfully fingered his richly embellished rosary, dangling from which was a beautifully carved ivory cross. He was, to Don Alvard, the embodiment of ecclesiastical hypocrisy, deceit, and smug vanity. It inspired in him a keen desire to run him through with his sword, and rip off the hypocritical veneer, and expose the coarse, common grain beneath.

Upon the order of the *legate* he had been attired as a papal envoy—a black velvet *manto* concealing a light chain hauberk. While this assured him of respect and comfort on his travels, he was to learn that it was a bit of clever trickery to excuse disarming him, it being so made that he could not attach his side arms in the usual manner.

The *legate* added a badge of identification — the seal-ring of his high office—a gold ring with a sapphire setting, similar to the ring usually conferred upon the newly created cardinals by the popes.

Sanatos had exhibited astonishment and poorly concealed vexation, when the Don appeared before him with his tremendous fighting-iron jangling about his heels—he had extended the blade to a length of five feet.

"Why! you are supposed to travel as a messenger of peace; do you expect to encounter and challenge Satan himself to mortal combat?" he exclaimed in a supressed voice.

"No—but should Satan challenge me?" replied the undaunted Don, standing erect and ready, as he placed his hand upon the hilt of the sword.

"Good!" ejaculated the prelate, with assumed admiration, which did not deceive Alvard.

Leaning forward, with a sly side glance, he said in a tragic whisper:

"One Cardinal Bambo now presides over the office of *datary,* at Rome. You will find him a very handsome and attractive man, and a jolly, good soul."

Don Alvard could not help noticing a sinister ring in the delivery of this speech, more than the words spoken.

One of the weaknesses of vain conceit always clung to these Catholic dignitaries, in their dealings with their inferiors; they did not give credit to any one for having the wit and sense to see through their flimsy false-pretense. This reference to Bambo concealed something in the nature of a jest; how was the Don to measure the intimate characteristics of pompous vatican dignitaries, that he should be warned of their good traits? He was more concerned about their faults.

Continuing, the *legate* said: "You will be received at Rome by a proper person to conduct you to the officials in waiting; your instructions are plainly set forth in this code," and he placed in the

Don's hand a letter. Bidding him a comfortable journey, Sanatos signified that the secretary would see him safely away.

Much to the chagrin of the wily Don, who expected to travel ahorse, he was ushered to a huge and cumbersome *vehiculo,* much resembling his own rattling old hay-wagon. To it were attached four prancing horses, eager to dash away—in itself suspicious, for at that period traveling coaches were scarcely known. Only royalty affected such uncomfortable luxuries.

"It looks like a guillotine," laughed the Don, as he surveyed the *coche.*

By the side of the *chochero* sat a huge *gendarme,* armed to the teeth. Two heavily armed outriders were mounted, ready to trail the *vehiculo.* This air of military preparedness did not escape Don Alvard, it only enhanced his suspicions—here was a real adventure. His big frame shook with laughter; he made no attempt to conceal his sarcasm, and utter lack of surprise and trepidation. He was doing a little fancy thinking himself, and it was not being lost on his retinue; side glances were becoming gaping surprise, and illy concealed consternation.

The secretary, with mock civility, approached and requested the Don to divest himself of his huge fighting-iron.

The fire-eating Don turned savagely upon him, and he drew back with an appealing look at the huge gendarme upon the seat by the *Cochero,* who only made a grimace, which did not escape the Don's alert eyes. Not even they could grasp that this giant had a mind as strong as his body.

As he approached the door of the *vehiculo,* he had other reason to believe that he was a victim of contemplated treachery; after he was once inside the thing, a heavy bar would drop into sockets and he would be a prisoner in a strong cage. Grasping the bar he ripped it from the side of the vehiculo and tossed it inside, entered himself and ordered them to proceed, in tones at once so authorative and commanding, there was no hesitation. The horses bounded away, tossing the huge Don about in a manner not at all to his liking.

As they left the palace of the *legate,* the Don had observed Sanatos peeping from a window and holding his clasped hands above his head.

This rough ride was doing its work. Alvard was growing more angry each moment. There was no longer a doubt regarding his position; he was the victim of conspiracy. The significance hidden in the request that he lay off his sword annoyed him, and his narrow escape from being encaged like a wild beast, angered him. Even so, at the rate at which they were traveling, he could not leave the vehiculo, and it suggested relays ahead, therefore, it was urgent that he take matters in hand at once. Already he had surmised that the course they had taken was exactly opposite to that which he had anticipated. He decided to call a halt. "Ho there!" he cried, but seemingly the sound of his voice was lost in the clatter of the *vehiculo.* He examined his cage minutely, and, upon finding a narrow opening running along beneath the seat of the *cochero*, at a venture, he jabbed his sword into it, coming near to causing a wreck, his blade having reached a tender spot in the man's anatomy, solving the problem.

The horses were thrown to their haunches and the *vehiculo* came suddenly to a halt, in fact, having no brakes it came near going on over the backs of the horses. Both the *cochero* and the *gendarme* found themselves sprawled in the dust of the road.

Regaining their feet their anger, which was manifest, quickly subsided upon seeing the giant Don standing over them splitting his sides with laughter. They sheepishly brushed the dust from their clothing and stood looking inquiringly at him.

The Don was himself now; he had solved the problem. He was a prisoner being taken somewhere. There was no honor involved in this case, therefore he would be the master, judge and executioner if needs be. Betrayal was manifest in every visible movement he had observed; he would conduct himself as sense and safety suggested.

No indication regarding their first stop, nor the course of their journey had been given him; he might be on his way to purgatory, instead of Rome, as far as he knew. This was his first experience in travel by *vehiculo*, and he didn't like it.

Suddenly he motioned for the outriders to take a position in front of the *coche*, then turning upon the others he demanded to know the course they were to pursue.

There was evidence of protest and wise exchanges of glances.

The giant gendarme ventured to ask why he made the inquiry and received a rebuff which convinced him that he was transporting a savage tiger instead of a timid, dummy messenger.

The Don placed his hand upon his sword, glared at the gendarme, and roared:

"It is my will! I give no reasons! Mount! and travel at half your former pace."

They took their places and he reentered the *vehiculo* and was driven at a more comfortable speed.

As he watched their actions he had greater cause to suspect treachery. He fell into a sad reverie as he contemplated the raw truth, that, the minds of men had been so poisoned by false teachings that few could be trusted. They thoughtlessly lent themselves to wicked, designing men, and turned against their own kind with no thought of justice or right —human conscience was dead.

The very message on his person, if he really carried one, might be designed to place him in the hands of the inquisitors, and that meant death. Did not the unsuspecting Uriah carry his own death warrant from the hand of the blessed David, in order that, that saintly king might prostitute his wife to bear him bastard children?

The sweet, fragrant, country air did not revive his spirits, it only carried his mind back there to

Pampero, where both the atmosphere and the minds of men were pure.

And then, that horrid picture of dead bodies, ravaged women and smouldering ruins rose up before him, and the savage desire for vengeance was rekindled. Sanatos had made a terrible mistake in his desire to destroy this man. He had turned a demon loose in Don Alvard's heart, and that demon would tear the heart out of the priesthood.

And now he was to come face to face with the first cause. Ah, this was joy. Nothing could daunt or discourage him; his world work had begun.

His precaution had brought them far short of the point where they had first intended making their noon halt. They were entering a small village where they would take some rest and refreshments.

Don Alvard commanded them to draw up to the front of the village tavern. Upon alighting he observed directly before them a steep declivity.

With seeming reluctance the *cochero* alighted; hostlers were called to care for the horses, and the Don and his retinue entered.

Mutton, bread and wine were placed upon the table and the hungry men fell ravenously upon the feast.

With a motion of impatience the Don exclaimed, as he pretended to search his person, "Ah! how careless!" And quickly arising he passed out of the door and toward the *coche*.

It seemed but a moment when he reappeared

in the door-way, but paused and looked outside, as though attracted by something there. Hurriedly motioning for his men to come, he bounded outside.

They were too late; upon reaching the door they saw the horses rearing and plunging as though in great fright, then they darted away toward the steep hill, down which they plunged pell-mell, the *vehiculo* swaying from side to side like a ship in the trough of a stormy sea. One of the lead horses fell, and the others tumbled over him in a promiscuous jumble of kicking heels and tangled harness. The vehiculo rolled over and over, finally landing in a state of hopeless collapse at the bottom of a deep ditch.

Don Alvard was in a rage, roundly cursing the hostlers, and flaying the apparently frightened landlord for entertaining such stupid and incompetent villians to serve travelers. Only the landlord knew that the jocular Don had nearly cracked his ribs with a friendly nudge.

Alvard ordered his own men to hasten to the wreck and to report to him the damages, insisting that the landlord and his men should leave their hands off.

It was noticeable, however, that the hostlers were not taking seriously the Don's savage resentment, in fact, the landlord and the Don were heartily laughing as they entered the inn. They soon came to an understanding by the use of ample silver which the Don poured into his hand.

Don Alvard quickly explained that he was carrying extraordinary messages to Tuscany, and it was urgent that he get rid of these men whom he suspected of being spies. He bargained for the immediate use of a strong courier's mount, and paid an equal sum for not supplying horses to any of his men for at least twenty-four hours.

To the dismay of his retainers, upon returning to make their report, they beheld Don Alvard mounted upon a large, well-accoutered *caballo* prepared to continue his journey.

They did not fully comprehend it, but this was to be his last and crucial test of their character. He merely informed them that his mission was one which would not admit of delay; they should return to their master, at their leisure, and explain to him what had occurred and that he had dispensed with their further services. He especially forbade the outriders following him.

The outwitted men were stunned to speechlessness, standing agape as the wily Don rode away.

Once he cautiously glanced back and saw them standing in a group, with their heads close together, and he chuckled softly to himself: "Have a care my lads, something tells me you are going to do something rash."

Three hours later his judgment of men and circumstances was vindicated. Four horsemen came galloping after him. Turning his own horse, he drew his sword and awaited their approach.

"Who instructed you to ride after me?" he demanded.

Instead of assuming an offensive attitude, the leader said politely:

"His excellency, the *legate,* instructed me not to permit you to get out of our sight until we arrived at Rome. I cannot recognize your authority."

The personal pronoun "I" had revealed the character of the leader.

"It is useless to bandy words. I instructed you to return. Were I a messenger to the Holy See, my word would be law, and you would have been subject to my orders. Your own statement convicts you. It is plain, you have acted under the instructions of the *legate* and you were conducting me to Rome to deliver me to the inquisitors. This is false-pretense and you are without authority to attach yourself to me against my will. It is no defense that you are only obeying the orders of your master; his orders have no basis of law. You are guilty of conspiracy against my life. I accuse, judge, condemn and execute such enemies. Your only defense is your sword. Draw!"

Before the astonished men could realize their danger, and place themselves on their guard, he had slashed them to pieces and they lay writhing upon the earth.

"From this day forward, thus shall die all such traitors," he exclaimed.

Dismounting, he searched the persons of the slain men, taking from that of the giant leader a bulky *gipciere* of letters and documents bearing the official lead seal of the Holy See.

Remounting his horse he rode rapidly away, nightfall finding him far from the scene of his encounter.

Snugly ensconced in a rose-covered cottage, where he had procured lodging, he felt an unusual comfort and relief, withal a sensation of safety.

It was a simple home of a wine maker, whose family consisted of a good house-wife, a buxom daughter of twenty, and himself.

The Don regaled himself with good wine and excellent conversation. As he entertained them with interesting tales of travel and adventure, promising to bring back to the daughter a good husband, should he ever again come this way.

While the night was yet young, he requested to be permitted to retire, being both weary and anxious to examine the papers in his possession.

By the sputtering light of a grease mat, he proceeded to his task. It was most important for him to know his present status before traveling further.

This cavalier was blessed with an intuitive sense equal to prevision. He had judged well in this instance. All men, at this period, were at the mercy of the intriguing clique at Rome. Disaster, without warning or explanation, fell upon unsuspecting communities. A sinister, death dealing power brooded over Europe like a vulture, and a feeling of impending evil struck terror into every heart. Fanaticism, born of hysterical fear, was a prevailing pestilence, flaring up at the least beck or call of the consecrated fingers of local priests, and destroying whole communities of innocent peoples without reason.

As the Don perused the messages as he opened them, he boiled with rage. The *legate*, Sanatos, had given him what purported to be a letter of instructions which he was to examine at his leisure while traveling; this he examined first.

"My much esteemed Don Alvard:

"It is with pleasure that I select you as my courier to bear important messages to his excellency, Cardinal Paul Bambo, who occupies the high office of *Datary* to His Holiness the Pope. This will bring you into intimate contact with persons in Rome, and may qualify you for future diplomatic missions.

"You may present this letter to his eminence as an open letter of introduction and hearty commendation. I warn you, however, my good Don Alvard, it would grieve me much, should you become so fascinated with the handsome and witty Cardinal Bambo that you may forget your affection for me.

                    "Yours most cordially,
                            "Sanatos—Legate."

This apparently cordial letter, so kind, so personal, puzzled the Don not a little, for he was stubbornly convinced, that, had the *legate's* original plans carried, he would have been betrayed to the inquisitors. Doubtless this Cardinal Bambo was his accomplice.

He now examined the papers taken from the person of the *gendarme*.

There were letters addressed to several persons
in Rome, mainly to persons attached to the Holy
See.   The itinerary of the journey, as originally
planned, would have carried him through the papal
states, according to attached instructions, one letter being addressed to the Grand Duke of Tuscany,
in which a complaint was made that certain terms
of a personal agreement made with the Duke of
Savoe had not been complied with.   He emphatically warned the Duke that he was using his best
offices to prevent the breach from being referred
to the Holy See for adjustment, the Duke of Savoe
being a lenient ruler.

Opening a letter addressed to one Cardinal
Gonsalvo, he read it with cumulative anger and
amazement.   Here was the revelation, the raw
truth.

"My beloved Gonsalvo:

"This communication, by the grace of the
mother of God, will be presented to you by my good
and faithful Sanzara, to whom I have intrusted
the responsibility of delivering to you the person
of the abominable Don Alvard de Balde.

"I know you will forgive me for not having
sooner accomplished for you this extraordinary
mission, but, you will agree with me I feel quite
assured, that, it was necessary for me to negotiate
a treaty with, and receive the unqualified acquiescence of his close and powerful relative, the Count
Bertram, Lord of Ognez, whom I found to be a
strong member of an ancient family of the province

of Guipuscoa, moreover, an ardent supporter of the
Holy See, being always in close and confidential
touch with His Holiness.

"Therefore, my beloved Gansalvo, it required
time and patience to bring about the consent of
Count Bertram to apprehend his wayward and
wicked kinsman, and deliver him safely to Rome,
and to the affectionate care of the inquisitional
court.

"I thank all the saints he is well off my hands,
for he is a very froward and dangerous person to
be at large. His impudent frankness is a bad example for those about him. I have tolerated him
only to consummate his final suppression.

"I have intrusted to Don Alvard a blank paper,
purporting to be an important message to that dog
Bambo. Let us hope and pray that you may find
opportunity to involve him in some manner with
this bear.

"You will find in a secret part of Alvard's *manto*,
a letter drawn for this purpose, if you can conjure
an excuse to use it. It purports to be a confidential
letter from Don Alvard, addressed to Bambo, showing an intrigue between them, concerning the Countess Milliette, now confined in the prison in Castle
St. Angelo—use it at your discretion.

"And, now, my good and faithful coadjutor, I
shall pray, night and day, to all the saints in heaven
and hell, that no accident befall our good Courier
Sanzara, and that he may reach you in safety, and
return to me early assurance that these extremely

delicate matters are in your possession. These are
dangerous times and we are playing with fire.

"By the same courier I am communicating to
Cardinal Ignatio and others matters relative to
Pampeluna.

"I recommend that you hold an early conference with them on this important subject. I feel
certain that France contemplates a *coup* to restore
the province of Navarra to the family of Jean
d'Albret.

"It is safe to predict that, France and Spain,
at an early period, will be at war over this disputed
border province. Pampeluna will be the objective
point in the first clash.

"Be conservative and express no opinions until
you again hear from me.

"The Holy See should not openly take sides in
this controversy in its present stage, there is much
to be gained by a cautious neutrality.

"I have almost forgotten to mention an important development in my negotiations with Count
Bertram. He has a son who was formerly at the
Court of Ferdinand, and now is at the Court of
Charles. This may seem trivial, but this favorite
son, now twenty-eight years of age, may inherit
all of the powerful estate of the Lord of Ognez,
which is very important. We must direct our early
attentions toward him with the view of training him
for future purposes, and bringing these riches into
the control of the Holy See.

"He is a wild and dissipated youth, and is given

to all the polite vices, especially wine, dissolute
women and gambling.   A king's court is no re-
formatory, and especially the court of a beer guzzling Hapsburg.

"The young man's name is Don Iñigo Lopez de
Ricalde.

"I am informed that you contemplate a visit
to Spain.   I recommend that you discreetly learn
what you can regarding this young man.   I have
a suspicion that he is maintained at court for some
ulterior purpose, the nature of which has not been
revealed to the Holy See.

"This is strictly *sub rosa*.   I am told he is in the
confidence of Borgia.

"Now my good friend, I commend you to the
blessings of all the saints.

"Affectionately,

"Sanatos."

Don Alvard pondered long over this amazing
evidence of duplicity.   He had little doubt about
his having been assigned the honor of escorting
himself to Rome and into the jaws of torture and
death.   As the perfidy of this betrayal gradually
tore its way into his heart everything turned red
before him, and he silently cursed the ungodly
power which rendered such things possible.   The
inspiration could only come from evil minds.   The
papal system was blasphemous; an outrage upon
nature, and a curse to humanity.

Another light dawned upon him, like the rising of the morning sun in a clear, blue sky.   His

case was merely incidental to a world-wide intrigue which was slowly but surely creeping like a murderous shadow over Europe. The murder of his dear ones was but one of thousands; the destruction of his beloved Pampero but one of endless similar outrages. He now recalled his knowledge of the Bible as taught him in his theological course, and he could not believe otherwise than that, ecclesiasticism, taking advantage of its *temporal power* over rulers, was closing down upon innocent, unsuspecting humanity to culminate its original aims and purposes. This was the end, when men would seek shelter in the mountains to freeze, starve and be eaten by wolves.

It was plain, his task was greater than a personal one; he must awaken and warn the world of its dangers.

In vain did he try to solve the identity of the "beloved Gonsalvo."

He now unhesitatingly broke the seal of the message addressed to Cardinal Bambo, finding it to be a blank, as Sanatos had said.

"Curse of Christendom!" he ejaculated. "What devil's mess is this?"

This intrigue opened wide his eyes to what was before him. It was no child's play. He would fight the devil with his own fire, and to a finish, but, first, he must locate his chief enemies and lay out his plan of warfare. He would go on to Rome and locate this "dog Bambo." Maybe he would be something more than the cur, Sanatos, had pictured him.

He especially desired to meet, face to face, this unknown but intimate enemy, Gonsalvo. Cardinals, Bishops and Popes did not inspire him with fear; they were very human. Only in their own self adulation were they superior to the common herd of humanity, and, withal, most ungodly men.

This intrepid avenger was now in the saddle to begin his life work in active service. A life of excitement, and extraordinary adventure was before him. He slept soundly, ate heartily, and was an iron hearted man as he approached the age of thirty. Fearing neither man nor devil, he was overflowing with blood-lust of justifiable vengeance. As he had lengthened his terrible fighting blade, he now extended his services to a wider field; he was from this day forward the avenger of outraged mankind. We shall always find him respectful to worthy women, kind to children and animals, fond of mutton and wine and always sitting or standing with his back to the wall with his sword free.

He had a purpose in assuming the name Don Alvard de Ricalde, by which name he will be known in his future adventures. He was feared as a Ricalde and hunted as a Balde.

Thoroughly aroused to the devilish nature of the intrigues of Rome, he buckled on his armor of steel and wit and was ready to match strength and skill with the evil forces which he believed were secretly and systematically raping the world.

It was a long and tedious ride to Rome, but,

in due time, and without important adventure, he arrived in that historic city.

He had stepped into the arena at the beginning of a prolific period of world affairs, replete with storms, revolutions and human catastrophies, the greatest that history records.

Having chosen his strenuous course he burned his bridges behind him, and neither asked nor gave quarter—it was always a fight to the death. Measured by the visible precepts, and shameless practices of the church, Don Alvard was wholly within the Christian code.

As he entered Rome he smiled broadly that he possessed the real signet, identifying a true messenger to the Holy See, he having taken this off the person of the unfortunate Sanzara. The ring with which Sanatos had dedicated him to the horrors of the inquisition he held for future uses.

"I'll make a collection of these baubles to make old Moses and Aaron turn over in their graves," he muttered.

"That reminds me, I may organize a crusade to go in search of the grave of Moses. That would be as reasonable as seeking the sepulchre of Christ. Neither of these ever existed."

CHAPTER IV
THE POPE'S EYES
A GUILTY CONSCIENCE BEGETS MORAL COWARDICE

THE novel experience of two pontifical funerals in a period of about sixty days, one of these being due to the sudden death of Pius III, who had occupied the throne only twenty-one days, was a strain upon the nerves of the superstitious and excitable Roman populace to arouse hysterical expectations of strange and thrilling manifestations.

God was having a terrible time trying to glue the garb of his local business manager to the papal chair.

The unfortunate Peter Piccolomini, nephew of Pius II, was one of the prime causes of this extraordinary sensation. He was elected to the office of pope as Pius III, and had died before he could warm the pontifical bed, or learn to wind the holy family clock, twenty-one days being the limit of his earthly association with God. The college of cardinals was working over time digging up dark horses, from dark places, for each new campaign.

When Julian de la Revere dropped into the papal residence (Nov. 19th, 1503) as Pope Julius II, he sniffed, contemptuously, and inquired:

"Are these the floral decorations of an inauguration or a funeral?"

Cardinal Paul Bambo, whose duty at that period

was to introduce the new incumbents into the papal
household, made the most graceful bow his poor
humped body would permit, and replied:

"Perhaps your Holiness forgets that, Alexander,
also, is only a short time departed, therefore, the
confusion of odors. One who dies of his own poison
does not leave a pleasing perfume."

"I might have recognized his odor upon seeing
you," tartly retorted the irritable new pontiff.

Bambo already had sensed the acuteness of the
nose of the nephew of the murderous Sixtus IV, and
he promptly replied:

"Am I to accept that as a suggestion that I may
retire from the pontifical advisoryship?" And the
hunchback cardinal looked at the new master of
the vatican with unflinching eyes.

The haughty and overbearing Julius looked
sharply at the dwarf for a moment, to see if there
was purposeful insolence in his question, then he
said:

"You have held this position for a long time I
believe."

"Since the incumbency of His Holiness Alexander VI," replied Bambo.

"Then I shall give you a trial, to see if you are
suited to my requirements," sullenly grunted Julius.

"I must respectfully inform your Holiness that
you have a wholly erroneous conception of my position. It is equally speculative as to whether I shall
care to continue in a gratuitous position. I am
member of the Sacred College. I have hitherto

served as private advisor to their Holinesses by courtesy, and upon their specific request. It will depend upon circumstances as to whether I shall further assume so arduous, and, usually thankless responsibility. Doubtless your Holiness will not require a person in an advisory capacity. Your secretary-ordinary will be quite capable of performing the routine duties which I have never performed."

The amazed pope stared in unfeigned wonderment at this frankly spoken statement. He could not believe his own sense of hearing, that this deformed piece of humanity could possess the soul of a man, and have the courage to assume this insolent attitude toward the vicar of God. But, this surprise was wholly due to his own lack of information and experience.

The popes at that particular period did not act upon their sole initiative, as he was soon to learn. The scenes were shifting so rapidly, the divine actors were forgetting their lines. He took no heed of the embarrasing fact that, his crown painfully lagged in settling upon his Godly brow, some weeks succeeding his election before he was officially crowned, notwithstanding his promises to Caesar Borgia, and the alleged bribery of several cardinals.

The church was in a precarious position, because of manifestly perverse pontifical policies.

Church history relates that, in the whole list of popes none was so guilty of notorious black simony as Julius II.

"Then you are not the acting-secretary?" Julius asked of Bambo.

"I am not, and my resignation as special counsellor is at your disposal," coldly replied Cardinal Bambo.

"I shall require time to consider this extraordinary situation," said Julius, and the cardinal withdrew from the Holy presence with a feeling of contempt for the new incumbent.

Julius had much to learn, notwithstanding he had enjoyed the emoluments of Bishop of Carpentras, of Albano, of Ostia, of Bologne, and Avagnon. He was a product of the old hard-shelled school of discipline, which submerged all personality and natural reason in the will of the superior. He could not evolute from the moth-eaten customs of the mediaeval ages; he could not understand the renaissance, or adjust himself to modern diplomacy.

The supreme position of pope made fools of such case-hardened bigots and the same system turned strong men into devils.

The fiery-tempered, vain and conceited Julius was no exception to the rule; he at once wanted to pose as a Joshua, and order the sun to stand still till he could admire his shadow, and then move on at his divine command. He expected the mountains to fall down and worship him as the only living God.

He was soon to learn that this alleged power in Joshua was a divine joke, and within vatican walls, the "I am God" stuff was *passe* — this was a political period.

Cardinal Bambo's attitude toward him was incomprehensible, and, to his bigoted mind, treasonable; he would punish, humiliate and dispose of him at the earliest opportunity. With this in mind he consulted with his closest confidantes, and learned, to his surprise, that, the vatican family fireside was no place to air vanity; it was the place where the pope was the least held in awe. Here the rigid external form and discipline of the church was hung on the back of a chair, and a floppy pair of old slippers sheathed the holy, but calloused feet. The mask was taken off the face, and the wrinkles ironed out by good living. The real cobbling, to mend the sole of the church, was done in secret. The chatter was taken out of the machinery where a little cussin' could be indulged in by papa. The Godly chariot was a clumsy *vehiculo* at best.

To his dismay, Julius was told, that, Cardinal Bambo was the only one who could perform vatican miracles without noise.

When banded men are under stress they are not polite. Just at this particular time the college of cardinals was under stress. Julius had been allegedly chosen in the hope of restoring some of the old fashioned church discipline, but it was soon learned that, that external form was wholly dependent upon the meanest egotism, selfishness, and stubborn bigotry, and an unpardonable forwardness. Moreover, there was not an honest bone in Julius' body.

Julius belonged to that papal clique bent upon the church supremacy over the civil powers of Europe; hence, his first important move was his attempt to enfranchise Italy and bring it wholly under the control of the Roman Court, that he might drive out all strangers, sow the seed of division between the rivals of the Holy See, and take advantage of the confusion to reestablish the Gregorian supremacy.

The true, underlying purpose in the struggle of the popes for temporal power has always been to bring about a condition whereby the civil laws would compel every human being to come into the church and pay a fixed tribute or tax for its maintenance. This is the true, Christian unity sought by Catholics and protestants alike.

Of all the popes, Gregory VII, Innocence III and Julius II were the most uncompromising enemies of kings, and the most ungodly temporal gods. They centered all their efforts upon establishing the doctrines of "infallibility," and the "temporal power," in the church.

The most outrageous duplicity of Julius was revealed in his treacheries, dishonesty and contempt for truth, in his negotiations with the sovereigns of Europe. He openly called the Spaniards, French and Germans, barbarians. It is a reflection upon the sanity of these nations that they permit anything Catholic to exist in their territories. Yet they are rank bigots with regard to the church, despite all the agonies they have caused.

Julius' was the most corrupt, destructive and hurtful influence ever emanating from Rome, for, when he could not dictate, he sought to ruin and destroy, keeping Europe in constant turmoil and warfare—confusion is an agent of the church.

The whole civilized world, including his associates, heaved a sigh of relief when Julius died. (Feb. 21st, 1513.)

At the time of assuming the pontifical throne, Julius found the kings of Europe doing their own family washing, and political bargaining, occasionally throwing in the church favors for good measure without consulting the Holy See, thus making of the church a mere chattel in political trade. In brief, he was rudely awakened to the responsibilities of his job, and the necessity for showing some human, if not Godly respect for those who could give him good advice, even though accepted grudgingly.

Among other things he found, to his deep chagrin, that, one hunch-back, Cardinal Paul Bambo, held a high place in the vatican councils, because of his peculiar fitness, and extraordinary fund of vatican knowledge. In fact, he was absolutely indispensable to the popes. Through the better part of three pontifical administrations, he had been a sort of fifth wheel in the turning of God's chariot, in its wild and eccentric course.

This situation was due to the fact, that, Bambo had labored for many years classifying and bringing order out of chaos, in the libraries of vatican records. His most important duties were those of custodian of the *archivio secreto*. Not even the popes dared quarrel with him, as Julius soon learned, which greatly wounded his false pride.

Behind his mask of hypocrisy, Julius was no fool, else he would not have been chosen pope, for the time had long passed when imbecils could be placed at the head of the church. Vain, self-conceited men usually make fools of themselves after they have assumed the uniform, and the tarnished glitter of high position—Julius did this.

When he discovered that a humped body might conceal a rare mind, he sent for Bambo. His anger knew no bounds upon being informed that Bambo could not be found. He finally was located in Venice, and Julius made a humiliating appeal for his immediate return to Rome.

Bambo returned and became so important to Julius he was named "the pope's eyes."

Toward the last, Julius became unbearably errotic and garrulous, and Bambo sought an excuse to again leave the Vatican. Julius ignored the best advice Bambo could give him, with the result, that, he went to his grave hated and despised above all his predecessors, leaving the church nearer the brink of destruction, and its pretense to a divine right to the temporal power shattered. He particularly abandoned religion, devoting himself exclusively to political intrigue, intended to embroil Europe in constant turmoil. He exercised no discretion, and possessed no element of greatness. It was only the terrible conditions of Rome, at the time of his election, when murder and robbery occurred in open day light in the streets of Rome, that permitted him to pose as a reformer, to cover his own simony. Caesar Borgia was the evil genius of this period, and he ruled Julius.

Bambo took secret pleasure in irritating Julius, this being the only means by which he could hope to be sent away from the Vatican. He wrote on the margins of Julius' favorite prayer book Spanish proverbs, which he knew the pope despised. On one occasion he wrote:

"Quien abrojas sicumbra espinas Coge." (He who sows brambles reaps thorns.)

Calling the suave and irritating Bambo upon the carpet, Julius engaged him in his customary abstruse argument, in which he quoted the offensive proverb, considering this a sufficient reminder of his displeasure. He invariably came out second best in these verbal combats, he generally retiring in a fit of anger. The learned and astute Bambo despised his pedantic false-pretense.

"If we are to maintain a spiritual heaven upon earth, we, also, must establish its antithesis, a well regulated hell," he said to Bambo.

"You have succeeded well, your Holiness, in laying the foundation for the latter institution as a concrete thing; but, do you know the primary significance of that word heaven of which you speak? Not the ecclesiastical meaning, which you know is the ecclesiastical government, but the root meaning."

"I admit, I am not a philologist; linguistic science has always been a tiresome bore to me," said Julius.

"My knowledge of these matters has always given me the privilege of speaking plainly to their Holinesses. Heaven is masculine, as evidenced by the prefix *he*. *Aven* means *nothing, nothingness, space, emptiness* and that is exactly the significance of the Christian heaven," grimly remarked the cardinal.

"That impeaches the very foundation of my infallibility," roared Julius.

"Both the church and the civil powers are equally resentful toward many of your decisions," mildly responded Bambo. "If you will permit me to point out a single fallacy which is the cause of much disputation, I respectfully suggest that your theory of infallibility intimates that God's vicegerency is subject to physical evolution. Other vicegerants have suggested a similar belief. Is the world to understand that this dignity, which has not been vouchsafed to many of your predecessors, is a special dispensation to your incumbency? Or is this gift of infallibility to be perpetuated in the future, and stand as an evidence of natural evolution in papal power?"

"Undoubtedly the infallibility of the head of the church must be a perpetual law," replied Julius.

"Suppose, then, that, at some future time, the

overwhelming judgment of humanity should declare this theory an untenable error, and without divine authority, what correction do you desire entered in your biography?"

"Leave the things of the future to future generations," hurriedly replied Julius. "To continue what I started to say, "there must be a suitable heaven to reward good and faithful subjects of the church for obedience, and a suitable hell for the punishment of those who will not obey the church. The urgent necessity for the enforcement of the will of the church is becoming more apparent each day."

"You arouse a very serious thought, your Holiness. Is the Holy See to regulate the operations of both heaven and hell upon earth?"

"The keys of both heaven and hell were surrendered to the church for that purpose, undoubtedly it must control both," cautiously replied the pope.

"Naturally, then, all divine instruction for the conduct of both institutions must be delivered through the vicegerent," said Bambo.

"Certainly," responded Julius, looking askance at the wily cardinal.

"The possession by you of the keys of hell, necessarily gives you full authority over the conduct of that institution," purred Bambo.

"Yes."

"Have you permanently locked the gates of hell to prevent humanity from entering, or Satan from coming out?" asked Bambo.

"No."

"Then, after all, hell is merely an agent of the Christian enterprise and an ecclesiastical invention."

"Hell is as real as heaven," said the Julius.

"More real than heaven, for he-ll means the *grave*, while he-aven means *nothing*," declared Bambo. "You declare you are the vicegerent of the God of heaven, why are you not equally the vicegerent of Satan in hell?" said Bambo.

"God rules over Satan on earth," whined Julius, weakening.

"Then, if God is so anxious to divert humanity to heaven, why does he not lock the gates of hell to prevent their going there, and prevent Satan from coming into the world to further extend evil? Thus humanity could be driven into heaven through the church. None has tasted of your heaven, while all have roasted in your earthly hell," said the cardinal.

"Ah, that is exactly our object in assuming the temporal power, which gives us legislative control, that we may establish proper statutory laws to compel the wayward and rebellious to recognize the saving power of the church," excitedly responded Julius.

"Undoubtedly, then, you do not control Satan upon earth, for surely you cannot attribute this stubbornness to God," mused Bambo.

"Satan is loosed upon earth to reveal innate wickedness in all humanity, which must be purged out of men before they may enter the kingdom of heaven," urged Julius.

"That is, to vindicate the doctrine of 'original sin.' Evil must be legislated into mankind; that is very practical," doggedly urged Bambo.

Julius began to exhibit irritation.

Continuing, Bambo said:

"I can see, also, that, this drastic coercion incidentally will develop the sale of indulgences. I am speculating regarding what the result will be when you have absolute temporal power, and good and evil are combined in a happy medium under one earthly control. Wouldn't God lose his prestige under such human arrangements?" said Bambo.

Pope Julius looked searchingly at Bambo, realizing the danger of his leading him into a trap, and an acknowledgment of error, then he slowly said:

"My good Cardinal Bambo, I should request that our conversation cease now, did I not know your cunning nature. I know that you are aware of the underlying principles of the church. Of course it is human. It could not be otherwise. It was a misfortune that mistakes were made in the beginning, and due provisions were not made for the future mental development of a rapidly increasing humanity. It is now too late to correct these miscalculations; the church cannot acknowledge these mistakes without admitting error and fallibility, and this would be fatal to the personal God theory.

Temporal power in the church means arbitrary

control, and that we seek as a measure of self-protection. Should the church lose its prestige now,
chaos would engulf the civilized world. It is essential to establish upon earth a living purgatory as
a well-spring of St. Peter. The legality of the sale
of indulgences is unquestioned by every authority
of the church. It is the future support of the church.
As the refining process enfolds humanity, the church
resources must of necessity expand until all men
are safely brought under the authority of Christ.
Of course it is human. God can only act through
men. It is in this manner that he manifests in the
flesh."

"That is very frank," softly replied Bambo.
"The present as well as the future fate of the church
rests upon the permanency of a colossal tariff, levied
upon cultivated evil; that is, evil created by statutory
laws made for this specific purpose."

"Why not?" demanded Julius, "Gold is refined
by fire; humanity is refined by temptation and trial.
He who comes out pure is worthy to take his place
among the angels; he who refuses to obey the dictates of God must go under the yoke. The church
must be supported; if the good cannot provide, evil
should be compelled to pay a license for its existence.
By placing the burden upon the sinful, the drawing
powers of the church are enhanced. Why is this
not proper and just, I should like to know?"

"And what is your authority for this policy?"
asked Bambo.

"God himself.   Look!" and Julius turned to a passage in the scriptures.

"I make peace, and create evil."   (Is. 45:7.)

"Do you suppose God creates evil merely for pastime?   No! he does all things to enhance his own glory.   It is not only a privilege but a duty for his vicar to follow in his footsteps, a priest is not supposed to question his authority."

Cardinal Bambo arose as he made reply.

"Your Holiness, it is inconceivable that men of your intelligence, parroting each other down through the ages, still pretend to believe that the church derives its power from an impossible divine source. Your formulae mean nothing to me, but they do impress those who have not the opportunity to know the truth.

"No power of the church has ever changed one law of nature, although it has defiantly opposed nature in a bombastic pretense of reflecting the will of an impossible and fabulous god, whose servants are human, and must be fed by human energy. The church is fantastically patterned after natures principles and forms, and must of necessity be fed, clothed and maintained by natural laws and processes, and this law is the very foundation:

"It is a fixed law in nature to cultivate, foster and extend that upon which a system depends for its life-giving substance and physical support.

"With each century, the world has grown wiser to the palpable truth, that Christianity merely is the concealing cloak, covering a predatory system, originally founded upon its own construction and interpretation of what is sinful; that it lives, thrives, and has its being, in an atmosphere of its own creation—cultivated evil. Should this conception of evil cease, the church would not stand for a day. Every known statistic proves that, enlarged congregations do not reduce or correct per capita evil, but they do enhance the fabulous wealth of the church.

"This vindicates your theory that, the church may be enlarged by making it a refuge for evil people willing to pay for protection. You must know, your Holiness, that the origin of that theory was that accursed institution which planted its defiant banner on Mount Palatine, seven hundred and fifty-three years before Christianity, and made it a refuge for criminals from all the clans of Europe—a retreat for the criminal scum of the civilized world. Every monastery of the early centuries was fashioned after this rendezvous. If it is your purpose to convert the church into this kind of vestibule to your new hell, I cannot subscribe to your theories. I warn you now, with all its prestige, the church cannot traffic in good and evil, playing one against the other, thus making a commerce of religion, and live.

"If you must vindicate that damnable doctrine of 'original sin,' by legislating crime into humanity by endless statutory laws, to save the face of Christianity, you will hatch out a brood of vipers from your own smug nest."

Purple with rage, Julius was standing with upraised hands, clinched till the blood ran down his palms.

"Stop! stop!" he shouted.

"Traitor to your vows as a priest! I excommunicate you a thousand times! Your morals cannot exceed your unruly manners."

Bambo responded with even more galling words.

"Although my language may not be pleasing to you, nevertheless it specifically reveals the secret purpose of your theory of infallibility. It is the theory of Gregory VII, and Innocent III. It is to be shield and buckler to foil reaction, from future illogical policies, intrigues and inevitable scandals. God can do no wrong, because he is under no law, because he cannot be reached.

"Where there is no law there is no transgression."

"The pope is God on earth, hence, the pope can do no wrong."

"It would seem to me that your distinguished uncle, Sixtus IV, raised sufficient hell, for all ordinary church purposes, when he debased the papal throne by conspiring against the lives of the Medicis. If he could so woefully underestimate the powers of that single Florentine famity, by what measure do you gauge the whole civilized world, whose enmity you seem bent upon provoking. I now place myself at your disposal."

Cardinal Bambo was now standing defiantly before His Holiness, strong and unafraid, in the belief, that, like his predecessors, he was an arrant coward.

The pope was trembling with both anger and fear. This crippled thing must surely have some great power back of him, to thus boldly assert his manhood in the presence of the greatest dignitary in all the world. Surely no other pope had ever been so affronted. It was contrary to all the traditions of pontifical dignity and sacredness.

Raising his hands high he cried:

"I forbid such treasonable utterances in my presence," and he made a motion as though he would strike Bambo.

"I have nothing for you to destroy but this poor, broken body, deformed by a priest. My soul is my own. You are not as formidable to me as you appear to yourself," snorted Bambo.

Julius struggled hard, biting his lips till the blood gushed from them. He knew not what course to pursue. Seating himself he drummed nervously upon the arms of his chair. Well did he know that he had accomplished his purpose; he had uncovered the greatest menace to the full accomplishment of his papal designs, yet he found it a living, writhing thing, which he feared to further arouse or antagonize. He knew that this frank display of independence, and defiance to customs and discipline, must be backed up by some great secret power, the nature of which he must ascertain before antagonizing it too strongly. This Bambo was not an ordinary adversary. He knew the underlying false pretense of all that the papacy stood for.

Suddenly turning upon Bambo he savagely exclaimed:

"You are the only person in my court daring to oppose me by expressing your odious personal views, and stubbornly antagonizing every thing I desire to accomplish. I am tired of this opposition and it must cease."

The hunch-back cardinal listened patiently, a sinister smile lurking about his thin, firm lips, which boded no good to Julius. As the pope paused, Bambo replied:

"I cordially agree with you, neither will I permit my own opinions to be bent to meet views contrary to reason and common sense. I am not of that school. I am not impressed with human infallibility. You must be responsible for your own errors. I am not a servant to blindly obey orders. If we cannot dwell together in amity, it is my duty to withdraw. I must suggest, however, for your protection, that, you keep a close and confidential espionage upon the *Archivio Secreto*, if you do not want the secret records of your bishoprics to become public property. The trafficking in benefices is becoming a stench in the nostrils of Europe, and is the source of much scandal. Moreover, your determination to press your proposal to excommunicate all kings, and deprive them of their kingdoms, is not acceptable to the college of cardinals."

After this impressive talk, with a calm, provoking smile, the hunch-back cardinal, whose father had once filled the papal chair, slowly withdrew from the holy presence, leaving Julius sitting in gloomy silence, marooned in his own desolation.

Going direct to the chief librarian, Bambo handed him his resignation as custodian of the *Archivio Secreto,* taking a receipt from him.

Writing a carefully worded letter to his other colleagues, he took his departure from the Vatican and Rome.

It was with grim satisfaction that he left behind him the inevitable troubles rapidly accumulating about Julius II.

The Medicis could not forgive Julius for being of the same blood as Sixtus IV, who had taken from them a life long sinecure—the treasuryship of the Holy See and given it to the murderous Pazzi, thereby establishing a deadly feud between these two strong Catholic families.

Cardinal Bambo had in mind the treacherous intrigues of this nature, chargeable to the blood of Francis de Albescola de la Rovere.

It was not possible for the bigoted and narrow minded Julius to rise above the level of envy and hate, and make friends of the powerful Medicis, whose enmity was more to be feared than the kickbacks of his own intrigues, which were making him the laughing stock of his colleagues, and drawing upon him the ridicule of sovereigns.

Bambo had watched the Medicis slowly but surely headed for the papal throne, and pitied the stubborn blindness of Julius, that he could not at least conceal his contemplated treachery against

Florence, especially with the knowledge that his
uncle, Sixtus IV, had brought lasting disgrace upon
the church, and the pontifical throne, by a similar
treachery.

But there was brewing a sweet revenge for the
much persecuted family of the Medici. Cardinal
Bambo, farsighted diplomat that he was, saw it
coming, and promptly went to Florence and made
known the fact of his retirement, and the reasons
therefor, in order to clear his own skirts of the
Julian treachery. He then retired to Venice, where
he remained in quiet and comfort, watching for
the time when the Medicis would wrest from the
family Rovere—the Franciscan—the family of
bishop—mongering, nepotism and simony, control
over the college of cardinals and the pontifical
throne.

Even this would not compensate them for the
foul murded of Julian de Medici by the hired assassins of Sixtus IV, under the borrowed shadow of
the elevated host.

Even though swift vengeance did overtake and
punish the tools of Sixtus, nothing could conceal
or excuse his evil purpose to exterminate, by criminal methods, the Medici family.

While the hanging body of his accomplice, the
bishop of Piza, insanely gnawed, in dying agony, at
the dead body of his hanging companion in the
crime, Francisco Pazzi, Sixtus, in his blind hatred,
excommunicated every thing and every body in

Florence, because of the discovery and exposure of his diabolical connivance in the crime.

Had Sixtus been tried before a jury of European potentates, the day of his hanging would have been perpetuated as a festival occasion.

Thus could an ordinary, common-grained man, fold about him the protecting cloak of the church, and defy all civil law. It was a common saying of popes, that, they had the right to kill with their own hands those who defiantly disobeyed their edicts.

That was Christianity in the sixteenth century. But the nations were looking on with grim disapproval. Even the Sultan of Turkey refused to give refuge to Sixtus' murderous Bandini, returning him to Florence to be ignominiously hanged.

All Europe resented this treachery of Sixtus. It brought the church into a conspicuous light, and defamed God through his wicked vicegerent. Italy, France and Germany, to save their own churches from toppling, openly repudiated Sixtus.

Although himself wounded almost to death by the assassins, Lorenzo de Medici earned the applause of Europe by his patient, conciliatory attitude in the better interest of the church, thus directing the public indignation more strongly against Sixtus. This doubtless sowed the seeds which were just now beginning to blossom. His son, John, or Giovanni de Medici became Pope Leo X, and the son of the murdered Julian later became Pope Clement VII.

This was the gloomy picture before Julius II. Right well did he know that the deformed Bambo, with his penchant for secret records, was wise to the rottenness of his own past life, and the murderous Rovere blood welled up in his own heart. He resolved to coax Bambo back to Rome and put him safely out of the way.

Few men had come into the same intimate contact with the popes, and none had the same just reason for holding them in utter contempt as Bambo. Not one had measured up to the full sature of honorable manhood.

Julius had been secretly warned against Bambo's canny knowledge of vatican secrets, and more than once had he wrought himself up to the point of laying violent hands upon Bambo, only being balked by the fear that violent action might precipitate the very exposure he most desired should remain concealed.

This hesitation had enabled Bambo to escape with his life. He was well aware of the perils of his remaining there.

Perhaps no other person experienced a greater sense of relief at the death of Julius than did Bambo.

It was like a vindication of Bambo, for him to receive from Giovanni de Medici, shortly after he was raised to the pontifical throne, an invitation to assume his former confidential position, including, now, the important office of *Datary*.

Bambo occupied this position of trust through the incumbency of Leo X, retired again during the brief administration of Adrian VI, and returned under another Medici, Clement VII, who was the posthumous son of the murdered Julian de Medici.

His previous service, under Alexander, Pius III, and Julius II, were his most strenuous experiences.

It was Julius who attempted to leave for himself a permanent monument in the erection of St. Peter's but it remained for Leo X to immortalize the sale of indulgences by advertising it broadcast and causing the Reformation. Nevertheless it helped largely to extend St. Peter's.

Bambo, after having labored hard with both Leo X and Clement VII, declared that the *office of Pope would corrupt God himself.* He left the post, temporarily, shortly after Clement was elevated, thoroughly disgusted even with the Medicis. Clement was tempted to recognize the organization of a secret espionage system to be called the "Company of Jesus." Bambo foresaw, that, should such a militant body be secretly turned loose upon the people, they would be surreptitiously enslaved by an invisible government, subjected to eternal espionage and inquisitional torment, and devoured by multiple taxations, until exterminated by devastating wars.

On the theory that the weaker the nations the stronger the church, it was a fixed policy of the popes to keep nations at war.

Bambo made a careful survey of the proposed new order and decided that this sinister power should not be permitted to saturate nations of people with faith in a premeditated and permanent state of mental and physical slavery.

There had long been a suspicion on the part of the Sacred College that Bambo had discovered some clue to the long lost history and records of the gnostics, and that this was the secret power he held over the popes, for only Julius had ever resented, even what appeared to be rank insolence toward popes, on his part, and yet he retained a strange and friendly attachment of all who knew him.

Of Bambo one thing was admitted; he was no hypocrit; he told the truth. He of all men best knew the fabulous nature of the ecclesiastical pretensions.

CHAPTER V

VOICELESS ST. PETER'S

THE GRAIN OF THE WOOD REVEALS THE WEAKNESS OF THE BEAM

O N March 18th, 1524, Don Alvard de Ricalde quietly entered Rome, experiencing no difficulty in convincing all challengers that he was a messenger of the Holy See.

He found suitable lodging for himself and his good horse, to whom he had given the Christian name of Belial, confiding to him the truth, that, they had engaged in a dangerous enterprise.

This intrepid man, raised in an atmosphere of personal freedom, was not hampered by any scruples of fear or uncertainty, nor was he given to wasting time. He immediately plumed himself for strenuous work. Nevertheless, had he been blessed with the presience of an Elijah or a Daniel, he would have been appalled at the experiences awaiting him, like so many gorillas, along his future path. It is even doubtful if he should have believed it worth the exhaustive labors involved to go forward to meet their challenges. But Don Alvard was not a man easily daunted. With his contempt for the church pretensions of divinely inspired authority, he accredited to himself the same divine authority, to justify his own acts on the opposing side. The church had little or no respect for the civil law, therefore, in so far as his attitude toward the church was concerned, he would have none, he was a law unto himself; he would accuse, judge and punish those whom he recognized as the foes of humanity, according to his own conscience, and with the same cruelty as exhibited by the murderous inquisitors. They studiously invented and devised new and novel forms of torture for the innocent people falling into their clutches, he would vie with them and punish them according to their well earned merits, even if hell itself became jealous. He had enrolled himself, as the champion of humanity, against the fabulous God of vengeance of the conscienceless, ecclesiastical enterprise, and he would carve his record in the bloody history of his time.

Rome was writhing under papal changes, no two popes having the same policies in the conduct of God's office, located in Rome, to govern humanity throughout the world.

When the martial Julian de la Rovere ascended the papal throne in 1503, as Julus II, he at once set himself about elaborating St. Peter into a vast Cathedral, as a monument to himself. Nevertheless, by his mean, narrow, bigoted policies, he gained for himself the hatred of all who came in contact with him. Had the Christian God been a reality, he would have repudiated him. His ten years incumbency worked great harm to the cause of the church.

When Giovanni de Medici became pope, as Leo

X, (1513) he posed as a patron of art and learning, and began to show his contempt for Julius by attempting the impossible task of crowding into his brief span all the reforms necessary to overcome the evil results of a thousand years of educational suppression, and cultivated ignorance, intolerance and bigotry.

No man has ever been so great that the papacy would not taint him with its poisonous fumes. Bambo was right, the position would corrupt God himself, if such a being existed.

Leo X found his self-imposed reformation a thankless task, and a hopeless aspiration.

Ecclesiastical depravity had inoculated the blood of humanity with a loathsome disease, and Leo was not a physician.

God having refused to grant his proud ambition, Leo turned to the devil for inspiration, and with startling results. Desiring to outdo the hated Julius, by completing St. Peter, and having not the wherewithal, he conceived that amazing traffic with the devil of licensing crime, thereby bringing about the unexpected Reformation.

Pope Leo's edict of the sale of indulgences, for crime, openly advertised to the world, was such a radical smack in the face of all that Christianity stood for, God became disgusted and has never since been heard from on earth. It caused the Reformation, and branded popes in the forehead, as political freaks. The consequence is, the proud Cathedral of St. Peter smells of crime as well as garlic, every stone was bought with tainted money, confiscated from the moulding ruins of feudal castles.

Even a Medici had to admit, to his dismay, that, the great political reptile, called the church, was a system of perpetual motion. He could not stop its momentum to examine it for defects, gathered in fifteen hundred years of constant wear and tear. The cumulative mistakes of his unerring predecessors clung about it like barnacles on a foul ship. Consequently, it had acquired so many eccentric motions it was dangerous to try to take the monkey-wrenches out of its wheels. The Catholic universe was out of tune, and Leo was not a piano-tuner.

All who were wise to the situation realized that, in due time, Christianity as a religion, would expire by limitation, and ecclesiasticism would seize political control of the world or cease to be. Through the ages it would cling to the moth-eaten Christian cloak as a disguise—an ecclesia is not a religion.

The forces were already loosened and set in motion to make the sixteenth century the most cruel and bloody period of all time, in order to bring humanity under abject terrorism. This was the sole purpose of the inquisition. The seeds of evil were widely sown and had taken deep root in human institutions. Those who had purposely sown evil, well knew that succeeding popes would reap and garner the harvest, followed by a host of sycophant gleaners. There was no hope for future humanity;

drudgery, ignorance and poverty for future generations were inevitable. Leo had sown crime that the church might thrive on evil. Well did he know that *every system cultivates that upon which it depends for maintenance.*

Finding that he could not master or mend the situation, Leo attempted to cast a glamour of glory over Italy, as a cloak to conceal the shame of the church, and to draw attention away from the glare of burning homes, wantonly being pillaged, and the innocent being slaughtered throughout the Christian world by brigands turned loose upon the world by the insane popes, in the name of their illogical and inconceivable Christ. The odor of burning flesh is a sweet savor in the nostrils of the Christian God.

Like the beating of the drums of Tophet, to drown the cries of the innocents being sacrificed by fire, the inquisition concealed the heinous character of the ecclesiastic exploitation.

Leo succeeded most admirably in concealing from the credulous masses of the world the most sinister and deadly encroachments of the most hateful thing ever incubated and hatched by the church of Rome—that monster, insane fanatacism, which smothered out of the human heart all love, and implanted in its stead hate, causing men to sacrifice their own blood kin in a blind frenzy to win the applause of the church, vindicating the damnable doctrine of hate placed in the mouth of its fabulous Christ.

"Think not that I am come to send peace on earth; I came not to send peace but a sword.

"For I am come to set a man at variance against his father and the daughter against her mother.

"He that loveth father or mother more than me is not worthy of me."   (Matt. 10.)

This is the sweet natured saviour in whose name the inquisition burned and tortured to death tens of millions of innocent men, women and children. Prince of peace?   What a lie!

Church fanaticism, which flourished under Leo X, debauched every decent human instinct, and inoculated the blood of humanity with the virus of incurable hate.   The best parts of Europe were desolated by inspired mobs of her own people, absolved by their hell inspired priests, in anticipation of the commission of these crimes which had blossomed out of Leo's traffic in indulgences.

This policy of persecution could not be suspended, because it was an inherent evil in the constitution of the organization, and constantly being suggested by inspired precedents in its canonized scriptures, to be put into practice and execution in the Christian dispensation.   For any pope to attempt to suppress these evils was to acknowledge the fallibility and error of the church.   These cruel interpretations had been preached by generations of evil minded men, posing as vicars of God, and claiming to be infallible, therefore, to repudiate their work would impeach the very foundation of Christianity, tarnish all saintly crowns, and reveal the claim of divine temporal power as a glaring false-pretense, which would smirch their own God.

In all ages, the church has sacrificed the people to save itself, as its God murdered the innocent bastard of David and Bath-sheba, to save the face of the church, and did not punish the murderous profligate, David, who is named the father of Christ. (Mat. 1:1.)

The peoples of the world owed little to their weak sovereigns of that period. They were too often puppets in the hands of the ruling popes, who placed their crowns upon their heads, then kicked them off, to show their contempt for what their sovereignty stood for—common mankind. Resentment of this was slow to reflect benefit to the people.

No effort to interpret the flimsy nature of the scriptures were permitted, hence the church glamour hypnotized, awed and terrorized the ignorant people into a blind belief of some vast, concealed power which gave men such strength.

This was the period, and these were the conditions prevailing, when Don Alvard de Ricalde added a couple of feet of steel to his blade, and whetted its edge, preparatory to his assault upon the human squid which had wrapped its slimy tentacles about all that humanity stood for. O, that the world might have had a thousand such men at that time.

Don Alvard, starting out into the world to right his own wrongs, and avenge the cruel and unjustifiable death of his dear mother and sister—one example out of thousands—as he came in contact with the ungodly crimes of the inquisition, he felt his cause expanding, and his desire for vengeance became cumulative. If the God of Christianity had set the precedent for the law of vengeance for wrongs, he would take full advantage of that law in his own case, for he was against human individuals who had committed unwarranted crimes against him, and the law did not protect him.

He became the wandering nemesis of ecclesiasticism, and the defender of persecuted humanity. He never sheathed his ponderous weapon so long as he could openly wield it against oppression and wrong. When he did sheath it, he had planted a tree whose leaves would heal the nations of the earth.

He was known and secretly dreaded, by the instigators of these evil deeds, because he killed in the open, and shouted his protests from the mountain tops. They did not seek him; he sought them, and only too frequently found them—they feared he would set Europe on fire against Rome, but the disease was too deep seated to be easily eradicated. It had eaten too deeply into the human constitution and made lesions which could not be mended.

It was a trying period for the bishops of Rome. That which the popes most dreaded, ridicule, was soon to have an ally in Don Alvard.

To his great disappointment, Bambo had found Leo X as treacherous as the preceding popes. While he was above the contemptible level of the Roveres, and did many things for which he received credit, endearing him to the Italian people, his good deeds too often cloaked some deep treachery. He was literally smothered in his uncontrollable hatreds. Under his rule the intrigues of the Holy See became deeper rooted, and bid fair to bear bitter fruits for future generations.

The pontiffs before Leo X had set the world on fire to "burn the tares," and Leo now found himself fighting the consequences to save the church, his fatal error being his advertised sale of indulgences for crime, which became the precedent for all governments to establish a similar system under the civil law, encouraging endless laws.

Taking advantage of this, Luther and Calvin, equal fanatics, fanned the fires of hell beneath St. Peter, and kept the popes dancing a holy jig to keep their own naked souls from blistering. The insatiable fires of the inquisition also singed the tender hides of many popes, as well as civil rulers.

Early in the sixteenth century, Rome began to mother the French masses to incubate the fanatical mob-spirit which gave to the Holy See power to practically smother the nation. The greatest powers of Rome were transferred to French soil, to secretly undermine the civil power and establish the church authority, developing some of the most contemptible rulers that ever disgraced their high postions.

Leo X literally choked himself to death in his hatreds, dropping dead from unholy joy upon learning that France had been expelled from Milan, although but forty-six years of age.

Luther was right, Leo had been caught red-handed trafficking with the devil, and making the confessional a secret bargain counter for the sale of privileged crime.

Adrian had no opportunity to manifest his just and frugal nature, but another Medici began to patch up the rents in the Christian church with very poor success.

Giulio de Medici, as Clement VII, botches the work of his kinsman Leo X, by refusing to divorce Catherine of Aragon, and denouncing the marriage of Henry VIII, with Anne Boleyn, thus sticking his nose into private family affairs.

Clement had just comfortably settled himself upon the papal throne when our hero, Don Alvard de Ricalde, kicked his caravan into Rome, looking for one handsome Cardinal Bambo.

Although impatient for action, the Don approached his task with caution. He knew no friendly element in Rome to which he might turn in case of an emergency, therefore, he deemed it wise to test every foot of his ground, and keep his hand upon his ponderous fighting-iron. He now possessed the rings of both the *legate*, and the one taken from Sanzaro. Concluding that Sanzaro's ring might possess the greater potency, he resolved to use that as his credential to the Vatican. Feeling sure a messenger from Sanatos could not reach Rome under several weeks, the dangerous Gonsalvo could not be stirred to action against him. He, at least, could determine the advantage or disadvantage of his having made the arduous journey to Rome.

He first made a visit to the Lateran of St. John, desiring to view the ancient home of the bishops of Rome. The gloomy edifice depressed him. Nevertheless, he was deeply impressed with this reminder of the glorious Rome under Constantine. The noble family Laterani must have been possessed of great wealth to have resided in so grand a palace at so early a period.

There arose in his mind the very question which had made it essential for the church to forge the false-pretense of a gift of this palace to Pope Silvester I, by Constantine. "How was it possible for the church to acquire the wealth which enabled it to possess so grand a palace?" Was it possible that the bishops of Rome had occupied this palace for more than a thousand years? Did God require such pretentions? Who had paid for all this? Credulous humanity.

A brass plate informed him that, in the year 1377 the papal household was removed to the Vatican, to which he now took his way.

If he had been impressed by the palace of the Lateran, he was astounded upon beholding the vast wilderness of St. Peter's. It was his good fortune to come first to the space which later became the magnificent *Piazza di san Pietro*, with its awe inspiring series of Doric columns which have put wonder in the minds of millions of travelers.

This approach to the church of St. Peter was about 1000 feet long by 800 feet wide and was temporarily laid out as a beautiful garden. The pavement which was laid by Benedict XIII, (1394-1417), and who, by the way, was a Spaniard, Peter de Luna, had cost the church some twelve thousand pounds sterling.

Don Alvard did not permit one interesting feature to escape him. His costume identified him as a papal messenger and his tremendous proportions and fearless bearing, commanded respect from all observers.

Turning to the right, he approached the *Portone di Bronzo,* which led to the entrance of the Vatican. There he encountered two huge guards who forbade further approach.

Don Alvard inquired the way to find Cardinal Bambo, and they directed him to pass into and through the great *basilica,* even then vast and barn-like, under the reconstruction of Julius II, which began in 1506, and had been continued through the pontificate of Leo X, who selected the great Raphael to supervise the work. Leo X met the expenditures by advertising broadcast, the sale of indulgences, thereby causing the disastrous Reformation. St. Peter's was founded on crime.

The quick eye of Don Alvard, as he passed slowly through the church, observed the utter absence of architectural grace and beauty. It seemed to him that several styles had been progressively patched together, one having died out before the

other had begun to breathe. It was neither austere
nor dignified, yet it was deathlike and cold, in itself a reflection of a common papal desire to inspire
awe and fear. It seemed to symbolize the approaching end of the three leading supervising architects,
Giuliano da Sangallo, Fra Giocondo da Verona, and
Raphael, none of whom lived to view the completion
of the structure.

Because of its rugged, uncouth character, Don
Alvard experienced a sense of lonliness; danger
seemed to lurk near; its silence was like an accusing whisper. He instinctively waited for an expected peal of thunder and a flash of lightning. It
well symbolized the fabulous St. Peter. Evidently
Voltaire experienced this same sensation when he
referred to the "thunders of the Vatican."

The best critics in the world have spoken ill
of the architecture of the greatest cathedral on
earth, but, Don Alvard experienced with a shudder,
the sensation of being in the living presence of the
greatest power on earth, by virtue of this eloquent
crudity. It was the crystallized expression of a soulless force, not a line of sympathy was permitted to
appear anywhere.

If architecture stands for anything, it is to reflect the spirit of the occupant of the structure,
hence, St. Peter's is perfect. Dante alone might
have added some warmth to its aspect.

This was no place to indulge in sentiment, or
to make mistakes, espionage lurked in each dark
recess; dead eyes peered from each mysterious

angle; it was a tomb not a church. What word of sympathy or hope could echo from these lofty arches, or from the musty, fluted surface of somber pillars, flaked with the dust of ages? They looked as though weary of bearing up their burdens.

To Don Alvard it was an empty sarcophagus long waiting to receive the dead carcass of the church.

Hearing the scraping of shuffling feet he instinctively placed his hand upon his sword; it was a sloven priest passing. Motioning for him to pause, he inquired the way to the offices of the *Datary*. Uttering not a word the priest pointed to a corridor.

Disgusted with the colossal church humbug, the Don walked toward the designated corridor. He had seen nothing suggesting the presence of God-like things; only the evidence of useless expenditure of wealth to rot in due time. The temple of God smelled loudly of garlic, doubtless left in the fetid atmosphere by passing priests. As a whole it was downright filthy, in, that, it was too vast to be kept scrupulously clean.

"If cleanliness is Godliness, this is a most ungodly place," thought the Don.

Coming upon another shambling priest, who seemed bent upon reaching his destination by skating, which motion was merely intended to keep his shapeless sandals upon his feet, the Don again made inquiry. The reply was the same poking of holes in the atmosphere as he pointed down the long corridor.

"Another dummy," exclaimed the Don, convulsed with laughter at the grim humor of it all. He did not know that these were *novitiates*, who had taken the vow of silence for atonement for some trivial slip of the tongue offensive to a grumpy old priest.

Finally he entered the ante-chamber of the *Museo-profano*, where he was indifferently directed toward the great *library galleries*, where he soon found himself in the library founded by Nicholas V. (1447.)

Here was a living structure whose architect had in mind some great future purpose. He roamed at will, no one seeming to have charge of the volumes.

He was no nearer to Cardinal Bambo than when he had entered the vast labyrinth, and he began to exhibit some impatience. Every sloven servant of God's vicegerency was apparently a dummy; he might as well be in the ante-chamber of a Turkish seraglio, in so far as human language was concerned. He mentally named it "voiceless St. Peter."
Suddenly he thought he heard the sound of a human voice; he listened, yes, doubtless a priest was mumbling a prayer in an adjoining closet. It matters not, he was going to suspend this prayer long enough to get some information out of the first man he had discovered with the faculty of speech. Now he more distinctly heard two voices, and he listened intently.

"Come! I'll trim my beard with the shears of St. Fortunatus, if I don't win this throw. Come!"

"By the Crown and Sword of St. Ferbronia, you loose!" exclaimed a boyish voice, with a laugh, "throw again."

"May St. Eutropius trample me with his hob-nailed shoes! What ill luck is mine!" grumbled the older voice. "Gut me with the iron hook of St. Vincent if I throw again."

Cautiously drawing back a heavy drapery, worth its weight in gold, Don Alvard peeped into a small ante-chamber, with a dusty tiled floor, and some rude benches against the walls.

A diminutive hunch-back, wearing a dirty cha-suble, as though coming from the usual mechanical mass, and a young page, anything but a *ganymede*, were tossing small pieces of copper at a mark on the floor.

So intent were they with their gambling, they did not observe the approach of Don Alvard until he was close upon them.

Looking down upon the sacred culprits he said:

"Did not your Christ cast the money changers and gamblers out of the temple?"

As the hunch-back priest looked up and ob-served the towering form above him he shrank back in surprise, crossed himself and exclaimed:

"Son of Satan! Where did you spring from?"

The giant looked down upon him with a good-natured, friendly smile, replying:

"Father of devils, no matter from whence I come,

both of us will be consigned to the same melting pot when we die."

The look of fright in the hunch-back's countenance turned into a broad grin and an expression of unfeigned admiration gradually spread over his good-natured face. He laughed heartily at the Don's retort.

"I desire to locate the office of his Eminence Cardinal Bambo," said the Don.

"There is no such person," tartly replied the priest.

"That is strange, I bear credentials, and important messages, under the official leaden seal, addressed to Cardinal Paul Bambo, *Datary* to His Holiness Pope Clement VII," explained Don Alvard.

The dwarf eyed him suspiciously, covertly looking at his dress, and momentarily resting his eyes upon his ponderous sword.

"I am the *Datary*," he said indifferently.

Don Alvard began to show impatience.

The page had left the room and they were standing alone. The Don gruffly addressed the priest.

"Come, I am not given to parley," and, with a quick bend of his huge body, he unceremoniously tucked the kicking cardinal under his arm and entered the nearest doorway. Carrying him like a rag-doll, fussing and protesting, he deposited him upon a table in the middle of the room.

"Now, will you stop trifling with a courier of the Holy See? Tell me how and where I may locate Cardinal Bambo."

"I tell you there is no Cardinal Bambo. I am Paul Bambo, *Datary* officer to the vatican," sullenly growled the dwarf.

"You are Bambo!" exclaimed the Don, staring in amazement at the dwarf.

"Then bless the saints for bringing us together without a third person to introduce us, for I shall tell you something to take the kinks out of you."

"You need not make sport of my deformity," growled the still angry dwarf.

"Deformity! God forbid! I am the one entitled to sympathy. I can neither sit at an ordinary table to dine, nor comfortably sleep in an ordinary bed. What one of us lacks the other has, therefore, to equalize this difference we should strike hands as friends," and the Don gently lifted the dwarf from the table.

Bambo regained his composure and usual good-nature, and smilingly shook the big hand extended to him saying:

"Perhaps you are right, we may both need friends. Ordinarily, you would jeopardize your life by thus entering this holy place and laying rough hands upon a priest of the pope's household."

"Ha! Ha! you have never seen me in action! Wasn't it Samson who pulled down the temple upon the heads of his persecutors? Well, the pope and every cardinal in the sacred college would jump through the smoked-glass windows of St. Peter, if I ever got loose in here," and the Don whipped out his long sword and fairly made it sing as he carved the atmosphere into ribbons.

Bambo threw up his hands in afright, crossed himself, rushed to the door and closed it. Placing his fingers upon his lips he returned to the Don saying:

"The wise man does not wholly rely upon his brute strength, against great odds and invisible enemies, until diplomacy is exhausted, and his back is to the wall. Strategy and caution save many scars, my friend. Super-strength and master-discretion are invincible."

The Don acknowledged this wisdom with a profound bow.

"You may be my master in diplomacy, my good Bambo. I will compensate you with strength with which I am well endowed."

Bambo assumed an air of business importance, bidding the Don to be seated.

"You say you have messages for me. It is an extraordinary procedure, but I desire for my own special reasons, to exhibit my official seal of authority, that you may feel yourself at ease in the exchange of confidences, for I have a strange feeling that your visit here presages important events. I am astonished that you did not fall into the official hands by your inquiries for me. Surely the discipline is growing lax."

Don Alvard also presented the seal ring which he had taken from Sanzara to Bambo, causing the latter to turn chalky white and to look askance at the Don.

"Is your important message from Sanatos?" he asked.

There was such a ring of savage resentment in his voice, Don Alvard hastily replied.

"Be not alarmed, good Bambo, it is worse than you believe, but fate is kind to both of us." He then presented to Bambo the letter of commendation given him by Sanatos, referring to Bambo as "handsome and witty."

Bambo read this and shrugged his deformed shoulders, his face showing his resentment.

The Don handed him an important looking packet, bearing the official lead-seal of court correspondence. Bambo broke the seal, opened the packet and found it contained a blank sheet.

He looked inquiringly at the Don.

The Don gave him the letter of instructions to Gonsalvo, which he had taken from the person of Sanzara.

Bambo exhibited signs of agitation as he perused this letter. Holding it trembling in his hands, he looked long and earnestly at Don Alvard, then he asked:

"How do you happen to be in possession of this confidential communication to Cardinal Gonsalvo? And why do you bring it to me?"

Don Alvard searched the now ashen face of Bambo to see if the question was friendly or otherwise, then assuming an attitude of suppressed anger, he replied:

"I have brought these matters direct to you, because I believe that we both are the victims of some devilish plot. We secretly are being betrayed into the hands of the accursed inquisitors. I know nothing of their hatred for you, but it is fear, and a desire for revenge, that directs their evil designs against me.

"I believed I would find in this despised Cardinal Bambo a strong man, whom they feared and sought to dispose of, therefore, a man who would appreciate knowing the truth. I believed that we might unite in a common cause for self protection."

Then the Don recounted his experiences in Savoe and his adventure bringing him to Rome.

Bambo sat thoughtful and gloomy; suddenly glancing up at the Don he said:

"You are an educated man, from whom did you receive instructions?"

Don Alvard related his educational course.

"Then you must have known Verosala, at Barcelona," exclaimed Bambo.

"My first friend," replied the Don.

"What has been your experience with Gonsalvo?" asked Bambo.

"None, that I am aware of," replied the Don.

"Come with me," and Bambo led him to a protected balcony overlooking the *Garden of La Pigna*.

"Now, do not expose yourself, but view the

priests below; this is the hour of their recreation in the gardens."

Several distinguished looking prelates were slowly pacing about the garden paths. As they listlessly fumbled their breviaries, and mumbled their mock devotional prayers, they reminded Don Alvard of a herd of sleek, fat cattle ruminating their cuds after the morning's browsing in rich pastures.

Occasionally they would gather in little groups and engage in earnest conversation, but not for long, this being contrary to the rules of discipline. Conclaves are not assembled in open gardens.

Don Alvard gasped, and tightly held Bambo's arm, exclaiming:

"Look! That is the hell-hound that led the massacre at Pampero!" and he pointed out a square built, dark visaged priest, who with another priest was walking toward where they stood concealed in the balcony, directly above the path.

Bambo quickly placed his fingers upon his lips, saying, "Wait, listen."

The two priests momentarily paused directly below them. They were engaged in a heated discussion, causing them to raise their voices above the usual tones heard there. The square man was saying:

"Yes, yes, but your altruistic ideas have prevented your receiving the red-hat."

"Altruism! May the mother of Christ curse me, if I am guilty of that crime," exclaimed the other. "I hate the mob of dumb cattle to which I must cringe and cater. The ox helps to turn the furrow, and the vat helps to make the wine; does it follow, that, because I keep them in order to perform their functions, I too aspire to become an ox or a wine-vat?"

The square man was shaking with laughter as he responded:

"If I were you, I would use some other simile, in view of your condition last evening."

"Ugh! you will not be serious," grunted the other, as they moved beyond the hearing of the listeners.

Turning to Bambo, the Don said:

"It was he who permitted the wanton murder of my mother and sister, and led the band of assassins who pillaged and destroyed Pampero."

Grasping the Don's arm, and quickly drawing him back into the room, Bambo softly said:

"Gonsalvo a murderer? I am glad we did not betray our presence. The game is ours," and he chuckled with secret glee.

"These men make popes, but just now, it so happens, I make and unmake cardinals. I am a hunchback, that is why I say I am not a cardinal. You saw no deformed men in that garden. Well, I do not take my recreation there. I sometimes play games with popes. Dwarfs and giants do not travel in herds or flocks. We are not of their class, my new made friend, hence they seek to outlaw us," and Bambo's emotions equalled those of Don Alvard.

"And that priest?" inquired the Don.

"That is Gonsalvo," was the reply.

"Curse of Christendom!" ejaculated the Don, grasping the hilt of his sword. "I shall kill him before I quit Rome."

"Wait," whispered Bambo, "you can get him at your leisure, wait till we have canvassed our position; he may be more useful to us alive than dead, just now. I promise you, however, he belongs to you, even though I myself would be delighted to strangle him."

"And that is Gonsalvo!" mused Don Alvard. "Now I add to my list Sanatos."

"No!" exclaimed Bambo. "Spare him to me."

"I do not feel that I can leave Rome until I have tortured the soul out of this murderous dog," urged the Don.

"On the contrary, you will leave Rome without coming in contact with him at this time, if you can possibly do so. He is too valuable for other purposes. I hope to confide to you a great secret and an important mission. Don Alvard, you must wait till I may explain it to you before involving yourself in dangerous complications."

Suddenly Don Alvard turned upon Bambo, looked sharply at him and said:

"This is extraordinary. I am in the church of Rome—the vestibule to hell, and the hot-bed of all deviltry. I have confessed to you my innermost secrets. I have confided to you sufficient to subject me to the inquisitional court, should you desire to betray me to this murderous beast, Gonsalvo. What

assurance have I that I am not betraying myself
to one of its high officials and subjecting myself to
grave personal dangers?''

In answer to this, Bambo turned his back toward
Don Alvard and savagely exclaimed:

"If you must have visible evidence, look! Is
that hump not sufficient? I was not born thus.
God originally made me beautiful. It was the hatred of nature's perfect works that caused a vicious
hearted priest to maim me for life. I, too, have a
sore heart to mend; I, too, am nursing a sweet revenge, one which, if I live to consummate my work,
will wipe out of existence this whole mangy tribe.
I have slaved and waited for all these many years
for fate to send to me a man; one who could take
the place of my poor broken body, listen to the unbroken soul within, and wield such a sword as you
have. My prayer has been answered as you will
learn. We must trust and have confidence in each
other. Humanity holds up her tired hands and calls
—we shall respond.''

Don Alvard looked the sympathy this speech,
delivered in tones of great anguish and bitterness,
had invoked in his own eager heart. He briefly
related to Bambo the facts of the massacre at Pampero, and the desolation of his own home, as an
apology for having expressed doubts regarding his
sincerity.

Bambo momentarily could not speak. He picked
up the papers lying upon the table, saying:

"Let us analyze our situation. Gonsalvo knows

nothing of your presence here. It may be weeks before Sanatos can communicate with him. While you are a marked man, because of your abnormal size, only accident will identify you. I doubt if Gonsalvo would remember you should he encounter you here; however, intrigue here is ripening into tragedy, and, mark me, trouble looms right close. I feel that I am near the time when I myself must act, assuming a different attitude toward the church; therefore, Don Alvard, frankly state to me your own attitude toward the church."

Don Alvard made an emphatic reply.

"I am not a believer in Christianity in any form. Having delved deeply into its origin and history, I am convinced it is a fraud and a snare, only intended to deceive and enthrall the weak-minded, uneducated masses. It is a necessary concealment for a premeditated exploitation of humanity, conceived in sin and executed in crime and iniquity, by the most sinister minds that ever invented snares for men. Their fictitious scriptures do not name one conspicuous character that cannot be charged with some form of sin. They cannot name one conspicuous character in the development of the ecclesiastical theocracy who may not be charged with duplicity in some form, from the forgery of the gospels to the murder of the millions of innocent beings. Their principal doctrines have been wilfully appropriated from every previous form of religion, and their practices include every previous form of worship."

Bambo held up his hands.

"You are talking treason in the house of the vicegerent of God."

"And I will go into the streets of Rome and make these same statements, and, within the hour, bring a mob of outraged people hammering at the doors of St. Peter," declared Don Alvard passionately.

Bambo smiled and laid his hand softly upon Don Alvard's arm, saying: "I am surprised that you are so familiar with the truth. It is a good foundation for the greater work ahead of you. I shall add new and startling things to your education. But, it is needless for you to recklessly expose yourself to loud threats and superfluous exhibition of your strength. It is not the loud thunder, but the silent lightning that executes.

"We have a better way. Rome was not built in a day, and that especially applies to ecclesiasticism. It has so interwoven itself with civil governments, and their political manipulations, that, it now is a fixed and integral part of them; in that, it is the key to party controversies, becoming the balance of power. It is the Christian church behind which it hides, which is vulnerable.

"No progress can be made until the nations of Europe overflow with population, and the church attempts to follow the people into strange lands. We will discuss this more fully at another time,

"It is sufficient now for me to say, if you and I are to join our arms and resources in a common cause, we must do it right. We both know that the church is a great false-pretense, erected on political power, and there is a single word which will break it—*ridicule*. I thus speak frankly to you, a perfect stranger, because you are a brave, courageous, earnest man. I trust you. The church is a much greater false-pretense than you believe. I hold the secret."

"In the work I have laid out, I fear neither pope nor devil, I am not afraid to speak the truth, and defend it to the death," said Don Alvard.

"Good! I am not condemning you. I am cautioning you. I too, have a score to settle with the priesthood and its secret monasteries; these are all we need challenge.

"Christianity is but the lamb's skin concealing the wolves, the external disguise. They must be rooted out of their hiding places and chastened by their own methods. Their secret places and practices must be held up to the sunlight and scorched by the scrutiny of humanity. Therefore, you must curb your enthusiasm and eagerness for physical action. I will teach you how to dig into the very vitals of papacy, by exposing the fictitious character of their alleged inspired scriptures.

"You may think it strange that I entrust to you my greatest life secret, but I am fearful that something may occur to prevent my leaving Rome in a manner to avert suspicion that a difference exists between myself and His Holiness. I will explain this to you as I reveal my story. It is His Holiness' practice to send those who differ with him on long missions, rather than expose the quarrel.

"I have labored unceasingly to place myself in a position to bring me into intimate contact with all the inner secrets of the priesthood. For many years I have been custodian of the sacred *Archivio Secreto*. I have equipped myself to qualify as secret legate at large, which will give me my freedom, yet leave me diplomatically attached to the Holy See. This provides me with a liberal expense account for myself and a secretary-companion. I shall have plenipotentiary powers, reporting only to the pope. In fact, my good Don Alvard, in all things pertaining to my diplomatic work I will be second only to the pope, thanks to my extraordinary knowledge of vatican secrets.

"You must surmise that there is a very urgent cause for this. There is, but I must reserve this until I can give you time to consider a proposal from me to accept the pleasing position of secretary-companion in my travels. Your duties would be to guard me against dangers while traveling from place to place, and to continue my work, in my name, should accident befall me, hence, you would be in my full confidence.

"I will allow you three days in which to superficially acquaint yourself with Rome, and to ponder my proposal.

"On the third day I shall ask you to again report here with your decision.

"Should you decide to accompany me, an inci-

dent of our leaving Rome will involve you in one
dangerous enterprise, which I feel I could not leave
unaccomplished."

Calling into the room a kindly faced man, of
about fifty years of age, he introduced him as his
confidential servant.   Maleano, who would join him
at his lodging, and, for the ensuing three days, would
act as special courier to conduct him to the interesting places in the ancient city.

CHAPTER VI

THE MYSTERIOUS PRISONER IN THE CASTLE ST. ANGELO

OF ALL ANIMAL KINDS, MAN IS MOST CRUEL TO HIS OWN FEMALE

MALEANO was no mean guide, moreover, he was extraordinarily well educated, and especially well informed as to the antiquities of Rome. This was the most interesting and instructive three days in the eventful life of our Cavalier, who was a willing and grateful student, eager for knowledge.

The giant Don stood, with folded arms, gloomily viewing the ruins of the *Forum Romanorum*, with its mutilated remains strewn in broken and mouldering heaps, and jagged, half decayed piles, as Maleano graphically delivered a most interesting discourse upon its early history and latter day vicissitudes, dwelling upon that period of Rome when the historic spot was a marsh, only 38 feet above the sea level, and, perhaps, frequently inundated by the Tiber, turning out both the money-changers and the fish-vendors. Here, before the small dealers were banished to the *Forum Piscatorium*, their loud smelling wares irritated the nostrils of the scribes and ranting philosophers; here, also, were located the *money-changers* and the *goldsmiths*.

Upon this historic spot, still loudly smelling of

the sordid Roman customs, were celebrated the funerals of the nobility. Greed for excitement, and desire for notoriety, gave license for converting trivial community events into public celebrations.

What a ravenous thing so-called human progression was, devouring even the historic hills to connect the capital with the Quirinal. What a jealous thing is human vanity; these vast arenas had been bedecked with gilded bronzes, rare marble statuary, and triumphal arches. At all of which time laughed, while all devouring decay gulped these vain conceits, as a hippopotamus fills his tremendous belly with a bale of hay.

It was a sad reflection upon Christianity, that, in the seventh century, when the last of these emblems of human vanity, the *Column of Phocas,* was erected, the crudeness of the architecture betrayed the tremendous decline in art, as its influences grew stronger. The most pathetically crude, and, at the same time, the most expensive structures in the world, are the temples of God, with their phallic fingers pointing to the sky.

For a thousand years, the most imposing and beautiful structures in the world, the grand castles of the decadent Roman nobility, were mere quarries from which the ravenous ecclesiastical enterprise pilfered its materials for the construction of its hidious churches.

Many boasted church columns, and huge corner stones, are but the confiscated parts of these castles, to appease the vanity and ravenous appetite of the church for carnal things. In like manner, Christianity plagiarized the doctrines of other religions.

With rage arising in his heart, the emotional and passionate Don listened, as Maleano pointed out the vast encroachments which had been made upon the walls of the ancient colosseum, the *Amphitheatrum Flavium,* the most imposing and colossal theatre structure in all the world, by the conscienceless popes, who had turned this property of the people into a quarry from which to mine the materials for their own aggrandizement. His mind reverted back to the gloomy St. Peter, as a specimen of degenerate architecture, reflecting the degeneracy of humanity under the ruthless hands of ecclesiasticism. The church was making as great inroads upon developing civilization as it was upon the material monuments of human hands. Its evil influence upon human progression was in exact proportion to the uncouth results as manifested in its gross structures.

Pointing to the summit of Mount Palatine, Maleano said: "There is the origin of the monastery as a refuge for those fugitives who for various reasons must flee from the world. That was the beginning of Rome, 753 B. C. It was an asylum for criminals of all nations. They fled to this place as a refuge to avoid punishment for their crimes. Here was erected the banner of defiance to the decent world. From Palatine its spread to Capitoline, Aventine, Esquiline, Mounts Coelius and Quirinalis.

"These six centers became the recognized places of refuge from the arm of civil law.

" 'Then ye shall appoint yon cities of refuge, that the slayer may flee thither.

" 'And they shall be unto you cities of refuge from the avenger.

" 'And of these cities, six cities shall ye have for refuge.'   (Num. 35:11, 12, 13.)"

Don Alvard listened in amazement, exclaiming: "Then, Christian duplicity is a thing of Rome!"

"Yes, disguised under the Greek word *Ecclesia,* signifying a legislative control.   Rome borrowed all the art and refinement it ever had from Greece, and the church borrowed the name of the governing body which ruled ancient Athens, the *Ecclesia* for its political purposes, concealing the truth, that secretly, it is a government."

"What devilesh hypocrisy," mumbled the Don.

"Come, now, I will show you the ancient pantheon, *(Sancta Maria ad Martyrs),*" said Maleano.

Upon arriving at this warehouse for priestly bones, the guide warned Don Alvard that this was the most sacred place in Rome, hence the name *pantheon.*   Its history held his attention closely until Maleano said: "Early in the seventh century Pope Boniface IV, consecrated it as a Christian church, (May 13, 609), dedicating it to all Saints. On this occasion twenty-eight wagon loads of bones, allegedly those of martyrs, were brought hither from the catacombs and dumped in a heap, this to be their future resting place."   To the horror of Maleano and a number of visitors, Don Alvard burst into a roar of laughter exclaiming: "In other words, the pope

moved the heavenly police-force closer to St. Peter.
Why, all these fake heroes died natural deaths as
fat, overfed priests.   What will happen at the time
of the resurrection, when the saints begin to quarrel
over these bones?"

Maleano held up his hands and urged the Don
to go quickly from the sacred place; this was blasphemy, the punishment for which was death.

The *pantheon* was the only ancient edifice in
Rome which had been kept in perfect preservation,
the word *pantheon* meaning *very sacred.*"

Nevertheless, the impious popes even confiscated
the copper off the dome and the supporting pillars
with which to embellish their own palaces and
temples.

They visited the catacombs, the first meeting
place of the Christians in Rome, and later a burial
place for the rotting carcasses of the Saints, including St. Peter and Saint Paul, who never existed in
actual life.   The monks with their brown, silken
beards, looked askance at the huge cavalier and
Maleano, showing them scant courtesy, and they
soon left the place convinced that church things
were gloomy and forboding.

One glance at the great tomb of Hadrian was
sufficient.   Don   Alvard   had   grown   impatient.
"Let's go back to the city," he said.   "I'm tired of
all these attempts to dignify rattling skeletons of
men whose sole mission in life was to keep humanity
in an uproar of hysterical excitement, or cast down

into abject gloom. I must give my attention to living things."

"Well, you know what the bible tells us," said Maleano.

"God is not the God of the dead, but of the living." (Matt. 22:32.)

"Yes, but the same Bible gives Christ greater powers than God himself possessed," replied the Don.

"For to this end Christ both died and rose, and revived, that he might be Lord both of the dead and the living." (Romans 14:9.)

"The purpose of this is clear," continued the Don, "for we shall all stand before the judgment seat of Christ.

"For it is written, as I live, saith the Lord, every knee shall bow to me, and every tongue shall confess to God." (Romans 14:10, 11.)

"This makes of Christ a priest to preside over the confessional." (Heb. 4:14—7:26.)

"Nevertheless, Christ himself says:

"I came not to judge the world" (John 12:47), remarked Maleano.

"This contradiction is made more emphatic by a positive evidence that this judgment refers to living men, for 'flesh and bones cannot enter heaven,' and this confession to Christ requires the bending of the knees."

"If you do not fully grasp the true intent and purpose of placing a master over men, I refer you to I. Peter 4:17.

" 'For the time is come that judgment must begin at the house of God; and if it first begin at *us*, what shall the end be of them that obey not the gospel of God?'

"Now, who is *us?*

"The paramount importance of this is evidenced by the fact that, the words *judge* and *judgment* appear in the bible more than one hundred times."

"What always greatly impressed me was a quotation from Collosians, often referred to by my friend and tutor, Verosala," said Don Alvard.

"Let no man therefore judge you in your meat, or in drink, or in respect of an holiday, or of the new moon or of the sabbath day." (Col. 2:16.)

"Then he would say, read I. Timothy 2:5.

"The *man* Christ."

Thus they bandied their Bible knowledge as they returned to the lodging of the Don, who had reached the conclusion that Rome was wholly controlled by Catholic superstition. He realized that Rome had been tarnished by ignorance more than by age. She was a victim of fanaticism more than of the ravages of time. He had absorbed quite sufficient to fatten the imagination of the most gluttonous mind. He had seen things in Rome he did not dream existed —evidences of a rich past, bankrupt by bigotry, and slowly passing out of living vision and memory that it might not cast a shadow in the path of the rapidly developing church power which dazzled and amazed sovereigns, and frightened ignorant humanity into different degrees of hysteria and insanity.

After a night's rest, and refreshment, the Don felt a great relief in again presenting himself to Cardinal Bambo. He had found Rome a wonderfully interesting, but slimy thing. Its grandeur was putrifying beneath the mould of its broken walls; its life was but the maggots thriving upon the rotting carcass. Nothing which he had read about Rome exactly registered with what he had seen. A growling monster seemed buried somewhere within this ruin of a once great city, like the tread of a lion in a darkened cavern. Death was manifest in the catacombs, but behind the grinning skull of Rome was something virulent which refused to die. Treachery was in the very atmosphere. A serpent had coiled within that grinning skull.

He found the hump-back cardinal in anything but an amiable mood. Some erratic instruction from His Holiness, had threatened to disjoint their plans and prevent Bambo's immediate departure. Only by the greatest diplomacy had he overcome the pending disaster, and he was now eager for action before the fluctuating mind of Clement could take another course.

Don Alvard thanked Bambo for the services of his confidential servant who had proven a worthy and well informed guide, conducting him to the most essential places and sights of the Ancient City. He also quickly made known his desire to accept Bambo's proposal, declaring his readiness to execute the task of which he had spoken.

"I want you to assist me in the release from

the castle St. Angelo, of the Countess de Milliette, niece to the Count Brabon of Castle Bonelle, who is my great friend and benefactor," said Cardinal Bambo.

"Why, that is the name mentioned by Sanatos, in his communication to Gonsalvo," exclaimed the Don. "Isn't that a remarkable coincidence?"

"Exactly so," replied Bambo. "Her uncle is not aware of her incarceration here, he having been deceived into the belief that she, of her own free will, had taken the vail and retired to a convent.

"I have not dared advise him of the truth because of his brave and intrepid nature. At no time has it been safe for me to do so without jeopardizing the life of both the count and his niece.

"This is one of the great court secrets, Don Alvard, and if there were an avenging God in heaven, he would visit an especially cruel vengeance upon those who brought this good and beautiful woman to this dire state, merely because the countess would not sacrifice her pure womanhood to the low-born profligate, the nephew of that moth-eaten cardinal Bishop of Tortosa, which match was proposed to strengthen the church. She was secretly brought here and placed in St. Angelo, the vilest hole outside of hell, where she will remain for the balance of her life if we fail to rescue her.

"I have suffered mental torture to save my friend from the clutches of the fiendish inquisitors, yet, to do this, it was necessary to sacrifice the poor countess. Because of my deformity, I cannot expose myself in such an enterprise. Your conspicuous proportions would equally expose you to recognition were you not a stranger in Rome, nevertheless, you have the ability to protect yourself in an emergency.

"With your approval, Don Alvard, I desire to take advantage of your presence here to attempt this rescue and fulfill a long cherished desire. I also want to leave the city with you, carrying the countess away with us.

I shall give out the report at once, that, I have taken my departure from Rome on a diplomatic mission. We must agree upon a rendezvous, where I may conceal myself and await you and your charge. The whole may be quickly executed and we can make our escape under cover of night."

"I am at your commands, and await your instructions," said the willing Don.

"Very good, very good," earnestly said Bambo, all aglow with the unusual excitement. "Feeling sure of your ability to carry out this enterprise, I do not hesitate to inform you, that, its execution may require your killing at least two men, but they are such villians, your only crime will be to cheat the gallows."

Bambo paused, but Don Alvard merely nodded to continue.

"You are an extraordinary man in appearance, not at all resembling a Roman. I will send Maleano with you to the keeper, a lazy, drunken, sleepy wretch. You will exhibit the seal-ring of Sanatos, which bears the Coat of Arms of Julius II. You must not present the other ring. You will request that you be permitted to procure the signature of the countess to a document which I will prepare, and to which I will attach the papal seal, therefore, do not permit the document to leave your possession. Your visit will be late in the evening.

"Customarily, the keeper summons his assistant who remains outside the cell door while he enters with the visitor. I leave to your discretion the means by which you dispose of these two wretches. I cannot commend their souls to heaven or hell. But, my good Don Alvard, if you are successful in this dangerous undertaking, and we succeed in quitting Rome in safety, I will confide to you things which will fill your life with enjoyable adventure."

"What provision have you made to disguise this countess after we have taken her to the street?" asked the Don.

"Maleano will have upon his person a suitable disguise for the countess. You will bring her to our adopted rendezvous and we shall immediately take our departure from Rome."

"And when shall we execute this delivery," asked the Don.

"At the hour of ten o'clock tonight, if you can be in readiness," replied Bambo.

"That is quite satisfactory to me, and I can see no difficulty in executing your plans. I believe my present lodging place will serve our purpose," said the Don.

Thereupon all preparations were made and

Maleano helped Cardinal Bambo to quit the Vatican and secretly enter Don Alvard's lodging place.

In the meantime the Don procured a suitable horse for each, the cardinal and the countess, and carefully looked over his own faithful Belial, finding him in excellent spirits, due to his grateful rest.

Bambo had officially prepared a safe alibi by having bid farewell to some of his associates early in the day, as though taking his immediate departure from the city.

A huge bell was vigorously clanging the hour of ten o'clock, as Don Alvard and Maleano made their way, by a secret passage used only by the Vatican, to the inner, spiral passageway of St. Angelo. Maleano knew every inch of the dingy old labyrinth, and, for his own safety, avoided coming in contact with the perambulating guards. At length they were challenged at the entrance to a lateral passage and gruffly asked their business. The guard, a burly ruffian, looked savagely at Don Alvard as he produced his credentials and demanded to be conducted to the cell in which the countess was confined.

"Move quickly," sharply commanded the Don, as the guard hesitated.

Before he could surmise his purpose or prevent it, the guard struck the wall with a sort of flapper, evidently intended to attract other guards, for hurrying steps were heard shuffling along the corridor behind them, and a similar villain appeared, to whom the first guard explained Don Alvard's mission.   The second guard demanded to examine the credentials.

The Don raised himself to his full stature, pointed down the corridor and thundered: "March!"

The guards were so overcome with surprise at this preemptory order, ringing with authority, they both stepped down the corridor at a lively gait, until a heavily barred door was reached, where they stopped.

"Open!" commanded the Don.

The bar was removed and the guards stepped back to permit them to enter.

"Enter!" was the Don's order.

The first guard entered while the second lagged back, and then an unexpected thing happened. Don Alvard seized the lagging guard, as though he were a dummy filled with straw and slammed him against the first guard with such violence, they both lay in a heap, stunned and helpless.

Bidding Maleano guard the door, he pressed the two bodies together, face to face, drew their surtouts up over their heads, and in a jiffy had them so securely bound they could neither move nor cry out.

Cautiously entering the dark dungeon, he called: "Is some one there?"

There was a rustling of straw, and a groan.

"Come forward, I am a friend," said the Don.

The drooping figure of a woman came slowly forward, her clothing literally in rags and tatters; her hair matted and tangled; her features and hands filthy, and her eyes staring out of their sockets with abject fright.

"Who are you?" asked Don Alvard.

"I am the Countess de Milliette," softly whispered the pitiful creature.

"I am your friend, come with me," and the Don gently helped her to the dungeon door where Maleano quickly cast about her the brown garb of a mendicant monk, drawing the cowl carefully over her head to conceal her matted hair and face.

"Can you walk?" whispered the Don.

"Yes," she replied.

They hurriedly returned to the secret passage, fortunately meeting none of the guards, and were soon in the fresh night air.

Don Alvard knew the countess was weeping, but knowing it was for joy or due to overwrought nerves, he said nothing.

Turning for a moment he viewed the gloomy, circular building and muttered: "Every brick in you is a symbol of a human tragedy. To cheat you of one single soul I would risk perdition."

The task was well begun, but it seemed too easy for the redoubtable rescuer. To thus rescue an important prisoner, right under the shadow of St. Peter, without a fight, seemed incredible. He felt as though the honorable thing would be to return, release the two guards and make them fight. He knew, from experience that such tasks were not to be called easy until they were accomplished. There was a danger point somewhere in every such enterprise. Therefore, bidding Maleano support the countess on the one side, he gently lent his aid on the other, whispering:

"I would gladly carry you, but we must not attract attention." Her arm trembled with excitement.

It was a long and tedious walk for the countess, weak from confinement and deprivation.

Arriving at the *via del corso,* they found it impassable, and filled with a festival throng. The narrow street was jammed from wall to wall with the usual Latin crowd, good-naturedly jostling, bantering and teasing one another. From the *Piazza del Popolo,* half way to the *Piazza Venezia,* was one continuous mass of heaving humanity.

At first this seemed to the Don a good stroke of fortune. They could mingle with the merry makers with little risk of being noticed as strangers.

For once the wily Don miscalculated.

A fun-seeking Latin crowd is to all intents and purposes a licensed band, to be converted into a destructive, fanatical mob upon the slightest provocation.

Don Alvard was about to learn a new lesson in civilized manners under stress of licensed revelry. He had not learned the purpose and latitude of the so-called festival mobs.

It was his extraordinary size which attracted the attention of the mob, and, from that moment, he became the butt of a thousand jeers and jokes, and the target of more material things, as the people

massed themselves about them, persistently plucking at the clothing of the trio.

With it all, Don Alvard kept his wits. He knew
he must keep his temper and concentrate his efforts
to prevent the exposure of the frightened woman
beneath the monk's garb.

Realizing that they might at any moment be
torn asunder, he whispered to Maleano to force his
way to the nearest divergent street, or public place
which they might enter, while he hovered over
them as a mother hen protects her brood from the
ravenous hawk.

Slowly they were shuffled along until almost
pushed into a narrow side street.

Pressing into this street the Don turned to urge
the others to go forward where the red-light of a
public house was visible. To his surprise, poor
Maleano was not in sight, and his momentary release of his hold upon the countess almost lost her
to the mob which now was pulling and hauling at
her garb. The Don was rapidly losing his temper.

Like the blades of a wind-mill his great arms
swept the crowd, tumbling many into a jumble upon
the street.

As he and the countess arrived at the entrance
of the public house, the proprietor stood in the doorway, attracted by the noise and confusion without.
Permitting the two to enter, he quickly closed and
fastened the door, as the excited mob filled the narrow street and began clamoring for admittance.

Don Alvard's sigh of relief was cut short, however, his troubles were only begun.

The grizzled head of a soldier peered from between curtains which shielded one of the stalls. Upon seeing Don Alvard he burst into ribald laughter, swearing he had seen the devil himself.

Then several heads appeared, and a hubbub of offensive epithets was aimed at the now thoroughly enraged Don.

With a sweep of his ponderous hand the Don cracked their heads together so hard they roared with pain. Two of the soldiers rushed out of the stall with drawn swords making for the Don, who quickly recognized them, by their peculiar uniforms, as belonging to the vatican Swiss guards of the pope, therefore, he knew he must defend himself against men worthy of his steel.

Pushing the now almost helpless countess behind him, he whipped out his long blade and put himself on guard. Seizing a metal waiter's tray from a table, by sheer strength of his left hand, he bent over the edge as a grip, and held the tray before him as a shield.

This feat of strength so surprised the soldiers, they momentarily hesitated, but they could not show fear at this stage of the contest, therefore, they plunged furiously upon him.

The swish of the Don's blade cracked like a whip, as it cut through the air, almost severing the head of the foremost soldier. With a dexterous motion he pushed the stricken soldier into the arms of his comrade, and with an overhand stroke he clave the head of the second guard.

A cry of dismay from the stall caused him to look there. He could hardly believe his own senses; the terrified face of Cardinal Gonsalvo was staring with bulging eyes. It was evident he had recognized Don Alvard.

A grim smile wreathed Don Alvard's face—his opportunity had come sooner than he had anticipated; but, he had no time to speculate, four other soldiers rushed from the stall and simultaneously assaulted him. Gonsalvo stood, terrified, holding back the draperies and trembling with fear. He was afraid even to attempt to escape.

The Don quickly put two of his sturdy assailants *hors du combat,* and had the other two well in hand. He had a purpose in mind as he gradually circled the room, drawing near to the stall.

With a lightning back stroke the keen point of his long sword made a terrible slash in the face of Gonsalvo, extending across the forehead, splitting the nose, lips and chin, the cardinal falling, screaming to the floor.

A moment later a stealthy hand reached from out the stall, picked up the sabre of one of the fallen soldiers and made a vicious slash at Don Alvard's head. The point of the blade ripped a long gash in the Don's left cheek. The Don saw the face of another priest holding the sword in his hand— he never permitted that face to fade from his memory.

No priest ever lived, who would not desert his own friends in time of danger, and flee for his own life. David set the precedent, even leaving his concubines behind him.

The two priests made their escape, followed by two well slashed soldiers.

The mob outside, hearing the tumult within, was now beating savagely at the door.

Don Alvard's wound was bleeding profusely, and the whole place resembled a shambles, with tables overturned and walls spattered with blood.

Seizing a cloth from the table the proprietor quickly bound up the wound, warning the Don that Gonsalvo would soon return with other soldiers— they must escape at once. Almost like a miracle a way was open. Other persons who were dining in the restaurant, unable to make their escape by the door, had discovered that a partition was made of flimsy materials, and had pressed out one of the large panels. Through this opening the Don and the countess passed out into a narrow way leading into another street, and hurried away to a darker and more secluded part of the city.

They had escaped, nevertheless, it required hours of dodging and hiding before they finally reached the rendezvous where they found Bambo much worried concerning them.

The countess wholly collapsed upon being assured of her temporary safety. Bambo wept as he saw her pitiful plight.

He now had the woman to revive and Don Alvard's painful wound to dress, both of which duties he quickly performed, as dexterously as a good physician.

"I understood you to say, that, this adventure would only require my killing two men; instead I I had to kill four, and carve my address on the ugly face of Gonsalvo," growled Don Alvard.

Bambo paused in his work and looked sharply at the cavalier, saying, as he pointed to his wound. "Ah, then you exchanged compliments; the soldiers were the pope's guards. Truly this is unfortunate. We must flee at once. The whole city will be searching for you. This is not murder, it is blaspheming."

They had a task before them. The poor countess, because of her long incarceration in St. Angelo, was so weak she now could scarcely stand. The excitement of the last few hours had shattered her nerves and she sat as though in a stupor.

Stepping to her side the Don pushed away the cowl and looked closely at her.

"You are safe, now, you must hold together till we get away from Rome. We shall take you immediately to your uncle," and he placed his huge hand upon the matted hair, attempting to smoothe it. A sense of horror crept over him as he touched it.

She looked at him as though not fully comprehending what he had said, but she did not shrink away from his comforting touch.

They were startled by a rap upon the door, and

Bambo opened it to admit Maleano. It was then
explained that, upon being torn away from them
by the mob the faithful servant had escaped and
made his way to the rendezvous to apprise Bambo
of the situation.

It being evident to Bambo that an immediate
departure was essential, he had sent Maleano for
certain necessaries for their journey. Among other
articles Maleano had brought some suitable apparel
for the countess, to take the place of the filthy rags
which only half covered her.

After she had hastily bathed her hands and face
she felt much revived.

The Don was impatient, saying:

"Come, we must be on our way."

A half hour thereafter the faithful Maleano sorrowfully bade them farewell and they took their
departure, but not by way of the *via del corso*.

Morning found them far from their dangers and
extremely weary.

They were fortunate to find, in a secluded place,
a comfortable, rural home willing to provide them
with lodging until they were in better physical condition to travel.

When the mother of the house learned that the
countess had long been confined in a prison, she
wept. She at once began to alleviate her condition. What a blessed sensation it was to the poor,
worn countess to have good, kind hands adminis-
tering to her needs.

Bambo was almost as helpless as the countess,

he not being accustomed to strenuous exercise, because of his physical infirmities. But, a day and a night's rest greatly improved them for travel; in fact, the countess appeared as a new being. The care and attention so refreshed and revived her, she could not adequately express her gratitude and thankfulness.

Don Alvard's face gave him considerable pain and she tenderly redressed the wound with her own hands.

The Don looked carefully at her and marveled at the change a few hours' rest had wrought. She was a handsome woman, despite the terrible ravages of the prison. The constant darkness had almost blinded her. She must have been blessed with a rugged constitution to retain the recuperative powers displayed. An overpowering feeling of sympathy swept the soul of the giant. Taking her hand he said gently:

"I am glad to see you recover your spirits and strength so quickly. It will be a pleasure to see you again in safety in your uncle's castle."

The tears came into her large, brown eyes as she responded:

"And you and good Cardinal Bambo, I can never fully express my gratitude or repay you, but I can devote the balance of my life praying for your comfort and safety. I know a soldier's life is not a comfortable one."

"The greatest happiness of a soldier is to play the

hero to a charming lady," gallantly responded the Don.

Bambo joined them and suggested that they take their departure; they were not yet safely beyond the long arm of the Vatican.

Suddenly, Don Alvard asked of Bambo:

"Who was the priest who talked with Gonsalvo in the *Garden of La Pigna,* on the day that you pointed out Gonsalvo to me?"

Bambo studied for a moment, then replied:

"That was Santillo; he is not a cardinal."

"He is a scribe," declared the Don, pointing to his cheek. "It was he who decorated my face; his time will come."

Soon they were on their way again. Their brief rest had filled them with good spirits, and they traveled with much greater comfort. Nevertheless, they were well fatigued when they arrived at the castle of the Count Brabon, where they were received with great joy.

The pathetic meeting of the countess and her good uncle started Don Alvard's blood to raging again. His mind went back to Pampero, and he was filled with a desire for blood vengeance.

Upon being informed of the facts, the Count Brabon was furious, swearing vengeance against Rome and all it stood for.

Don Alvard assured him that, he need not endanger the lives and properties of himself and niece, that he would make it his duty to duly reward those guilty of the crime against so gentle a woman as the countess.

Bambo also cautioned the count against permitting it to become known that either the countess or himself had taken shelter under his roof, as that would immediately bring upon him the accusation that he had had a previous knowledge of the rescue from St. Angelo and the flight from Rome, in which four of the vatican guards had been killed, and the handsome features of the all important Cardinal Gonsalvo spoiled for life.

The wise count agreed that it would be better to bide the time when a suitable punishment might be measured out to the guilty.

Don Alvard soon learned that Bambo was very much at home with the count, and, that, he himself was not to feel embarrased because of the cordial entertainment extended to him. After a few days' rest the countess showed great improvevment and devoted much time to Don Alvard who found her to be a lady of much talent and learning.

So grateful was the fair lady to again have her freedom, and find herself snugly tucked away from danger in her uncle's castle, she wept and laughed with joy. She heaped praises upon Don Alvard as her hero, and the Don actually began to feel an extraordinary flutter about his own big heart.

Bambo very bluntly cautioned the Don against becoming too sentimental regarding the countess: they had strenuous work before them. He declared that, the Don having taken the vows of a priest of vengeance, he was wedded to a life of celibacy. Love and hate cannot dwell together; he must be as cruel in his loves as in his hates.

In their confidential interviews the countess said:

"I wish you could always be near me. I feel so safe when I hear your voice."

He responded with feeling:

"My work calls me, but should you need me, I will circle the world to come to you."

CHAPTER VII

THE CONFESSION OF CARDINAL BAMBO

AN INJUSTICE DONE IN ANGER MAY REACT IN WRATH

CARDNAL BAMBO had given to Don Alvard his full confidence. Long and earnestly, they had discussed some all important subject, the count good-naturedly eliminating himself from these conferences. Finally it was announced that the Don was to accompany Cardinal Bambo upon some mysterious pilgrimmage, and preparations were made for an early departure.

On the very morning named for their going, Bambo fell seriously ill, doubtless due to the long and arduous journey from Rome. For several days his life was despaired of. It was apparent that the cardinal would be confined to his sick room indefinitely, which wholly disarranged their plans, much to the discomfiture of the restless Don, causing him great distress of mind, although, each day he remained near the countess, gave him sweet compensation and pleasure. He well knew this was the real danger of his remaining there. Truly, love is a wonderful force. The countess had greatly softened the hatred which thrilled his every fibre.

Nevertheless, the Don's mind was not at peace by any means. It was very doubtlful if any sentiment could ever cause him to abandon his designs against those whom he called his enemies.

Cardinal Bambo summoned Don Alvard to his bedside.

"I shall make you my confessor, my good friend," he said. "It grieves me greatly that I am compelled to, at least temporarily, abandon the work for which I have so long labored to equip myself. I am overtaken by an ailment which is a complication of the wounds which I received in infancy, resulting in my permanent deformity. I fear that I may never again recover sufficiently to assume my former activity, and complete my life work. Life is altogether too brief in this world.

"My good friend Count Brabon assures me that I may remain here in comfort till I die, or sufficiently recover to permit of my going to Venice, there quickly to end my time.

"Now, I am about to consign to you a burden which you may find irksome, but it will bring you in contact with the very elements which you seek, and, in the end, it will fully compensate you for all your troubles. It is my desire that you take up my life work, combine it with your own and carry it through to the end, therefore, listen well to what I tell you—the secret will be sacredly locked in your bosom I know.

"My true name is Paul Barbo. I am the illegitimate son of Peter Barbo, who was Pope, from September 16th, 1464, to July 28th, 1473, as Paul II.

"My father, it was unfortunately true, was not a lovable character. I became the innocent victim of his vanity and folly.

"He was a vain and handsome man, and, at the time of his elevation, was cardinal bishop of St. Marc. In his vain conceit he desired to take the pontifical name of *Fermosus,* signifying *beautiful,* but was finally persuaded to take the name Paul II.

"His enemies were so numerous, they were like a swarm of bees about him, he having the faculty of bringing upon himself the enmity and hatred of all the kings of Europe.

"As a test of their attitude toward him, he attempted to unite them against the Turks, but signally failed.

"Instead of making the strong and powerful Medicis his friends, he deliberately invited their enmity, by his vain, overbearing and pompous nature, and his tendency to treat lightly their own pretensions. Subsequent events have proven how wrong was his judgment.

"The controversy with the Medicis arrived at a point where some adjustment of differences was essential. This was attempted by a commission, negotiating through the new cardinal of St. Marc at Venice.

"This mission failed, and bitter resentment was expressed by all factions.

"As a child, I had inherited my father's beauty, and having free access to the cardinal's palace, I frequently visited there in the company of my tutor.

"A young prelate, who was a member of the commission, while passing through a corridor, saw me and paused, because of my beauty, inquiring

who I was. My tutor innocently told him the truth,
at which he became enraged. Swearing a mighty
oath that, another *Formosus* should not arise to
plague them, he seized me and hurled me through
the window to the gardens below, with the result
which you see."

Don Alvard was gradually recharging his heart
with hatred for priests. Placing his hand softly
upon Bambo's arm, he asked:

"Does that prelate live today?"

Cardinal Bambo, raising himself upon his arm
to more emphatically express himself, answered:

"Don Alvard, I requested that you not kill Sanatos as long as I am capable of acting for myself.
I want you to spare him to me. Should I be deprived of strength, and the pleasure of killing him
myself, I want you to avenge me in your own way.
His cruel hands made me what I am, a thing to be
despised, shunned and laughed at by men. My
humiliation and shame no man can know. I only
hope he may live to feel and know that I am
avenged."

The Don bowed his head.

"Now, let me continue my story.

"I assumed my present name to protect myself
against constant insult and persecution, because of
the evils of, and hatred for, my vain father. For
thirty years I have stealthily crept to the positions
which I have held in order that I might inform myself of the innermost secrets of the priesthood. I
have a reverence for Pope Nicholas V, for having

established the vatican library, for it became the focus for manuscripts long hidden away in the private personal libraries of cardinal bishops. The adoption of the *Archivio Secreto* was an inspiration. It was the very cornerstone of St. Peter. My researches have uncovered the secret foundation of the whole ecclesiastical power. I am convinced that not a half dozen persons other than myself know that this great mystery exists, so closely has the secret been guarded.

"Pope Leo X knew the truth, and he also knew that I had made myself master over this church mystery, and I intend to maintain this poistion as long as I live. Its secrecy is vital to the continuation of the Roman Catholic church—it is the great *revelation*. When it is revealed the church will cease to be as a religious body, and humanity, like vultures, will tear out its vitals.

"A great day of reckoning is before the exploiters of Christianity at some time in the future — maybe in a few years, maybe in centuries. The longer it is postponed, the more will the churches be reviled by those who have been deceived.

"The ancient archives of the wisdom and knowledge of the gnostics became the foundation of the Roman priesthood. It was, originally, the scientific knowledge of the world, possessed only by the learned few. The Roman priesthood concealed this wisdom from those without the order by allegory, romance, figure and symbolism, and secretly taught it to the initiated as traditional with Christianity, hence, even the priesthood at large does not know the inner mystery, the key to which is still lost.

"The priesthood absorbed and smothered gnosticism, but evolved from it a system so ingenious and so attractive that the origin of the underlying principles was lost sight of by the acting priesthood until it was forgotten.

"The all important gnostic records were delivered into the hands of selected agents called church-fathers — *Clement of Rome, Ignatius, Polycarp* and *Hermas,* to harmonize and adopt them to the use of the Christian enterprise, by clothing them with mystery, and weaving them into a fabulous mesh called inspired scriptures. This work was done in secret monasteries and gradually brought into practice.

"Don Alvard, these so-called scriptures conceal the *inner code* of *the monastic priesthood,* which, when interpreted, reveals the premeditated exploitation of humanity under the guise of the Christian religion. You must search the world for the key.

"These treasured records were handed down from century to century, for several hundred years, the actual custodians of the original *Archivio Secreto* being the popes themselves, so closely was this secret guarded. This was unfortunate for the church.

"It was these church fathers who retired to monasteries and worked out a code for the underlying foundation of the Christian enterprise.

"The Christian religion would have died before

it was born, had it been based upon naked truth. Even so, it could not give to its Christ a divine origin for several centuries after his alleged birth.

"Clement, Turtullion, Eusebius, Ignatius, Papias, Carpocrates, Cerdon, Marcion, Appelleus, Valentinus, Titian, Ptolemaeus, Heraclon, Simon, Magnus, Basilides and others, were the early spirits of the great work.

"These were the great gnostics who laid the foundations of Christianity.

"The writings of Clement and Ignatius are replete with evidences of gnostic training before the monastic orders were absorbed into the Christian scheme.

"Not one word of the gospels was spoken by the characters into whose mouths this alleged language was put by these writers.

"Alleged sermons and exhortations were placed in the mouth of a fictitious Christ, yet it is admitted that it is not even known in what language he spoke.

"Christ is said to have spoken in Hebrew, yet the Hebrew language was not spoken in Palestine in his time, which renders his preaching farcial. The good of his teachings was taught ages before the Christian era.

"There never existed such a being as Papias, yet the larger part of the sayings of some of the apostles, especially John, were attributed to his pen. Not one word of this fiction may be traced to such an individual. Nothing is known of his birth, life or death, or when or where he resided.

"But, even in the spurious works of Papias, Paul is ignored and his language not even known.

"These manifest discrepancies regarding the language spoken by Christ and Paul are flippantly excused by the following:

" 'The manifestation of the spirit may be by speaking in diverse tongues.' (I Cor. 12:10.)

"But that does not enable a whole people to understand diverse languages.

"Eusebius himself said:

" 'Papias must have been a man of small mind, if we may judge by his own words.'

"The Greek and gnostic Christians repudiated Papias, classing his alleged writings as Hebrew romance. *Papias* is *pater, papa,* the origin of *pope,* the father—the priest.

"To remove Papias from the origin of the gospels would leave them without authorative evidence which would wholly destroy the Christian church, and yet his own words condemn him as a fictitious character, conjured out of the fertile mind of the church fathers. Not one authentic word of his birth, life or death, is extant, yet, the multiplicity of his alleged writings are made the very foundation of the Christian dispensation, with no originals to be found.

"Carpocrates was a gnostic, celebrated for his gnostic teachings—his famous theory was: 'The idea of the possession of property forms no part of a divine plan.' Which challenged the accumulation by the church of vast wealth, such as it possesses today.

"The third name in the secret Christian code signifies possession—Cain, who was dispossessed by the church, its original intent being to confiscate all property.

"Cerdon and Marcion were both known gnostics.

"Valentinus was one of the most famous gnostics in the early history of the church.

"Appelleus was excommunicated for his gnosticism.

"Titian was converted from Christianity to gnosticism.

"Ptolemaeus and Haraclon were both high gnostics.

"Basilides was a gnostic, and he wrote an elaborate commentary on the gospels.

"For nearly three hundred years after the alleged birth of Christ, there existed no authentic gospels, and but few of the church doctrines of the present time were then known. The immaculate conception was not heard of for more than a hundred years after the alleged birth of Christ.

"It was manifestly essential to manufacture the gospels, if Christianity was to be successfully exploited; they could not be wholly borrowed from other religions as were practically all the Christian doctrines.

"It required more than five hundred years for the Roman priesthood to absorb and submerge gnosticism, and secretly confiscate its accumulated wisdom and knowledge, that these might not rise up and reveal the duplicity of the ecclesiastical theocracy. For fourteen hundred years the world has been sifted to destroy every scrap of evidence of the original gnosticism.

"Now, my good Don Alvard, I have thus, in some detail, explained the origin of the Christian scheme, in order to impress upon your mind the importance of the work I am going to impose upon you. I will now come to the gist of my story.

"Gnosticism is not dead. No power on earth has been sufficiently strong to destroy the recorded wisdom of the gnostic brotherhood, *because it is the true revelation, and is subject to the laws of natural tradition* — the one great gift of nature which the Christian powers have withheld from mankind. Some secret power has hovered over and protected it.

"In transmitting this secret work to you, Don Alvard, I am acknowledging the greatest confidence one human being can confer upon another. It is the fear that the secret might die with me, that urges me to pay you this tribute, as well as my belief that you are worthy of the trust.

"The revelation is deeper than gnosticism. I entrust to you the secret that there exists a code key which reveals the fictitious character of the bible and you must find it.

"As you are aware, early in the fourteenth century, the Holy See was transferred to Avignon, by Clement V, out of pique because he could not bring the Romans under abject obedience to the church, thus revealing that there was no authority for the making of Rome the official center of the Catholic universe. This was a fatal church error.

"Rome spelled the divine nature of the church. *R=master. O=light. M=wisdom. E=power.*

"At this time Clement also suppressed the Templars, as much in fear of this military order, as in the desire for political profit—only the ecclesiasts should remain an oath-bound secret order. Religion signifies *oath-bound.*

"The world could not know that this was one of the great turning points of the Christian enterprise. So enraptured were they with political intrigue, not even the sacred college was aware that the *Archivio Secreto* was being ravished. In 1305 a serious chism threatened, the breach not being healed for a long period.

"After the death of Clement V, April 20th, 1314, the papal throne remained vacant for two years, before the election of the pedantic pompous John Eusius, as John XXII, Aug. 7th, 1316, revealing the wide gulf between Rome and Avignon.

"During this period chaos reigned in the indifferent library, and the greatest scandals were revealed by promiscuous access to the secret vatican records. Great inroads were made upon the sacred archives, and tremendous volumes of the most important records disappeared. Hence the valuable books and manuscripts were confiscated and scattered to the four winds—especially to the great Medici library at Florence, through a Tuscan,

Bishop of Bologna, who afterwards became Pope Nicholas V, and made himself famous by the restoration of valued works to the Vatican library. But it was not in his power to restore the most valuable records.

"A sacred trust had been handed down, from pope to pope—the inviolable custody of the mysterious system which not even the rank and file of the priesthood was permitted to know. This consisted of complete gnostic records compiled and tabulated for the perpetuation of the system—as the foundation of the Christian system, and the secret scriptural code, for the conduct of the church.

"The invaluable records wholly disappeared and the church was hopelessly at sea, and without a rudder. From sheer necessity the Vatican had to plunge into the political intrigues of Europe to conceal this great loss, and attempt to strengthen a protective temporal power to offset the loss of evidences, which if made public, would reveal the fallacy of its alleged divine origin. The evidence that high church interests held the secret was in, that, it was not exposed.

"During the long period in which I was the custodian of the *Archivio Secreto*, I solved these mysteries. The confiscation of the gnostic records was a direct assault upon the powers at Rome by the monastics, who long antedated Christianity, who in fact did not fully concede their absorption into the Roman system.

"The powerful Benedictine Monks, at the Mon-

astery of Montserrat, near Barcelona, were long
known as the custodians of the loot of the earlier
crusades.   Untold wealth was deposited in the
church and monastery, accumulating in such quantities it lost its identity, the Benedictines becoming
the wealthiest monastic order in the world.   This
wealth inspired a desire and ambition for self- government, and political power, independent of the
church.

"This order became a menace to the world. It
defied the Vatican, and it soon became known that
it possessed and was exercising some strange power
over the popes. The truth gradually revealed itself—
it possessed the lost gnostic records, together with
certain church secrets, with which it could club
the church to death if needs be, but it preferred
to hold in tact the Christian organization for its own
purposes.

"But, it is I who hold the great mystery. This
fear of the Benedictines is unfounded. I made the
discovery that, they have not had in their posession
these priceless records for a long period of time. A
chism in the ranks of the order was its undoing. A
small band of seceders confiscated the gnostic works
and disappeared, no one knows where.

"This is the strangest situation in christendom
today. No attempt was ever made to reveal the
gnostic system, although it was the true revelation.
I have found a curious intimation that this was due
to an early loss of the symbols which should have
accompanied the work, but which had never been

found. I am in sole possession of the truth that, there exists a scriptural code of which gnosticism is the basis. Therefore no one possesses the complete system. You now understand why I am so solicitous regarding these lost records. They are essential to the fulfillment of my purposes, as they are to the revelation of the church mystery. This gnostic work is not religious, it is scientific—*therefore the antagonism between Christianity and science. Exposure* is the greatest fear of the church.

"Don Alvard, my roving mission was to go in search of the lost gnostic records; I know they still exist. But, now, I may not continue this pilgrimage, therefore, I select you as my successor. If you find them you will hold in your hands the greatest power on earth, the key to the scriptural code together with the secret ecclesiastic system. These mysteries represent the power to destroy the greatest parasite that ever burdened humanity. For fifteen centuries it has fostered sin to vindicate its doctrine of *original sin*.

"I have long been in a position to know that, the Benedictines, Dominicans and Friars have combed the earth in a determination to find a clue to this lost treasure, thereby bringing themselves into bad repute by their persistent inquisitions. To these fiendish monks is entrusted the espionage system of the inquisition.

"The Holy See itself is now secretly organizing a pernicious system of spying and espionage for the same purpose. It will ransack the world. The

anger and shame of the church, that it is no longer
on safe ground, is one cause for the drastic and
cruel inquisition.   Its lawless *search* and *seizure*
goes further than the monastics ever dared go.   It
purposes placing over all mankind an inquisitional
espionage to guard against the revelation of gnosticism, and that system will continue as long as gnosticism is unrevealed.

"I now entrust to you, my good friend, the continuation of my work.   I give to you my credentials
and authorize you to assume, at your discretion, my
name.   There will be times when the credentials
of a cardinal will procure for you desired audiences
and favors which might be denied a cavalier.

"My letter of credit will be honored as you require funds.   Should I require immediate funds, I
confide to you that my friend, the count, will provide.

"From time to time, as opportunity permits, I
should like to have some word from you, telling me
of your adventures.   I will pray for your success.

"As Bambo, be a gentleman; as a cavalier, you
will often find that a dissembling poverty and appearance of bravado, will prove your best disguises.

"Good bye, my good friend; let nothing daunt
or discourage you.   These are your broad instructions," and he handed to the Don a package of
papers.

Don Alvard sadly left the presence of the man
with a perfect mind concealed in a deformed body.

In the beautiful gardens of Count Brabon, situated on a terrace overlooking his magnificent estate, Don Alvard had spent many happy hours with the now gentle and contented countess. There he sought her to bid her good bye. He knew her favorite retreat, where he could find her talking softly to her birds, which knew her so well they would flutter about and nestle upon her person to feed upon the crumbs she brought each day for them.

He hurriedly presented himself, in a brave effort to go with seeming indifference, but this was wholly impossible upon viewing her sweet, happy face. A truly wonderful transformation had taken place. She was now beautiful as an angel; he knew he loved her and believed she entertained for him a sentiment stronger than mere gratitude.

"I am about to take my leave," he said, in a faltering voice.

She did not respond, but placed her hands over her face and he saw tears trickling between the fingers.

"Ah, my dear countess, I have made you unhappy. I dare not say, though, how unhappy I am, that duty compels me to forego the extreme joy of remaining near you," and he looked away off over the valley to conceal his own emotions.

She arose and extended both her hands.

"I know the truth," she gasped. "My uncle has told me all, I will not detain you. I know your vow. I know your mission. Do your duty well, my good protector. If you slay with your own hands, every

living priest, when your task is done, return to me.
You need not speak, I will wait. At any time you
are hard pressed, make this your safe retreat. I
will be here to greet and comfort you."

He raised her hands to his lips and kissed them,
then pressed them to his bosom, looking far away
to keep her from seeing his tears.

She took from her neck a strong silver chain
to which was attached a locket.

"Keep this near your heart till we meet again,"
and she placed the token in his hand. He did not
attempt to embrace her or kiss her lips, but again
kissing her hands, he bowed gravely and left her
in a heap upon the seat, with her face buried in her
hands.

He did not turn back, nor did she raise her face
and look after him. Each felt what the eyes would
have revealed. It was a sad parting, rendered more
so by the tragedy which seemed to engulf their
lives.

CHAPTER VIII

THE SIEGE OF PAMPELUNA

It Is Wiser to Dissemble Than to Appear too Wise

DON ALVARD de RICALDE was again astride his saddle and on the road to nowhere. Desiring to avoid another arduous journey to Italy, if possible, he spent two months prowling from city to city, in vain search for some clue which might direct him in the way he should go to quickly solve the task set for him by Bambo. He felt a sort of religious responsibility to fulfill with credit the mission imposed upon him. He smiled upon fully realizing that the cardinal's letter of credit relieved him of all financial worry. His conscience did not trouble him that the expense of his journeying was being financed by Rome.

Gnosticism was as a blank to Italy. Nevertheless, his travels were edifying to the extent that he found the Roman Catholic power in complete control. He had been amazed at the mumbling and meaningless street parades in Rome on every occasion, whether funeral, wedding or holiday, but this same mummery prevailed throuhout Italy, and was always fronted by a blear-eyed, pompous priest, bearing a banner or cross, and accompanied by boys clad in flimsy, dirty semi-chasubles, and a lot of absurd and imbecile flubdubbery, behind which trailed, like a sloppy tail of a garment, those who chose to bask in the priestly shadow. It sickened him to think that human beings were so grossly ignorant. He had quite enough of Italy. He foresaw, that, as long as it lived as a nation, this would be so.

He had slowly directed his travels to the northward, in order to eventually bring him into Spain and to the pleasing city of Barcelona, where he had received his education. Finally arriving in the beautiful old city, travel-worn and weary, he felt much inclined to be alone, that both mind and body might enjoy much needed rest and recuperation. Moreover, he had much about which to think.

It was with deep sentiment that he recalled the happy, hopeful years of his sojourn here. He quietly visited the old haunts of himself and former comrades, living over again the comforts and pleasures of University life. He frequented the splendid health baths and ate with high relish, smiling to again see the same *panzudo Paranza,* come swinging his *caldera* with its toothsome *potage.* It had the same old room-filling odor and a flavor, much enhanced by the exaggerated appetite of a ravenous cavalier. Within forty-eight hours he was filled with new life and ambition.

When Hamilcar Barcino planted his staff at this spot, (200 B. C.), he must have relished the salubrious climate, and partaken of its curative waters, for it had for seventeen centuries perpetuated his name and been famous as a health resort, as well as being one of the great commercial cities of Spain.

Ferdinand and his savage hearted queen, Isabella, greeted Columbus here upon his return from America in 1493—the very year in which Don Alvard first kicked his brawny self into the world. His mother had always told him he was laughing when he was born, and even at thirty-one, that roguish smile, which put funny wrinkles all over his face, was a mirth provoking thing; but, his frown was a thunderstorm.

It was not characteristic for the vigorous Don to remain idle for a long period. Feeling recuperated and in need of action he sought his old friend, Verosala, finding him employed as custodian of public records of the City of Barcelona, a most honorable position, consequently he found Verosala a happy, prosperous and amiable man. At the time of his visit he found with his friend one Carrabello, who had conducted a party of refugees from the province of Navarra.

Carrabello wept as he told them that Southern Navarra was being overrun with French soldiers, and, that it was common report that, they were preparing to lay siege to Pampeluna with the view of recovering the territory which had been taken by Ferdinand and his coadjutor, the wily Bishop of Toledo.

This was a vindication of the warning which Sanatos had given to Gonsalvo, that France would attempt to restore Navarra to the family of Jean de Albret, therefore, it was no surprise for him to learn of this bold French move.

The French well knew that the indifferent Charles would scarcely take notice of such movements, being little in Spain and not even taking sufficient interest to learn the Spanish language, preferring to guzzle beer with his rollicking friends in Flanders. Any display of resistance on his part would be for theatrical effect.

Here was adventure; the Don craved a close-up experience of warfare.

Bidding his friends good bye, he turned Belial's nose toward the city of Pampeluna, where, in due time, he arrived, to find the place gorged with Spanish troops in anticipation of war. To him they did not appear to be the invincible Spanish soldiery of repute.

As he rode into the city, a company of dandies, gorgeously appareled, and displaying much gold lace and *plumaje*, galloped past. Their air of superiority caused him to pause and make inquiry as to their identity. Upon being informed that this was the king's own guards, representing the court of King Charles, he remarked:

"It looks like a parade at a country fair. They will be made acquainted with sterner stuff than posing about a king's court, with its lax habits and loose morals. At the first sight of real warfare, half of them will throw themselves into the river Agra."

Almost before the city could realize it, the French made their assault upon Pampeluna.

As Don Alvard had anticipated, the Spanish

soldiers were not equal to the well trained and disciplined French.

He realized that the city would quickly be overwhelmed. In fact, the prompt capitulation of the Spaniards smacked strongly of disloyalty, but, what could be expected of soldiers who scarcely knew their king.

He was so thoroughly disgusted, he resolved to extricate himself and go on his way. But he found this no simple task, being trapped so completely that he could not cut his way out. It was the most trying situation in which he had ever found himself. It seemed as though he would not be able even to reach and enter the citadel and surrender with the other soldiers, could he find no way of escape.

Suddenly, the French artillery, at close range, began to pour shot into the citadel. A large breach was opened up and the Don found himself going through it along with French soldiers, they believing him to be an agent of the Roman court.

Dropping into a narrow passageway, he found, huddled like sheep, the pet guards of King Charles. Several of them had died by their own hands, while the others were half crazed with terror.

Observing one of the soldiers frantically attempting to reach a window, and failing to do so, draw a dagger which he was about to plunge into his own heart, the Don struck the *punal* from his hand, took him by his collar and dragged him back to the window.

Raising himself to the opening, and finding the ground but thirty feet below, he lifted the soldier to his side. Before he could restrain him, the terror stricken man sprang aimlessly out of the window.

Don Alvard, holding to the sill, carefully let himself down to his full length and dropped, with no worse results than a severe shaking up.

The soldier was not so fortunate, both his legs being broken in his fall.

Regardless of his groans, Don Alvard tossed him across his huge shoulders and plunged into a ravine which led them to the river Agra, and near the place where the Don had stabled his own Belial. Concealing the injured man in the shrubbery, he hastened to procure the horses to enable them to flee away from Pampeluna and to safety.

The Don conducted the injured man to a small monastery hospital near the town of Azpeitia in the province of Guipuscoa. The urgent necessity for medical attention caused them to stop there, where he also remained a few days. The man was so badly hurt he came near dying at once of shock and pain. His condition prevented the Don questioning him, therefore, he did not address him by name, but learned that his father had a castle located also in this same province, to which place he would be transferred as early as he could make the journey.

His few days' rest gave the Don an opportunity to ponder his future, and plan his next destination.

He decided to start upon a pilgrimmage to Mont-serrat.

Enjoying the interesting journey, the Don arrived at a small village at the foot of Montserrat, where he encountered a traveling monk who introduced himself as Francisco Rienzi.

Cautiously questioning the monk, he was surprised to learn that he had only arrived there a few hours previously, and had come from the same monastery where Don Alvard had left the wounded soldier; by a coincidence they had not met there, and the monk had anticipated his departure only by a few hours.

He confided to Don Alvard that, he was preparing the way for a later pilgrimage, to be made by a distinguished soldier who lay wounded at the said monastery, and, who, because of sensational revelations made to him in his hours of delirium, and of the fact, that, his wounds received in battle at Pampeluna, would incapacitate him for further military life, had decided to devote the balance of his life to religious devotion, beginning with a pilgrimage to the church of the Benedictines, at Montserrat, to make his first confession.

Don Alvard almost fainted upon being informed that this penitent, made so under the stress of fear of death, was none other than Don Iñigo Lopez de Ricalde, of Guipuscoa, whose father was Count Bertram, Lord of Ognez.

Curbing his inclination to reveal his own identity, he asked of Rienzi if it were permissible for a

traveling soldier to visit the Monastery of Montserrat, not revealing to him that he himself was
journeying there.

The monk assured him that it was, and invited
him to accompany him the balance of the way,
which invitation he accepted with suitable expressions of gratitude.

The monk gave him a glowing description of
the old church, saying:

"This wonderful place is well worthy a visit,
especially by an educated person like yourself, with
leisure to acquire knowledge. It is resplendent
throughout with gold, and is stored with rarest and
most costly treasures gathered from the whole
civilized world, the offerings of penitential kings
and princes, surpassing the wealth of the celebrated
church of St. James at Compostella.

"Before the altar of the Virgin Mary stand sev-
enty-five golden lamps."

"On what theory did potentates contribute this
great wealth to lie dormant in an isolated church?"
asked Don Alvard.

"There are several theories advanced to apologize
for this, but there are also many causes, practically
all of which resolve back into the one basic cause,
the right of the church to receive gifts under the
ancient edict of Constantine," replied Rienzi.

"But the alleged 'donation of Constantine' was
declared to be a clumsy forgery," quickly replied
Don Alvard.

"Nevertheless, it is authentic that, from the year

321 Constantine permitted the churches to acquire landed property, and he allowed individuals to enrich them by legacies, donations and gifts.

"This privilege gave rise to a multitude of misunderstandings, and, most likely, was the cause for the forgery of the 'donation of Constantine,' and Pepin as well. It is not even now safe to dispute the authenticity of either. As late as 1478 persons who expressed such doubts were burned at the stake at Strasburg. An unchallenged falsehood of long standing is easily established as truth under the coercive influences of bigotry and intolerance. This story of the donation of Constantine was invented in the latter part of the eighth century and was even transcribed into the canonical compilations of Gratian, Theodore and Balsamon, in the twelfth century—although known to be a fiction.

"The two great sources of church wealth have been large donations inspired by fear, and the proceeds of crusades and confiscations. Secret intrigues of spoilation are an essential element in the conduct of the church. There is much mystery associated with these donations, which fill to overflowing these secret storehouses. Here you find the process of the sale of indulgences on a tremendous scale."

Rienzi paused, because he observed on Don Alvard's face signs of astonishment.

"I am surprised to hear you practically condemn the church for this accumulation of wealth. You are not a church fanatic," said the Don.

"You may think it strange that I, apparently a Benedictine monk, should speak thus frankly to a stranger," said Rienzi, "but I have a reason. I believe I may give you my confidence, as I need help at this particular time, and you are a Christian soldier, you can understand these matters, where an ignorant, bigoted, lay Catholic would at once incite a mob to burn me at the stake."

"Proceed, I will neither incite a mob nor report you to the inquisitors," said Don Alvard with a friendly smile.

"I believe you," replied Rienzi, "therefore, I shall make known to you my true mission here. This injured soldier, lying in the hospital which I have just left, is the son of a wealthy Lord of Ognez, who is a devout Catholic, whose father had previously been *tesorero* of the Holy See for the province of Guipuscoa. Don Iñigo informs me that great iron bound chests, stored in the strong room of his father's castle, contain lists of distributions of the proceeds of crusades. Therefore, it is a safe conjecture that much of the wealth stored here at Montserrat came from such sources, coming in through the ports of Bilbao and Sebastian on the north, or through Barcelona on the east. Up to a late period it was the privilege of the crusaders to outrage the women and loot every town on the line of their travel not specifically exempted. The treasure thus accumulated was divided between the church and the state, the soldiers being paid, and given a free hand to outrage."

"Then these crusades were not to express the divine wrath of an angry God?" exclaimed Don Alvard.

"No, they were only holy crusades because they were inspired by the pope," replied Rienzi.

"And what could a poor soldier of fortune like myself do to further your cause—the purpose of which you have not made plain?" asked the Don.

"You have struck the key note," quickly exclaimed Rienzi. "I take it you are not a religious enthusiast, as is this Don Iñigo, therefore, you would not be troubled with scruples should occasion require you to dissemble."

Don Alvard laughed, saying:

"I know of no experienced Roman soldier with scruples. I would be willing to publicly weep and pray with the best of them for eight hours a day, but I should reserve the right to curse privately for eight hours; it would be no ones business what I did the other eight hours, eh?"

Rienzi laughed heartily with the Don, promptly throwing off all pretense of disguise, seeing in the big, hearty man an adventurous cavalier like himself. Continuing he said:

"I do not now hesitate to inform you that I am anticipating Iñigo in a journey to Montserrat, the secret purport of which is to learn the satus of a vast fortune in loot stored here. He, of course, will come as a weeping and praying penitent. It will be several months before he will be sufficiently recovered to make the arduous journey. During

this period I shall remain at Montserrat and obtain
all possible information, by close espionage and
liberal bribery.

"Don Iñigo can neither disguise his *limp* nor his
nose, hence he can neither prowl, nor travel incognito.   He will be kept out in the open as a target
for public opinion to shoot at."

Don Alvard eyed Rienzi sharply, saying:

"You are forging ahead of your story. By what
you have said, I sense a deep plot back of this game.
While it is not my nature to be inquisitive, it seems
to me I should first be made aware of your plot,
so I may intelligently consider such details as you
may desire I should know."

"That is true," exclaimed Rienzi, "and you have
not identified yourself to me señor."

"Let us visit together this wonderful treasure
house, filled with divine plunder, as trusted cavalier
friends, ready to help one another in emergencies.
We may later determine if we may profit by a
closer exchange of confidences," suggested Don Alvard.

"That is very well said," replied Rienzi.   "I
will continue my disguise as a monk, and you accompany me as a Christian soldier. I am sure, with
my credentials, we may search out the secret places
of Montserrat."

"And I," said Don Alvard, "will simulate a revival of the spirit of the Catholic zeal of Ferdinand's
time, and give out the impression that I am organiz-

ing a crusade to sweep from Spanish soil the remnants of Mohammedanism."

"Very good," replied Rienzi, "we may permit Don Iñigo to exercise his fanatical hysteria until his zeal is exhausted. Let us commend him to the tender mercies of the priesthood, for who loves a cripple? The church welcomes influential persons who are rich, unfortunate, eccentric and unlovable, because they nurse a selfish grudge against the more fortunate of God's creatures, who do not seek the foolishness of the church to make them happy, therefore, they willingly give their support to the church, the enemy of human pleasure and joy.

"From this day let it be the Christian fakir, the pious zealot, Ignatius. He is sufficiently rich and weak minded for them to weave about him a wonderful, apocryphal halo of his exemplary life, with no reference to his debaucheries and evil mongering at the courts of Ferdinand and Charles. They will fill his ignorant, untutored mouth with words of wisdom, and, perhaps, they may Saint him, who can tell. Only a derelict could afford to father the diabolical scheme being hatched through the connivance of that master plotter, Francis Borgia, and I suspect that Iñigo's own father is selected as an early victim."

Don Alvard stared at Rienzi curiously, as though trying to fathom some deeper meaning to his utterances.

"I am puzzled to have you thus expose your

own contempt for a system with which you seem
to be closely allied. I am in a position to know
that, your protege is a dissembler and a pious fraud.
I know the nature of Iñigo's mental ailment—but,
your attitude I cannot understand."

"You amaze me!" exclaimed Rienzi. "Have I
made a mistake in giving to you my confidence?"

"Not at all," quickly replied Don Alvard. "On
the contrary, you have enlisted my sympathy, and
your frankness has released to you my confidence.
I warn you, this Iñigo is not a mad-man. But I
must know more of your Christian standing. I
must assume that, you are playing the role of an
interested observer, rather than directly participat-
ing in the plot at which you have hinted."

"As our acquaintance progresses, you will find
your conjecture is correct, but one must be discreet, with the very air saturated with the espionage
of the diabolical inquisition," replied Rienzi.

"And one must have an impelling motive to assume so dangerous a role," softly said Don Alvard.
"I have no particular objective, hence I am not inspired by some prodding motive; but you are
directly in pursuit of something, hence, there is
motive in what you do. I offer you my services,
either as van or rear guard, but from long tried
experience I suggest that we not be identified as
other than casual acquaintances. Close proximity
will bridge the narrow span between assumed es-
trangement and secret cooperation."

"Again you amaze me with your astute wisdom.

You are not the soldier you appear to be?" exclaimed Rienzi.

"I know of no better name than a soldier of fortune and adventure. I am a free man. Men who are wise to the situation must be dissemblers. *"It is a natural animal instinct to blend with the surrounding foliage when dangers lurk near.*

"No law that men ever made, morally, mentally or physically binds men to forget their God given natures, and submerge themselves in an unidentifying mass to be molded into putty images.

"It is living, individual identity that men seek, not a foolish promise of an impossible individual immortality after death," declared the Don, dramatically.

"You are a philosopher and a learned man. You have my deep respect. I cannot urge you to more fully identify yourself to me now; but, may I ask, does this Iñigo know your full identity?" asked Rienzi.

"No," quickly responded Don Alvard. "And I think it best that he be not informed. I especially suggest that he should not know of our having met —perhaps we may be of service to each other sometime."

"I pray we may become very dear friends," replied Rienzi.

Thereupon they made preparation to journey immediately to Montserrat.

CHAPTER IX

ALL ROADS LEAD TO MONTSERRAT

HYPOCRISY IS ITS OWN WORST ENEMY

BENEATH that cultivated hypocrisy, which only too often approves of Ehud's tactics, lurks a primitive longing for a respite from the artificial life of greed and selfishness, which breeds enmities, betrayals and treachery between men. Both Don Alvard and Rienzi felt this longing for frank comradeship, and childlike confidences, and they relaxed under the hypnotic spell of a mutual admiration for the novel sights they encountered on their ascent to Montserrat, wholly forgetting, or at least suspending, the more sordid aspect of their mission.

The early part of their journey was rugged, slow and difficult, but, as they approached nearer the summit, broad resting places were found, from which vantage points splendid views were to be had of the country below. As these panoramic scenes came into view, they indulged in expressions of admiration bordering on childish glee.

The road began to broaden, and evidences of culture were manifested; stone walls, hedges and flowering shrubs began to greet them with beauty and fragrance. Evidences of human skill in landscape gardening helped to soften the rugged sides of the road.

"The determination of man to improve upon the face of nature, to appease his insatiable desire for new thrills, is one of the first causes of human slavery," said Don Alvard.

"Hunger is the first cause. As long as men will pay for these things, hungry men will expend their energies for wages with which to buy food," replied Rienzi.

Occasionally, they had met descending, pilgrim monks—bare-foot fanatics, leaving Montserrat, gorged with the ambition to beat and beg their way about the world as "Christian Mendicants," rendering no service for what the people chose to give them through superstitious fear.

"The world is being filled with these lazy beggars," said Don Alvard.

Ascending, vegetable, fruit and wine vendors slowly passed them, prodding their weary donkeys, urging them up the steep way to supply many idle, hungry mouths above, for which they would receive a moiety in money and the balance in prayers for some loved one whose feet still lingered on the eighth step of that wonderful purgatory of the insatiable church of Rome, which coined a profit out of the souls of men. Purgatory! the fountain of plenty, the fruit of cultivated human credulity— what a joy to the chuckling priest, and, as the protestants declare, founded on no warrant of scripture whatever.

Now, like a spiral, the road took a wide sweep, landing them upon a broad, level terrace, with a magnificent view of the far reaching world beyond, deeply inspiring to men with minds for the great things of earth.

They were amazed to behold, frowning down upon them, the battlements of a tremendous fortress, the grim and gloomy walls of which were slashed with the ballastraria of an ancient period of the bow and battering-ram. These walls hoar with antiquity, still possessed the unspoken power to challenge their approach with a demand to know the purpose of their visit.

Long and intently they surveyed this grand and imposing spectacle—surely men were strange creatures, judged by their hiding places. This was but a system of artificial caverns.

Wonder of wonders! How was this stupendous mass assembled? Its gloomy towers, graceful minarets, and impregnable walls, were the creations of architectural skill. It must have required ages of time and generations of men to complete the colossal task of building.

But, what was more essential, from whence came the tremendous monetary cost of erecting this monument of egotism and selfish isolation? What good purpose did it serve to humanity?

Why do men shirk their duties toward humanity at large, and seek the selfsh indolence of silence and solitude? If this is a lawful prerogative, and all thinking men should avail themselves of the privilege, what would become of civilization?

Passing through a great arch leading into an

outer plaza, the pilgrims were greeted by a somber
faced monk, aged and decrepit, coming out of a
half-tumbled-down lodge nearby.   His duty was
more to collect alms than to dispense information.
His filthy garb, his unkempt person and his attitude of utter uselessness, all bespoke the decay of
ages, which now began to appear by closer inspection.   All that the hand of man creates is subject
to decay—time never tires.

Placing some coins in the withered and crumpled
hand of the monk, they began another spiral ascent
which brought them to a higher level, upon which
rested the principal buildings of the celebrated
monastery and church, grim reminders of the va-
garies of half demented men, seeking aloofness from
the common mob, in the belief that they are special
dispensations and super-beings.   Despite the uncertainty, as to the status of the other, Don Alvard
and Rienzi experienced the same thrill of disgust,
and a thought in common, as they viewed the vast
establishment of organized fanatacism.   This had
no thought of humanity or the advancement of civilization.   It was founded upon pure, unadulterated
selfishness and conceit, a world in itself.   It was
the inner circle of ecclesiasticism, battle scarred
from its own schisms.

Antiquity was the hall-mark of everything visible—the vast cathedral; the long gray building containing the filthy unkempt cells of sloven monks;
retreats where fanatical penitents retired to chas-
tise their bodies, mortify their souls and insult

nature, to "wash away" their worldly sins—merely
a pretense of making amends for their crimes
against men, with hypocritical tears of a heart-tear-
ing hysteria, born of moral cowardice and superstitious fear.   Here and there were shrines, sur-
mounted by ponderous crosses, where strange beings with accusing hallucinations, brazenly cast
themselves down upon the worn bases to draw attention to their repentant zeal—pure hyprocrisy.
Tortured by an unknown emotion they would clasp
their hands, and apparently drop into a state of
ecstatic silence, or indulge in a moment of secret
meditation, the nature of which they and God alone
knew.

Like Mount Palatine at Rome, seven centuries
before the Christian era, this was a refuge of criminals who fled the world to escape punishment for
their crimes.   Their penitence was the rankest false-
pretense.

Even in its infancy, Christianity had been suspected of evil secret practices and rites; here it
roosted in safety.

To the contrary, there was no lack of comfort
and even luxury, for the executive forces of this
rendezvous of righteousness.   It was no tomb, it
was a living, writhing thing.

"It reminds me of a putrifying body, alive with
maggots," whispered Don Alvard.

There were schools for *novitiates*, and training
quarters for a militant service.

Priests, monks, pilgrims, novices and penitents

were coming and going in a false-pretense of importance, like bees in a hive, all vieing with each
other which could exhibit the greatest evidence of
zeal and insanity, which they named devotional
piety.

Rienzi was right, his credentials gave them cordial welcome. They were provided with comfortable quarters and given freedom to roam at will
through the dismal, withal, interesting place. This
was safe, for one could not steal anything without
killing a guard or bribing a custodian, and, should
one fall off the walls, he would land outside the
jurisdiction of Montserrat.

It was eventide when they strolled. From the
cathedral came the notes of a splendid choir, singing the eventide canticle.

As the commencing words: "O sing unto the
Lord," came rolling into the soft, fragrant air, it
inspired a strange sensation in them; there was
something hypnotic in the chant.

Don Alvard paused, placed his hand upon
Rienzi's arm and said:

"My friend, I may tell you a story, at some
suitable time, which will chill your blood; then
you will curse the power which thus borrows the
mantle of beauty, and steals the voice of love, to foster the most hateful system that was ever conceived
by men."

They had been informed of the hour when they
would be received, first by the secretary-ordinary,
then by the superior of the monastery, at which

time they were to make known any especial reasons
for their visit.

At the appointed time they were ushered into
a large, comfortably furnished reception room, in
the palace of the superior, where there were a large
number of visitors awaiting the audience. It was
a Mecca for frenzied fanatics.

Don Alvard, ever on the elert, was hardly prepared for the surprise awaiting him. A sweeping
glance about the room gave him a quick scrutiny
of the faces. He was shocked to see, there, the face
of Bambo. That astute person displayed neither
surprise nor emotion. The Don pressed his finger
upon his lips and passed him by without recognition.

Rienzi was spokesman for both, and they were
granted the freedom of the institution. They were
properly assigned to their sleeping quarters and bid
each other a good night's rest.

After retiring to his humble but quite comfortable cell, the Don impatiently waited for some word
from Bambo, feeling certain that his astute friend
would communicate with him.

Late in the night there came a tapping upon
a heavy door between his and the adjoining cell.
A voice softly called: "Open. It is Bambo."

The Don expecting this visit, had not extinguished his light. Observing a latch upon the door
he loosed it and Bambo entered, joyously greeting
him.

After brief explanations, Bambo recited, that,
having recovered his strength and health, he had

decided to visit Montserrat, to learn what he could regarding the history of the lost Gnostic records before seeking the Don's whereabouts.

They rapidly exchanged their adventures and experiences since their separation, the Don relating how he had gone to Pampeluna, and how he had come in contact with Don Iñigo who proved to be his cousin. He then informed Bambo of his chance meeting with Francisco Rienzi, and the seeming friendship which had resulted, suggesting that, perhaps, he might be useful to them.

Bambo was silent for a moment, then slowly said:

"I am not sufficiently acquainted with the true identity of Rienzi to quickly pass upon his character, but there is a never failing rule by which to judge men, and that is by the company they keep. By this rule Rienzi is not above reproach, and even suspicion, for he is a close associate of Francis Borgia. That is quite sufficient to put us fully on guard. Anything bearing the brand of Borgia is to be suspected.

"Since Alphonso Borgia was pope, under the name of Calixtus III, (1455-1458) the Borgias have never ceased conspiring to again seize control of the college of cardinals. Deceit, treachery and even murder are in the Borgia blood.

"Calixtus III was convicted of nepotism.

"Alexander VI was Roderigues Borgia, father of the notorious Lucretia and Caesar Borgia.

"Calixtus elevated two of his nephews to car-

dinalships which they dishonored by the publicity
of their evil conduct. He heaped secular dignities
and emoluments upon a third nephew, making him
Duke of Spoletum, general of the Holy See, pre-
fect of Rome, Governor of Castle St. Angelo, and,
attempted to make him king of Naples. Such was
his bartering in Godly perquisites—and this is
called Christianity.

"He also attempted to arm the Milanese against
Prince Ferdinand, forbidding his taking the throne
as king. Therefore, no Borgia will ever again be
trusted in Spain.

"We are here in the secret hiding place of ecclesiastical intrigue. One must challenge and disarm
his own shadow to feel safe."

Bambo displayed agitation and excitement as
he recited these things to Don Alvard.

"Then you know Francis Borgia," said the Don.

"I know him to be the most dangerous man in
the Catholic world today," replied Bambo. "He
is cunningly training the See of Rome toward the
establishment in the Americas of a militant Catholic
Empire. He is responsible for the secret dispute
now on regarding the distribution of the spoils of
the looting of Mexico, the most heartless, inhuman
and contemptible enterprise ever projected by men.
The wanton assault upon a helpless, harmless nation, and the merciless torture and murder of its
people, was wholly for plunder, a portion of which
was to go to the church.

"That villainous countryman of yours, Hernan

Cortes, who is pictured as a saint planting the blood stained Christian cross upon Mexican soil, is friendly to Borgias projects. They propose to extend the same murderous conquest throughout the Americas in the name of the church. In simple, under cover of extending the Christian religion into new lands, they propose to grab every foot of territory that can be made to stick under a papal grant or decree, and colonize the new world before other nations are aware of their purpose, and to establish a Catholic Empire. This is a sinister thing. It will annihilate the primitive American peoples by robbery and cold blooded murder.

"I am informed that a demand has been made upon Charles for a division of the gold taken by force from Montezuma, amounting to 600,000 marks. Also of the vast quantities of precious stones and jewels. Is that a Godly calling? All this is to be covered by a glamour of heroism, as were the murderous crusades.

"Borgia is secretly organizing a militant order as a wing of the church, to carry forward this speculative work for the church, that the latter may not be directly accused of imperialism and self-aggrandizement. Rienzi and your cousin, Iñigo, are secret agents of this enterprise, without doubt, and, if you want to know the truth, Borgia and Gonsalvo are bosom friends."

"Curse of Christendom!" exclaimed Don Alvard, "may we never shake off this accursed agent of Satan, Gonsalvo?"

"Not as long as we travel his highway," replied Bambo. "But the other man, Borgia, he is rich and powerful; he is a ghost, here, there, everywhere. Your own brother may be his secret agent, and always with secret intrigue hidden beneath his cloak. His boasted ambition to exploit the new world, and plant there universal colonies under the paternal control and protection of the church, is but a preparation for colossal plundering expeditions—and, mind you, I prophesy that he will succeed, and that America will be dominated by an invisible ecclesiastic power to the end its governments.

"Eventually, Rome will make peace with the hated heretic protestants and they will unite as a balance of political power to rule the new Babylon. Every nation on earth will add to the 'mixture and confusion' of the new world, by sending there, their ignorant criminal and poverty stricken surplus to strengthen the Catholic power, which has always established refuge for crime. They propose to colonize crime in America.

"The very fact that Borgia has entrusted to Rienzi this delicate pilgrimage to Montserrat is sufficient to arouse suspicion regarding his character, for Borgia does not make mistakes in choosing his agents. He is posing before the world as indispensable to the Catholic propaganda. I have already discussed with both Leo and Clement, the possibilities in establishing a *Congregatio de Propaganda Fide,* which sooner or later, will be estab-

lished, to promote these identical exploitations.
Only a fear that the sovereigns will openly resent
this bold move has held it back. A foundation must
first be laid in the new world. Borgia has assumed
that task. The *Index Librorum Prohibitorum* has
long ago muzzled free speech."

"An assumed frankness is often a clever disguise. Rienzi perhaps is well aware of this. It is
possible he knew you were coming here."

"It is important, then, that we learn from Rienzi
how closely attached to Borgia he truly is," suggested the Don.

"On the contrary, it is better that we show no
interest which might put Rienzi on his guard. It
is of much more importance to ascertain to what
extent your uncle has been involved through this
renegade son, Iñigo, for the church undoubtedly is
reaching out for control of his rich estate. I prefer,
however, to leave these matters to your discretion."

"My discretion very distinctly warns me to see
no more of Rienzi at present. I hate this villainous
intrigue, and shall have nothing further to do with
it. I give my worst enemy a chance, but these
sneaking cowards stab in the back, or from ambush,
therefore, we need not have scruples about betraying them. I have found no honor in the Roman
code," doggedly grumbled the disgusted Don.

"That is too true. You will find the precedents
in Ehud (Judges 3:21) and Joab, (II Sam. 3:27)"
softly replied Bambo, with a sigh. "Now let us talk
of other matters.

"In the belief that I might soon locate you, I have acquainted myself with the truth regarding the lost Gnostic records. I have learned there is a whispered legend that the seceding monks fled into the Pyrenees Mountains, at the source of the river Lobregat.

"After a careful examination of a secret map, and an analysis of the stories available, I have secretly prepared a course which will at least determine if there is any merit in this legend. I have ascertained, also, that there is an obscure road leading away from Montserrat which will enable you to take your departure from here unnoticed, by your starting in the early dawn.

"I must confess, I have a fear that, Rienzi has another spy trailing him, and you may become the subject of his espionage. After you have been shown over this remarkable place I would suggest that you take your silent departure from here.

"Early tomorrow morning, if you will stroll along the north wall, you will be met by my own confidential courier who will be your guide during the day.

"Upon your departure I will return to the castle of my friend, Count de Brabon, to remain there indefinitely, for I foresee turmoil at Rome. Of course it is speculative as to when we may meet again after you leave here.

"I must warn you of a grave danger which you will encounter on your journey. You will find yourself on the border of a desert which you must avoid.

It will be necessary for you to make a wide detour to safely arrive at a small village, half French and half Spanish, named Andorra. The legend comes from that town. It may mean nothing, nevertheless, it has all the ear-marks of truth. There you may find some valuable clue.

"I will explain now my seeming haste in getting you away from here. You must give out the impression that you contemplate a longer visit. There is a person here whom I fear. He is a cardinal disguised as a Benedictine monk. I have secretly ascertained, that, he is here on a mission from Rome, although he is a Spaniard, named Salviso. Not an hour ago I saw him in confidential conference with Rienzi, hence, I take it, he also represents Borgia, and, that, some urgent scheme is being incubated. He is the most insistent inquisitor I have ever encountered. Should you come in contact with him, be most discreet. He spends most of his time in the secret archives. You will know him by a mole on his chin."

"Shall I take no chances and run him through, if he gets troublesome?" asked the Don.

"No," laughingly replied Bambo. "Don't crowd Satan too much," and he arose and fervently held to Don Alvard's hand in bidding him good night.

It annoyed the independent Don, not a little, to realize that his responsibilities multiplied with his contact with the plans and opinions of others. Instead of relying upon an intuitive good sense, and a hitherto friendly fate, he found himself wondering

what others might think, should he do this or that
and trimming to these influences. Now, he was
resolved to throw off the restraint and begin the
very next day to consult no one, but to concentrate
upon one main object and seek the shortest way
to its attainment.

Casting off his troublesome thoughts, as he
would remove his big buskins, he slept soundly.

The crowing of a cock warned him of Bambo's
instructions; thereupon he hastily arose, donned his
outer clothing and walked upon the plaza, with his
long sabre clanking about his feet upon the pavement. This was contrary to the rules, for pilgrims
were not permitted to carry side arms after having
spent the first night at Montserrat.

Observing a lone monk seated upon the low wall
and gazing over the vast plain below, he approached
and bade him a good morning, believing he was
Bambo's courier.

The monk savagely resented the greeting, asking:

"Why do you, a clanking soldier, intrude thus
upon my morning meditations?

His cowl had fallen back upon his shoulders
and Don Alvard quickly recognized the monk described by Bambo.

Taken aback by the monk's strange attitude toward him, he sharply retorted:

"Such impious discourtesy could only come from
a sinful heart," and with a bow he turned to leave
the monk.

"Do not be so hasty to take offense, brother, I was only trying your mettle, come, is that not inspiring?" and he waved his hand toward the landscape.

Don Alvard folded his arms and looked gloomily below.

"You are a visiting stranger; have you seen the wonders of this place of God?" inquired the monk.

"Will you lay off your mask and show me these wonders, Cardinal Salviso?" responded the Don, with a sardonic grin.

"Ah, you know me?" excitedly exclaimed the monk. "Then you are from Sebastian."

Don Alvard placed his fingers upon his lips and looking cautiously about said:

"Indulge not in personalities, we may be here on the same mission. I cannot talk to you here. It is sufficient that I am not from Sebastian."

"Are you what you appear to be, a soldier of the Holy See?" asked the monk.

"Are you what you appear to be, a Benedictine monk?" asked Don Alvard.

The monk looked confused, hesitated, laughed and drew his hood over his head.

"You do not answer," said the Don. "Then I must draw my own conclusion. However, it matters not now, but, your kind intimation that I should view the wonders of this monastery suggests, perhaps you could introduce me to the custodian of the *Archivio Secreto* of the establishment."

The monk looked sharply at him and asked:

"When did you arrive here?"

"Last evening I had the pleasure of listening to the evening canticle," replied the Don.

"You have conversed with no one since your arrival?" inquired the monk sharply.

"Ah, can one not escape the inquisitor even at Montserrat? I held brief converse with his eminence the superior, with the hostler, and, now, I may add, with one distinguished prelate disguised as a monk," suavely replied the Don.

"Come, let us be frank, what is your mission here?" bruskly asked the monk, with assumed authority.

"Yes, let us be frank, what is your mission here? You are wearing a disguise. Let us ask to be taken before the superior to make frank avowal of our purposes," and the Don grinned.

The monk scowled, drew his garb about him and took a step away from the Don, saying:

"I am afraid you are not what you seem."

"And you?" questioned the Don, laughing, and he watched the monk disappear.

Bambo's private courier made himself known to Don Alvard, and they spent practically the whole day viewing the wonders of the great institution— endless displays of the relics of past ages.

"I once had the pleasure of spending several days in the *Archivio Secreto* at the Vatican," cautiously said the Don, while they were passing through the great libraries.

"Wait a moment," said the guide, and he approached a venerable monk and they held a whispered conversation, touching hands with a clink of silver coins.

Motioning for Don Alvard to follow, he led them through a long, dark corridor, at the end of which a door opened into the secret archives of the Monastery of Montserrat.

"Only cardinals and bishops are permitted free access to these ancient writings," whispered the custodian.

"Ah, this, then, is the depository of the Gnostic records," cautiously said the Don. "See, I bear the credentials and seal-ring of a cardinal."

"There is a sad story connected with the Gnostic records," said the monk.

"Yes, so I have heard, but I never have known the whole story," replied the Don, who felt the perspiration beginning to gather on his face. Was it possible that he was about to be told the truth?

"I will tell it you briefly," began the monk. "There, where you see the priest reading, is the most sacred spot in this monastery, the secret alcove where were deposited the treasured Gnostic books of wisdom, which formerly were kept in the *Archivio Secreto* of the Vatican — or rather in the possession of the popes.

"They could be read only by the past masters of the Benedictine order, who made special pilgrimages for that purpose. They alone knew of their existence here.

"Many years ago, a schism in the order occurred,

and all of these Gnostic records disappeared, together with a number of monks, who named themselves the *last of the Gnostics*. They subsequently have not been heard from."

"And no clue has since been found?" asked the Don.

"Only once," replied the monk. "A few years ago, some mysterious word warned the superior of this monastery where the seceding monks could be located. A company of trusted crusaders was sent to investigate this rumor, but not one man ever returned."

"You mean to say they wholly disappeared?" exclaimed the Don.

"They at least never returned here, and, in so far as I am aware, no word was ever received regarding them," was the reply.

"What course were they supposed to have taken?" asked the Don.

"One of the great secrets of this monastery is, that, they were led by a shepherd to some mountainous region at the source of the river Lobregat. A great eathquake changed the whole aspect of that region at that time, and, it was generally accepted, that they had perished," was the monk's answer.

"May I approach and greet the reader in yonder alcove, that I may get a closer view of it?" asked the Don.

"Certainly," replied the monk, and he stood awaiting his return.

The secret alcove was some distance from where

they had been standing conversing. The Don strode
to the reading prelate who looked up in surprise
as the Don greeted him:

"Well, my good Cardinal Salviso, are you attempting to reconstruct the Gnostic wisdom?"

The Cardinal bounded to his feet and angrily
exclaimed:

"Fiend! Who are you?"

Don Alvard laughed, replying:

"I make an engagement to meet you again, at
which time I will answer your question to your
satisfaction," and he returned again to his guide
who remained with him till he was safely within
his cell that night, where Bambo again visited him
in a state of great excitement.

"Rienzi has taken his departure," he informed
the Don, and then they talked till it was time for
Don Alvard to sleep, for he desired to ride away in
the early morning while it was yet dark.

At the break of day he found awaiting him,
Bambo's courier, who refused the money which the
Don offered to him, and, as he shook his hand to
bid him good bye, he whispered:

"I am Bambo's friend, we are both Gnostics.
God speed you."

"Give this letter to Bambo, will you," said the
Don. It was a letter for the countess.

The Don rode away from that gloomy rendezvous for rogues, feeling as though he were escaping
from a prison.

CHAPTER X

THE LOST GNOSTIC MONASTERY

CULTIVATED IGNORANCE IS THE GRAVE OF KNOWLEDGE

OUR cavalier was again on the way toward the unknown. Uncertainty dominated his meditations as he trudged the weary and monotonous trail. During a long and irksome day he had traversed a mean mountain road, encountering not one living creature.

As night approached, unspeakable loneliness began to press him down to the earth. Even the patient and uncomplaining Belial seemed to be standing still while the two sides of a blank and lifeless gorge passed them by, so monotonous had become the hourly grind of unchanging scene. It seemed that his poor, tired horse was merely lifting his feet up and down without moving forward.

As night seemed to close upon them like a deadly, invisible hand, they emerged upon the rim of a desert. As far as the eye could reach spread a flat, desolate plain which must have been a veritable furnace in mid-day, for the smothering heat reached them in firce waves, as though challenging them to come on and be roasted.

In no pleasant state of mind the Don dismounted to give his good, faithful Belial a moment's breathing spell, while he pondered their situation. It required a brave and stubborn heart to not turn back at that critical point, and a world of courage to go forward, upon discovering, that, due to some unfortunate mistake not a morsel of food nor a mouthful of water had been brought with them. There was not a sprig of grass in sight for the poor, weary beast. This was a grim calamity at the very beginning of their journey. He munched a dry crust as his own meager meal while he thought, finally pushing a portion of this crust into the muzzle of Belial who nodded his head gratefully as he tried to find it.

It was indeed a trying plight with no visible way out.

Upon observing a full moon in the sky, he boldly decided to cross over the desert by night to avoid the heat of the day, and another long and tedious detour, which might require many days' travel in an uninhabited country offering neither water nor food, and little better shelter than the desert. He afterwards admitted that this was a foolhardy decision, nevertheless it terminated in the greatest good fortune, demonstrating how finely balanced is the fate of humanity, for the results of this arduous journey were destined to overturn world powers and change the trend of civilization.

Undaunted, he looked at the sky for a guiding star, and plunged into the seething sands. All that terrible night he and Belial blundered through the clogged course, stopping only for brief periods of rest. At last morning dawned with its horrors visible everywhere. The rays of the sun were

like red-hot rods as they began to prod the scant
shrubs to route out even the insect life to destroy
it. The sky was like a polished brass dome closing down upon them and the plain was bespangled
with visible heat vibrations, the waves rising like
a mist from the super-heated sands.

In vain did he search the horizon for some beckoning shadow which might momentarily shield them
from the glare of that brazen dome above them, but
not even a shrub could be seen sufficiently large
to cast a shade for them. It was a desperate situation. It was absolutely essential that both he and
Belial should rest for a brief spell.

With great hearted sympathy he placed his arm
over the bowed neck of his weary horse and apologized for having thus displayed a streak of insanity.
Then he put it up to Belial if it would not be more
comfortable to die now, than later in the blistering
day, but Belial declared that he preferred to burn
on earth than take chances of a million years of
torture in a Catholic hell, otherwise it mattered little
where or when they died, just so they died quickly.

For once in his fighting career the courageous
cavalier found himself menaced by a crafty enemy
whom he could not challenge to stand up before
him and be punctured by his mighty fighting-iron,
which just now added so much to Belial's burden.
It was not a problem to be solved by mortal combat. Only wit and grim endurance, could conquer
so crafty an enemy. The Don became angry, cursing his own bad judgment, and scolding Belial for

not exhibiting ordinary horse-sense by refusing to
go into the desert.

Looking up into the sky, he exclaimed in alarm:
"Curse of Christendom! old comrade, look there!
Our time is come," and he pointed to the heavens,
black with vultures.

"That is a bad sign, Belial. Let us pray for
the powers of St. Ephesus and recommend that our
children adopt his coat-of-arms."

Real calamity was impudently staring them in
the face, and leering at them from every angle.
Death was patiently trudging along with them and
beckoning for his allies, the vultures, to keep pace,
for it was but a matter of short time when he would
deliver the stroke which would give these desert
ghouls a banquet.

He laughed aloud and yelled at the top of his
voice.

" 'Come on all you fowls that fly in the midst of
of heaven. Come and gather yourselves together
unto the supper of the great God. That ye may eat
the flesh of kings, the flesh of mighty men and the
flesh of horses.' (Rev. 19: 17,18.) But, this once
you may stand by and lick your hungry chops, for
these two kings will fool you, won't we, old comrade?" and Belial nodded his buzzing head as
though agreeing with all his master had said.

"Let us make another spurt, old cardinal"—he
had previously given to Belial this distinguished
title—"and I promise to saint you before I die if

we don't pull through." Then they again began to plod through the stinging sand.

A new menace now loomed in the distance. Far out upon the desert a well defined sand-storm was visible.

Nearer and nearer circled the scavengers, now swooping down close upon them, then rising with impatient screams that their victims held on so tenaciously. Their stench sickened the Don as they fanned the fetid air in his face. Their impudence alarmed him as they grew bolder.

He had realized that his faithful horse could no longer bear his great weight, therefore, he trudged along, dragging his "caravan" after him. He dared not look back to see how tired the animal was.

Suddenly, Belial gave a lunge, nearly upsetting his master. Turning quickly, to his horror, a vulture actually rested upon his saddle, only taking flight upon his approach.

With an oath he drew from its scabbard, which hung from his saddle, his long blade, and made a vicious slash at each bird bold enough to come near, until he finally brought one to the earth. Crippling it so it could not fly, he left it fluttering upon the sand to attract the others.

"That ends our troubles from them, Belial," he said. "How like human beings they are; the moment one falls the mob pounces upon him to tear him to pieces."

Strange to say, the vultures left off following

them and now circled about and hovered over the spot where the wounded bird had fallen. It was evident they were tearing it limb from limb.

Night was again approaching, and the Don and Belial had but a few ounces of energy left. Neither man nor beast had a morsel of food or a mouthful of water. In his half delirium, the Don raved, but he was kind and gentle to his poor horse who staggered painfully. They were now leaning close together, for sympathy. Belial's sad, weeping eyes seemed a premonition of the end. If he went down it was doubtful if the master would struggle further, for his strength and courage were fast waning.

Pausing for a momentary rest, the Don scanned the horizon, concentrating his gaze toward what appeared to be a low range of hills. If they could hold out to reach this country they doubtless would find succor.

"Curse of Christendom! Belial, this is a suitable place to offer our carcasses as a sacrifice to Moloch, but if you will stand up, old comrade, we are not yet ready to die an ignoble death.

"Look there!" and he placed his arm affectionately over the weary horse's neck and pointed to the hills.

"Ha! You do understand!" he exclaimed, as Belial raised his head and peered off into the distance to where he had pointed; he seemed to understand that, that was the promised land.

"You are a Jew, Belial. For forty years Moses pointed out the promised land to your ancestors.

That was the only thing that would keep them moving." And he patted the side of his face, much to the good animal's satisfaction. "But, I'm not going to fool you as God fooled old Mose, we'll reach the promised land."

Thus, alternately crawling forward and resting, they tolled off the time, and measured the remaining grains of energy left to them. It now required the greatest mental effort on the Don's part to keep going in one direction. He found himself inclined to leave a straight path to bend to a curvilinear course. This greatly puzzled him. Here was something new, but he did not know that it was a common physical law, which takes possession of exhausted bodies traveling in a straight line.

Looking back to where they had left the wounded vulture, the Don had cause for new alarm. The sky was literally black with the carrion birds and they were still coming in long, black ribbons from all directions. It was plain these ravenous vultures would not hesitate to attack them and torment them to death, did they remain another day upon the desert. It was a demonstration that animal life could not dwell there.

But, what was of equal interest, the sand-storm, which had been visible, was now a low, rolling wave, so dense it seemed to be an elevation across the plain. It did not seem to be moving, nevertheless it was now close upon them. It was more alarming, too, that the clouds of vultures suddenly rose in a fighting, tumbling mass and began to form

long lines leading before the storm. To Don Alvard's relief they took a course at a right angle
from where they were standing, intimating the direction of the storm, which, if his conclusion was
correct, would leave them out of its destructive
course.

"We are not worthy of that horrible death,
Belial; a discreet retreat is better than an abject
surrender. We must use our last ounce of energy
to turn the end of that storm, and reach the protection of the hills tonight."

With bowed heads they doggedly counted off
the weary miles. From time to time he would stop
to scan the desert behind them, and give Belial an
affectionate pat on the cheek to encourage him. It
was the flickering spark of life remaining in the
faithful beast which kept them going.

At last they could go no further, grateful night
was covering them, yet it only gave relief from the
direct rays of the sun, the atmosphere remaining
stifling. Nevertheless, they slept.

The morning dawned, with a crisp, refreshing
breeze blowing little whirlpools of sand about them.
Belial was already on his feet. Don Alvard arose
and looked sharply about, the cool air meant something. The atmosphere was clear, the sand-storm
having disappeared towards the heart of the desert.
The range of low mountains were now plainly visible. Ah! there was something still more encouraging. There, within an hour's walk, could be
plainly discerned a clump of trees, which gave the

hope of water, for the green of the foliage was
bright in the dancing light of the rising sun.

Belial was nearly gone, but his master encouraged him with friendly taps and boastful conversation. Pointing to the oasis he proudly exclaimed:

"There, Cardinal, a feast fit for a king awaits
us. Am I not king of this desert? Are you not my
good and faithful Cardinal? O, if Bambo could see
us now! Forward!"

Within the hour they had approached sufficiently near to the green spot to draw some conclusion as to its nature. It consisted of large willow
trees with a lower growth of thick shrubs, doubtless, alder bushes, both of which held out a promise
of water. The Don could not help wondering at
the effect the close vision of the green had upon the
horse; he was as much elated as the Don himself
as they staggered to its grateful rim.

At last life was again in their grasp. In the
midst of this oasis was a large pool of cool, clear
water, surrounded by an abundance of rich, green
grass. It was more, much more, being a rookery for
numerous water fowls, especially a nesting place
for plover, hence the Don would also find ample
food for his own hungry maw.

His first care was to use due precaution in the
partaking of the water by both, each sparingly
quenching his thirst. Belial displayed every evidence of gratitude upon being relieved of his burden and permitted to feast upon the tender, succulent grass.

The Don now began to forage for himself, finding plovers' eggs in abundance, and many young birds about ready to leave their nests.

Never before had he felt so grateful for life. Truly nature was unconquerable, yet a generous opponent. She had held his life in her hand and had given it back to him. He was impressed by the fact that this same consideration had been shown for man and beast alike. In fact, Belial would have faired even better than he, had there been no birds nesting here.

Viewed from every angle, he could not see one single evidence of the miraculous intervention of a character resembling the Christian God. He could trace every feature of the case to natural circumstances and causes, and, the composite picture seemed perfectly to reflect the original source of the whole Christian idea.

Gathering a quantity of eggs and young birds, he was prepared to partake of a feast of his own.

Belial was so tired that, upon being given a more hearty drink, he lay down and nibbled the grass about him as far as he could reach, occasionally giving vent to a healthy snort of satisfaction.

With flint and tinder-box the Don made a fire, and prepared his own meal, enjoying it equally as much as Belial had his.

Both now lay in the cooling shade of the drooping willows and slept through the day. It was indeed a joy to awaken and find it was not all a dream.

He now went upon another foraging excursion,

gathering all the eggs and birds he could find for his evening repast, and to provide some food for the further journey.

To his delight and amusement he saw Belial lie down and roll over several times, then rise and shake himself vigorously.

He laughed aloud and exclaimed: "Feeling pretty good, old comrade, eh! I am, too, Cardinal. The moon is quite full, it will give us light to travel tonight, and we shall reach the mountains by morning."

As the sun disappeared, a soft wind began to move the drooping willow foliage, and started the alders to jiggling. The air was perceptibly cooler, promising a much more comfortable journey. The Don rubbed Belial down with bunches of dry grass, which grooming the good animal seemed to relish. He then harnessed him for the night's trudge to the mountains. He provided himself with a strong willow staff and shared the hardship by walking along with Belial.

Thus they alternately traveled and rested, through the moonlit night, so silent and ghostly it almost frightened them. With the early morning again came that refreshing breeze from the mountains trying to cool the desolate sands.

Notwithstanding they were much stronger since their rest and recuperation at the oasis, they felt extremely tired and sore. It was with great relief that they found a well defined, beaten path leading into a wooded valley, indicating the presence of living things, hence water and food, for animals at least. The Don was unable to determine the character of the animals making this trail, but it doubtless led to water in the valley. This proved to be true. They came upon a splendid spring, two small deer bounding away as they approached, indicating the wild nature of the spot. In the soft earth could be seen tracks, also of animals with padded feet, but whether dogs or wild beasts the Don could not determine.

There was ample food for Belial, but he was not so fortunate in finding any available source of food for himself. He had husbanded his birds, but these were scarcely a mouthful for the big man. Taking a strong hitch in his belt he sparingly nibbled the delicate bones, cracking them for their marrow.

While he sat brooding over his extraordinary plight, he observed something to shock him, and put his blood to tingling. There, in the soft earth, were the imprints of naked, human feet, along with the padded tracks. These tracks had been made long previously, nevertheless, they were human, and the tracks of Benedictine monks, for the shepherds of this part of Spain wore sandals lashed onto their feet and ankles by heavy thongs made of goat-skin. But, the animal tracks; if they belonged to dogs, these animals must have been of tremendous size.

Don Alvard was himself again, alert and ready for adventure. His death inspiring journey had not been in vain. "After all, he mused, "when one starts upon a journey to locate an unknown place, perhaps the feet have more sense of direction than the head, but I am convinced that ecclesiasticism got its original idea of hell from that desert."

A substantial trail led from the spring toward the mountains, but he felt the necessity for a brief rest before going forward, and they spent some hours at the spring.

"Come, Belial, our work is before us," said the Don, as he began to arrange the pack. "I don't know what we shall find, but this path will lead us to somewhere."

There were no new indications of human presence as they proceeded along the rugged way which grew more difficult and tortuous as they ascended.

The gorge now began to narrow until there was barely sufficient room for them to pass. There were no indications of recent travel over the trail. It was utterly desolate and deserted, with scarcely a sprig of verdure visible. The rough travel necessitated frequent pauses for rest.

Before reaching a sharp turn in the path, Belial drew back suddenly and emitted a snort to do justice to Gabriel's trumpet, signifying that he had sensed something around that corner unpleasant to his alert nostrils. Don Alvard felt a cold thrill trickle down his spine, the whole surrounding was spooky, with little fighting room in which to wield his sword.

"I can best defend us upon your back, Belial," he said, and he climbed into his saddle. Drawing his long sword, he cautiously urged Belial forward, very much on the alert for surprises. Turning the sharp angle in the trail, his vision was on a level with an overhanging cliff which sheltered a shelf-like projection. It was plain that there was something abnormal about this shelf, but he could not at once determine the nature of the phenomenon in the gloom.

Slowly he approached, and, finally recognized, what appeared to be a human form, lying upon the projection, as within a sepulchre.

The most courageous man experiences a sensation of dread upon suddenly being confronted by the evidences of death, in a lonely spot—a false sentiment, born of superstition, nevertheless creepy.

The body was wrapped in the cassock of a Benedictine monk. Prodding it with the point of his sword, the cowl fell back, exposing the mummified face. Desiccation had preserved the body from disintegration. It was the remains of a dead monk, which he concluded, had sought this spot, inaccessible to wild beasts, to breathe his last.

Seeing the bones of the hands still interlaced, as they had been folded across the chest, he lifted from them, on the point of his sword, a rosary of amber beads, strung on a silver wire.

"Curse of Christendom!" he muttered, "even here, in this Christ forsaken wilderness, this emblem of Catholic mummery is paramount. Did I not know the absolute hypocrisy of it, I should be impressed with superstitious awe. But, old rogue, I'll wager

it will require more than counting beads to expiate
your crimes, else your Christian God would not have
deserted you to rot in this desolate spot. The resurrection will never remove your rotting body from
this place."

Prodding about the cassock, his blade came in
contact with a hard object which he hastily uncovered, revealing a copper treasure-box common to
that period.

He also found, attached to a girdle, a leathern
pouch, now hard and brittle. Cracking it open,
he found therein a gold crucifix, and the key to
the box. Attached to the key, by a silver wire, was
a copper talisman, wrapped in a thin lead-foil.
Nothing else of value was found.

Don Alvard thrust all these into his own capacious traveling pouch, to be examined at leisure, and
proceeded on his way.

He was thrilled now with the sensation of having found a field in which the earlier Benedictine
activities had been cast.

It being most essential that they reach some
suitable place for rest, and where water and food
might be found, he urged Belial along the rugged
way. He was growing ravenously hungry. The last
carcass of a plover now was brought forth. As he
looked at the delicate bones in his own huge hand,
he laughed, saying:

"Poor little bird, the strong eat the weak."

Upon reaching the other arm of the cliff, he
came out upon a platform which afforded a mag-

nificent view of a valley below, a grand and beautiful spot, wholly surrounded by high, steep mountain cliffs. Like a silver cord a stream of sparkling
water wended its way into the distance. He wondered if this might be the river Lobregat.

Herds of cattle were lazily grazing, or lying
along the cool banks of the stream. Nowhere could
he see a human habitation. In the bright, clear
atmosphere it resembled a well executed oil painting.

He was disappointed that the trail did not lead
toward this paradise, which sadly recalled the happy
home of his youth, which was such a peaceful valley. On the contrary his path took a sharp right-
angle turn and started on a gradual ascent, carrying
him deeper into the gloomy mountains—there was
no alternative but to proceed or turn back.

Pausing, he muttered: "Curse of Christendom!
Old mate, if we do not soon locate some place of
rest and recuperation, we shall have cheated the
buzzards only to go the way of the lonely monk, or
perhaps be devoured by gregarious jackalls.

Dismounting, he approached the edge of the cliff
and peered below. Quickly he withdrew, and, seeking another spot, he again looked below. It was
evident that he had made some discovery, for he
looked from side to side as though expecting to find
a way of descent. Finally, he pushed Belial back
close to the wall, and stretching himself upon his
stomach, peered long and earnestly at something
below. Some big idea was incubating in his fertile

brain, for he searched the mountain side as well as the plain.

Slowly arising, he retraced his trail, whipping the scant shrubbery on the edge of the cliff. With a grunt of satisfaction he found a break in the path concealed by shrubs. Returning he led Belial to this point and cautiously began the descent. For half an hour he followed the trail which abruptly terminated in a valley surrounded on all sides by high, sharply defined cliffs.

Along one side of the cliffs ran what appeared to be a deep, sheltered balcony, the whole almost concealed by a profusion of flowering shrubbery in a tangled growth. With these were intermingled fruits, berries and nuts, from all appearances of spontaneous growth, and without cultivation. The floor of this plateau was matted with a rank growth of grass, clover and wild oats. Here and there could be seen goats, sheep and cattle, rolling fat, and wholly unconcerned at this intrusion.

This is what Don Alvard had seen from above. Curiosity brought the animals closer to see who had come to visit them. The udders of goats and ewes were gorged with milk, to the satisfaction of the hungry Don. Here was food for the plucking—ripe grain, fruits and milk.

"We have discovered the lost monastery, Belial, but there seems to be no one at home," whispered the Don, deeply impressed with the surroundings.

Assured of food in abundance, the Don deemed it wise to make a closer inspection of the place before presuming to plant his flag of occupation and possession by discovery. Leaving Belial to brouse, he passed to the cliff where he made a most grewsome discovery. Beneath the overhanging walls was a long row of cavern-like cells hewn out of the solid rock. Each cell contained, on either side, a projection which doubtless served as both bed and seat. There were twenty of these cells with forty of such benches. On each of the projections lay the mummified remains of a Benedictine monk. Judging by the mould and accumulated dust, the bodies had lain thus for ages.

Don Alvard recoiled at this horrifying discovery, believing it probable that death had been due to some contagious disease, which had completely wiped out the colony. With this uppermost in his mind, the very atmosphere seemed saturated with pestilence.

The romance had faded, the paradise was a snare. He hastily withdrew, determined to at once supply himself with some food and depart from this sepulchre.

At the end of the balcony he observed a much larger compartment, which, doubtless, had belonged to the superior, but no body was in this room. There were portions of antique furniture, some broken picture frames, and other decaying articles lying in confusion about the cell.

Night was approaching, and the long shadows began to move about over the place like ghosts, the sensation becoming more uncanny each moment.

Don Alvard felt himself being shut up in a tomb, with all these desiccating monks dancing in glee about him. The bravest heart would grow sick here. He experienced the creepy fear of the unknown which all humanity feels under similar circumstances.

Mechanically, he walked toward Belial. He was standing in the open thoughtfully surveying his strange surroundings when an ominous sound reached his ears; he distinctly heard the savage half smothered growls of beasts, seemingly coming from somewhere in the earth, certainly not from the open space.

Drawing his sword, he approached Belial and stood on guard.

From somewhere out of the blank wall came an aged monk, holding in leash two tremendous, bristling Asiatic Mastiffs. With his snow-white hair and beard whipping the air, the monk made a picture which never left the mind of the Don—Father Time had come to question youth.

He stood looking at Don Alvard in speechless surprise for a moment, then, in a commanding voice, he demanded:

"Are you friend or foe?"

Don Alvard smiled and replied:

"I do not know, I have dropped in here by accident, and I do not know whether my life has been miraculously saved or put in greater jeopardy. Until I know more about my adventure I prefer to be received as a trusted friend."

"You speak well.   Are you an inquisitor?" asked the monk.

"God forbid!" exclaimed the Don.

"Are you a Roman Catholic?" was the next query.

"Regardless of what you may profess, I am not a Christian," replied the Don.

"But you wear the garb of a soldier of Rome."

"As a disguise, as you will learn."

"And what accident brings you here?"

"Fate, I believe," said the Don.

"Have you any information concerning this place?"

"Only that which I have gleaned since coming here, and I am quite willing to go and forget rather than remain overnight with it."

"Wait," said the monk, and he as mysteriously disappeared, taking the great dogs with him, and soon returned alone. His whole aspect had changed. His good natured, twinkling eyes were friendly, and there was no room for doubt in the sincerity of his greeting.

"Stranger, you are most welcome here.   I am the only living, human being to greet you.   First make your tired horse comfortable.   Let him mingle with the herd; they will make him feel at home, I am sure.   Here is the fountain at which they drink and the water is pure and sweet.

Don Alvard relieved Belial of his galling accoutrements, the good beast gratefully acknowledging the favor by a vigorous shaking of his whole body.

"If I could have human friends as loyal as this animal, life would be sweet," said the Don.

The monk only smiled and nodded, saying, "Come with me."

Leading the way, he took the Don into a comfortable apartment, half cavern and half wood construction with an extension which overlooked the valley below, now lost in the gloom of settling night.

"These are my outside quarters, and I live right well, you may feel at ease," said the monk as he prepared two large grease mats to give them light. "You must be hungry. It is our good fortune that you arrive on my roasting day. See, here is a haunch of roast mutton, as tender and juicy as a young lamb. Here is brown bread from flour of my own making, and, I say with some pride, here is the best wine to be found in all Europe," and he placed these upon the table and motioned for the Don to take one of the seats. "Let us feast while we get acquainted."

What a feast. No wonder the Bible dwells upon "mutton, bread and good wine on the lees."

As the host carved the mutton he remarked: "There is my cooking furnace, you will find this mutton most toothsome." And he placed a large portion upon the Don's platter. Nothing ever before tickled the cavalier's palate like this, and the monk chuckled as he watched him eat with vast relish. The monk himself ate like he enjoyed it.

The Don having finished his repast, with a deep

sigh of comfort and contentment, he settled back
in his crude chair, and looked gratefully at the
monk, saying:

"Let us get acquainted. I am Don Alvard de
Ricalde. I was on my way to Barcelona, and, to
avoid the heat, attempted to travel at night and lost
my way upon the desert. It is a miracle, exceeding
the raising of Lazarus, that I live to tell you the
story and sit at your table to enjoy this excellent
hospitality."

"Have you not the slightest knowledge as to
where you are, and what this place is?" asked the
monk.

"Yes, and no," responded the Don, "but that is
a story in itself. It was incidental to my trip, that,
I undertook a mission which caused me to stagger
into this place. That I will make clear to you in due
time. It is sufficient, now, to say, that, it is wholly
friendly to you. I believe that you are going to inform me that this is the lost Gnostic Monastery. I
can assure you that the outside world believes this
is a myth."

"You are quite right. I do tell you that this
is the last stand of the Gnostic brotherhood. I am
Monetho, the last living master," said the monk.

"Ah, I am most grateful to fate for having guided me," softly replied the Don.

Monetho arose, saying: "Come, I will introduce
you to the Gnostic Masters, night or day; a visit
is the same to them."

CHAPTER XI

THE TOMB OF GNOSTICISM

THOUGH PLACED IN A SEPULCHRE, IMMORTAL WISDOM LIVES

THE venerable man, with joyous eagerness, lifted one of the grease mats and bade Don Alvard follow him. Passing along the outer ledge, he opened a concealed door, exposing a dark passageway cut in the virgin rock. Now lighting two antique, wick lamps, he handed one to the Don, and carried one himself, leaving the original mat in the passageway which extended some thirty feet where it apparently terminated in a blank wall.

Placing his lamp upon a projection, Monetho reached high above his head and pressed upon a concealed lever, enabling him to swing a large section of the wall upon an invisible pivot, exposing beyond, a circular chamber.

This chamber was provided with a bench-like projection around its walls, and a vast round table in its center. All neatly cut out of the solid rock.

Passing to the table, Monetho pointed to great piles of materials thereon, saying:

"My brother, behold the greatest treasure of this world, the records of the Gnostic wisdom."

Don Alvard was amazed. There, in systematic order, were piled indisputable evidences, not only of the previous existence of gnostictism as a system

of education, but also of its antinquity. The forms
in which these records were preserved testifying to
their authenticity.

Monetho explained their significance as they
walked around the stone platform.

"The papyrus rolls, and waxed tablets contain
the Egyptian legendary wisdom. These clay tablets and tiles are Babylonian. These yellow parch-
ments are not necessarily Syrian because they are
in the Syriae language, any more than these rolls
in the Hebrew, are Hebraic, for duplicates are found
in other languages, proving a progressive study and
translation—Gnosticism embraces all.

"It is important for me to explain to you the
true significance of Gnosticism, before you may
fully understand the nature and purpose of the
Gnostic brotherhood.

"Originally Gnosticism was a school, founded
for the grand purpose of gathering from the past,
and present, the accumulated wisdom of human
observation and experience. It drew its wisdom
from all schools, its outer mark being the word
Gnosis, *to know*.

"Therefore, a Gnostic is born, not made. While
he may not be an initiate into the nominal organized Gnostic Brotherhood, making him an active,
working Gnostic, nevertheless, every living creature
is a born Gnostic to the extent of his natural, or
acquired knowledge and understanding, and his
ability to transmit that knowledge to other living

beings, hence, *Gnosis* not only means *to know*, but also means *to teach*.

"Gnosticism, then, is revealed nature, and understanding is the light by which that revelation is manifested. Human thought and reason are the highest powers of revelation, and are possessed in some degree by every normal human being.

"The Gnostic Brotherhood is a secret thing from necessity. It was brought together in order to prevent ecclesiasticism from crushing out all knowledge from the masses, in order that a super-class might be raised up as a secret priesthood, to monopolize all avenues of education and learning, which would enable the church to work humanity into a plastic mass. The unit man, with individual thought and personal rights, was to be suppressed."

"What are your logical supports for this theory?" asked the interested Don.

"It is not a theory, it is a living historical fact," quickly replied Monetho. "It is recorded truth that, ages previous to the Christian scheme, the richest wisdom the world will ever possess was rapidly being evolved by deep and learned minds. The foundations of all we know today, were hoar with age when the Christian era first began. It was five hundred years before the ecclesiasts had entrenched themselves behind political powers sufficiently to give them the power to suppress education. This was called the *'extinguishing of the gnostic lamp.'* In plain words, the human world was plunged into abject ignorance. Again we may point to historic

fact; from 486 to 1495, a thousand years of abject
ignorance prevailed. Sovereigns were not permitted to acquire knowledge, because of the fear that
they might learn the truth and revive the Gnostic
spirit; the ordinary priests were not permitted to
seek education, for the fear that they might become
wise to the chuch duplicity and teach others. Even
bishops could barely trace out their Latin. Men
who dared to advocate education were promptly
burned at the stake.

"The horrors of this wilful outrage upon progressive humanity, in its most critical formative period,
may be estimated by a casual examination of the
character of education the church proposed as a
substitute for the accumulated wisdom of the ages,
as found in the absurd, childish, ridiculous books
of Genesis in the Christian scriptures. It was not
intended that the masses should know the truth.
(Matt. 13:13.)

"The most awe inspiring thing in nature is
the sun; hence, in order to inspire superstitious fear
in ignorant humanity, sun-worship in its concealed
and modified forms is, always has been, and will
be to its end, the secret doctrine of ecclesiasticism.
There could be no revelation without the sun, hence
Christ is made to say:

" 'I am the light of the world.' (John 8:12.)

And the fake Hebrews are made to say:

" 'For our God is a consuming fire.' " (Heb.
12:29.)

"Ah! I see the light!" exclaimed Don Alvard.

"The light of Christianity is concealed sun-worship, proving conclusively that, the ecclesiasts even plagiarized their God from Egypt and Babylon."

"Worse than that," replied Monetho. "They deliberately stole this from Gnosticism, and suppressed the underlying truth, that, the sun-worship of the Egyptians and the Babylonians was a definite educational system, giving credit and reverence to the sun as the great revealer of nature's truths. Those nations gave to the world a broad knowledge of mathematics, astronomy and constructive science.

"Without this knowledge Genesis of the Christian Bible could not have been written. Without this baby-like effort to conceal the stolen property of Gnosticism, Christianity would have no foundation.

"Now, my brother, I am going to reveal to you the underlying secret of the fall of man, used as an excuse for the existence of a burdensome church and priesthood, and to be perpetuated for the same reason.

"A garden means a place of culture.

"Later, as you take up the study of the ecclesiastical code, you will find that Eden means pleasure, delight.

"Ecclesiasticism, in the beginning of its great Christian exploitation, found mankind making rapid strides in the general dissemination of true knowledge and wisdom. It visioned a world filled with joy, and the delights of enlightened civilization. Through the meanest selfishness ever betrayed by a human institution, it surreptitiously turned mankind out of this supreme state, debased him in ignorance, and accused him of bringing this calamity upon himself through disobedience to its will. The intimation that the original sin of man had a sexual bearing is the merest false-pretense to cover up the truth, and make marriage by the church one of its great sources of income. Nature evidences this.

"Nothing need be reverenced without a logical reason. Christianity has never given such a reason. Its God has never been demonstrated; its heaven has never been located, and its teachings have been illogical.

"This precious collection tells a story of the evolution of knowledge up to the Christian era. Following the papyrus rolls, the wax-covered tablets, and the baked tablets and engraved plates of Babylonia, are these parchment leaves, revealing the broader expansion of learning, necessitating the economy of time by convenience in examining the records.

"You may not be aware of this, and it is essential; it is the practice of ecclesiasticism to add importance to its assumed knowledge by a pretense of original wisdom interpreted into the true knowledge. I will make this clear. In an attempt to convey the impression that everything ecclesiastical is original, and dates back to a divine origin, it coins words of its own as the missing links in a chain of 'inspired' evidence. But, it is a curious thing about these coined words, that, they must be inserted into the ecclesiastic code in order to make them understandable to their initiates. This exposes the artifice. For instance, it is declared that the advance from the papyrus rolls, and the cumbersome tablets, to the convenient parchment leaves, was the invention of one Attalus II, king of Pergamos. An analysis of this by the ecclesistical code makes quite an interesting story.

"Attalia means *that which increases*.

"Attalus means *increase*.

"Increase means to augment, extend, enlarge, dilate, expand, enhance, aggravate, magnify.

"Attalia was supposed to be a coast town of Pamphylia, meaning *a mixture of nations*, the chief town of which was Perga, meaning *very earthy*, where Paul preached. Paul means the *church worker*, and he preached to the common, earthy, Adamic masses. Pamphylia was a nation made up of every tribe—keep this in mind, it has a bearing upon the colonization of America, in which all European and Asiatic nations will contribute each its quota of its effete population.

"Pergamos was in Mysia, meaning *criminal, abominable*. This has specific reference to the above.

"Attalia merely signifies the increased facilities for recording knowledge, and in the storing and transportation of such records, by the use of parchment leaves over the old and more cumbersome methods.

"It is alleged that this invention was introduced in the year 150 B. C. The truth of the matter is, parchment leaves were a novelty in Rome two hundred and fifty years after this alleged period.

"Pergamos merely signfies the elevation of learning. It is alleged to have been the seat of the celebrated library which later was transferred to Alexandria in Egypt. This has reference to the location, at Alexandria, of the philosophical schools, following the conquests of Alexander.

"On its face, this is an attempt, on the part of the ecclesiasts, to create an impression that they had enjoyed access to this great library previous to the Alexandrian period, in order to deprive Gnosticism of the glory which it achieved in the compilation of the wisdom of all schools, into a composite, religio-political form of government.

"There is no evidence of such transfer. To cover this myth, the small town of Bergnia is selected as the former site for Pergamos, in Mysia, as the former seat of this fabulous library which was allegedly bequeathed to Rome by King Attalus III, in the year 133 B. C. By an alleged misinterpretation of this imaginary gift, the Romans included and appropriated the whole kingdom, with all its moveable property. In the beginning the jealous ecclesiasts declared that, in this plunder was a library equaling the Alexandrian library, admitting that they were not one and the same. This left open the question as to what had become of this library in Rome. It was urgent to trump up some plausible reason for the absence of the library, and why the Romans possessed no such learning and knowledge as the Egyptians—the town of Pergamos was a myth.

"The excuse invented was wholly in line with the level of ecclesiastical morality.

"It was brazenly declared that Mark Antony made a gift to his mistress, Cleopatra, of the Roman library, allegedly the property of the Roman people, and transported it to Alexandria. There is not one single evidence that Mark Antony ever possessed such authority, nor would the high strung Roman people have permitted him to make this royal gift to a historical prostitute, in a heretical country."

Don Alvard laughed, saying: "If the devil himself wore a crown, ecclesiasticism would accept him. This pious fraud is sickening. Isn't it strange that the more essential things attaching to Christianity are associated with crime? This country, Mysia means *criminal*. Pergamos is in Mysia. Therefore, even had this fabulous library been a fact, this is an acknowledgment that its possession had a criminal origin."

"Well, the church developed out of Rome, and the beginning of Rome was Mount Palatine, a rendezvous for fugitive criminals for many centuries preceding Christianity," said Monetho.

"It has been the one ambition of the church of Rome to pose as the highest educational power of the world, hence, the alleged source of its wisdom, Pergamos, signifies *height, elevation*."

"It seems to me you have revealed an ugly policy of the church, for this false-pretense of a gift of the Kingdom of Bergnia, together with the minor gift of the library, is identical with the *forged 'donation of Constantine,'* of all his sovereign powers, accompanying his decree which permitted the church to accept donations, possess property and erect churches. 321 A. D., four hundred years after this decree, this abominable forgery appeared."

"Exactly so," replied Monetho, "and there is another important link in this chain of usurpation. From the time of the parchment leaves, book-making was exclusively in the hands of the monks which enabled them to conform their work to the ecclesiastical requirements, for the monasteries were absorbed into the Christian system. Here you have evidences of the very early custom of placing covers upon sheaves of parchment leaves to protect them from wear and accident. This was wholly the practice of the Gnostics.

"Here, you see the later forms of printed books, while the process was slow and tedious, nevertheless, it was a wonderful advance over the early methods. These records, in printed forms, were produced during the thirteenth, fourteenth and fifteenth centuries, and in absolute secrecy, by the Gnostics, in order to perpetuate their system and assure the preservation of the Gnostic wisdom, for they especially adjusted their progression to the natural laws of evolution.

"This was the assembly room of the last Gnostic masters. Let us rest here while I impart to you some essential facts which you should know before

we proceed farther. I desire also to know more of
yourself. I especially desire to know the source
and nature of your knowledge concerning the
Gnostics. Before you begin, however, I shall disa-
buse your mind of some false ideas regarding the
association of Christianity with Gnosticism. It is
not true that they developed together, and it is
especially not true, that Gnosticism crystallized into
the Christian church. This was an assumed pose
of the church.

"The Ophite and the Naosseni Gnostics, of the
second century, have nothing to do with the original
Gnosticism. These were coined out of the fertile
imagination of Irenaeus, as is proven by their falling under the Ecclesiastic Code, which was invented
centuries after Gnosticism.

"Ophite is derived from the same root as Ophir,
signifying *fruitful*. Gnosticism was the fruitful
source of wisdom. It also was the figurative place
from where the Hebrews drew their gold, symbolizing a past golden age. In truth, it pretends to
account for the alleged wisdom of the Jews. Gold
means wisdom.

"It has not been located because it never existed.
Naosseni is Nahshon, signifying *enchantment, that
fortells, serpent.* The serpent is the symbol of
secret wisdom. 'Be ye as wise as serpents.' (Matt.
10:16.)

"Now tell me what you know about Gnosticism."

"Few words will suffice to tell you all I know
of Gnosticism, in so far as it relates to these records.

Only recently have I been informed that some great
mystery enshrouds the connection of Christianity
with Gnosticism.   In my theological studies, of
course, I was familiar with the different Christian
ideas of the Gnostics, and the fierce opposition to
them of both the Jews and the Christians.   I seemed
to grasp, that, there was much in common between
Gnosticism and Christianity at an early period; in
fact, my tutor and I would often marvel at the
truth, that, the evidences were so strongly in favor
of the Gnostics having first attempted to assemble
the leading features of all religions, with the view
of placing these before the world in a spirit of
frank comparison, as mankind could absorb the
truth.

"The Gospel of John seemed to have taken a
middle course between Valintinus' Gnosticism and
Marcion's Gnostic dualism.   The alleged use of the
Gospel of John by Justin Martyr may or may not
be true, but the Gnostics of the second century
did use a gospel resembling that attributed to John.
Such things, I am superficially informed about,"
said the Don.

"I am glad to know this," gravely replied
Monetho.   "It is a good foundation upon which to
erect a new Gnostic structure.   Then you have taken
a course in theology; have you taken orders, or
directly allied yourself with any church?"

"No.   My religious researches took a curious
bent, due to my having formed a close friendship
with one of my instructors at the University of Bar-

celona, one Verosala, who was an avowed atheist.
He took great delight in confounding the pious
Christians by showing that their scriptures and gospels were neither authentic nor honest. He especially accused the Christians with being satisfied to dine
at second table to the Jews; Christianity being
based upon and presupposing the Hebrew religion.
These discussions gave me an early distrust in the
Christian pretenses, and I was reluctant to take
any part in the debates. But, now, my good Monetho, I am deeply interested in the church of Rome,
so deeply, in fact, I have made a vow to spend the
balance of my life killing priests."

Monetho looked startled, but did not speak.

"I now know, beyond all doubt, that, Christianity, as it is portrayed by the Church of Rome, is
an evil thing. I am against it. I doubt if anything
can alter this sentiment in my heart," and the Don
showed signs of excitement.

"You must be prodded by some more urgent
call than mere speculative investigation to arouse
in you such a bitter and vindictive resentment toward priests," remarked Monetho, as his keen eyes
searched the Don.

"Yes, a very personal reason which I think I
should explain to you before we proceed. I desire
that you should know that I am not a mere adventurer, but have a righteous cause. My life is dedicated
to the avenging of my wrongs. More is the pity
that there are not a greater number of priests, for
the entire priesthood is not sufficient to expiate

the crime." Then he briefly related to the deeply inerested Gnostic master his woeful tale.

Monetho remained silent for some minutes to permit the agitated Don to recover his composure.

Arising, he said softly: "Yes, my brother, yours is a sad story, but it is an individual case with but a single heart to bleed; humanity has a greater cause. The crunching of the iron heel of Christian hate into the vitals of humanity leaves many ugly scars. Come."

CHAPTER XII

THE LAST OF THE GNOSTIC MASTERS

<small>VISIBLE DEATH FILLS THE BRAVEST HEARTS WITH
SUPERSTITIOUS FEAR</small>

OPENING another secret way, Monetho, entered a large cavernous chamber, bidding the now fascinated Don to follow.

Pausing, he softly said:

"I trust, my good soldier, that the spirit of Gnosticism still seeks a body in the outer world, and, that, you have been sent here to receive the inspiration direct from these lifeless masters, to go forth and do battle for humanity, and rekindle the torch of progressive education for the cheated masses.

"I now give to you another good and sufficient cause for the unsheathing of your consecrated sword at the treacherous tread of ecclesiasticism."

Passing along the wall, he lighted grease mats which quickly flared up in apparent anger, throwing a gruesome and baleful glare throughout the chamber. The shadows cast by the fluttering flames seemed to set in motion a multitude of fantastic figures, filling the room with ghostly life.

With all his courage, the brave cavalier started back in alarm, and unfeigned trepidation, amazed at the picture before him, made more gruesome by the volumes of dark vapor arising from the burning grease mats. He stood speechless, awaiting Monetho's explanation. He had had no adequate means of anticipating the horrors of this chamber of death, to prepare his mind for the shock.

As the first surprise subsided, and he recovered his wits, understanding flooded him with deep emotion. Like the savage rush of air into a vacuum, rage welled up in his whole fighting being.

"Curse of Christendom!" he exclaimed. As his mind reverted to the scenes in the outer caverns, he recognized this as a part of one terrible tragedy.

Monetho came and stood silently by his side until the impressive scene could sink deeply into Don Alvard's consciousness, there to remain an indelible picture of human infamy.

As the deeply moved cavalier turned an inquiring gaze toward the aged monk, the latter slowly waved his hand about the chamber, saying:

"Behold! the last of the Gnostic masters, symbolizing the ecclesiastical suppression of human intellect."

There against the rough-hewn walls, seemingly wavering and swaying in the flickering light, were eleven crude, wood crosses. Upon each cross was a human form, whose mummified face, as brown as parchment, peered with sinister leer from beneath the cowl of an enshrouding cassock. They seemed like things alive in the garb of death, boldly questioning, with deep sunk eyes, this intrusion.

"Here, my brother, you view a greater crime

than the mere taking of human lives, because it deeply wounds all humanity.

"This, too, was done under the murderous call, 'God wills it,' of a Franciscan pope, whose own God could not spare him the humiliation of exposure in a murderous conspiracy against the Medici of Florence. This was the master stroke of ecclesiasticism against Gnosticism.

"This is the last remnant of the original Gnostic brotherhood—the desiccating bodies of eleven dead, and this shriveling body of mine, the last living one."

There was a sad huskiness in the aged man's throat, as he uttered these words, and, for a moment, he looked far away, as though trying to peer into the abstract *hyle* of Gnosticism, in search for the souls of his comrades.

"This is the true crucifixion of humanity. They were sacrificed upon the cross because they declared that the cumulative knowledge and wisdom of the ages was the heritage of humanity at large, and, that, all men are born in innocent equality, and should not be deprived of equal opportunity to acquire knowledge and understanding of nature's purposes in physical and mental evolution. They advocated an open revelation of all knowledge, that all men alike might have access to the true good-spirit of creative nature. You doubtless know that the word *God* is the sanscrit *good*.

"It was logical that nature should reclaim her own by this reunion, because these brave and self-sacrificing philosophers defied that autocratic, usurpative ecclesiasticism at Rome, and decreed, that, by their sacrifice, these master records should not remain buried in the secret places of the Vatican while humanity was being steeped in ignorance, stupidity and cultivated evil, the God of desire—*Evi* means desire, *El* means God, becoming the Christian devil.

"If there were no other evidence that Christianity, the invention of ecclesiasticism, is but false-pretense, its utter helplessness in times of great stress, and its inability to hold fast to the Gnostic secrets, are quite enough—the true apocalypse is not to be made by ecclesiasticism."

The eleven crosses, leaning pathetically against the slanting walls, seemed to nod assent.

Thick wood pins pierced the hands and feet of the hanging bodies, this having been the original means by which they were attached to their crosses. Their strong cassocks formed a kind of retainer to hold the bodies in tact.

At the right hand of each lay a sheaf of manuscript, rolls of parchment, or volumes composed of sheets of parchment in piles, fastened at the edges with thongs, the pages being covered by legible writings and figures, in Greek, Latin, Hebrew and sanscrit.

To these Monetho pointed, saying:

"These are scientific, not religious, yet they are the foundation of the Christian church. Of those outside the priesthood who acquire this knowledge

they say: 'Behold the man is become as one of us.' "
(Gen. 3:22.)

Passing from one stone to another he pointed
to the inscriptions thereon, which named the scientific subject of which each was master.

1—The Alchemy of Nature, the basic chemistry
of the universe.

2—The Ancient Astrology, treating of the laws
of planetary systems.

3—The Medicine of Nature, the secrets of vegetation.

4—The Genesis of Organic Life, the fishes,
the fowls and beasts.

5—The Human Universe—man.

6—Physiology and Anatomy.

7—The evidences of a premeditated evolution.

8—Body and Mind.

9—The philosophy of cause and effect.

10—Evolution of animal thought.

11—The purpose of death and disintegration.

12—Immortality.

"These are the subject heads of the Gnostic
philosophy. They, with their collateral branches,
comprehend all that it is possible for human thought
to evolve, and all that the human mind can comprehend.

"These are the things which all men should
know without a paid intermediator. To deprive men
of initiative thought is to break their mental continuity in the universal, cyclic evolution—a horrible
crime against nature and her necessary contacts.

"My brother, let me tell you that which the ecclesiasts know, if they have a knowledge of Gnosticism, yet they dare not reveal. Only by the cumulative evolution of initial thought by the individual being, may the spirit of man attain the immortal state. The ecclesiasts conceived the idea of coining human energy by the sacrifice of constructive human thought, that this energy might become a productive power to help the church to amass carnal wealth. This sacrifice of the great masses is a visible and pathetic thing. The mind is weakened, not alone to brutalize the physical body, but to guard against the acquirement of knowledge and understanding which might cause a recognition of the church hypocrisy and stir rebellion against the usurpative church power.

"Mankind, as the highest evoluted being, by a mental contact with nature, has a spiritual evolution which progresses only during the life of the body, merging into the great universal *hyle* through a process of constructive, understanding thought. All carnal pleasures and joys are the carnal fruits of this system. At death, individuality ceases, and the universal mind has been enriched to the extent to which acceptable wisdom has contributed to its nourishment. The ecclesiasts are not bashful in admitting this truth.

" 'If we have sown unto you spiritual things, is it a great thing if we shall reap your carnal things?' (I Cor. 9:11.)

"The immortal part of man is that essence which

he contributes to the universal mind during his
living, waking period. At death, the material, fruit
yielding tree, the body, disintegrates and passes
back into the great reservoir of substance to be
reincarnated in other systems. Individuality ceases
with the death of the body.

"The church attempts to suppress thought by
confusion, and by submerging the unit minds into
a plastic mass during physical life."

Don Alvard for once in his life was thoroughly
stunned. He knew not how to reply to Monetho's
speech, but stood looking, alternately, at the monk
and the gruesome symbols of martyrdom.

"Come, and I will tell you the awful story,"
said Monetho, and he extinguished the burning mats
and led the way back into his comfortable living
quarters.

Again seated at the table, with a flagon of good
wine before them, Monetho began.

"Your good priestly friend told you the truth
regarding the disappearance of these Gnostic records during the removal of the Vatican archives
to Avagnon, and I will remark here, that, this papal
move marked the departure of the Roman church
from its own Christian pretenses, to follow a strictly
political course. It was practically a repudiation
of St. Peter, for Rome and St. Peter were as insepar-
able as the old and new testaments.

"He also told you the truth of their secretly having been removed to Montserrat; but, it will be

necessary for me to tell you their subsequent history
which he could not know.

"The popes have, for centuries, strenuously denied having in their possession the complete Gnostic
system, for the good and sufficient reason, that,
the Christian revelation was the Gnostic revelation,
and they had not in their possession the keys and
symbols essential to accomplish this purpose. This
is the reason why the alleged Christian mystery has
not been revealed. Moreover, an admission that
they possessed these all important records, would
have heralded to the world that this known wisdom had been purposely suppressed by them, in
order that they might selfishly elaborate a great
exploitation, and, in the end, pose as the founders
of this philosophy. Hence the Benedictines were
safe in their possession, as long as Catholic hands
could be kept off them. In fact, when they disappeared from the great Benedictine Monastery at
Montserrat, the Roman Catholics were suspected of
having been the cause of their sureptitious removal
and a schism was threatened.

"Through all the centuries, an immortal Gnostic
line has been kept alive. Of necessity, it has been
a secret order. It long ago would have redeemed
its pledge to humanity, had Satan's hordes not visited us.

"The inner circle consisted of the 'immortal
twelve,' held together by a vow to recover the Gnostic records which had been confiscated by the Roman
priesthood. As one died, or was martyred for the

cause, another was carefully chosen, from a select sub-organization, to take his place, the master body always remaining twelve.   They   mingled   with priests, bishops, cardinals, and even with popes.

"It was authentically established that, the great bulk of the records secretly had been transferred to the Benedictine Monastery at Montserrat.   Over a long period of years tried, working Gnostics were gradually initiated into the Benedictine orders and were slowly concentrated at Montserrat.

"This subordinate body of Gnostics, forty in number, was intrusted with the dangerous task of seizing and carrying away the Gnostic records, and bringing them to this retreat, which the immortal twelve had previously prepared.   Here they were to receive from the masters the proper training and instructions for passing out into the world and organizing a system by which the original plans of Gnosticism would be executed, and nature's traditional message be delivered to mankind.

"Our project was working admirably; we developed here a paradise.   The wild cattle, which you saw in the plains below, are a remnant of our herds.   The stream which you saw, is the river Segre, which flows into the Ebro.   Forty of our working apostles were prepared to take their places out in the world and organize *ternary* bodies of teachers, when the storm came, like a stroke of lightning from a clear sky.

"A body of forty horsemen, heavily armed, and, without one word of parley or explanation, dashed

into our midst. Separating the masters, distinguish-
able by their garbs, from the others, knowing them
to be monks from Montserrat, they drove the forty
into their cells and murdered them in cold blood,
leaving their bodies where you saw them. In this
region dead bodies do not putrify and decompose,
they merely desiccate and mummify.

"They then began to torture and persecute the
eleven masters, I having fortunately escaped, although I was secreted where I could behold, with
horror, all that was done. They could not torture
from the masters the location of the treasured records. Finally they compelled each master to bear
from the mountain-side the rude cross upon which
you saw their bodies hanging. One by one they
tortured and crucified them in the presence of the
others, but in vain. They left them hanging in a
row fronting the outside gallery.

"I was an eye witness to this cruel tragedy.
They searched in vain, finally leaving without having discovered the coveted records.

"Later, I removed the crosses and their burdens
into the secret inner chamber, where are all the
master records, the records in the first chamber
being the library for the working members.

"I will now tell you the strangest part of this
story.

"While all of the working forms of Gnosticism
were actually in the possession of the Benedictines,
neither they, nor the Vatican ever possessed the in-
terpreting keys and symbols, by which, alone, the

works could be deciphered.   Therefore, you may
well imagine my anguish upon discovery that the
marauders had confiscated the master's set.

"The situation was reversed.   I, the last living
master, possessed the system, and they possessed
the keys and symbols.   I however, felt most certain
that, in anticipation of losing the records, the astute
Benedictines had made duplicates, in which event
they would possess the complete Gnostic system.
*They would be in possession of the fabulous keys
of St. Peter—wisdom, symbolizing heaven, and ignorance hell,* which the church had never possessed.

"These keys have more than once revealed the
fabulous nature of the Gospels alleged to have been
preached by Christ, Peter and Paul.   They caused
the alleged rupture between Paul and Peter, merely
signifying the difference between church factions,
Peter symbolizing the church and Paul the working
priesthood.

"The Jewish Christians insisted upon maintaining the Jewish institution of the Sabbath.   Paul
protested against this, urging that the Christian
enlightenment freed them from the observance of
a sabbath, and from other restraints

" 'Let no man therefore judge you in meat or
in drink or in respect of any holiday, or of the new
moon, or of the Sabbath day.' "   (Colossians 2:16.)

"Paul symbolized Gnosticism.   Peter merely
was a symbol of the Roman church.   Paul knew that
the Sabbath was contrary to nature, as taught by
the Gnostics.

"Anyone reading 1st Corinthians, Chap. 12, must believe that Paul was a Gnostic, or at least, the author was a Gnostic, for no such individual as Paul actually existed, the name merely signifying—the church worker.

"In this connection, I want to impress upon your mind, my brother, that Gnosticism brought down upon itself the hatred of the Roman priesthood when it began to exhibit the tendencies of Plato and Pythagoras to reveal the truth, and, that, hidden beneath the letter and figure of Christianity was a mysterious, secret code, which could only be received by the inner priesthood, supposedly having superior minds, while the multitudes had to be satisfied with the merely outward or apparent meaning, the husks. This mysterious code was the invention of the priesthood, or rather the system of monks directly preceding Christianity.

"Words are put into the mouth of their own Christ which substantiate this.

" 'Unto you it is given to know the mystery of the Kingdom of God; but unto them that are without, all these things are done in parables; that seeing they may see and not perceive; and hearing they may hear, and not understand, lest at any time they should be converted, and their sins should be forgiven them.'   (Mark 4: 11,12.)

"Does that sound like a saving institution?

"Here also is the evidence that, there were hidden mysteries, to be revealed only to the elect.

" 'For there is nothing hid which will not be

manifested, neither was anything kept secret, but that it should come abroad.' (Matt. 4:22.))

"There is a sinister sense to this strange Gospel. Christ is speaking in private to his close associates and Christ is merely the head of the church.

" 'Take heed what ye hear.

" 'For he that hath, to him shall be given; and he that hath not, from him shall be taken even that which he hath.' (Mark 4: 24,25.)

"This is the promise to his apostles of a revelation of Gnostic mysteries which were to be concealed from the masses. That has been the constant policy of the Roman church. It strove with the Gnostics for five hundred years before it believed it was in a position to plunge humanity into the blackest ignorance, in fulfillment of this policy. You know the result; for a thousand years it held the world in that condition of stupidity which enabled it to assume control of all the educational systems by which it moulded its fanaticism, intolerance and bigotry. Only very recently have signs appeared of an emergence from that night of educational intolerance.

"Gnosticism was the consensus of philosophies held in common by all the schools, hence its meaning, *knowledge, to know.* Gnosticism welded together these fundamental points in a sublime school. The Jews and Christians could not maintain their illogical dogmas should this school be permitted to live, hence, they both openly antagonized the Gnostics, painting them in the blackest colors and literally burning them.

"Unfortunately, Gnosticism had no political aspirations, therefore, it did not srengthen itself with such affiliations. Gnosticism was the rising sun of civilization, peering above the horizon of dawning scientific understanding.

"It is quite easy to explain why the Gospels accredited to Paul were written in the Greek language; they taught the secret Gnostic wisdom. For this reason Marcion repudiated the whole of the new testament except Paul. It was the Gnostic tendencies of the Greek philosophers as against Peter, the fabulous voice, representing the ecclesia of Rome—the one striving to reveal the Gnostic wisdom, and the other seeking to suppress it. Death and the sepulchre were the end of revealed Gnosticism, hence *Paul*, the worker, superseded *Saul*, the *grave*.

"The only authority for the so-called four Gospels of the new testament is one Irenaeus, (A. D. 190) and here is the language in which he expresses this authority.

" 'They (the four Gospels) should be four in number, neither more nor less, because, they are four universal winds, and four quarters of the world' —Gospel means *good-story*.

"This may be declared the sole foundation of the four Gospels.

"Irenaeus himself, being at heart a Gnostic, could not refrain from betraying this, even in his fictitious gospels, causing words to be put in the mouth of Christ accusing certain learned men of having confiscated the keys to knowledge, meaning Gnosticism, the Greek word Gnosis meaning *knowledge, to know.*

" 'Woe unto you, lawyers, for ye have taken away the key of knowledge; ye entered not in yourselves, and them that were entered in ye hindered.' (Luke 11: 52.)

"And these keys were never returned, for they are the keys and symbols of Gnosticism, preserved through all the centuries by Master Gnostics. Hence Christianity has not been able to make the revevlation promised to mankind. If it has, why has it selfishly held it back for all these bloody centuries?"

"The alleged gospels of Peter smacked so strongly of Gnosticism, they were suppressed, and new gospels of Peter were adopted, and censored from Rome. The plethoric bishops of Antioch had to be muzzled. Too many dangerous words were being charged up to Peter, that is, from Antioch, which merely signifies opposition—for instance:

" 'For as much as ye know that ye were not redeemed with corruptible things, as silver and gold, from your vain conversation *received by tradition* from your forefathers.'   (I Peter 1:18.)

"The ancient Gnosticism was transmitted *from generation* to *generation* by *tradition,* the keys revealing this to be the recorded tradition of living nature.

"The Gnostics declared that, he who could see and hear could, by natural thought sequence, attain to full understanding of the wisdom and knowledge of nature, thereby becoming a Gnostic without initiation into the brotherhood. The ecclesiastical theory and policy was opposed to this, leading the human mind away from the truth by symbolism, figure, fable, romance and parable. Hence the frank acknowledgment in Mark 4: 11,12.

"Peter was the voice of the ecclesiastical power at Rome, sent to warn Paul that, he must cease preaching the Greek Gnosticism. It was simply a difference of opinion between the *good-story* of Paul and the church of Rome.

"This was the alleged quarrel between Peter and Paul—between the church and the working priesthood, a difference of opinion between the workers in the field and the pope at Rome.

"Now I will continue my story of the raid. Naturally I expected another visitation, and I waited in terror until I had made due provision for my own personal safety, which I will later explain to you. To the present time no one has intruded upon my seclusion. You are my first visitor.

"It seems evident to me, that no duplication of the original Gnostic records had ever been made. At least, no evidence has appeared to intimate such duplication. The world seems wholly ignorant of the great secret powers of the system which the keys would have revealed."

As Monetho paused, Don Alvard smiled broadly, asking:

"Has it ever occurred to you, that, possibly, the looters were overtaken by calamity, and never returned to civilization? I was told that a rumor had long been prevalent, that, a great earthquake had caused vast changes in these mountains, about that time, and it was believed the crusaders had been engulfed."

"I had no means of knowing of this legend. Nevertheless, it was an error; the great earthquake happened two years previous to the visit of the crusaders. This eliminates that theory," replied Monetho.

"Well, some mysterious power has protected you. It is a fact, that, the pillagers never returned; but, truly, my friend, fate plays many strange pranks in dealing with humanity. I'll wager my helmet against another noggin of your excellent wine, that, we are the only living human beings with a positive knowledge of the complete Gnostic system. That I may show good faith, I present to you, as the true Master Gnostic, what I believe to be the Master's signet ring."

Arising, the Don drew from his pouch the articles which he had taken from the cadaver on his journey up the mountain trail, and handed to Monetho the ring and the key.

Monetho stared at him in blank amazement, not fully comprehending this new turn. The Don urged him to take the articles in his own hands.

"Why! Yes! This is the master's ring," he faltered. "Tell me how it came into your possession."

The Don related the simple facts, then also placed the box upon the table. Fitting the key into the curious mechanism called a lock, it was readily opened.

Monetho wept with joy upon beholding the contents—the master's working outfit.

The cavalier watched Monetho with pleasure as he mumbled over the contents of the receptacle. It was a priceless treasure. Don Alvard, better than any other man, knew and appreciated the tremendous power which fate had placed within his grasp. From his own experience in the outer world, he knew that, the soulless power at Rome would gladly destroy half the human race to wrest this treasure from him, and regain possession of the Gnostic system, now enhanced in value by the working symbols, by which its mysteries could be interpreted.

While Monetho was the master in possession, he was the master by proxy.

This was the great *revelation,* which Christianity had promised to humanity. It had slipped away from it and it was unable to fulfill the promise, proving the fallibility of its alleged divine mission.

Don Alvard softly said: "I have been guided by fate on the most sacred pilgrimage ever accomplished by man—a pilgrimage to the tomb of wisdom, to witness the resurrection of the inherited rights of humanity. God! what vengeance is mine."

"Yes, my good brother, you will learn from my teaching that, you have been purposely guided by the all knowing universal mind, and that same inspiration will give to us the power, and the means, to safely deliver to human kind the message which should have been given to each man at birth, through all these wasted Christian centuries.

"To build is a single task, but to tear asunder and rebuild is a double labor. To reconstruct the mind of mankind is an immeasurable thing. Where the law of nature originally intended that each human unit should begin with instinct, and, by a logical evolution and experience, develop reason, in the absorption from natural manifestations a true knowledge and understanding of basic principles, an unnatural and perverted system of an evil power has guided the human mind away from its normal course, and filled it with superstitious fear, intolerance, bigotry, hatred and fanaticism.

"My friend, it will require a thousand years to purge the blood of humanity of this poison. Like a virulent disease it has undermined the constitution, and caused lesions which may not be mended. Generations upon generations must come and go before a pure race may be evolved out of the present state of cultivated degeneracy. Increase in population will necessarily require the distruction of hundreds of millions. This age must pass away. You and I will not live to see the full return of Gnosticism, because it begins at the birth of a race. When the mental continuity is broken, it cannot

be mended. But we may have instantaneous vengeance, by secretly irritating the enemy. It is a
strange fact, that, when a poisonous reptile is
wounded, it continuously inoculates itself with its
own virus unil it dies. This is the only remedy for
fanaticism. It must run its course. This is the principle upon which the Christian church has sown sin
and evil in the world, and sits watching humanity
destroy itself, that it may possess the world."

Don Alvard had listened patiently to Monetho's
gloomy picture, convinced there was too much
truth in it. Placing his hand upon that of the sage,
he said gently: "I can well understand your deep
feeling in the matter, but let us not dispute upon
any point about which we may hold a difference of
opinion. We may devise a system of tests to guide
us in our work. I lay no claim upon this treasure,
and I gladly acknowledge you as its true master,
and I shall abide by your wisdom in whatever course
we may decide upon. I place myself under your
tutelage and at your disposal. Nevertheless, ow-
ing to your long seclusion, I may safely lay claim
to a better knowledge of the temper of the outside
world than you can have. To offset this, you possess
the secrets of this great power; therefore, we may
make a full and frank exchange of views regarding
the best methods of delivering the great message to
the world."

Monetho almost joyfully acknowledged the
wisdom of Don Alvard's suggestion, saying: "I
wholly agree with you, my spirit would not rest

in peace, I am sure, were these precious records
to die with me, yet, I would prefer eternal torture
rather than they should again fall into the possession of that priesthood of evil which has hitherto
deprived mankind of its natural rights."

A broad smile wreathed the Don's face as he
said: "My good Monetho, one of the best minds
in Rome told me that I am possessed of an uncanny
knowledge of human nature, as well as super-human
strength, yet, I am but a young man in age.   I
know that wisdom and judgment belong to age, and
impatience and impetuosity to youth, therefore by
tempering my lack of patience with your wisdom,
we have an invincible combination.   If you and I
have been chosen as agents for the restoration of
the Gnostic wisdom to men, we should assume, without question, that, the same guiding power will
reveal to us his will in the execution.   Nevertheless,
we must expect, that, cunning will meet cunning
when we venture out into the world with our campaign.   We must not attempt to reach our goal
too quickly and stumble into the devil's own ambush."

"Very good," responded Monetho.   "Let us assign our duties according to our qualifications.

"I shall remain the secret custodian, and you
will assume a militant role out in the world," en-
thusiastically exclaimed Monetho.

"That is good, replied the Don, with equal
pleasure.   "You will be my Moses, and I will be
your Aaron.   You will place in my mouth the words

to be spoken, and I will trumpet them broadcast."

"Yet, bear in mind," said Monetho, "I shall not pose as a god to the people, nor to Aaron."

"Ha, ha," laughed Don Alvard. "I'll venture I could take you to Rome and swear I had discovered the unknown supulchre of Moses in the land of Moab, and dug you out of it, and word would be passed throughout the whole Catholic world that, Moses was resurrected as the second coming of Christ, and the Jews would be vindicated."

"A thousand more absurd things have been coined by Rome," said Monetho, then continuing. "It is not now so much a matter of time as it is of organization and discretion. It is of first importance that you take a superficial course in the Gnostic teachings. I must inform you of the unfortunate truth; the Gnostic continuity, once so well established from generation to generation, is broken.

"But, you must be very weary. In my zeal, I had forgotten your strenuous experience on the desert."

"Who could remember bodily weariness or think of sleep, after my sensations here? I regret the necessity of sleep," said the Don.

"Nevertheless, we have three masters who must be obeyed; *hunger, thirst* and *sleep* and, under differing circumstances these may become our most persistent enemies, betraying us to death," said Monetho, arising and motioning Don Alvard to follow him.

A passage led out upon a sort of balcony, from

where the wonderful blue sky was visible. A myriad of glinting stars were having a merry time of it, signaling to the inhabitants of the earth, seeming like a living thing watching over them.

"See the unsleeping eyes of nature looking down upon us. This is your first Gnostic lesson. You will learn to converse with all the earth through their mediumship," softly said Monetho.

At the end of the balcony was a sleeping place.

"The Gnostics were named vile by the Christians because they indulged in personal comforts and pleasures," said Monetho. "Here is a comfortable couch; these sheepskins are dressed as fine as silk, their wool is sweet and clean. You will need their warmth before the morning. Sleep well, my brother. I fell a great elation that you are here. Good night."

"Good night, my generous host, may your own sleep be sound and refreshing."

CHAPTER XIII

THE MAKING OF A GNOSTIC WARRIOR

NATURE AND NIGHT HEAL THE WOUNDS OF THE DAY

MORNING came, a great and glorious morning, with a sky so beautiful, a sunlight so caressing, and a serenity which soothed the body and calmed the mind.

Don Alvard first looked down upon the valley; a splendid picture in the first blush of the morning sky. Here, and there, he again saw the herds of cattle lazily grazing. A winding stream was dancing and glinting, and flocks of birds were fluttering along its reed cluttered banks, or settling in the tall grass.

"Is it not beautiful?" asked a soft voice. It was Monetho who had silently entered. "A substantial breakfast awaits you, my brother."

The Don cordially greeted the monk, and for a few minutes, listened to his story of the glorious life led here by the Gnostic brothers; a life free from worldly cares, and the bickerings of ambitious men. Then he followed him into the living room, where a meal fit for the gods awaited him. Fruits and berries, crushed grain, and pigeon's eggs, with wine which took the place of water. These were served with goat's milk as rich as cream.

After the meal they strolled into the grounds, where they visited with the little flock. Belial had become one of the happy family and came to be caressed by his master.

"I will introduce you to my closest companions," said Monetho, and he led the way to a cliff in which was a secret door leading to a long shelf like piece of ground on which were a well cultivated garden, and a comfortable little cabin. Deep niches were cut into the wall containing stores sufficient for a siege.

The two fine dogs, which the Don had seen on the previous day, were running at large. They stopped, sniffed, bristled and growled, upon beholding a stranger, but, at a word from Monetho, they came forward and greeted them in a perfectly friendly manner.

"This is my retreat. Look!" and Monetho waved his hand; the view was perfectly wonderful. "Here I live. I am quite happy."

As the days drifted into weeks, and weeks into months, Don Alvard began to absorb this same happiness. The peaceful, restful life softened him, and the utter irresponsibility left him free to think without mental irritations. The bodily comforts of the place were extraordinary.

Thus, many pleasant months slipped away while he took his course of studies in Gnosticism, each day's work bringing him more fully into the truth, giving him a clearer vision of his future task.

As the end of his course approached, he was a changed man, feeling a calm self-assurance which concealed his former bristling nature. Grimness took the place of savagery; thoughtfulness served where impetuosity once inspired his acts, and he could see and understand the potency of diplomatic approach. Bambo was vindicated.

Monetho was most patient and painstaking, as a tutor, and his pupil was alert, apt and receptive, moreover, deeply grateful. A strong affection grew between them, and both sadly manifested their sorrow at the approach of the day when the student must go out into the world to become a powerful teacher. The Don felt strong in the self-assurance that, by discretion, diplomacy and his great physical strength, he was invincible in any emergency.

Monetho had taught him foundation lessons in new sciences, and things of which he had never dreamed. He was mentally equipped to cope with the best minds of the world on the subjects upon which they had specialized, the subjects essential in his work.

His surroundings were not devoid of physical entertainment. From time to time he made excursions, even into the rich meadows below, always bringing to Monetho some pleasing trophy of these jaunts—and sometimes strange ones; for instance, he brought his pockets full of young rabbits; again, his bonnet full of squab pheasants, and to cap the climax, he carried home a young bull calf because of its peculiar markings, for all of which Monetho generously blessed him.

One of these exploring expeditions brought unexpected and far reaching results. He had frequently been tempted to follow his original trail higher into the mountains, finally starting upon this adventure. He trudged the rugged path to a point where it suddenly terminated in the debris of some great convulsion of nature, either an earthquake or a landslide. Great heaps of broken granite, and limestone, in grotesque piles, blocked his further progress. This was the most profound demonstration of the powers and forces of nature he had ever beheld, therefore, he viewed it with awe and admiration while resting a bit before he started to retrace his steps.

He was on the point of leaving the spot when he was attracted by the sound of falling waters. A narrow ravine led to a waterfall. He was hardly prepared to meet the picture of tragedy which confronted him. The ground was strewn with the desiccating remains of men and horses.

Ah! truly, death inspires dread and fear, he thought, as he experienced the same sensation which came over him upon discovering the dead monks in their cells. He counted thirty-nine dead bodies, all clad in the armor of crusaders. The erosion of time had eaten most of the exposed steel, but an examination revealed that the armor of some was of beaten silver, artistically etched, and lined with well preserved plates of steel. The accoutrements of the horses also were of the same character.

Don Alvard smiled grimly, as he looked down upon the grewsome scene. It seemed a miracle that Monetho had previously warned him, that, should

he come upon a spring in the mountains he must
not partake of its water, because it was poisonous.
He had before him, as though written in letters
of fire, the whole story.   These thirty-nine bodies,
and the single body which he had previously found,
were the forty murderous marauders.   They had
partaken of the forbidden waters upon arriving at
this point.   They had believed they could cross the
mountain range, but had found that nature had
anticipated them.   Here they duly paid the penalty
of their heinous crime.   The single individual to
escape immediate death from drinking the poisoned
waters was the monk lying upon the shelf below.
He had attempted to reach the plain below but had
succumbed at this point, dragging his body to the
shelf to escape the claws and teeth of ravenous
beasts—a victim of his own criminal folly—nature
had avenged herself.

Had the Don been reared in the superstition of
the Roman Catholic church, he would have concluded, that, providence had avenged the Gnostics;
as it was, he knew that the accident of adventure
had cheated the gallows and the devil.

"I shall now proceed to properly equip myself
and Belial with raimen befitting our noble station,"
he mused and began to gather together suitable
parts of the better class armor.   He chose a pistol-
proof corselet or cuirass; a hauberk of linked silver, lined with pliable steel plates; breeches of similar construction; a helmet with visor; a splendid
pair of silver gauntlets, with buskins to match, and

a pair of large jingling spurs. To these he added
suitable accoutrement for Belial, and sundry side
arms.

Attached to the bodies of several of the crusaders were leathern pouches which had become
so hard and brittle he had to crack them with a
stone. Every pouch contained gold and silver coins.
He very carefully conveyed these to his own capacious pouch and made sure that he had not overlooked anything of value. Most of the arms of the
crusaders were practically destroyed by rust, but
he found one noble blade with a hilt made of gold,
and beautifully inlaid with gold, silver and mother
of pearl; this he appropriated. For Belial he had
silver mountings, saddle parts and stirrups.

Looking at the burden he had imposed upon himself he made a wry face and began to gather it up,
finally, with difficulty, he managed to keep it in
his grasp and started down the trail. With many
pauses, gruntings, and a few suitable military ex-
pletives, he landed his junk in the presence of the
astonished Monetho, who threw up his hands and
exclaimed: "St. Jupiter shrive us, who have you
murdered and robbed?"

The almost exhausted Don mopped his perspir-
ing brow and laughingly said:

"If you have a drop of Jew blood in you, you
will offer me a pretty sum for this junk. It is much
embellished with silver—but, I am not offering it
for sale today, for I am rich in gold and silver,"

and he poured a great pile of coins upon the ground. He then related the facts of his adventure.

"This is a great relief, my brother. We know now that we are the sole possessors of that which makes of gold and silver common dross. The Gnostic treasure is safe." He examined some of the coins, saying: "This will be useful to you when you go out into the world."

The Don labored for many days to make for Belial a suitable saddle, from some excellent leather made by Monetho, which he embilleshed with the silver mountings of the dead crusaders. He and Monetho also reconstructed the garments for himself, and, with such success, that he stood forth a grand and commanding figure, whom no man would care to challenge to mortal combat.

Day by day they had checked up for the departure of the cavalier. It was agreed that he should assume the attitude of a bold, swaggering, itinerant soldier of fortune, looking for any adventure which might redound to his advantage. At suitable times he would assume the role of Cardinal Bambo. They partially reviewed and discussed the cities he should visit in his itinerary, subject to such changes as in his discretion should be made.

A code had been worked out concealing the Gnostic vocabulary upon which the bible was founded, in order to provide against accidents by which it might fall into alien hands.

At last, the eventful day arrived, and a sad day

it was to both of these earnest men, when Don Alvard rode away from the tomb of Gnosticism.

Never before, in all his equine experience had Belial beheld a creature like that which attempted to bestride him. He had been amazed at the new toggery, with its polished silver mountings, which had been packed upon him but he was alarmed at sight of the gold and glitter which proposed to take roost upon his back. The Don had polished every silver surface until it rivaled the sun itself. He had welded the golden hilt to his five foot blade, making of his fighting-iron a thing to hang upon museum walls to be admired and gaped at by future generations.

Having bade an affectionate farewell to Monetho, he was essaying to comfortably attach himself to the pile of flubdubbery with which he had embellished his snorting charger who felt so mortified that he resented the approach of the sun-kissed giant.

The angry Don stepped in front of Belial and drew his sword threatening to cut off his ears if he cut any more undignified capers.

Evidently Belial understood, for he offered no further resistance, nevertheless, it was manifest, that any self-respecting horse was within his rights in protesting against being loaded down with such junk.

Don Alvard de Ricalde, the most dangerous individual in all the world, was on his way; riding toward groaning, bleeding humanity, a fighting nemesis; an avenging cloud upon the Christian horizon, whose lightning would sooner or later fall somewhere, and death would spatter the earth and hell open wide her gates to welcome the souls which he would release from their sodden husks.

CHAPTER XIV

BETWEEN LOVE AND DUTY

The Fake Healer Likes Not His Own Nostrums

O F ALL the refined weapons of intellectual warfare, ridicule in a master's hands, is the most subtle, irritating and destructive. It is like unto the sowing of pernicious seeds, which may not be discovered until a rank and poisonous growth has sprung up amidst favoured plants and flowers. Had the ridicule it richly deserved been applied to Christianity, in the early centuries, it would have withered before it could have produced its bitter fruits. Fifty million human lives would have been spared through the middle centuries, and the God of Abraham, Isaac, Jacob and the popes of Rome, would have been deprived of the sweet savors of burning flesh.

The sowing of seeds may be done by a single hand, without the aid of a great organization, and this may saturate the garden with pernicious weeds which many hands may not suppress. If the gardner is kept busy fighting these weeds, he must, to this extent, neglect the cultivation of his own products, and his garden runs to ruin.

It was on these principles that Monetho and his apostle, Don Alvard, planned their campaign.

Christianity had sown ignorance which blossomed into intolerance and ripened into fanatical bigotry and superstitious fear. A turn had come where incredulity had observed the period of a second sowing with wondering eyes, turning upon the exploiters and questioning them regarding the sincerity of their teachings.

The sight of blood renders the average human being queasy. Only experienced butchers are hardened against such squeamishness, and the sickened world had begun to turn away from the gruesome sight of roasting men, women and children, even though it had the sanction of God, because they could not be coerced into expressing a blind faith in manifestly absurd and illogical doctrines which were contrary to ordinary human observation and experience.

The time was ripe to unsheath the deadly weapon—ridicule.

Had not the church so intricately interwoven itself with civil governments, thereby making sovereigns mere puppets of papacy, a Gnostic reaction would quickly have taken the world by storm, and a wave of eduction would have revived a faith in science and philosophy to sweep Christianity into the rubbish-heap. But *fear* was king, and false-pretense is shield and buckler to cowardice. These are hard to reach even by ridicule.

Don Alvard went forth with the battle cries of the church fathers ringing in his heart: "Fight the devil with his own fire." "The end justifies the means." "A lie is not a lie when uttered for the church." "Crime is not crime when committed in the name of the church." "Pious fraud for the good of the church is condoned by God."

This code of morals was digusting to Don Alvard, when applied to normal things, but as a measure of warfare, and retaliation against a known enemy, he felt justified in using it.

"I am within the ecclesiastical code; my cause is as just as the cause of Rome; the civil law is inadequate to protect me from a deadly foe; self-protection is the first law of nature; I shall force their own deadly nostrums down their own throats; I will give every adversary an opportunity to draw and defend himself, and my sword shall remain unsheathed till my work is done or until I fall." This was Don Alvard's challenge.

Monetho had inspired him with confidence even greater than that of Bambo, yet he still felt bound to Bambo as the first cause which had brought him into the magical influence of the call of Gnosticism. His brief training under Monetho had more than corroborated Bambo's belief in Gnosticism, and he longed to reach his old friend and tell him the story.

Cardinal Bambo had intimated that, he would go from Monteserrat to Barcelona, and remain there for a while to take the benefits of its medicinal waters and the salubrious climate, after which, he would retire indefinitely to the castle of his friend and patron, Count de Brabon.

Don Alvard traveled directly to Barcelona as his first starting point. He very much desired to

consult with Bambo.   At Barcelona, by diligent inquiry, he learned, that, after a brief sojourn there,
Bambo had gone by ship to Italy.

Making provision for the good care of his horse,
Belial, he also sailed for Italy, in order to economize
in valuable time.   Without pause he traveled to the
castle of Count de Brabon.   It is needless to say
that he was doubly inspired to make this journey,
Bambo being a gratifying excuse.

The Don was warmly welcomed, the count cordially inviting him to remain as long as possible.
Bambo was overjoyed to see him again, eagerly
awaiting the time when he would relate any adventure which had befallen him during the anxious
months he had had no word from him.   Little did
the cardinal think that the doughty cavalier had
interpreted the dream of his life.

The dear countess' greeting was more than cordial.   After a few hours of interchange, she bade
the anxious gentleman be patient until the tired
Don had rested; then she invivted him into her
pretty garden, where she gave him sweet assurance
that she had not forgotten her affection for him.
Bambo had delivered his note to her which she drew
from her bosom to show him how much she cherished it.   Bambo had previously told her of the arduous journey which the Don had undertaken, and
she declared how she had worried all the long
months of his absence.   "And you have changed
greatly.   You are so gentle and quiet.   Tell me all

that has happened.   I know you have had some serious adventures."

Don Alvard was deeply touched by this delicate and affectionate interest in his welfare, on the part of the countess.   He was a changed man, and he felt the change now more than ever before.   His future forbade his indulging his sentiments with the only woman toward whom his lonely heart had truly yearned, now pouring out her sympathy and affection in his ear.   It was a difficult position.   He interlocked his fingers, arose, and paced back and forth until he could command himself.   The countess watched him with deep concern.

Coming and standing in her presence, and looking down upon her, with unmistakable adoration, he said:

"Yes, my dear lady, I am changed, and this is the brightest, yet the darkest moment of my life. Your voice, your face and your actions all tell me the old story.   You are willing to have me tell you that I love and adore you, which God knows I do. But there is a power stronger than love, sterner than ordinary duty, gripping my soul, and imperiously pointing the path which I must tread.   Listen, I will tell it you first.   It is a wonderful story." Dropping into a seat by her side and taking her hand in his, he related all that had occurred to him after he had left Montserrat.

She listened breathlessly, not permitting a word to escape.   She was entranced, slowly relaxing as his story unfolded until he had ended.   They sat in silence for quite some time; then she said gently:

"I understand, we must make great sacrifices. You must fulfill your mission.   It is a sacred charge."

"Let us not grieve now," said the Don.   "Should we longer keep your uncle and the good cardinal in suspense?"

"No, that would be selfish," replied the countess, looking smilingly up into his face, as she took his arm and they returned to the salon, where Bambo was impatiently pacing the floor, the count having walked out.

Don Alvard excused himself, leaving the countess with Bambo until he passed to his chambers to bring the all important matters which he was to deliver to the cardinal.   Upon his return the countess retired, leaving them alone.

"Ah, my good Don Alvard, you do not know how impatient I am to hear of your journey."

"You must be calm, my dear friend, for I have tremendous things to impart to you," replied the Don.

Bambo looked critically into the cavalier's grave, almost sad face.

"Gnosticism lives; we have it completely under our control," said the Don.

Bambo pressed his hand upon his heart, caught his breath, and inclined his head for the Don to continue.

"We have what no institution, not even the Gnostic order, has had for these many years, the com-

plete Gnostic records, including the master's working key and symbols." And Don Alvard paused
to let this sink deeply into Bambo's understanding.

"Tell me the story," softly whispered Bambo,
and great tears of joy coursed down his cheeks,
which had grown wan and creased.

The Don himself was so touched, he turned
hastily to the package of manuscript to conceal
his own agitation. Placing this upon the table, he
proceeded to faithfully relate to Bambo all his adventures since leaving him at Montserrat. They
paced the floor of the great *salon;* they walked in
the gardens, and they talked until late in the night.

"We have it in our hands to crush the papal
power," said Don Alvard.

"And deluge the earth with human blood before
mankind can get from under the crash," replied
Bambo. "Monetho is right, we are not now dealing
with an institution. It has inoculated civilization
with its foul disease, and before mankind can even
understand the meaning of Gnosticism, it must be
taught the true intent and purpose of Christianity,
in order that it may see the logic of repudiation.
This simply means that, the disease must run its
course. No, Don Alvard, neither you nor I will see
the final fall of Christianity, for it will burn itself
out as a fire consumes a mass of rubbish, and humanity will remain as a charred body, possessing no further elements of combustion. When human intellect ceases to be a factor in the world, human energy
will have dropped to a non-productive zero. Then,

Christianity will be no more for lack of nourishment, and one-half of humanity will starve to death."

"Then why trouble ourselves farther about it?" asked Don Alvard, in a tone of half impatience.

"Ah, my friend, your question has a deeper significance than you think. I have not said that the human race will become extinct with the end of Christianity. Gnosticism will rise as the true healer of mankind. It is as necessary to lay the foundation of an enduring Gnosticism, as it was to spend a thousand years to establish Christianity. We alone have the power to begin this work. Is there no glory in knowing that we hold the lost link of continuity in mental evolution, and may restore it to the human race? That is why we should trouble ourselves farther. What is a period of five hundred or a thousand years to the life of this planet? Nevertheless, in that time a new race must be raised up to people the earth; the original thinking type must be resurrected."

"Will you examine this vocabulary?" said Don Alvard. "I am surprised to find it more complete than we thought it would be," and he placed before Bambo the volume which he and Monetho had carefully prepared.

Bambo examined the work for some time, with frequent grunts of satisfaction. Placing his hand upon the volume, and looking at Don Alvard, he asked:

"Did Monetho say it would require centuries
to dislodge Christianity before you prepared this
volume, or afterward?"

"This work was graudally done over the period
that I was there," replied the Don.

"He was thoroughly familiar with this?"

"Yes, he laid great stress upon it as evidence of
Christian duplicity, saying that it was not Christianity which must be eradicated. In so far as its
religious pretensions are concerned, it had suppressed itself; it is the mental state of humanity
that must be corrected; purged, he called it. He
declares, that, the doctrine of universal sin has
brought the human race down to a brute level, and
this could only be corrected by a long and patient
evolution."

"I quite agree with him," said Bambo. "We
must hold this *exposé* in reserve for a safeguard.
It is not difficult to demonstrate the fictitious character, or even dishonesty, of the scriptures and the
so-called gospels."

"You say dishonesty, of what nature?" asked
Don Alvard.

"Dishonesty in translation is the smallest offense," said Bambo, drawing a Bible, which lay upon
the table, to him and opening it.

"Here is a corrected translation of the alleged
Hebrew scriptures. In the first chapter of Genesis,
and the first three verses of Chapter two, the Hebrew word *Elohim* is used in every instance. It is
the plural form of the word, and the only way to

translate it honestly is to render it 'the gods,' making it read:

"'In the beginning *the Gods* created the heaven and the earth.'

"'The spirit of *the Gods* moved upon the face of the waters.'

"'And *the Gods* said let there be light.'

"'And *the Gods* saw the light that it was good, and *the Gods* divided the light from darkness.'

In the latest translations this word is made singular.

"And, thus, in more than thirty instances this deliberate perversion of the truth is revealed, but this is trivial.

"This absolute dishonesty, on the part of paid translators, to prevent its reading as it was originally written, convicts Christianity of wilful misrepresentation. Had it read, '*the Gods*' it would have revealed its Gnostic origin. But, the scriptures contain much greater deception.

"The Gnostics were called the *Elohistics*, therefore the Christians found it necessary to do that which distinguished them as Jehovahistics.

"Now, turn to your Gnostic vocabulary and see what the word Jehovah means; *Jehovah, self-sustaining.* They were establishing a self-sustaining priesthood, to be nourished through its external organization, the church. The fabulous fathers, Abraham, Isaac and Jacob never heard of *Jehovah,*

"'And I appeared unto Abraham, unto Isaac and unto Jacob, by the name of God Almighty, but

by my name Jehovah was I not known to them.'
(Ex. 6:3.)

"And, it is true, not until Moses' alleged bringing
of the Israelites under the law, which enabled him
to levy a burdensome taxation, was the priesthood
self-sustaining; the same is true of all governments.

"Don Alvard, by your persistent hardihood and
courage you have rendered a great service to mankind. We have here the interpretation of all the
Christian mysteries. The idea of a *great name*, associated with a court above all civil courts, has ever
been the paramount object of the ecclesiastical
forces. We cannot examine it now, but you will
find, at the proper time, that, the very first name
succeeding the deluge, *Shem*, betrays this. Look
at the word *Shem*, it means *name*, *fame*, to *put* or
establish.

"In this connection I will call your attention to
another important evidence of duplicity.

"The conception of the Grecian philosophers
was, a powerful king, father of Gods and men,
Ju-pater. Associated with him is *Ju-no*.

"They have with them, the Lords of land and
sea, wisdom, beauty, love, light, darkness, war and
song. *Ju* is *Jehu*, meaning mighty; *pater* means
father. Therefore, Jehu and Jehovah are merely concealing forms of *Jupiter*.

"They are served by attendant spirits.

"They have messengers to send to distant points
and to men.

"Now, change the names of these Gods to angels, suppress the sexual passions; read *our father Jah*, for *the father Ju*, and we have the old testament idea of *God* and *heaven*.

"Contrast this with the conceptions of the thinking Gnostics:

"The Creator is a force occupying all space, which the limited mind of men cannot perceive. It is the universal mind pervading all things. It treats the largest body and the smallest particle with equal consideration and justice. It is present alike, in sun, moon and stars; governs the universe with unchangeable laws, and constructs with the same precision the mountain and the grain of sand.

"Even the words of the Gnostic thinker are plagiarized, although they do not apply to the Christian system.

" 'Oh, Lord, how manifold are thy works, in wisdom hast thou made them all; the earth is full of thy riches.'   (Ps. CIV:24.)

"This is pure Gnosticism—the universal mind personified."

"You are more deeply versed in the subject than I thought," said Don Alvard.   "You practically agree with Monetho.   To quote his words, 'ecclesiasticism, like a loathsome disease, has poisoned the human system and must run its course.'

" 'It required five hundred years to submerge Gnosticism; it may require a similar time to purge humanity of the virus of error, and its evil fruits.'

"I foresee that I have a hard and thankless task before me."

"Yes, my good Don Alvard, you have an endless task set for you. You will encounter great hardships, but all this may be softened and modified by your own attitude toward the cause. You must make your own comforts and pleasures as well as use discretion with regard to the lengths you go in combating hardship. We may go further into this phase later. What I most desire to know is, to what extent Monetho initiated you into the underlying philosophies of Gnosticism."

"Naturally, I could only assimilate a superficial understanding of the nature of the Gnostic science —and it is a science. Monetho was very patient and persistent in convincing me that Gnosticism had nothing in common with morbid forms of religion.

"The one central theme is, that, natural evolution, in endowing animal kind with sense organs, anticipated the culmination of the senses in the supreme reasoning powers of man, the highest evoluted animal being. Man was to rise to a plane to form an essential mental contact with the Universal Mind, blending the mechanical mind of the organic being with the abstruse mind of creative nature. This gives a logical reason for progressive, animal evolution. Moreover, it intimates, that, nature, as a whole, is an organic, thinking, reasoning being, and visible creations are his parts, each part performing a specific function in the exercise of the whole. This theory does not set up a single part as a personal God, because, the creative power in itself is the executive power, hence, no part of this

power can be delegated without weakening the
original whole, and giving abnormal powers to parts,
to the detriment of other parts. The God-like power
is a creative power, an indivisible, primitive force,
and, material, physical and organic creations are
but extensions of the one body, and having specific
functions which alone endow them with life—which
is mental attachment to the parent whole. The living bodies aspire upward, toward a state of freedom, and the dead gravitate downward, toward a
state of inactivity and subject to the physical call
of nature in future constructive operations.

"The two attitudes are symbolized by the two
basic sciences of nature, Astronomy and Chemistry.

"These two sciences, suggested to the ecclesiasts
the idea of *heaven* and *hell,* and by these two words,
in their primary significance, the ecclesiasts are convicted of secret plagiarism. Here is Monetho's
analysis of these words:

" 'Throughout the scriptures, many words which
secretly carry God-like significance are placed in
the masculine gender by the prefix *he. He+aven,*
meaning *nothing, nothingness, empty. He+'ll. He*
means *male, El* means *God* or *power.* This at once
distinguishes between the spiritual and the material,
establishing *God* and the *Devil.*

" 'This resolves itself into *Good* and *Evil.* The
word *God* in the original sanscrit is *good.* And even
a more subtle plagiarism, as the basis of the doctrine of *original sin,* is the word *devil,* derived from
evil. Evi+el. Evi means *desire. El* means *God;*

hence the devil is the *God* or *power of desire,* and
desire arises between living physical beings, the
idea of the fall being suggested by the tendency of
material bodies to gravitate toward the earth,
whereas, spiritual things aspire upward.

" 'Again, in this connection, they betray themselves by symbolizing the common masses of humanity as the productive earth. *Adam* means *earth,
Earthy.* Productive humanity is symbolized by the
fertile earth.'

"This now brings us to the very essence of the
subject.

"According to the Gnostic philosophy, the original intent of nature was to evolute its physical creations to a mental, or spiritual understanding, whereby its highest organic beings would attain a mental
state in common with the Universal Mind, knowing
all wisdom in common. This original belief suggested the name:

"Gnosis, *to know, knowledge.*

"You will at once realize the vast significance
of this. All worldly knowledge was to be widely
disseminated among humanity, in order to develop
the unit, thinking man to his highest power, for, only
during his life in the flesh, could he contribute
acceptable wisdom to the Universal Mind, the greater body requiring this essential food to enable it to
provide the organic, physical being with material
food. This is specifically illustrated by hunger,
thirst, the desire for sleep, and a myriad of other
calls of nature.

"The call of the mental man is as urgent as that of the physical.

"It is a manifest truth, that, this mental contact is broken by death, and individuality ceases. Moreover, should this contact with the Universal Mind be perfected in the human race, all men would be equal, therefore, it was essential to break the system teaching such a doctrine, that some men might be wise, and pose as gods. This is frankly admitted.

" 'And the Lord God (the master of the order) said, Behold, the man is become as one of *us.*' (Gen. 3:22.)

"The *Lord God* here is the high priest. *Us* is the priesthood.

"This is the same identical Lord God mentioned throughout the scriptures, and who becomes the Christian God, manifesting in the figurative Jesus Christ, symbolizing the crucified humanity. This crucifixion was made real by the debasement of mankind to a level of brute ignorance. The resurrection was to be the rehabilitation of the intellect of humanity.

"This is recorded by authentic history; the 'dark ages' (486 to 1495) pathetically symbolized the darkness which fell upon the earth as the time of the crucifixion.

"But the church had not the power to raise humanity out of the mire, hence it turned to political intrigue.

"By this horrible crime against nature, mankind

has never been permitted to mentally rise above
the gaseous plane, which is the atmosphere of this
planet, whereas, he should have been in direct mental contact with every other planet in this system.
His own organic construction reveals this as a physical truth. The power to attain this contact is the last
evolution in physical being; it is born, bred and cultivated in the cells and tissues of the living body;
hence, nature intended to evolute mankind as a unit
system. Ecclesiasticism debased the system to a plastic mass, to be controlled by super-men for commercial profit. This also is confessed. That same Lord
God promises those who will surrender their individuality, and grovel at his feet, they shall be of
his chosen people, and shall have *Canaan* as their
portion. *Canaan* means *merchandizing* and *trading*.
These are named Jews, to distinguish them from the
Gentiles, the non-believers.

"Monetho declares that ecclesiasticism made
the fatal error of destroying the Gnostic masters
before the complete system was understood, for not
once has a master Gnostic arisen among the ecclesiasts, the false-pretense of the prophecies to be ful-
filled in the future being but predictions of what
the church proposed to accomplish by political intrigue in the future, the masses to remain in a state
of ignorance and controlled by a cultivated superstitious fear. To the priesthood, the line of prophets is simply a code. I was so impressed with
this I have carefully saved my original translation;
here it is:

"The line of major prophets:
Isaiah=the salvation of the Lord.
Jeremiah=the grandeur of the Lord.
Ezekiel=the strength of the Lord.
Daniel=the judgment of the Lord.
Hosea=the help of the Lord.
Joel=the will of the Lord.
Obadiah=the servant of the Lord.

"This evolution foretells a state of servitude for the masses in the glorification of the master of the ecclesiastical order.

"The suffix *iah,* terminating several of these names, signifies *light* or *fire.* The suffix *el* means *God* or *power.*

"The minor prophets mean quite a different thing, signifying action.

Jonah=he that oppresses.
Micah=he that humbles.
Nahum=he that comforts.
Habakkuk=he that persuades.
Zaphaniah=he who gives impressiveness.
Zechariah=he who remembers.
Malachi=God's messenger.

"Clearly, this line of so-called prophets conceals a preconceived scheme of propaganda and procedure, as the priestly instructions for the inner circle."

"Yes, this is familiar to me," said Bambo.

"One thing which greatly impressed me," the Don continued, "was Monetho's explanation that the original Gnostics were trained through several generations. Under no adverse influences, and a continuous practice of ritual exercises, the adept is born in the fifth generation, knowledge alone, not being sufficient to bring one into the universal contact. Nevertheless, an intimate understanding of the system raises the disciple above his fellow-men sufficiently to make him their master. It is on this theory that the ecclesiasts deprived the greater masses of the opportunity for higher education. Science and philosophy are taboo, because they expose the duplicity of the church."

"That is quite true," said Bambo, "but my mind is not clear regarding the theory of universal contact. What is the medium? There must be a medium, or at least a point of merger."

"The transmission is through the vibratory *hyle*, which is the thought pabulum of matter. In dreams, and subconscious visions, independent of any conscious effort, thoughtful persons frequently have surprising glimpses of the universal mental world. Thoughts, then, must begin as nebulous spirals to develop into concrete forms.

"Monetho especially impressed upon me that the designed forms assumed by all material bodies are conceived in the universal mind, and are manifested in the material world through our external sense organs. He demonstrates this by the creative powers of man, who apparently conceives a thing in his mind and constructs it with his hands, but to construct he must gather the materials, else his conception will not be realized.

"Thus all visible nature consists of composite aggregations of ideas."

"You will readily recognize this as the alleged Platonic doctrine of ideas. Everything in this lower and material world has a celestial and immaterial archetype, an original pattern or model, before the thing is made."

"Yes, yes," exclaimed Bambo. "This is a hateful doctrine to the ecclesiasts, nevertheless, they attempt to use it in their blundering Genesistic creation.

" 'And every plant of the field before it was in the earth, and every herb of the field before it grew.' (Gen. 2:5.)

"This does not agree with the geocentric theories of the ecclesiasts necessary to nail their doctrines to the earth. Theirs is an earthy institution, dealing only with earthy contacts."

"Monetho insists that Gnosticism, in a broad sense, is equivalent to the universal *hyle*, therefore it is vindicated by its own manifestations. It is the reservoir of all human knowledge. It is the interpretation of potential wisdom into understandable knowledge. This demonstrates the Platonic theory as a universal truth, by establishing its own original authority by visible creations. Gnosticism deals only in demonstrable facts. Nothing is left to conjecture requiring blind faith. It existed before man appeared upon this earth, writing its records and traditions upon the face of the earth for man to interpret. It is an exposition of co-eternal principles which, by constant contact, observation and experience, man learns to understand."

"And, Monetho's understanding of these powers; in their highest form, they enable the adept to do what?" asked Bambo.

"They bring the adept into direct communication with the Universal Mind, enabling him to read and vision the Platonic ideas in their original conception, proving conclusively that the human mind is a co-related part of the greater mind of the whole being, dormant until awakened and trained to action.   There can be no argument to dispute that, creative nature endows its creatures with the mental powers to perform their alloted functions, therefore, as these creatures evolute to higher states, their intellectual powers will be increased accordingly.   We recognize man as the highest evolved being.   By a Gnostic examination, he is logically the goal of physical, organic life and this is the point where Gnosticism and ecclesiasticism take divergent courses.

"Gnosticism declares that the mind of man is in touch with the universal, creative mind while living, maintaining a compensating exchange to justify his being.   This is verified in many ways, none better than by respiration.   When respiration ceases, death of the body ensues, and disintegration distributes the gross elements.   All individuality ceases, and contact with Universal Mind is impossible after death.   The immortal part of man is the wisdom which he has contributed to the uni-

verse while his organic being was capable of respiration. No individuality is involved in human immortality; the exchange is definitely limited and for
mutual purposes, else no visible compensation would
be, and physical life would not be limited by time.

"The ultimate object of mental exchanges is undoubtedly for the betterment of the physical
world."

"Again I can see the tendency for the ecclesiasts
to covertly refer to the Gnostic beliefs," said Bambo,
reaching for his Bible.

" 'For dust thou art, and unto dust shalt thou
return.' (Gen. 3:19.)

' For that which befalleth the sons of men befalleth beasts; as one dieth, so dieth the other; yea,
they have all one breath; so that a man hath no
preeminence above a beast.

'All go unto one place; all are of the dust, and
all turn to dust again.

'Who knoweth the spirit of man that goeth upward, and the spirit of the beast that goeth downward to the earth?' " (Ecc. 3:19.)

"It is rather a strange coincidence that the first
quotation is found in Genesis 3:19, and the second
in Ecc. 3:19," remarked Don Alvard.

"Not when you analyze it," replied Bambo. Ec-
clesiastes is used as a disguise, or *nom de plume* for
the Hebrew, *Koheleth,* meaning one who speaks in
an assembly, the assembly being all who give their
hearts to the acquisition of wisdom. This is closely
associated with Gnosticism, hence, there is an ele-

ment of secrecy about it to conceal this. It is apocryphal, meaning *hidden*."

"Here in the code I find the word Kohath, meaning assembly, congregation, obedience, to make blunt," remarked Don Alvard.

"And this clears it up; blunt means pointless. Applying this to an obedient congregation by a speaker in disguise, could not mean the dissemination of wisdom. One may readily appreciate:

" 'And he said unto them, unto you it is given to know the mysteries of the Kingdom of God; but unto them that are without, all these things are done in parables.'

" 'That seeing they may see, and not perceive; and hearing they may hear, and not understand.' (Mark 4: 11,12.)

"Christ told this in confidence to his apostles, in secret, after leaving the congregation."

"It seems a pity that the masses, who contribute all the church support, cannot understand they are not of the church, but are only contributing members.

"That which is preached to them is senseless chatter to inspire fear and awe."

"I will continue," said Don Alvard. "Gnosticism brings the *Atomic hypothesis* of the ancients through the realm of speculative theories and into the world of facts.

"Assuming that the atom is the smallest particle of matter, it becomes the unit of transmission of mental force. The force which we call mind traverses the *hyle* from atom to atom, the flash being to all intent and purpose, instantaneous; hence, time and distance have no meaning in the universal wisdom. Sound cannot manifest in the realm of thought, because sound is a sequence of conflict and opposition. We have an excellent illustration of this in dreams, which sometimes cover long periods of time, and vast distance, in a single moment of sleep. The word alone, in its manifold forms of expression, can manifest sound or its equivalent, where some other sense assumes the function of the ear. This especially intimates a thought transmission, giving all human kind, trained as adepts, a thought in common, for the *hyle* permeates all things."

Bambo stared in amazement, exclaiming:

"Do you mean by this, that, were you and I adepts, and you here, and I in Rome, we could communicate with each other?"

"If you were on the planet Jupiter, or anywhere else in this planetary system, I could communicate with you," declared Don Alvard.

"Then the ecclesiasts conceived the idea of appropriating to their especial purposes and ends, the whole universal *hyle*. This is a startling thing. Don Alvard, it is a new vindication of the Gnostic theory of universal knowledge, and explains the necessity for the ecclesiasts to suppress Gnosticism, and destroy all avenues to scientific and philosophical thought and learning. They believed in the theory, and desired to bar all but their own selected or chosen kind from the acquirement of this blessing of nature. But they were too worldly and gross to develop the sense. This comes near to solving the nature of the Christian God. Let us examine the Bible."

"Here it is, the purpose is to bring all the world under the power of the Universal Mind through those who required the mental powers of the Gnostic adept, in order that:

" 'God may be all in all.' (I Cor. 15:28.)

" 'God was manifest in the flesh.' (I Tim. 3:16.)

" 'No man hath seen God at any time.' (I Jno. 4:12.)

" 'God is a spirit. (Jno. 4:24.)

" 'Not the God of the dead, but the God of the living.' (Mark 12:27.)

"I can understand the purpose of the retirement of monks to caverns. Meditation was a part of the Gnostic training. This is why Christianity absorbed the monastic orders.

"This fully corroborates the Gnostic theory. It is clear that ecclesiasticism has attempted to confiscate this universal power and personify it upon earth."

"Yes, that is undoubtedly true, but even ecclesiasticism had been anticipated first by the Babylonians, Assyrians and Egyptians, in their worship of the planetary bodies and second by the Jews in their worship of fire. They were all seeking light." said Don Alvard.

"Ah! that is a suggestion; let us see what the code says about this," excitedly exclaimed Bambo.

"The Gnostic code or the ecclesiastic code?" inquired Don Alvard.

"The ecclesiastic."

Babylon signifies *mixture* and *confusion.*

Assyria means *happiness.*

Egypt means *oppression* and *trouble.*

Darkness means *ignorance, adversity, misery.*

Light means *intelligence, joy, prosperity.*

"The Jews and the Christians say:

"Our God is a consuming fire."   (Heb. 12:29.)

Christ says:

"I am the light of the world."   (Jno. 8:12.)

"This Christ character is the last product of the ecclesiastical system, and we are very positively informed that this 'Christ light' is the universal mind manifested in the flesh of men on earth.

" 'This then is the message which we have heard of him, and declare unto you, that *God is light* and in him is no darkness at all.'   (I Jno. 1:5.)

"This necessitates the worship of an invisible personification of intellect and wisdom as God, and visible light and knowledge as Christ, personified in a human head of the church.   Otherwise God and Christ will be in direct conflict.

" 'Christ is the head of the church.' (Eph. 5:23.)

"The pope at Rome is the acknowledged head of the church, therefore, the pope is the living Christ, and God on earth."

"Is that plain enough?"

"I will now tell you the hopeful side of this story," said Don Alvard.

"While it is true, that, we cannot restore a conscious reciprocal contact with the universal mind, we are by nature in living contact with the greater being through planetary influences. As long as we have life in our bodies we shall have this afferent connection with nature, more physical than mental, because of our mechanical organic processes, which are a part of nature itself. It is a fact, also, that the heavenly bodies cast off nebulous spirals.

"An excellent illustration is, we frequently find a person with a limb broken or injured in a manner to render it useless and incapable of performing its normal functions, yet it remains alive by the circulation of the blood, therefore, the life element is in the blood, hence, we find this in the Christian Bible, (Gen. 9:4.)

" 'But flesh with the life thereof, which is the blood thereof, shall ye not eat.'

"This is strictly a physiological problem. Physiology was a theme of Gnosticism ages before Christianity. The circulation of the blood was known and discussed in Egypt before Christianity was invented.

"But, that which is of vastly greater importance is, nervous force is essential to inspire action in physical mechanism, therefore, the seat of will is in the nervous center.

" 'Not every one that saith Lord, Lord, shall enter into the kingdom of heaven; but he that doeth the *will* of my Father which are in heaven.' (Matt. 7:21.)

"In the ecclesiastical code *heaven* means *control, government*. Thus we have the seat of *will* located in the brain. If nervous contact is destroyed, paralysis of the part ensues, but life in that part continues, that other members of the body may not die because of the misfortune of the one. By this process humanity was intellectually paralyzed.

"This is all Gnostic, and the ecclesiasts knowingly appropriated it to their purposes, and brought every power to bear to destroy the original Gnostic system. The spiritual fruit of the human system is understanding knowledge. This tree is prevented from bearing fruit which will perpetuate its kind. Humanity has been deprived of the power to complete its cycle by a natural process which would have merged it into the universal hyle. That process is by individual, independent thought, guided by that same universal influx which controls the compensating respiration of organic life. Mankind has been steeped in ignorance and stupidity until its efferent nervous force extends only to the fleshy tissues of its own body. Men would not have been useful to ecclesiasticism, else they also would have been rendered blind, deaf and dumb, this being the only manner by which their *afferent system* could have been rendered equally dormant. Do you now grasp the horrors of Christianity?"

Bambo was spellbound; he could only listen.

"I will now hasten, quoting the teachings of

Monetho," said the Don. "Gnosticism was preparing the way to bring the whole world into the immortal contact; it had accumulated all the available knowledge of the intellectual world; it was formulating schools for propagating the great revelation. The far reaching possibilities of the system were known only to the Masters, and they were a unit as to the necessity for bringing all mankind into the intellectual light.

"At Rome a secret priesthood conceived the idea of establishing a tollgate through which humanity should pass, and pay a tax, to acquire this goal. A schism was inspired in the ranks of the Gnostics, and the seeds of dissension were sown as the seeds of foul weeds in a perfect garden. By promises of great emoluments, many Gnostics were corrupted. Ecclesiasticism selected some of the strong leaders, gave to them the Euphonius name, 'Apostolic Fathers,' and laid the foundation for the corruption and final destruction of Gnosticism. The system of mental starvation, and taxation, has enslaved humanity ever since, barring men from the only immortality, *for the universal mind is atomic memory*.

"If Gnosticism had not been smothered to make an exploitation of humanity, the whole mental world would have attained the immortal state, and all men would have enjoyed a mind in common. The evoluted mentation of man was the only natural process by which this could be accomplished.

"The Roman priesthood, with premeditated afore thought, strove to make a commerce of the highest gift of nature, and, for fifteen hundred years, it has jingled before the eyes of hungry, struggling humanity the promise which it could not fulfill, while it ground out of men the carnal things which it coveted.

"'If we have sown unto you spiritual things, is it a great thing if we shall reap your carnal things?' (I Cor. 9:11.)

"I am deeply impressed," said Bambo. "I foresee terrible things for the future. My heart bleeds for humanity. Every indication points to the fulfillment of the words placed in the mouth of the fictitious Christ.

"'Think not that I am come to send peace on earth; I come not to send peace but a sword.

'For I am come to set a man at variance with his father, and the daughter against her mother.' (Matt. 10: 34, 35.)

"And for what purpose is this threat made? A wholly selfish purpose:

"'He that loveth father or mother more than me is not worthy of me.' (Matt. 10:37.)

"Thus do they set up the institutions of marriage, fatherhood and motherhood, and penalize them by black-mail.

"'The meek and lowly Nazarene' actually becomes the agent of this nefarious system."

"The secret code goes further than this," said Don Alvard. "Jesus is born of *rebellion* and takes refuge in revolution. Jesus here symbolizes humanity.

"Mary means *rebellion.*

"Galilee means *revolution.*

"Jesus, symbolizing humanity, was carried into Egypt, meaning *oppression.*"

"This is quite sufficient," said Bambo. "Let us plan our campaign.

"Just a moment," urged Don Alvard. "In this connection, this has a bearing upon that all important problem of the wealth of treasure concealed in the monastery at Montserrat.

"As you are aware, the word *Jesus* is the Greek form of *Joshua.* An analysis of Joshua reveals the whole secret of Jesus Christ. *Christ* is not a proper name. *Joseph,* the adopted father of Jesus, means *increase. Jo,* an abbreviation of Joseph, *increase,* plus *shua* is *Joshua.*

"Shua means *wealth.*

"Hence Joshua signifies that, increased wealth is the *saviour* and *salvation* of the Christian enterprise.

"The figurative wealth of the church is the contributing congregation, cultivated from the *increase* in population. The literal wealth is a different thing. As Joshua made his plundering raids for the fictitious Israelites, to set a precedent for the church, and David his raids of murder and pillage, to set a precedent for kings, and prevent the latter from accusing the church of crime, the popes, assuming to be Jesus Christ, the head of the church, in the 10th, and 11th centuries, deliberately aroused in all Europe a state of fanatical and hysterical frenzy,

and organized that horrible and murderous insti-
tion, the Crusade, and plundered the East, costing
millions of innocent human lives and unknown
treasure."

"We must invent a new kind of hell to punish
this in this generation," soberly said Bambo. "Let
us retire now, and tomorrow begin our organization."

CHAPTER XV

THE PLAN OF BATTLE

FATE WAITS PATIENTLY FOR TIME TO BECKON

THE morning was beautiful. Don Alvard had slept again the sleep of adolescent youth; he had dreamed of a delightful voyage, in a sea filled with sunlit islands, with a sweet and lovely woman wearing a mask. She had removed the mask and he had recognized the countess, when he was awakened by the notes of a brown thrush at his window. He indulged himself for a few minutes in a pleasing remembrance of his dream, then arose, dressed and made his way silently to the garden.

Although early, he found Bambo strolling thoughtfully about among the semi-tropical trees and flowers.

Upon seeing the Don the pathetic hunch-back betrayed extreme joy, as he bade him a cheery good morning.

A servant promptly appeared and asked if they would like their breakfast served in the garden, which they promptly approved.

There, midst the sweet odors of roses, and fragrant shrubs, these two earnest men planned the future of mankind.

"My good Don Alvard," said Bambo. "I have slept little, but I am not weary. I am so filled with our subject, sleep seems like a waste of valuable time. I am so elated over the vast possibilities before us, I deeply regret that I cannot go with you out into the teeming world; but that is not possible. Therefore, I shall lay before you a plan which I believe, in a general way, will most effectively replant the seeds of Gnosticism.

"Naturally, I make no attempt to dictate to you a rule of procedure, and I expect you to exercise the broadest discretion in what you deem best to do to forward our cause, therefore, my suggestions are quite brief.

"Retain my credentials as Cardinal Bambo, and alternately assume the role of a traveling cardinal, having plenipotentiary powers, and that of a broken soldier of fortune, as occasion suggests.

"Begin, diligently, to sow the seeds of weeds, and the tares of discord, in the papal gardens.

"Buckle at your side two weapons in addition to your ponderous sword—ridicule and sarcasm.

"You are familiar with precedents to amply justify this method of warfare.

"Scruple not to resort to intrigue, deceit, hypocrisy, and subterfuge in dealing with any agent of the church.

"Fear not to resort to the sword or fire in a mortal combat with your enemies. I have the power and authority to absolve you in advance of any act you may perform.

"The church has flooded the world with its fabulous saints. In my name I authorize you to saint anything, person or place. Sow your saints right alongside theirs, and especially caution the people against paying money to anyone in offering prayers to your saints. You will be amazed at the results; the ignorant masses care little to whom they offer their prayers. Do this in my name and garb. Marry, bless, curse and absolve, in my name. Let Rome know that the poor, despised Bambo lived.

"There is no counter blow to ridicule which brings contempt upon their false-pretense. They will only gnash their teeth and rend their garments.

"Use your discretion and judgment in selecting permanent local agents, to carry on the work, but never confide to any one your next move, purpose or objective point.

"Conceal your identity as long as possible, and always dissemble when you are among strangers. This mystery will establish you as a nameless nemesis. The church will shun you instead of seek you, and the priesthood will flee from you as the earthly personification of the devil.

"Do not pose as a teacher of Gnosticism, but quietly and casually discuss it with learned thinkers, and gradually sow the Gnostic seeds. The wind can scatter seeds, but it does not cultivate them, leave that to the local conditions and forces.

"In your travels choose your own time, direction and purpose, being guided by circumstances more than by personal comforts and desire.

"I here present to you a list of financial agents,

located throughout Europe, who will honor your drafts upon Rome, made in my name, without question.

"And, now, my good soldier of the new cause of mankind, I must briefly speak of personal things. I am aware of the sentiment which has developed between you and our beloved protegé, the countess —youth must be served. I cannot advise you, but I can impress upon you the fact, that, the grandest duty that ever devolved upon any one human individual rests in your heart and is subject to your will and discretion. I do not believe you will shirk any personal sacrifice to fulfill faithfully the obligations of your mission to the best of your ability.

"Nevertheless, I am not by nature cruel. I do not advise that you wholly break off this perfectly natural longing of the soul for companionship. Our lady has suffered too much already. She looks up to you as her god. Both she and the count are heart and soul with us, and we must now take them into our confidence and councils. Therefore, I can only presume to suggest, that, for the time being, let your affections assume a Platonic aspect and let time and circumstances solve the future. Let us begin our organization here. I have so much faith in both of you, I believe I may leave the matter of your sentiment to your discretion.

"I especially suggest that you make this place your fixed rendezvous for rest and recuperation when hard pressed, keeping your visits here secret as long as you can."

Don Alvard listened very patiently to Bambo until he intimated he expected some response, when he said: "I have listened well to all you have said; my beliefs fully coincide with your instructions. You may trust to my discretion. I will make any sacrifice of personal sentiments to attain success in our undertaking.

"And, now, my field, I discussed that with Monetho. I shall immediately quit Italy and return to Spain, where I best know the people, their language, customs and temper. Who knows, maybe I can repair some of the ravages of the late fanatical Catholic sovereigns, Ferdinand and his dictatorial and blood-thirsty queen, Isabella. There are ten thousand human lives charged up to her ravenous appetite for burning human flesh. These murders were made festival occasions, with thousands viewing in ecstasy, the victims writhing in agony, while fiends made 'dog-faces' by applying burning torches to their faces.

"Since coming in contact with Gonsalvo, Santillo and Sanatos, I am hopeful that my surmise may be correct, that, their present plots may cause them to pay an early visit to Spain."

"That is very good. I fully agree with you," said Bambo. "I will now give you an opportunity to suitably smooth your departure from here," and he smiled up into the Don's sober face as they arose from their breakfast table.

The Don was soon joined by the countess and they walked toward her favorite spot at the end of the terrace overlooking the valley. Her sweet face, and her soft and gentle manner, did not conceal the sadness in her eyes. She knew he was about to take his departure. The Don's hearty greeting only caused her to smile happily for a moment, as her kindly, dark eyes softened, and a blush momentarily suffused her cheeks, which had become ruddy and healthy. The Don hesitated for a moment, then looking admiringly down upon her, he said:

"You are a wonderfully handsome woman this morning."

She made no reply but coquettishly took hold of his arm with both her hands, and thus they walked along the path almost in silence, in the direction of the cozy spot where she held communion with her birds and her heart.

The Don wore the dress of a gentleman while at the count's home, and was a distinguished figure. Only the scar marred his otherwise handsome face.

Looking up at a window they saw the good-natured count waving his hand at them, his face wreathed in a generous smile. They acknowledged his salute, then passed on, pausing now to look out upon the broad expanse of land belonging to the count—a glorious view in the morning sunlight. As far as the eye could vision stretched the cultivated fields below. Here and there could be seen the pretty villages and homes, with their pink and yellow walls and red-tiled roofs. Herds of cattle lazily moved, as they grazed. Flocks of sheep were moving before their shepherds, and people seemed like so many ants crawling about. It was a wonderful picture of comfort and ease, beautiful and inspiring.

Don Alvard was young, he had a heart like other human beings. Nature is a dangerous agent. Nature was tugging hard at his conscience, and a beautiful, soft woman was pulling hard upon his arm. He looked down upon her with unfeigned admiration, and unconcealed affection; they belonged in that picture. She looked smilingly up into his face, and tears came into her eyes.

"We must enter into a treaty. Helen—may I call you Helen?" he said, and there was a clutter in his voice.

She clung closer to him, laying her face close against his arm, and looked dreamily out upon the inspiring landscape.

"Is it necessary to rend our own hearts to mend others?" he gently asked.

She looked up at him with startled eyes.

"I could be strong and courageous, did I know that here I had a true and loving woman praying for me," he whispered.

Her face was averted but her hands encouragingly pressed his arm.

"I cannot ask you to be my wife. It would not be just, in view of the strenuous work before me. You would not want me to forego my duty, I feel quite sure, no matter what our love may be; but, dear Helen, with my assurance that I leave my heart in pawn with you, I know you will be my guardian angel as I face the many dangers before me, and I cannot fail or fall."

"My Alvard, it is foolish for us to dissemble. We have linked our souls together, and no power on earth can tear them asunder. I am well aware of the necessity for your going away from me. I would not have you forego this great mission for all the world. It is a strong link in our lives. I will pray for you hourly; for your safety, comfort and success—and that you may soon feel a yearning to return to me which you cannot resist." Then she dropped into her accustomed seat, covered her face with her hands and wept.

Raising the drooping form, the much agitated Don placed his hands upon her shoulders, looked longingly into her face and asked:

"Helen should I choose to alter my plans, would you have me forego my work?"

Quickly she raised her arms and placed them about his neck, sobbing:

"No! No! My soldier, you must not do that. I am brave. I will live but to love and encourage you. O, how much better than lying in that lothsome dungeon. Yes, I shall think of that, and think of you, and be content."

"Then my sweet guardian angel, I will come to you for love, comfort and rest, not as Pope Gregory VII sought the amorous embraces of his Countess Matilda, at Canossa, but to renew my life and courage from a fountain of unsullied purity.

You, my dear Helen, shall be my well-spring. I will visit you perhaps more often than we now think, but, in all events, I shall keep my heart pure and undefiled for your sake, no matter where my duties call me. I have learned to be a good dissembler with my enemies, but I cannot dissemble with you. My soul burns to love you. I shall enshrine your image in my heart and address my secret prayers to you each day, and before entering upon dangerous enterprises. I know you will respond and give me courage and strength. I shall feel your power. I cannot fail, with you as my Gnostic Goddess."

The countess leaned her head against his bosom, and he silently pressed her with his great, strong arms. She slowly raised her face and they bound their alliance with a solemn kiss.

Now taking his hands in her own, she said:

"My lord, I am satisfied. You now have made me very happy, knowing that I have your love will sustain me during the long night of your absence. I will watch for the dawn of the bright day of your coming to me. You have granted me much more than I anticipated. Yes, I shall hear your prayers. You cannot fail. Now kiss me once and let us go within, where I know they are impatiently awaiting you. Be brave and let them know we are true Gnostics."

Passing into the castle, they found the count and Bambo in quite a state of hilarity, Bambo having superficially gone over the ground of their great discovery with the count, who was greatly enthused.

The count assured the Don that, he expected him to make his home the hub of his operations, and a place of refuge for rest and recuperation.

Then a long conference ensued in which plans for the future were discussed.

On the following morning the eager Don was supplied with a splendid horse and servants to conduct him to the nearest seaport from whence he would take ship for Barcelona.

Arriving at Barcelona, he found his good horse, the Cardinal Belial, ready for action.

We do not follow our hero through the first stages of his work, in fact, we shall lose sight of him for a long period of time. Nevertheless, sometimes as the astute Cardinal Bambo, and, at others, a dashing, bombastic soldier of fortune, and still other times as a savage, garrulous villain looking for trouble, and usually finding it, he sowed a veritable whirlwind of destruction for the Christian faith, and was known as an evangelist of uncertainty. He sainted everything that rendered him service, and anathematized all who angered or antagonized him.

Priests were horrified to find their congregations dwindling, and their former parishioners diligently praying to Saint Brisket, Saint Garlic and a multitude of other edibles and drinkables, which quickly accounted for delinquencies in the church offerings.

"Who is Cardinal Bambo?"

"Who is Cardinal Belial?"

These questions went booming into Rome.

CHAPTER XVI

THE ADVENTURE AT SAN PESTE

IT IS NO CRIME TO STEAL FROM A THIEF OR LIE TO A LIAR

"CURSE of Christendom! Stand up, you rattle-box! If you lie down here I'll carve your leathern hide into bits and feed you to the buzzards. Pull yourself together till we find a soft spot to fall!"

The poor emaciated, overburdened beast to which this unchristian language was addressed, groaned aloud and leaned his weary head sadly against his master, as though grateful for the suggestion that he might be put out of his misery, and inviting him to carry his threat into execution. He had counted off the bone crushing miles until his head was in a whirl, and his mind a blank. His marrow was consumed, his strength was shot; little did he care whether his jingling carcass was handed to jackal or buzzard. Well did he know, too, that his rough spoken master was ready to quit, only his tremendous courage sustaining him.

The master looked sorrowfully at his faithful companion, and there was compassion in his voice as he patted the horse upon his lean, scrawny neck and said softly:

"Forgive me, old comrade, I know how sore and tired you are, but cheer up; *dum spiro spero*.

"See! we approach a place of human habitation. We shall fill our famished hides to bursting here, if I must murder the whole population. I'll wager my buskins against a biscuit it's a fanatical, Catholic town.

"Curse of Christendom! Cross yourself Satan, there's a church steeple. That means a priest with a fat ponch. I can't ride in there as Cardinal Bambo."

Looking sympathetically at his beast, standing with bowed head, he said:

"But you are no Catholic, neither are you a dissembler, therefore, I shall salute papa for you," and he made the sign of the trinity. "That means bread, mutton and wine—or a big fight."

They made a sorry spectacle, standing like spectres in the soft, evening twilight, looking down upon a small village, ensconced in a dark foliage, and slowly blending into the shadows of the rapidly approaching night. Here and there lights began to twinkle like stars, and ghostly sounds began to rise up to them, as though goblins were creeping out of the earth to have a night's frolic.

He was a raw-boned man of tremendous proportions, at least seven feet in height; long of limb; leathery of muscle, and, for so large a man, exceedingly alert and quick of motion. Travel-worn, weather-beaten, and sun-tanned to a nut brown hue, he was the epitome of the hard soldier of fortune, awaiting an odd stroke of fate to direct him to new adventures which might redound to his profit.

Great, hidden energy and self-reliance were reflected in his every movement, reminding one of a coiled python, or a crouched tiger ready to spring upon its prey.

His horse was a cadaverous, ragged old bone-rack, scarcely able to bear the burden of the curious collection drooping all over him. He could no longer stand up under the added weight of the bulky cavalier, and had abruptly stopped to protest in groans and wheezy coughs. His equally weary master was no brute, notwithstanding his rough language. He understood the situation, and quickly alighted to inspect his caravan. Moreover, it was his wont to approach strange places with due precaution, both for advantage and for personal safety. He was now ready to place his forces in concealment while he reconnoitered the approach to the village.

He literally pushed his tired beast, load and all, through the hedge at the road-side, in order to hide him, that he might approach the town unobserved and by a path not visible to the public highway.

Seeking a secluded spot on the edge of a small stream, which was sheltered by the concealing foliage of drooping willows, he began to unload his junk. This consisted of sundry cooking utensils, rattling pans, water gourd and skin-bottles; a battered hauberk, half rawhide from patching, a pair of ancient tin breeches, with eccentric plates at the knees, a strange looking package resembling a Persian rug, and, lastly, his tremendous fighting-iron, the length and heft of which necessitated its

being strapped to a long strip of wood to prevent
its lambasting the ribs out of the unhappy Belial
in transit.   The scabbard had been removed from
the blade and was now badly warped.   Straighten-
ing it over his knee he carefully examined the huge
blade and pressed it into the case.   A conspicuous
feature of his sword was a hilt of extraordinary
beauty, being wrought in gold and silver, embellished with inlays of mother of pearl and jewels.
It was his wont to say that, he had wrested this
sword from the hands of a giant Mohammedan in
battle.

He now lifted from the horse's galled back a
saddle which must have seen service before the
Christian era.   Its flapping skirts almost reached
to the ground, the big stirrup cuffs finishing this
reach when the cavalier's feet were lolling about
in them, brushing up the dust on both sides.   A
large rosette of frayed leather adorned the outer
surface of each stirrup, resembling abandoned birds'
nests.   He carefully deposited the saddle upon the
sward and removed from the horse's head a bridle
fully in keeping with the saddle, nevertheless, this
well battered piece of horse toggery was richly
embellished.   His beast looked through silver
mounted blinkers and champed a bit of pure silver.
This was reverently deposited upon the saddle from
Noah's ark.

Spreading his long legs wide apart, he placed
his hands upon his hips and chuckled gleefully as
he watched his tired animal thrust his muzzle deep

in the sweet, cool waters and quench a thirst which had threatened to blow him up. The horse having satisfied his thirst, walked into a rim of luscious clover up to his knees. Slapping his sides the cavalier said:

"Your're not carniverous. I thought you would suck that stream dry." Then to prevent his straying, he attached a rope about his neck, leaving ample play, and tied the other end to a willow limb.

Now turning his attention toward himself, he began to decorate his person with accoutrement to put to shame the gorgeous array of any oriental potentate. First he donned the tin breeches, then the battered buskins of Jove himself. The hauberk was next strapped to him with a broad belt having a buckle as large as a tin platter.

Taking up the steel helmet he attempted to straighten the pathetically drooping plume, which surely must have ornamented the rear end of a camel. Placing the bonnet upon his head, he adjusted the metal chin strap, then attached to his belt his ponderous sword. And, now, ye Gods! opening the strange roll, he unfurled and vigorously shook, a faded purple robe, elaborately overwrought with gold lace, worn away and broken in a hundred places. This royal horse-blanket he draped over his person with the grace and eclat of a dandy at a king's court. "Even Solomon, in all his glory, was never arrayed like this."

Ah, but there was method in all this dissembling; he was an actor dressing for his part in a drama,

sometimes a comedy, but leading to the greatest of
all human tragedies. Don Alvard de Ricalde was
no clown, nevertheless, even his beloved Belial
laughed outright as the cavalier reared himself and
proudly kissed his hand and trudged to the top
of the ridge to peer at the village.

Making a cautious survey, he observed the small
church, nestling in the midst of a grove of silver
poplars, and went directly to it. A half open door
enabled him to peer within. He was as much in
need of rest as he was of food. The temptation to
enter and indulge in a recuperative sleep overtopped
every other thought, therefore, he cautiously entered and made a survey.

Some burning candles cast a ghostly glow over
the interior, revealing rows of rude, wood benches,
a chancel formed of a leaning wood rail, like a
wobbly fence, a crude *fald-stool,* an ancient type of
ambo, and other equally as crude fixtures.

He stood, like a grim specter of antiquity, and
surveyed this strange pen, into which human beings
crawled to worship the Christian God, while the god
of nature beamed his smile and blessings without.
What could this hypnotic spell be which made moles
of men? What was the power which could impell
humanity to turn its back upon the day, with all
of its visible glories, to worship the night, and an
invisible and unknowable deity?

With a shrug of contempt he strode to the rear
of the church and stretched himself on a bench and
slept only such a sleep as is superinduced by sore

muscles and weary bones—from long training he did not snore.

It was early morn when he was awakened by a noise about the chancel. Cautiously raising his head he observed a priest pantomining at the altar. Concealed by the gloom of his position, he watched him, wondering how a man of ordinary intelligence could practice such mummery. Arising, the priest made the sign of the cross, and went to a picture of a black-faced virgin, hanging upon the wall, looked cautiously about, and turned the picture, revealing a concealed ambry or alcove, out of which he lifted a leathern pouch, from which he took an ample handful of coins, thrusting them into a hidden pocket beneath his cassock.

Returning the money-bag to its hiding place, he tip-toed out of the church.

"The Virgin Mary truly conceals a multitude of priestly secrets," murmured the interested observer, as he lay quite still for a while.

Arising he walked down the aisle and confiscated the bag of money, saying:

"This money coerced from the poor, should be in circulation. It is no crime for me to levy a tax upon priest or church. I shall be my own judge. Confiscation is their commonest practice. I am a crusader, now, therefore, I am wholly within the church code. I acquit my conscience of a sense of dishonesty, and I shall duplicate this raid whenever opportunity offers."

He left the church exclaiming:

"Curse of Christendom! Even the church provides." Emptying the coins into his own pouch, he cast the other bag into the shrubbery.

Making his way over the ridge, he discovered Belial lying belly deep in the sweet, red clover. He imagined he saw a smile of satisfaction upon the faithful animal's face.

"You selfish rogue," he said. "Here you are stuffed to bursting and I have not had a mouthful of provender in three days. Wake up old comrade and hear the glad tidings. Don Alvard de Ricalde is again upon earth, and amply provided with the wherewithal to revel and feast. We shall breakfast early and blend the feast into dinner. Arise! my beloved, and let us hie to yonder village bin and take our place in the concourse—a bullikin of the best wine is mine, then a fatted fowl with frills, much highflown conversation, some women and ribald song. The most glorious morning follows the most gloomy night—if one only has faith; that's it, faith, Belial. You don't have to be a Christian to exercise faith. 'Faith is the substance of things hoped for.' (Heb. 11:1.) We hope for bread and hay."

While the strong hearted Don was delivering himself of this cheer inspiring harangue, he led Belial to the brook and allowed him to drink; then he piled upon him the cargo of junk which was his daily burden.

"Bear your burden patiently, Belial; patience, they say, is a virtue. Doubtless you will be sainted when you die, nevertheless, you will be bait for buzzards if you die in the right place, just the same as the Christian saints, who are feasts for the worms. Yes, I'll introduce you here as St. Belial. Your coat of arms in the calendar of saints will be a *pitchfork* and a *muzzle*.

Leading the caravan to the hedge he shoved it out into the highway, following it himself, nearly tearing his antique armor off his bulky person.

Mounting the staggering beast, he rode gravely toward the village, as though greatly fatigued. The first person he encountered was the self-same priest who had so generously replenished his purse. Upon seeing the priest, he softly muttered: "Blessed Mere! the saints are good to me; they commend me to the tender mercies of the village *padre* at the edge of the town. It will be my recommendation to enter with him, in godly conversation. Am I not myself a cardinal by proxy?"

The priest was a man of pompous mien, austere and dignified. Nevertheless the experienced eye of Don Alvard penetrated this ecclesiastical disguise before the prelate discovered his proximity—little did he think that he was so near death.

Attracted by the clatter of the Don's wabbling outfit, the priest turned his saintly head, and, upon observing the odd spectacle he hastily crossed himself, then stared at the uncouth stranger. Despite his godly austerity, he burst out laughing, holding his galloping stomach as he rocked his body back and forth. Suddenly stopping, he exclaimed:

"The saints protect us, I know not whether to flee or stand. Out of what mediaeval war-chest did you spring?"

Don Alvard leaned upon the pommel of his saddle, calmly looked the priest over and said:

"Whither art thou perambulating, father, at this ungodly hour? Will you join my caravan? We will make a triumphant march into yonder citadel and capture it without struggle or the shedding of human blood."

The priest laughed again most heartily, as he took a mental inventory of the Don's accoutrement.

The Don continued: "If reliance may be placed in external appearances, yonder tavern should yield savory provender and liquid accompaniments for a hungry soldier and his comrade in arms."

The priest suddenly drew back in alarm, exhibiting great fear, and, apparently contemplated flight.

The change was mutual. Don Alvard thrust his crane like neck toward the scared priest, and, in his excitement his Adam's apple bobbled up and down like a ball on a cord. With livid face and gleaming eyes, he exclaimed: "Curse of Christendom!" and slipping from his saddle, he drew from its scabbard his ponderous sword. With a snort of anger he crept toward the priest who was struggling to meet his anger with wit. Looking carefully about he raised his finger to his lip and whispered:

"Not yet, we need each other here, sheath your blade, also your anger, till a more opportune time."

Don Alvard eyed him with suspicion and re-

covered his self-composure. With a sarcastic shrug
and laugh he put away his sword.

Looking suavely at the priest, in marked contrast to his previous display of anger, he said:

"I have ridden long and far. I am weary. *Adonde
esta la mejor posada?* I desire food and rest for
myself and beast."

"Come with me to my residence," eagerly replied the priest.

Don Alvard instantly flared up and angrily retorted: "Not I! Do you take me for a pauper and
offer me charity?"

"You look the part," bluntly replied the priest,
with some show of bravery.

"I am not then, and I do not care to stand with my
back to the wall in any man's house to procure
food."

"What do you mean?" demanded the priest,
he having somewhat recovered from his fright.

"Is it necessary for you to ask that question in
the light of day?" hissed the Don, and he pointed
to the disfiguring scar, now purple, which marred
his face, and he made a menacing stride toward the
now much frightened priest.

"Be just, remember the circumstances," whined
the priest twisting his fingers and cringing before
the enraged giant.

"Let it be a truce till I leave this place," said
Don Alvard, "but one false move on your part, and
I will cheat Satan, and leave your foul carcass roast-

ing in your burning church, you cowardly hypocrite."

"Sufficient," replied the priest. "I will vouch
for and protect you while you sojourn here."

"I require neither of you," grunted the now sullen Don. "Remain upon your knees and pray for
your body and soul while I sojourn here."

The priest coldly bowed and pointed to a public
house. "Go there; Popeyes is the proprietor. Then
he turned and walked away.

Don Alvard led his caravan to the dilapidated
inn, which the priest had pointed out, and was met
at the portal by an ugly man with protruding eyes
and much hair.

He looked at Don Alvard and his outfit in great
surprise, and quickly motioned to some one inside.
Several men and women crowded in the doorway
and boisterously strove to get a view of the stranger.
No one there had ever before seen such a character.

Don Alvard looked Popeyes over with eyes of
fire, and laughed loud and boisterously, turning the
joke onto the proprietor.

"Well you are rightly named. What are you,
hostler or host?" he said, and, to the great amusement of the crowd, he tossed Belial's bridle-reins
over Popeyes' head—next to the *padre* Popeyes was
the most important personage in the town.

That outraged individual frantically disentangled
himself, gesticulated wildly, and screamed:

"I have no place for paupers! I will not give you
credit! Get away!"

The Don almost burst his leathern belt suppressing his anger, but gained ground by laughingly saying:

"Father Santillo recommends you to me; he will
probably visit me here. Shall I go tell him you have
refused me comfort?"

Popeyes perceptibly weakened, and motioned
for a hostler to come forward and take the traveler's
horse.

The Don gave specific instructions regarding the
entertainment of Belial, warning the hostler that the
horse had been sainted for extraordinary services.
Shortly thereafter Belial had his nose buried in
toothsome oats and hay, and was kicking himself
to see if it was not all a hallucination. In the meantime, his resourceful master had so far won the affections of the people of the inn, he was regaling
himself with a huge leg of mutton, sundry fowls,
and an abundance of excellent wine—Popeyes was
noted for his good wine.

The Don, with all of his worldly experience, was
an entertainer, his conversation flowing as freely as
his wine. With quite a party gathered about his
table—the ladies being seated and treated, and the
men standing, in respectful defference, against the
wall. Popeyes and Beppo Pescola, his closest friend,
and chief entertaining loafer about the inn, stood
near the hilarious stranger and speculated regarding
his identity.

As keen of ear as of sight, the Don had caught

the drift of their half whispered conversation, and began to send their minds a wool-gathering.

One of the now merry ladies asked of the Don if he had ever been in love.

"In love!" he roared, loud enough to ring the village church bell. "Why, in Barcelona I loved a woman so hard I broke three of her ribs hugging her."

This produced a roar of laughter, and Beppo remarked, "He is from Barcelona."

"Again," continued the boisterous cavalier, "I kissed my lady love, in Pampeluna, so ardently, she lost her front teeth."

"Not so," whispered Popeyes. "He is from Pampeluna."

Suddenly the Don whirled upon them, and pointing his long finger at Beppo, he demanded:

"From whence would you have me come?"

Beppo braced up, and in a wavering voice replied. "If you should happen to hail from Sebastian?"

"For your convenience, then, I am from Sebastian; then what!" said the Don.

"And should you be Corporal Magiola?"

"For your pastime, I am Corporal Magiola," roared the Don, springing to his feet and dragging forth his ponderous sword.

The room cleared instantly, and the Don stood uproarously laughing.

Beppo crept into the doorway, cringing and twisting his hands, and, in a wee small voice, said:

"And you should happen to be my brother-in-law, whom I have never before seen?"

In surprise, the Don looked contemptuously at the cringing figure for a moment, then growled:

"God forbid! the only Pescola I ever heard of stole the cross off the church in Pampeluna and was hanged."

Slowly reseating himself, he savagely glared at them, as he beckoned the ladies to return. Popeyes and Beppo withdrew.

It was full noon before he arose from his bounteous repast—whom Father Santillo recommended must be well entertained, hence, all the women of the place partook of the lively Don's generosity. There seemed to be no bottom to the capacious pouch from which he brought forth his coin. Covetous eyes awaited the hour when, wine soaked, he would drop asleep in his chair, as many another had done, when they would pounce upon this pouch like so many ravenous vultures.

But, all the wine in Popeyes' cellar could not put Don Alvard under the table. Popeyes had taken a deep dislike to the self-reliant stranger, from the first sight of him, and he was determined to humiliate him if possible. The tattered and battered appearance, of both the cavalier and his horse, bespoke hard service of some kind. It was very possible that he was an important messenger of distinction. Nevertheless, the chances seemed strongest that he was merely a wandering adventurer. In any event, Popeyes would remain on the safe side and only tempt the Don to betray himself. To this end he quietly inveigled into the house a comely wench to whom he entrusted the finishing touches of putting the Don under the table—drunk.

The Don was regaling his listeners with stories of his adevntures, when Popeyes peered through the door, then pushed the timid figure into the room.

Now, this battered hulk of humanity; this disguised giant, was wise in his day and generation. If Popeyes had told him in advance, he could not have made his trick plainer. The moment the Don's eyes lit upon the seemingly demure figure standing bashfully against the wall, with averted eyes and modest mien, he recognized the town huzzy, and the inn keeper's favorite.

Arising, he strode across the room, Popeyes having entered, and to the amazement of all present, he roared:

"Curse of Christendom! I'll choose my own company. Don't go out and invite the whole neighborhood. What money I have left I shall distribute to the poor, and I shall not ask your advice."

Gathering the half dozen women, who had arisen in alarm from the table, in his flail-like arms, he pushed them back and bade them be seated.

Cautiously, some of the more intrepid men slipped back into the room, remaining against the wall and near the door, and slyly bandied small jokes at the expense of the Don.

Suddenly there arose a hubbub about the door. The Don put down his mug and listened. A crowd, headed by Father Santillo and Popeyes, began to press into the room. Popeyes dramatically pointing his finger at the Don, said:

"There is the thief! Look at his poverty! Yet he has his pockets lined with money. Look at this. I found it in the shrubbery, near the church, when I went to early mass."

In his hand he dangled the identical bag which the Don had confiscated from the concealed *ambry* in the church.

Continuing, Popeyes said: "Down in the meadow you may find where his starving beast spent the night, destroying the clover and defiling the ground and stream."

A menacing crowd now began to fill the room, some with staves, others with knives and other weapons, apparently bent upon immediately dispatching the stranger without the formality of a trial. The mob had been organized too adroitly— the Don saw the hand of Santillo in it, and decided upon quick and drastic action. Slipping his hand into his pouch he filled it with coins, slowly arose, shot out his long arm and grasped Popeyes by the throat. With a dexterous twist he stood the terrified landlord upon his head and shook him vigorously, silver coins seeming to pour out of his pockets and jingle about the floor.

Casting him across the room, the Don pointed to the coins, demanding of the priest: "Identify your dirty money, you professional mob maker."

The priest, now as badly frightened as Popeyes,

attempted to push his way to the door, but, with a bound, the enraged Don collared him and viciously jerked him back into the room. Up to this moment no attempt had been made, on the part of the mob, to assault him, but now, a murmur went up that the beloved village priest should be thus manhandled.

"Tell them!" roared the Don. "Tell them that I am not a thief!"

The shaking priest turned toward Popeyes, saying: "It would seem that there is the thief; he has both my pouch and my money in his possession."

Roughly turning him about, the Don shook his finger in his blanched face, saying: "You, best of all men, know that, when I take anything, I know it is my own, and he who calls me a thief must die!"

To the wise priest this was a frank acknowledgment that the Don had confiscated his store of money, and he knew his opinion of money so accumulated. The Don looked into his face and laughed heartily, as he pushed him toward the door and ordered the mob to instantly leave the room.

Going to where Popeyes was standing, shaking in unconcealed terror, he demanded his score declaring that he would no longer remain under the roof of such an ungrateful landlord, who so little merited his liberal patronage. He also demanded that the hostler be sent to him that he might give him instructions concerning the harnessing of Belial, that he might immediately proceed upon his journey.

The hostler came timidly into the room. The Don winked and pointed to the coins which had not been gathered up from the floor and nodded for him to help himself, which he quickly did. Then he was duly instructed and left to bring Belial—he held a different opinion of this stranger.

The Don promptly settled with Popeyes and demanded that all the ladies who had helped to entertain him be sent into the room. They entered with less trepidation than the grumpy landlord. The Don bade them gather the balance of the coins from the floor and divide them equally between them. Thanking them for the joy they had afforded him, he strode out to the platform, where the grotesque Belial stood awaiting him. His flapping saddle-skirts, jingling pans, and gourd and bottle, made a picture to make a dead man laugh. At a respectful distance the crowd stood intently interested in the proceedings. Don Alvard glared about and growled:

"I will crack the bones of any one who smiles while I am in sight of this town."

Mounting, he slowly rode away. At once the most comical and the most terrifying personage that had ever honored the village of San Peste with a visit.

As the Don rode past the villa of Father Santillo, he saw that disappointed individual standing sullenly in the doorway. Approaching, he slouched himself down in his saddle and grinned as he spoke to the priest:

"You have seen me; that is sufficient for the present. Until we meet again, pray for I shall surely kill you in due time."

Then he slowly continued on his way, the priest watching him until he disappeared from sight.

"What fate dropped me in San Peste?" the Don asked himself. "It was out of my way. Seeking one evil I find another. Surely fate is with me. I had no particular business there. Santillo is Borgia's friend and agent; this is a rendezvous, for Santillo is not a man to bury himself in a smelly little village, away from the beaten path of civilization. This is not the end of this adventure. Turning in his saddle, he looked back, but could only see the top of the church spire, with its wooden cross peeping at him from the foliage of the giggling silver poplars.

His purpose in traveling through this country, disguised in his uncouth outfit, was to locate at another point, exactly what he now believed he had found by accident in San Peste. The discovery of Santillo, there, emphatically identified this priest as a part of the great conspiracy which he was trailing.

He could not kill him now, he needed him to identify his associates. As he pondered this adventure he was quite well pleased with the net results.

As much as he pitied his faithful Belial, he was the best part of his disguise. A strange and wonderful comradeship bound them together, Belial exhibiting an almost human affection for his master.

When night came they sought a suitable spot and lay down together to sleep the sleep of the just.

CHAPTER XVII

THE ADVENTURE NEAR SALAMANCA

HE WHO DRAWS THE SWORD WITHOUT A JUST CAUSE INVITES DISASTER

DON ALVARD opened his eyes to discover St. Belial free from his stake, and nibbling the scant grass about his buskins. Having rested well, he laughed heartily as he pushed his big foot against Belial's muzzle, saying: "You old rogue, you would eat the shoes off your good master's feet." But Belial only rooted his feet out of the way to enable him to get at an unusually succulent tuft.

Arising, the Don slapped his face and demanded to know how he had released himself. They were good pals, these two brawny animals, deeply attached by companionship in tremendous hardships. The great bulk of the giant cavalier was as much a burden to himself as to the good, faithful steed.

Breakfast consisted of the remains of last night's mess, and the Don did not consume much time in partaking of it. As he began to pack up his belongings, he picked up a book which he had found somewhere in his travels. Turning it over and looking intently at it, he grunted: "Curse of Christendom! A fine bit of Christian history this. I understand why Bambo and Monetho both should caution me ever to be on the alert for it. I shall be hung, drawn, quartered and boiled in oil, if I am caught in possession of such evidence against the Roman church."

If his friend, Santillo, could have seen him now, carefully primping himself as a cardinal, he would have concluded, that, the uncouth adventurer, whom he had seen at San Peste, was a most versatile character, and far from being the poverty stricken cavalier he appeared to be. As a truth, he was the most virile and dangerous anti-Catholic agent in all the wide world, with a well defined purpose concealed beneath his rough exterior. He was no wolf hiding beneath a lamb's skin; he was a roaring lion, challenging the whole Christian power, in a skin almost as tough as that of a rhinoceros.

As he harnessed Belial, he observed a package which he had not previously noticed in his outfit. Picking it up he found it was a large bag of gold and silver coins carefully wrapped and bound. He laughed heartily, as he held it up and jingled it. A note attached to the bag proved it was a gift from the household of the gentleman where he had last been cordially entertained.

"Use to the best advantage of our cause," read the message.

This generosity sobered the Don and set him to thinking of the future. He had made splendid headway, having thoroughly sown the seeds of the new Gnosticism through northern Spain. He could now feel assured that the good work would develop as he gradually wended his way southward.

It was a beautiful morning, as he trended toward the smoke of a distant city, visible from the elevated ridge along which he was riding. Coming upon a well traveled highway, he rode leisurely as became a cardinal. A heavy, black and gold cloth concealed the warlike nature of his accoutrement. His tremendous size made him conspicuous enough.

St. Belial suddenly tossed his head, bringing his master out of his reverie. Turning in his saddle he saw approaching three horsemen. Drawing aside as though to permit them to pass he felt for the hilt of his sword which was attached to a long, flat piece of wood strapped to Belial's side.

The horsemen, who came dashing up, reined in their steeds near the Don. Upon seeing that they were approaching a prelate, the captain, for they were a detachment of Spanish soldiers, saluted, saying: I trust your eminence will pardon our seeming disrespect, but it is so seldom a cardinal travels alone, we did not think the horseman preceding us would be so distinguished a person. Permit me to accompany you for a while."

The Don bowed assent, and the captain motioned for his companions to go in advance.

"I am glad of your company, my good officer, for it is very lonely. I am going to Salamanca. If I am not mistaken, it lies where we see that smoke arising," and the Don pointed toward the town.

"Yes, that is Salamanca. I, also, am traveling to that place," replied the captain.

"Are you in garrison there?" asked the Don.

"No, I am on an inquisitional mission," cautiously replied the captain.

"Ah, that is strange. I, too, am on a similar mission, but of a confidential and diplomatic nature. I am Cardinal Bambo, of Rome," and he displayed his cardinal's ring. "Perhaps I may be of assistance to you while at Salamanca."

"And I to you," replied the captain eagerly. "I am Captain Braganza, of the flying dragoons of the inquisitional office."

"If it is not confidential, my good captain, may I ask the nature of your mission?" softly inquired the Don, and he looked sharply at the complacent soldier, being careful to conceal his left cheek.

"Naturally, I consider every commission confidential until it is executed," said the captain.

The Don held up his hand, saying: "To be sure, to be sure, that is the duty of a good and faithful soldier. I am not inquisitive. I was only seeking to make conversation along lines which might be of mutual interest."

"It is very possible I may wish a friend in Salamanca. May I have the pleasure of calling on you there?" said the captain.

"Then you are not of Salamanca?" quickly asked the Don.

There was something sinister in the soldier's eye at hearing this question that caused the ever alert Don to secretly unclasp his outer cloak.

"No," was the captain's answer and he seemed to be thinking deeply.

"Were you a captain at the siege of Pampeluna?" the Don suddenly asked.

The captain was startled and half checked his horse. "Yes," he stammered. "I was in that siege. Why do you ask?"

"Have you come from San Peste?"

The captain turned sharply and stared at the Don, asking:

"Why are you asking me these questions?"

"Because, you, having been at San Peste, would naturally, have had a conference with the good priest, Santillo, and doubtless, he informed you that, should you encounter on the highway an uncouth and poverty stricken individual, armed and accoutred for battle, it would be your duty to inveigle him into the nearest town where he could be delivered to the inquisitors, when one Frances Borgia would pay you a handsome reward. I am the man you are looking for," and the Don dropped his cloak from his shoulders onto Belial's haunches.

The captain was a few paces in front of the Don. To draw and turn upon him was a dangerous move, if the Don had a concealed weapon. Nevertheless the daugthy captain shouted and took the chance. He wheeled his horse and drew his sabre in one motion. But to his horror he was confronted by a giant with a sword of such length it extended beyond the head of his horse. It was no indication of cowardice, but of good sense, for him to avoid a contact until his companions were by his side.

Don Alvard sat ready and smiling.

"Don't do it. You know me, captain," he said quietly. "I have put twenty opponents *hors du combat* in as many strokes. I want some conversation with you before I kill you."

There was that about this grim spectre now bristling with virility, which commanded discretion on the part of the three soldiers.

"Captain Braganza, you have drawn your sword against me, and brought two others to your aid, therefore, I must kill you," cooly said the Don. "I give you two minutes to cast away your swords. If you do this without hesitation, I will spare you; refuse and I will not grant you time to pray." With this he maneuvered Belial in anticipation of a dash by the three soldiers. His discretion was well rewarded; the three plunged their horses upon him simultaneously. With a dexterous motion he came in contact only with one sword, that of the captain. Before the unfortunate man could escape, the Don had badly wounded and disarmed him. Reaching out his long arm, he thrust the captain out of his saddle and sprang from his own horse on to the saddle of the captain, but none too soon, for instead of fleeing away, as he had anticipated, he appropriating the captain's horse to prevent this, they came at him again. With an unencumbered steed under him, he felt at ease, dispatching the two men so quickly that, the captain stretched his hand toward him and begged to be spared.

Replacing Captain Braganza upon his horse, he mounted one of the other horses, and leading Belial

directed the captain to precede him and leave the
highway. For an hour they rode silently on, notwithstanding the captain's weakness from loss of
blood.

At last the Don commanded him to halt. Dismounting, he assisted the wounded man from his
horse. Then he bound up the wound which rendered his right arm useless.

"Now, my good captain, we are safe from prying
eyes and inquisitorial ears, let us continue our interrupted conversation. Your life depends upon
your readiness to give me the information I crave."

The captain only bowed his head in shame and
humiliation.

The Don continued: "I knew Santillo would
attempt to entrap me, that is why I spared him, for
it is a part of my mission to kill him. I desire to
know where Frances Borgia may be found. Where
is he?"

Captain Braganza raised his head and looked
at the Don as though he expected him to take his
life, therefore he maintained a dogged silence.

"I warn you," said Don Alvard. "If you do not
speak, I shall kill you for my own protection, but
if you speak the truth, and frankly, I will permit
you to ride into Salamanca, under oath not to betray
that you know my identity. Your two companions
are dead, they cannot betray you. Speak quickly.
Are you in the hire of Borgia?"

"Yes," said the sulky captain.

"Where is he?" asked the Don.

"He is now at the new cathedral at Salamanca. I was dispatched to overtake you and follow you to the nearest point where I could have you apprehended and held for his instructions. He preceded me to Salamanca three days ago."

"Ah, I am well pleased with this day's work. I will know Frances Borgia in future," said Don Alvard.

"I did not think to find you disguised as a cardinal," innocently suggested the captain, who seemed very sick and willing to talk.

The Don looked sharply at him to see if there was concealed sarcasm in this speech. Could it be possible that, Borgia and Santillo were not aware of his masquerading as Cardinal Bambo and sowing counterfeit saints wherever he went? Thousands of Spaniards were now secretly sending up prayers to St. Potatoes, St. Garlic, Saint Beuf, St. Mutton and many things which the Don, as Cardinal Bambo, had beatified.

It was known that the Spaniards had found the Peruvians adoring *Potatoes* and *maize,* as symbols of divine sustenance, why not the Spaniards?

He called this the "new dispensation." Where the ancient totem worshipers worshiped some special animal, and the Christians had worshiped the lamb in the similitude, the "new dispensation" gave power to every man to bless his own food, naming it a Saint, and this food carried the blessing into the tissues of the body. Then he clinched this by saying, that, this was the principle of the Eucharist, which, in primitive times, was celebrated by the eating of a fish as symbolizing Christ.

It was the "new policy" of the church to dispense with expensive churches with their idols and their fat priests, and transfer the Christian religion to the hearts of men, according to the original Christianity. It was for the people to choose which policy they would adopt.

"Know ye not that ye are the temple of God and that the spirit of God dwelleth in you?" (I Cor. 3:16.)

"What? Know ye not that your body is the temple of the Holy Ghost, which is in you?" (I Cor. 6:19.)

"For ye are the temple of the living God, as God hath said." (II Cor. 6:16.)

"In whom ye also are builded together, for an habitation of God through the spirit." (Eph. 2:22.)

"Lo, I am with you alway, even unto the end of the world." (Matt. 28:20.)

"I am in my father, and ye in me, and I in you." (John 14:20.)

The people were amazed at the simplicity of the new doctrine.

These were the quotations of the traveling cardinal, and his arguments were equally unanswerable.

"If God, Christ and the Holy Ghost are in you, why have the priest praying to imaginary spirits up in the air? That is spirit worship, or why wear out your clothes kneeling before an image, if the true God dwells within you?

"If they are in you always, why look elsewhere for them. Bless the food you eat and keep it for your own God within. Don't fatten some selfish priest with it."

This silent work of Don Alvard had so upset the church work in certain localities, complaints were sent to Rome with urgent requests to apprehend this Ghost of a Cardinal. No word had yet reached the Don that this cardinal had been identified as himself. They were searching for a diminutive hunchback, not a giant.

These thoughts crowded into the Don's' mind as he cautiously contemplated the captain.

This adventure would surely identify him as the alleged cardinal Bambo, yet he could not kill this ignorant, helpless man in cold blood, even if he had had designs upon his life as he willingly should have killed a hypocritical priest.

"Now that you know who I am, be frank with me," said the Don. "Is Borgia accompanied by one Francisco Riengi?"

"Yes," replied the captain.

"And a cripple, named Ignatius?" asked the Don.

"No," replied the captain, "he has gone to Venice."

The Don smiled at this suggestion that his cousin, Iñigo, had been sent to Venice in quest of the real Cardinal Bambo. This was valuable information he was receiving from this wounded soldier, who alone had it in his power to betray him in a dual role.

"Tell me," said the Don. "What is Borgia's mission to Spain, and especially to this part of the country?"

"He is returning from Portugal where he has been in consultation with the organization in that country concerning the new world," said the captain.

"What organization?" asked the Don.

"The company of Jesus," was the prompt reply.

"Ah, then, they have extended this spy system to Spain and Portugal," mused the Don.

Suddenly the wounded man half arose, fell back upon the ground, his face turned purple and the blood rushed out of his mouth and nostrils, and, with a gasp, he died.

The Don had arisen in alarm and looked down upon the man with astonishment, not knowing the cause of this sudden collapse. He now made an examination and found what he had not previously known. Instead of a superficial wound in the arm and breast, his sword had penetrated the lung and he had been internally bleeding to death.

"Surely fate again has intervened in my behalf. This man undoubtedly would have betrayed to Borgia that I and Bambo are one," mused the Don, as he stood looking upon the fallen man.

It occurred to him to search the man's person, and it was well he did; thereon he found the itinerary of Borgia from the time he had left Rome, and the course he would pursue returning there. This was of very great benefit to him, enabling him to safely evade espionage. He chuckled as he looked over this paper then thrust it into his pocket. Beneath the blouse of the captain he found a pistol, powder and balls. The pistol was not loaded which accounted for the captain's having not used it. These the Don appropriated, carefully loading the pistol and concealing it in his belt beneath his robe, a new weapon for him.

He carefully looked over the accoutrement of the horses; and equipped St. Belial, and the big, strong horse, which the captain had ridden, to the best advantage. Leading the third horse over the ridge to prevent his following them, he removed the bridle and frightened him away. He stood watching the animal flee until he disappeared among the hills.

There was nothing else to do but leave the captain where he had fallen. Therefore, mounting the larger horse, and trailing Belial, the cardinal rode away from the spot, taking a course which would lead him near to Salamanca, but he did not enter the city.

Only a few years previously, the great Gothic cathedral at Salamanca had been completed, which, with the university, made this city conspicuous in western Spain. Great Catholic dignitaries made it a place of pilgrimage. Its three rocky hills, on the river Tormes, made it a picturesque and interesting city. From an eminence the Don observed these interesting features, then turning his horses into a road leading in the opposite direction, he rode away, sad and depressed that it had been necessary to take three human lives in defense of his own. But this human sacrifice was chargeable to the ecclesiastical system.

CHAPTER XVIII

THE COFFIN AND GRIDIRON

THE JINGLE OF GOLD, AND THE CRY OF POVERTY, ARE
ALIKE IN ALL LANDS

DON ALVARD'S mind was so occupied with
speculative meditation, the day was well
spent when he realized the urgent necessity
for finding food for both himself and his animals,
and a suitable place of rest for the approaching
night.

Almost before he could realize it, he was entering into a strange little settlement, consisting of
a single, narrow street between two rows of squat,
one room adobe huts.

The place at first glance, seemed wholly deserted, no sound and apparently no life, greeted him.

Riding slowly through the street, wary and on
the alert for surprises, he approached an open
square, in the midst of which stood a more preten-
tious building, which proved to be what he had
surmised, a public house. About the door, there
appeared some villainous looking men. They stood
stupidly looking at him, with no other apparent interest than dull curiosity.

He was shocked upon seeing a sign above the
door consisting of a coffin, and a large gridiron.

At one side the door was roughly painted:

> *"El que hace ataudes."*
> *"Emprendedor."*

At the other side:

> *"Parrillas Taberna."*
> "Coffin-maker"   "Undertaker"
> "Gridiron Tavern"

For effect the Don crossed himself upon reading this satanic greeting. Already had he resolved to pause here only a sufficient time to procure water and food. There was no visible indication that he could procure provender for his horses.

Observing a trough into which trickled a stingy stream of water, he led his animals to it and remained with them until their thirst was thoroughly satisfied. Seeing a runt of a boy standing like a dumb hitching-post, he placed the reins in his hands, bidding him hold them until he came for them.

The cluster of ugly visaged men made no pretense of offering help, but remained about the door, stolidly looking at the stranger, and, with anything but friendly faces.

The Don raised his hands and said:

"St. Brisket be with you."

At this salutation some of them made the sign of the cross, as they sluggishly made way for him to enter. They seemed amazed, however, to observe dangling beneath the Don's *manto* a huge sabre, which hammered about his heels as he stooped to enter.

Within he found a dingy, ill-smelling room, filled with dirty, uncouth men; some seated at rough tables gambling; others leaning idly against the walls, in sullen mood, while others were sprawled over the bar drinking. A strange silence pervaded the place.

Pausing, the Don asked for the proprietor. A man with blear-eyes, thick lips and a main of hair and whiskers, falling almost to his shoulders, came rolling toward the stranger. He held in his hand a long-handled fork, dripping with grease, most of which ran down his lathered apron, with which he had been tending roast mutton and toothsome chops. The pleasing odor of these, delicately flavored with garlic, filled the whole room and teased the Don's nostrils.

The Don hardly knew whether to draw or salute, but for safety he slipped his hand beneath his cloak and felt for his pistol. Then, with one of his bravest smiles, he asked the landlord of the *coffin* and gridiron if he might procure food and wine.

The human lion, whose arms hung down his sides like those of a gorilla, roughly boxed away from one of the tables some men who were seated gambling, and bade the Don seat himself.

Passing behind the bar he selected, with his own hands, a bottle of wine, picked up a mug and brought them to the Don's table.

Pointing at the mug, the Don said:

"Bring another for yourself."

The man made a huge grimace, humped up his

big shoulders, pointed to the grill and shook his head.

All the inmates now concentrated their attention upon the stranger, some laying down their cards, some turning their backs to the bar in order to face him, some staring insolently at him, while others covertly watched him from beneath low, animal brows.

The Don felt a squeamish thrill pass down his spine, for this direct attention seemed to have something to do with the placing of his wine upon the table, but his awakening suspicion was enhanced when a sharp rap of the iron fork upon the grill caused the men to reverse their attitudes like so many automatons.

It was too serious to treat lightly; he was puzzled. His keen instinct warned him of pending danger.

Observing one man standing aloof from the crowd, and apparently of a superior cast, he motioned for him to approach.

The man came forward in a hesitating and uncertain manner, as though reluctant to accept the invitation. Don Alvard's blood was aroused, he quickly interpreted the man's actions as the embarrassment of fear, for he glanced toward the grizzled cook at the grill before starting toward his table.

The Don asked him to join him and to bring another mug.

The man hesitatingly drew up another stool, again glanced cautiously toward the grill and seated himself at the table. To the Don's surprise he leaned forward and whispered: "Don't touch that wine, I will order another bottle. I'll explain later —but I have no money with which to pay."

The human gorilla, upon seeing what had occurred, pretending not to have fully understood the Don's original order, hurried to the table, rubbing his hands and giving his attention, also, to the other man, who timidly ordered another bottle of wine, watching him closely as he selected the bottle from the shelf and brought it to the table, placing it in front of the guest with a flourish and rushing back to his grill.

Reaching across the table, the man filled the Don's cup, which was still empty, then his own, and raising his cup said: *"Saludo"* and they drank together.

The Don, now thoroughly alive to a new situation, covertly watched the shaggy proprietor-cook, and saw quite sufficient to convince him, that, that individual was poking extra holes in his mutton because of impotent rage at the act of the man who had joined him.

"Parla Ella Italiano?" asked the man.

The Don nodded.

Cautiously referring to the proprietor, the man said in a low tone:

"Eun uomo buono da nulla."

"Egli guarda me, non voi," responded the Don,

"Cio che voi dite e verissimo," said the man.

"Ditegli che venga qui," said the Don.

The man called the cook and ordered mutton, bread and cheese.

The lion said something surly and turned his back upon him. Returning to Don Alvard, he said: "As I thought, he is angry that I did not permit you to drink the wine, which I am sure is drugged, if not poisoned. I do not believe he will serve either of us food."

The Don smiled grimly saying: "Then we shall help ourselves, but let us get our bearings first. May I ask you to tell me something of yourself."

The man nodded, saying: "Mine is a desperate story. I am supposed to be one of the owners of this nitrate and salt-peter mine. These villains here, have practically confiscated the mine, having made no accounting or return for two years. It is impossible for me to leave here because my horse was confiscated. And while they do not openly say so, I know that I am a prisoner. Look at me; I am a gentleman by birth, but, now, I am a beggar; I have no money; I am half fed, and in daily expectation of being murdered. I have seen three travelers partake of poisoned wine and die in convulsions in the dirt there. My name is Carlos Rizzi, and my home is at Toledo."

At this moment, the Don, looking through an opening, which served as a window, saw his two horses being led away at some distance from where he had left them in the care of the boy.

Arising quickly, he went to the door. All the loungers in the room were aroused, crowding to the

door as the Don went without. The Don roared at
the boy to return with the horses. The boy hesitated and the shaggy, lion-headed proprietor roared
to the boy to bring horses back, which he did.
Don Alvard stationed him where he could watch
them from the hole in the wall, and returned to his
table, where Rizzi had remained, and the conversation was resumed.

"Who is the local lord over this colony of
rogues?" asked the Don.

"I need not answer, whispered Rizzi; "look!"

A man had just entered the low doorway; a
regular brigand in appearance. He wore a tremendous *bigote* and his jet black hair fell in long greased
ringlets about his broad, thick shoulders; his dress,
of excellent material, was a reproduction of that
worn by Hernan Cortez, and his boots were highly
polished. He carried no sword, but in his broad
belt were two silver mounted pistols.

Beel-zebub, the name which the Don had given
to the shaggy cook, pointed to the Don's table, and
the new arrival promptly presented himself.   A
scowl passed over his villainous face as he saw
Rizzi seated with the Don.

"I am Señor Don Miguel Diego, said the brigand, bowing to the Don.

The Don merely held out his great hand, saying:
"I am honored to know you. I am the Cardinal
Bambo; will you join us?"

"Thank you," replied Don Miguel, and called

for a stool, then turning to Rizzi, he impudently wagged his head for him to go.

"I prefer that he remain. I desire to finish our conversation," said the Don, and he waved his hand for Rizzi to keep his seat. Suddenly he exclaimed: "Ah, a cup, my guest must drink, and he nodded to Rizzi who arose quickly and brought a cup, and Don Alvard placed the bottle of poisoned wine in front of Don Miguel.

There was a hurried, gasping exclamation and a shuffling of feet, and the grizzled Beel-zebub reached out to grasp the bottle, but Don Alvard anticipated him by taking the bottle and saying: "That's right, *Mesonero,* bring a fresh bottle of wine. A strange exchange of glances passed between Don Miguel and Beel-zebub.

"I am here by accident of travel, Don Miguel," said Don Alvard. "And right glad I am to pass through so historical a spot."

"And what, pray, is historical about this God forsaken hole, your Eminence?" asked Don Miguel, eyeing him sharply.

"Why, if I am not mistaken, it was the discovery of this very mine which gave rise to the use of the name St. Peter, the 'rock.' Salt was sanctified into Saint and Salt Petre into Saint Peter. 'The salt of the earth,' the rock on which the church is established, merely signifies the elect. You probably know that the origin of the word 'salt' is unknown."

"You astonish me," said Don Miguel.

"Your community should be a peaceful one," said Don Alvard.

"Why so?" asked Don Miguel in surprise.

"Because, they must be saturated with salt. In St. Mark we are told, 'Have salt in yourselves, and have peace one with another,'" laughingly replied the Don.

"Does that signify that this is a peaceful community?" asked Don Miguel, pointing to a pile of oblong wood boxes in one corner of the room. "They are coffins for the men who die here, and more than one half of these deaths are due to murder."

"Evidently there is such a thing as getting too much salt in ones system," said Don Alvard. "But we are not getting it here. We have waited for more than an hour for some food."

"We? Who are we?" asked Don Miguel, looking savagely at Rizzi.

"Being lonely, I invited him to dine with me, and I now extend the invitation to you; that, perhaps will bring mutton and bread," said Don Alvard.

"I only dine with gentlemen," muttered Don Miguel, with a savage look at Rizzi.

Like a serpent, Don Alvard uncoiled himself and seemed to tower above the others.

"Do you mean to apply that to me?" he demanded, looking keenly at the Don.

"Take it as you please," growled Don Miguel.

"Put your hands flat on the table," whispered Don Alvard, and Don Miguel saw the muzzle of a

pistol pointed at his breast from between the folds
of the Don's cloak. "If you move, I'll kill you.
Rizzi, step behind him and take his pistols."

Don Miguel was as pale as a sheet and sat mo-
tionless, while Rizzi took his pistols out of their
holsters.

This was done so quickly it had attracted no at-
tion. The Don said: "Rizzi, stand at the door and
cover the crowd. I will get us something to eat
and we will go. I have a horse there for you."

Rizzi was quite equal to his task; bounding to
the front of the room, he yelled: "Put your hands
up and keep them up."

With a single blow, Don Alvard knocked Don
Miguel senseless upon the floor. Drawing his sword
he bounded to the grill. Snatching a large, convenient copper vessel from the wall, and holding
it toward him, he commanded that the frightened
cook cast into it a roasted leg of mutton, the freshly
grilled chops and four loaves of bread. Backing to
the end of the bar, he seized two bottles of wine
and thrust them into the receptacle; placing the
vessel near the door, he yelled to Beel-zebub to
come forward, but he held back. Drawing his pistol, Don Alvard roared: "Come!"

The grizzled cook came sulkily forward.

Passing to the table, the Don poured a cup of
the poisoned wine, cast the bottle upon the ground,
pointed to the cup and commanded him to drink.

The cook started back in terror. The Don
sharply prodded him with his sabre, pressing him

toward the table. With shaking hand, the frightened wretch grasped the cup.

"If you drop it, I'll run you through. Drink!" roared the Don.

Out of sheer fright the man swallowed the fatal draught, and a gasp agitated the shrinking crowd.

"Shoot the first man who passes out of the door. Come, I will get the horses," and he took up the vessel and passed out of the door, followed by Rizzi.

The horses were there; they mounted and rode quickly away.

"We are safe!" exclaimed Rizzi. "There is not a man with intelligence enough to follow."

"What about Don Miguel?" asked Don Alvard.

"I thought you had killed him," replied Rizzi, in surprise.

"No, only knocked his senses out of him," laughed the Don.

"Very well, we are still safe. Don Miguel's mule train left only two days ago and will not return for a fortnight. His own *caballo* broke his leg a few days ago and he cannot follow. At last I am again a free man," and Rizzi wept with joy.

Suddenly he turned upon Don Alvard, exclaiming: "Why, I never knew that cardinals wore armor and sabres and pistols."

Don Alvard laughed aloud, exclaiming: "What do you think could take a lazy, gluttonous cardinal to a den of murderers like that? He would send a priest whom he would pray might be martyred and sainted."

"Then you are not a priest?" asked Rizzi.

"I am not, but I need not explain to you why I wear the garb of one," said the Don.

"Not at all," replied Rizzi. "If you were the devil himself I would feel grateful to you for having brought me away from that hell."

It was growing darker; they had traveled at a rapid pace for two hours, and the Don suggested that they seek a suitable spot, some distance off the trail, where they could spend the night. A small cove, with a gushing spring, looked inviting, and they dismounted, unharnessed their horses, examined their supply of food taken from the "coffin and gridiron," and found they were quite well provendered.

"There is so little for the horses to nibble, we must divide with them our rye bread," said the Don, and he broke two of the large loaves in fragments which the horses ate with a relish.

"I made sure this wine was not poisoned by taking the bottles from the bar freshly served to the patrons," said the Don.

They partook of a good, substantial meal of mutton, black bread and wine, and then prepared themselves for rest and conversation.

"I regret that you did not kill that brute, Don Miguel," said Rizzi.

"Why," asked the Don.

"He is a powerful, vindictive man, acting as agent for the Spanish inquisitors. They have confiscated our nitrate mines and attempted to ruin us. Why he permitted me to live, I do not know, for murder is a profession with him," declared Rizzi, in a voice betraying deep emotion.

"Why have you not killed him?" asked the Don.

"I am not a murderer for one reason, but this man was always armed and was so closely guarded it was impossible to get at him had I been so inclined," said Rizzi.

"Ah, you betray your weakness," said the Don. You knew this man had robbed you; you knew him to be a murderer; you believed that your life was in momentary danger, yet you raised no hand in self-defense. I regret that I did not know all of this while I was there. We should have recovered possession of the property. By St. Bunion, I have a notion to return there and have it out with Don Miguel."

Rizzi looked his amazement but did not speak.

"But, I have other matters calling me," muttered the Don.

"You have put into my mind a desire to accomplish what you have suggested, therefore, advise me," eagerly said Rizzi.

The Don smiled to see how he had put some fight into the despondent young man. "You can do it with utmost ease, if you follow my advice. Select ten men; arm them well; fall upon this place; take Don Miguel prisoner; confine him in some secret place; convert the murderes there into a chain gang and work them by armed guards. With this brigand out of your way, you may return to Toledo and legally justify taking possession of your own property by force," and the Don waited to see the effects of his words.

Rizzi threw up his hands exclaiming: "And bring down upon my family the bloody, unscrupulous inquisitors."

"Now, I have drawn out your real trouble, my good man," said the Don. "Remain in your present state of mind, and you will not only permanently lose your property, but you will encourage the very thing which you most fear. To justify their dishonesty, they will conjure up excuses for putting out of the way any who might complain. In fact they had begun this process by detaining you."

"What course, then, should I take. I have not the experience to devise such a plan. Are you so engaged that you could not become my adviser and leader in this venture?" asked Rizzi.

Don Alvard looked thoughtfully at the unhappy young man for some time without answering him, and finally said:

"I believe you honorable and worthy; tell me the history of this persecution."

Rizzi told him the story. For many generations these mines and certain other extensive salt mines, had been in the possession of the family Rizzi, which was very wealthy. The Rizzis were not religious fanatics, being heartily opposed to the inquisition. Under the fanatical reign of the murderous Isabella, the grandfather became a defender of Don Pedro Aranda, bishop of Calahorra, who was being per-

secuted by Torquemada, who had been made grand
inquisitor by Isabella. So closely was the inquisition allied to the crown, it was recognized as a direct
assault upon the Spanish nobility. No Spaniard
could escape its vindicative power, from the decisions of which there was no appeal. It found means
to persecute any one whose property it coveted.
The grandfather fell under the ban, becoming a
victim of Torquemada's wrath; his salt properties
were confiscated, and he was banished. The father's nitrate mine had not been confiscated directly,
but a meaner way was found. An inquisitional
agent, Don Miguel Diego, was placed in charge of the
property and never afterward could they get any
report of it. Rizzi's father was an old man, and
was afraid to arouse the old enmity by making
strong representation. The son had gone to the
mine with the consequences already related.

Don Alvard listened intently to this story, and
when Rizzi paused, he said:

"Your story, though sad, is not a new one. It
will interest you to know that my life is devoted
to righting such wrongs. This inquisition exhibits
two phases of 'divinely authorized' theft.

"When the civil laws are allied with the church
laws, the civil laws are nullified, because the governing laws cannot be both civil made and 'God
inspired,' and it is the power of the church which
brings about the alliance. Under such conditions
there is no recourse.

"The church laws are bare-faced false-pretense.

Fear of these laws is forced upon humanity by some form of coercion. I have never yet found a thinking person who had a respect for the so-called church authority, yet, practically all men fear it, and cringingly obey it.

"In this circumstance, believing my cause to be just, and dedicating my work to suffering humanity, I am a divine law unto myself. I indict, I judge and I execute. I believe I may help you to recover possession of your property. It will necessitate my first going to Madrid. I understand that the king has just returned from his beloved Flanders, with his beer guzzling retinue, which evidences that he needs money. He cares nothing for the Spanish people you know. Not enough to learn to speak their language. But, the clink of gold sounds alike to all ears and in all lands."

"And you will aid me?" exclaimed Rizzi. "My father will reward you well."

"I want no reward until I have accomplished my work," said the Don. "I must first learn what I may be able to do for you. You must return to your father at Toledo and remain quiet until I arrive there. Do not become impatient should it require longer time than I now believe it will."

With few other preliminaries they went to their rest.

On the following day they traveled together to a point where they separated, Rizzi to go on to his home, and the Don to make his way to Madrid. It was a hard and hungry drive for poor St. Belial.

The Don had hoarded remnants of their last feast to tide him over to the next smile of fate, but his beast must go both hungry and thirsty.

CHAPTER XIX

THE DISTRESS OF COUNT BERRASTA

'TIS SPORT TO FOOL THE HYPOCRITES AND LAUGH AT
LEISURE

AS Don Alvard awoke, the sun was glaring down upon him like a suspicious eye wondering at the revelation of this strange cavalier, and his battered old war-horse.

It actually angered him that this was so. The devil himself would not have passed them by unnoticed.

Well seasoned to rebuff, the Don knew not chagrin when men laughed at him, for such offenses he had a ready remedy, but, he felt a quickening sense of shame when nature seemed to make sport of his homely plight. Stopping on a slight elevation, he looked back at the eastern sky, waved his hand and exclaimed:

"Laugh, Sol! We'll have to take it from you, but I'll whittle to fragments any human being who laughs at us this day."

In this morose and sullen mood, he started on his day's journey. His recent experiences were souring him, and were putting him in a temper.

He had passed a bad night, again dreaming that he was back in San Peste, and playing over his anger provoking experiences while there, therefore, he was in a bad humor this morning. He was a sight for the Gods. His tangled hair and bristling *bigotes*, resembled mats of twisted copper wire; his eyes, red and bleared, were like vent-holes in a charcoal-burner, as they peered from beneath shaggy eye-brows; his long corrugated neck, with its conspicuous Adam's apple, resembled the neck of an ostrich struggling with a half-swallowed orange. Having slept in his ancient hauberk, it was all awry, giving him great discomfort. Through sheer indifference, or some strange hallucination, he had drawn on his slatted, tin breeches which now flapped aimlessly about his hairy legs like wind-whipped sails about broken spars. His royal *manto* was rolled in a long coil and thrown loosely across Belial's back, its ends whipping the jangling pans, and beating an irritating rat-a-tat-tat upon Belial's lean ribs. His huge feet were encased in the flat, badly worn sandals, which patted his heels with Belial's each jiggling step, the ponderous stirrups fanning up clouds of dust on both sides. With his battered bonnet cocked on one side of his head, the whole ensemble resembled some grotesque beast, or bird, attempting to take flight and unable to rise from the earth.

Yes, he truly looked the human derelict, cast upon an uncharted sea, without compass or guiding star, to aimlessly drift into the great unknown.

Regardless of the Don's ill temper, this was a dangerous disguise, for, beneath this uncouth exterior, there lurked a master-mind, and the venom of a rattle-snake; a fearlessness which never shirked danger, and a courage to conquer. Don Alvard de

Ricalde was a standing challenge to surprises. Upon the slightest provocation, his fertile brain would incubate a new and startling adventure, to coin calamity into good fortune; sorrow into joy; evil into good, or disaster into a happy termination. For, whatever he did, he had a ready and plausible apology, or ample justification, safely within the Christian code of his period. He knew no law but his own will; no judge but his own conscience, and he believed that his code was more within natural law than the edicts of the church, insisting, that, as long as the usurpative church was permitted to exercise its power over humanity, the unbelieving individual should have the right to resent its encroachments, on the grounds of justifiable self-protection.

The world recognized this as a dangerous, nevertheless logical attitude. The church at this period was admittedly a usurpative organization, seeking to culminate its exploitation in a permanent temporal power, to enable it to dictate legislation to compel all men to contribute toward its maintenance, and confess its absurd doctrines, to bolster up its bigoted priesthood.

No one knew this truth better than this trudging nemesis.

After two days of hard and hungry travel, the intrepid Don unexpectedly fell upon the text for his next great adventure.

No bigger hearted Samaritan ever lived than this veteran of the dusty ways. Although he always turned such opportunities to his own profit, in order to further his own work, nevertheless, he scrupulously served the good, and meted out condign punishment to the unjust, and the evil doer.

As usual, Belial trumpeted something out of the ordinary. Don Alvard saw some life in the road ahead of them, but, not until they had come to the spot, could he determine the nature of it.

A traveler was lying by the road-side writhing in distress, his horse having stepped into a gopher-hole, had thrown his master heavily to the ground, dislocating his right shoulder.

Don Alvard quickly dismounted, exclaiming:

"Curse of Christendom! What have we here?"

The man groaning, raised his left arm, and placed his hand upon his right shoulder, intimating his wound was there.

"Pobre hombre," murmured Don Alvard, in sympathy, tenderly raising the traveler to a sitting position.

The traveler wept as he pointed to his beautiful, richly caparisoned horse, lying groaning nearby, he having broken his leg.

The Don lifted the traveler to his feet and they stood looking at the suffering beast, agreeing that it was necessary to dispatch him out of his misery. Accordingly the Don drew his sword.

"Soi medico. I kill to cure. *Les lastima un buen caballo,"* and he killed the horse.

Lifting the suffering traveler onto the back of Belial, he took the reins in his hands and trudged doggedly through the deep sand until they came into view of a peaceful looking peasant cottage, surrounded by well cultivated fields.

Drawing near to the cottage, they saw a young woman standing holding a rope to which was attached a goat. The Don quickly turned to the stranger, exclaiming:

"Ah! *Amigo*. I envy you your convenient wounds."

"La muchacha es linda."

Hailing the young woman, he said:

"Buenos dies, Señorita."

"Como esta vd, Señor," was the cheerful response.

"Donde viva vd, Señorita?" asked the Don, and the maid pointed to the cottage.

"Go, if you please, and inform your father, and your mother, that, a wounded cavalier craves temporary comfort, for which he will amply reward them with money." The young woman promptly obeyed.

Therefore, when they arrived at the gate they were cordially welcomed by a flock of squawking geese, two barking dogs, and the farmer's comely wife, with interesting eyes, and a red and yellow *manto* cast over her head.

In a soft, friendly voice she greeted them with the hearty, Spanish ¿*"Como esta vd?"*

Don Alvard gracefully acknowledged the greeting asking for the man, who was in the garden near by. A little man came excitedly to where they were standing and eagerly inquired what was wanted, the following words ensuing between him and the Don:

¿"Escuche vd?"

"Si Señor, comprenda," and they lifted the hurt man from the horse and carried him into the yard, placing him upon a Spanish blanket which the good houewife had spread upon the soft, green sward.

Don Alvard, in his long course in the school of necessity, had become proficient in the minor surgery of first aid operations, therefore, bidding the Spanish farmer hold the stranger, to prevent resistance, he proceeded to make an investigation of his wounds. Placing his big knee upon the chest of the stranger, he made an effort, so the patient believed, to rend him asunder. To the contrary, however, with a sharp click the dislocated scapula was drawn back into its normal place and tightly bound there with a sheet supplied by the housewife, almost instant relief resulting.

The outcome was, that, ample silver, much more than was expected by the humble cottagers, gave Don Alvard two days' rest, and provided for the comforts of the sick stranger until he was sufficiently recovered to continue on his journey.

It was warm, and a comfortable hammock was provided for the invalid beneath the shading boughs of a maple. The pain having now subsided after a night's rest, the Don and the stranger entered into earnest conversation.

"I am grateful that it was not necessary for *el medico* to kill me to cure me, as he killed my poor *caballo,"* laughingly said the stranger, as they adjusted themselves for a quiet visit. The Don made a careful survey of the man, finding him above the average. He was of athletic build, and possessed the soldierly bearing of a man of physical training, although a pigmy in comparison with the colossal person of the Don himslf.

Upon being assured that he could not travel with safety under several weeks, he wept in vexation, confiding to the Don the story of himself and his mission.

Almost before he could realize it, the doughty soldier of fortune was in the midst of a new adventure, born of pure accident, in which one man lost the leading role, and the other assumed it.

The stranger, after apologizing for not having previously introduced himself, made known that he was the Count de Berrasta from Savoe, and was accounted the most accomplished swordsman in the whole of France.

As a secret envoy of the Duke of Savoe, his most ardent patron, he was making a journey, *incognito,* to Madrid, to enter the lists at the annual tournament, believing that his extraordinary skill might win for him fame—being already rich, he was not seeking fortune.

As the count thus identified himself, and frankly confided his ambitions to Don Alvard, the latter began to bristle, and writhe like a python preparing to seek food.

Continuing, the count said: "And, my good

Señor, I will confide to you my greatest aspiration. I have heard much regarding one great Sebastiano. I thought it very possible that, by my superior skill, I might even be successful in a joust-at-arms with this celebrated personage, in as much as report says they have not been able to find an opponent for him."

Don Alvard had received his cue. With burning eyes, he slowly arose and glared savagely at the count, then burst into boisterous laughter. The terrified count tried to shrink deeper into his hammock, cringing with mingled alarm and pain.

Stepping back a few paces the Don whipped out his tremendous sword and made it sing as he cut the air, about the count's head, into ribbons. Holding the blade high above the count, he roared:

"Curse of Christendom! Thank all the saints in the calendar that accident has interceded in your behalf. My dear child, this blade has played with a score of men at one and the same time, and left them to drown in their own blood. Do you think you could cope with it?"

Despite his wounded shoulder the count struggled to a sitting position, exclaiming:

"Why! What do you mean?"

"Did you ever participate in a joust-at-arms?" demanded the Don.

"No."

"Did you ever see this Sebasitiano?"

"No."

"Then you do not know the utter foolishness of your ambition," said the Don.

The count fell back into the friendly folds of his hammock and lay there blinking and unable to speak.

Laughing solftly, the Dan sheathed his sword and again seated himself by the count.

"Fate plays strange tricks upon all of us, my dear count," he said, in a friendly tone of voice. "She has saved your life by twisting your shoulder, and placed in my way an extraordinary opportunity. Now listen very intently to what I have to say.

"It has long been my practice to prowl about, from place to place, preceding the Jousts, to find some intrepid fool to meet the invincible Sebastiano. You surely must realize, then, that no ordinary man, well informed of his prowess, would seek him as an adversary.

"Amor con amor se paga."

"It is impossible, now, for you to attempt to arrive at Madrid in time to enter the lists. You may not again participate in athletic feats for many months, in fact, it is well known, that, no champion has ever recovered his full confidence after having received a serious wound incapacitating him for a time. The whole muscular system shrinks from new dangers."

"La verdad es Amorga," moaned the count.

"It grieves me to have to admit that all you say is true. Surely misfortune frowns heavily upon me at a most inopportune time."

"Ah! but a fortuitous combination of circumstances cast me at your service, to turn ill fortune into good fortune for both of us," earnestly insisted the Don, "and, perhaps your comparitively simple hurt has saved your life for some useful purpose. Fate is no respecter of persons. To accomplish her ends, she smites a king as readily as she does a rustic."

"Como?" anxiously inquired the disappointed young man.

"I will make the matter clear to you. It so happens that, I have been unsuccessful in finding for Sebastiano an adversary for the coming tournament. He is not a rich man, and is beginning to feel indisposed to risk his life further in jousting, for the mere amusement of the nobility, and the pittance which he receives as his wage. He is like all public idols, an ordinary man in his revelries, having spent his money faster that he has earned it; hence, he is always the slave of some noble who lends him money in order that he may pose as his master, and bask in his popularity. He has reached the point where he must replenish his purse quickly. I can see the way by which you, a young and ambitious court favorite, may take back to Savoe the credit for having put in the dust this invincible hero. *"Perro que ladra no muerdi."* You may do this without risk. Sebastiano, for whom I may officially speak, will eagerly embrace the opportunity to reap a harvest of gold, to enable him to secretly retire to a comfortable country life which he craves."

"Quien todo lo quiere, todo lo pierde."

"But my honor, my good Don Alvard?"

"Your honor! No matter how fastidious your honor, did you now return to the Duke of Savoe with the woeful tale of having met with an accident, with not a scar on your person, you would be publicly branded as an arrant coward, and a shirker. Jealous rumor is cruel in its injustice. You could not take these farmers with you as your witnesses; you would be accused of having bribed them if you did. What I have to propose to you involves no risk, and assured success will return you to your native country the greatest hero in Europe."

"What is your proposal?" sullenly inquired the count.

"Does any one in Madrid know you?" asked the Don.

"No, it was my purpose to slip into Madrid and challenge Sebastiano under an assumed name," replied the count.

"And you speak of your honor. You have already compromised your honor in your own conscience. You do not know the Spanish idea of honor in the arena. In this circumstance, failure would not only mean your disgrace, but would forever bar your patron sponsor, the Duke of Savoe, from all the courts of Europe," said the Don, in apparent disgust.

"Yes, Señor, you are very right. I should sooner take my own life than be the cause of so great a calamity."

"My proposal is this. I shall select a suitable friend, in whom I have implicit confidence, and who is a stranger in Madrid, and have him enter the lists as the Count de Berrasta, the secret entry of the Duke of Savoe."

"No! No!" exclaimed the count. "I could not risk disgracing my good patron by a false entry, appearing openly in his name, and being defeated, therefore, I cannot delegate to you so hazardous a prerogative."

"Ha! Ha!" laughed the Don, as he strode back and forth. "Why, you yourself proposed doing exactly what you now condemn. You are bound, in any event, to forego the tournament, and return to Savoe with the lame excuse that you met with an accident. I propose to save you from this humiliation by selecting a substitute whose failure would be impossible. Even though should he fail through accident, your alibi is perfect. You could boldly repudiate the imposter and save your reputation, and protect that of your patron. *Cada oveja con su pareja.*"

The count half arose, in his surprise and demanded of the Don a full explanation of this astonishing proposition. Here was a master-plotter indeed. He had actually forced him into a compromise by his own foolish words which he had not seriously meant. The Don realized that the count was deeply impressed by his logic and he was filled with enthusiasm.

Suddenly pausing, and looking down upon the count with amusement twinkling in his eyes, he said:

"So you have never seen this fabulous Don Sebastiano? You would not know him did you meet him face to face?"

"No."

Don Alvard de Ricalde was himself again. His fertile brain had functioned, incubating and hatching a new and extraordinary adventure. It was now his purpose to drive it home in his usual unanswerable and dramatic style. Looking cunningly at the count, from beneath his shaggy brows, and with a sinister smile lurking about the folds of his battered cheeks he said to him, who now recognized in the Don a new and dangerous being, having especially noticed the long, white scar upon his face turn a livid purple.

"It is a strange coincidence that we should have met in this manner. You have enlisted my hearty interest and sympathy, and to no small extent, my affection, therefore, I shall confide in you as you have in me. I am Don Sebastiano in disguise."

The count attempted to arise, but the Don gently pressed him back upon the hammock.

"Calm yourself and listen. What I shall tell you is well worthy of your most careful consideration. You would have been wholly within the Spanish code had you entered Madrid *incognito* and challenged me to mortal combat. It is considered extremely smart, among the Spanish nobility, to dissemble, and even to cheat, in the games. No man

need consult his conscience in these matters. Honor?
Bah! But your failure in such circumstances would
have disgraced you. With an iron-clad alibi you can
turn identically the same trick, with absolute cer-
tainty of success. I will explain.

"Having hitherto found it embarrasing to enter
Madrid openly, because of my poverty, and inability
to provide for the usual personal pomp it demanded,
I am assuming a new role, entering as an itinerate
soldier of fortune seeking adventure. The present
king is a reveler, bringing to his court, on each such
occasion, his friends from Flanders, and he is better
entertained by a clown than by a pompous hero
whom he considers a rival in the public esteem. I
am thoroughly disgusted, and am ready to adopt
any measure which will enrich me and permit me
to retire from public life. I know that I am but a
mechanical part in these annual entertainments, I
not belonging to the nobility. The day I fall I will
not live even in memory. I find it necessary to devise new methods for keeping myself before the nobility, for the man does not live who can successfully
compete with me in the jousts—that is my only
specialty. Afoot, and unarmed, a boy could put me
hors du concours with a stone. Add to extraordinary strength, my tried skill and long experience,
and no school can turn out an athlete to successfully
compete with me, either with sword or jousting-
stick. It has so long been merely a courageous
sacrifice on the part of lovelorn youth, sent into the
arena by señoras who had grown tired of them,

my conscience accuses me of wanton distruction of human life. I am tired of the game. I now ask you if I do not look the part?"

Raising himself to his full height, the doughty cavilier expanded his huge chest, and stretched his ponderous arms heavenward, with every muscle of his mighty body rigid, revealing a terror in human form.

Count Berrasta, despite the pain the effort engendered, sat up in his hammock and stared in amazement at the new being before him, and fell back, exclaiming:

"Basta! es suficiente!"

The Don relaxed and looked down upon him, as a giant would look upon a sick child.

"Fate has been kind to only dislocate my shoulder," softly said the count. "I never dreamed that Don Sebastiano was such an extraordinary being."

Yes, Don Alvard had won; the count believed. The balance was a mere matter of details.

Bending over the stricken man, the cavalier frankly confessed:

"I am in the game for money. The days of glorious sacrifice, to make the world stand agape, or scream with hysterical excitement, have passed. They are all reaching out for the coin. Glory soon tarnishes when the jingle of gold does not accompany it. It is true, I am a poor man. I have spent my earnings upon those who praised me and made me a pawn in their political games. You are rich and noble. You can afford to buy the glory of a

public idol as you would buy rich jewels with which
to decorate your person. But, whether purchased,
or won in combat, it is the same tarnishing thing;
the same notoriety; the same public-applause,
which do not belong to a man who must clink his
wage into his hand as he counts it. It means nothing to me. The whole of Christendom is rank hypocrisy and fraud. There is not an honest fiber in
it. Together we can do that which will fatten us
with laughter for the balance of our lives. It is
a great amusement to fool those who are always
seeking new ways for fooling humanity. As for
these tournaments there is nothing honorable about
them; they are conducted by gambling noblemen
for their own selfish ends. I admire the precaution
of your Duke of Savoe; he is an astute man and
knows the truth.

"Like their bull fights, they are arranged to meet
the insatiable desire for blood by the Catholic fanatics, and for some novelty in cruelty, a little less
disgraceful than the public execution of human beings by burning at the stake in the presence of kings
and queens, of which Spain had more than enough
under the Angelic Catholic Isabella.

"It would afford me great satisfaction to eliminate myself from future participation in these
despicable and barbaric pastimes of kings. This
seems to be an inspiration. I can make for myself
a large sum of money, and assign to you the glory
of a great coup. If you are willing to take a chance
on that, I can put it through without a jiggle."

"What is your plot?" asked the count.

"I will go to Madrid and select a friend who will safely impersonate you. No one will know him. I will permit him to defeat me and we, both, will immediately take our departure from Madrid. I also will despatch to you a fresh horse to enable you to return to Savoe. You may remain *incognito* and not a living soul need identify you."

CHAPTER XX

THE STAFF OF JOVE

M ADRID, the capital city of the proud and haughty Spain, was just at this particular time writhing in the excitement of a great event.

Charles V, the beer guzzling Hapsburger, had concluded a treaty with Francis I of France, and the very Catholic populace was in the state of laughing and weeping hysteria customary on such national occasions. Formerly these exciting periods of mental stress had been duly relaxed by Queen Isabella, the ex-nun, by the public burning of human beings. But, the stench of burning flesh was not agreeable to the olafactory nerves of visiting Sovereigns from other countries, and this gruesome pastime gave place to the more delectable sensations of seeing men kill each other in deadly combat, and men kill bulls.

It so happened, that, the celebration of the happy peace pact between Spain and France was united with the great annual tournament, hence, Madrid was doubly enthralled.

The nobles were straining every nerve and spending a lot of money, in their desire to gain the good will of Charles V, who had never ceased grumping, because some of the nobles, disgusted with a king who was so lazy and indifferent he would not take the trouble to learn to speak the language of the people he was to rule, had openly snubbed him.

Charles had slipped into the battered old chair of the hapless Ferdinand, who had been cuffed about by his lovely tempered queen until he did not know whether he was king, soldier or gardener, coddling that preposterous Hapsburg belief of "divine appointment." Nevertheless, he left his heart and his manners in Flanders, where his rolicking friends cared more for ribauld song, and good company, than for statescraft.

Under the cunning influence of that mangy old cur, as Bambo called him, Cardinal Ximenez, the zealots, Ferdinand and Isabella, had come near to disrupting, and wiping out of existence, that national institution called the nobility of Spain, and with no visible benefits to the Spanish people, but a world of benefit to the Catholic church.

The indifferent Charles, not speaking or understanding the Spanish language, could not grasp the significance of this remarkable situation, mistaking the eagerness to please him, on the part of the nobility, as personal popularity.

On this rare occasion extensive preparations had been made for an extraordinary entertainment of many sovereigns of other nations who had accepted invitations to attend the festivities. All the world seemed to be sending delegations, and Madrid was mad with joyous expectation. The air was filled

with music and exciting chatter, and good-natured
jostling sometimes took on the aspect of jousting.

Frantic jesticulations, and loud conversation,
gathered excited crowds to hear the controversies
over the merits of entrants for coveted honors. This
attracted all attention, for this became the basis for
the wagering of everything the average Spaniard
possessed, to the very coat upon his back, the Spaniards being inveterate gamblers, whether a coarse
woolen surtout or a gold laced bit of vesture, it was
in pawn till the eventful day.

Today was the last day for *entroda,* and a great
crowd besieged the offices of the final *junta comision,*
or *deputacion,* which arranged the details and conduct
of the tournament.

Under these circumstances Don Alvard had boldly crossed the little Manzanares and entered Madrid.

A peculiar situation had arisen; there were several entries made for the jousts, easily recognized
as mere duels between rivals for the hand of some
fair but devilish Spanish maiden, therefore, they
were of minor importance. It was sorrowfully announced, that, no worthy opponent had been found
willing to do combat with the great public idol, Don
Sebastiano, the magnificent, the pet of all Spain,
and especially the favorite of all the amorous women.
At the mere mention of this calamity, groans were
heard on every hand, deploring this misfortune, for
he always killed, and Spain had been educated in
watching the throes of dying humanity. They had
anticipated feasting their eyes upon the glorious

Sebastiano in action. Such was the state of hero worship at that benighted, Christian period. Notoriety has posed as popularity in all ages of Christian enterprise and will be to the end—a notorious mountebank is vastly more important than a popular savant.

Don Alvard had managed to hold his faithful Belial together barely long enough to reach Madrid. There he was rudely informed that it was useless for him to attempt to enter the lists, they were closed. But that which set his blood boiling was the insulting treatment he received at the hands of the strutting servants hanging about. They finally succeeded in gathering the usual Spanish mob to banter and tease him to madness, but he kept his good temper, desiring if possible to get in touch with some higher authority.

He quietly went about securing a comfortable place for his exhausted nag, and dragged the bundle of bones and battered toggery into it, bribing the hostler to take good care of him, whispering that a cardinal had sainted Belial for extraordinary services in the Crusades.

Then the doughty warrior started looking for trouble. After many rebuffs, and much difficulty, he managed to force his way to the attention of an under secretary. With a few pieces of silver, and some whispered conversation, he bribed his way higher, finally finding himself the butt of a jeering assembly of Spanish Grandees who had given him audience only because of the secretary's comic description of him.

While he was openly insulted, he took it good-naturedly, although grinding inside his tattered hauberk with deep and savage resentment. He well knew that only mild and unsophisticated manners would win him recognition. He could bide his time to make these smart boobs apologize, within their own hearts at least. His was a big game, and he must play it well, his time of triumph would come.

The room in which he stood for his lathering was the great *museo* of Arms of the Arena, the walls on every side being gridded with the pikes, spears and swords of fallen aspirants and heroes, who had entered the arena that, *"once too often,"* known to athletic sports.

His glance had swept the array of past misfortunes without fear. He was deeply impressed, however, by one tremendous shaft, twenty feet in length and he wondered what giant could have poised this gigantic weapon in battle.

The Grandees were justified in their making sport of this seeming derelict of the desert. He was one mass of dust, from crown to foot; he had walked until no soles remained attached to his tattered buskins, which were now twisted awry about his scrawny shanks. The mass of ragged chain stuff, half covering his body, could not be dignified by the name of vesture, leathern patchings having wholly disguised the original design. A pair of warped and twisted tin breeches, as hard and brittle as sheet

steel, encased his log-like limbs. His hair was matted like tangled wires, and his face bristled with
a stubby growth of beard. His whole appearance
resembled some strange type of cave-man, disguised
in ancient toggery, resembling nothing these gentlemen had ever seen before.

His battered, visorless bonnet, with its pathetic
plume drooping down upon his shoulders, was placed
at an angle to give his face the appearance of being warped from its normal position, the long scar
adding to this delusion.

The committee was awaiting the arrival of the
king's personal representative and friend, the rich,
noble and powerful Duke de Arraza. His word
was final in all matters particularly interesting to
the king's party, and the nobles who were so fortunate as to openly boast of the favor of the eccentric Charles.

The displeasure of the king, that, no man in his
kingdom would sacrifice his life for his amusement,
by meeting the idol of the arena, Don Sebastiano,
had been heralded abroad to inspire the sycophant
fools, but none had come forward to the sacrifice.
Consequently, the whole national festival was gloom-
ing, the committees were grumpy and the populace
was making sport of them.

The displeasure of a king was something to be
dreaded, often taking uncanny turns. Charles was
likely to go back to Flanders with his own friends
and leave the invited guests to be entertained by
the disgruntled nobles. A national scandal threat-

ened.   This was the feverish situation when the
Don appeared.

The Duke was in a rage when he entered the
committee room, but, upon observing the uncouth
giant standing meekly before his jeering colleagues,
he was struck with a sense of awe and interest.

"*¿Que es eso?*" he exclaimed.

Don Alvard's sature seemed to rise up an extra
foot, as his body straightened and his inner resentment prodded him.

A Spaniard can be insolent in any utterance,
if he chooses to be, and the attitude of this pompous person was most offensive to the sensitive Don.
Nevertheless, he gulped down his anger and held
his temper.

The Grandees were laughing uproarously, merely hoping to appease the Duke.

"*¡Silencio!*" he commanded.

Motioning to Count Sclassa, who was coldly
looking on, he whispered a few words of conversation and then motioned for Don Alvard to follow
them into an inner chamber.

"Señor, be good enough to tell us your mission;
have you any specialty which would recommend
you to us?   And the Duke bent a friendly face upon
the Don, placing him more at ease.

"Not meaning to be offensive, may I speak freely
in the presence of a third person?" and the Don
bowed politely toward Count Sclassa.

"The count is my most confidential associate
and friend," replied the Duke.

"Permit me, then, to say, I am not the clown I look," proudly said the Don. "I am master-at-arms of the old school, seeking new opportunities to exercise my skill. I bear, here, the ring of the Duke of Savoe. I am the Count Berrasta, of Savoe, come to participate in your tournament as an entrant of my noble patron, provided I may find a spot which may enable me to carry back to him evidence of some small credit."

The Duke and the Count both laughed.

"Your noble patron is timid, or else he is sending to us a surprise—and I suspect the latter, therefore, Señor, if we pit our wit against his, you will abide by the consequences?"

"You will find me willing to abide by your imposts. I must stand or fall upon my own merits in any event. The responsibility of taking defeat and shame back to my patron rests solely with me," replied Don Alvard with dignity.

"Esta muy bien," said the Duke, cautiously glancing at the count. Then continuing, he asked of Don Alvard.

"What experience have you had in jousting?"

"None whatever. I have never even witnessed a joust-at-arms ahorse," he frankly replied.

"That is much to be regretted, for we have open but one number which would seem to challenge skill and apparent great strength," said the Duke.

"¿Que es eso?" inquired the Don.

Ignoring this question, the Duke asked:

"Do you know of the prowess of our Don Sebastiano in the jousts?'"

"I have heard the report that he is a most formidable man-at-arms," replied the Don.

"He is thought to be invincible, hence, we have
not found an opponent for him in this tournament,
much to the displeasure of the king. We have invited several distinguished, royal guests to attend
our festival and we are now confronted by real disaster, because we can find no Spanish gentleman
brave enough to face our Sebastiano. Such a man
could make himself rich and famous in a day should
he, by accident, defeat him." There was a note
of eagerness in the Duke's voice, quickly discerned
by Don Alvard.

"I am more interested in the riches, what would
such a contest yield?" asked the Don.

"If his adversary failed he would have no use
for money. But, if he succeeded in mastering the
mighty Sebastiano, he could revel in wealth and
fame," said the Duke, and Count Sclassa nodded
approval, both exhibiting unfeigned eagerness.

The Don laughed, a soft amused chuckle, and
asked:

"And if I engage to toss his body into your box?"

There was that air of self-confidence in the Don's
manner to cause the Duke to look sharply at him
for a moment before asking:

"Have you the slightest reason for believing that
you could best Sebastiano?"

Don Alvard rose to his full height, stretched forth his great arms and proudly said:

"I am physically the most powerful man in all Europe. I am an invincible swordsman, having bested a dozen men in a single bout. The man does not live who can master me in any game of strength, skill, agility or wit-at-arms, on foot or ahorse. Were it permissable, I could take my common fighting-iron and best the terrible Sebastiano with his coat of mail and jousting stick."

So vehement was this utterance, it brought Duke de Arraza and Count Sclassa to their feet in admiration, half alarm.

"Muy bien! muy bien!" they exclaimed.

"With your pardon," said the Duke to Don Alvard, and he drew the count aside, and, for a few minutes, they conversed earnestly.

Returning to the Don the Duke asked:

"What suitable accoutrement have you for such an encounter?"

"My naked skin and my fighting-iron."

The Duke shook his head disappointedly.

"I have a plan," said Don Alvard. "I am a plain spoken man. Within your hearts you desire this Sebastiano to bite the dust—"

The Duke frowned, raised his hand, saying:

"Mas bajo."

Don Alvard also raised his hand and continued "—therefore, the greater his humiliation, the greater will be your satisfaction. I am not looking for glory, I need money. I am familiar with all of the weak

points of athletics, and I know men. This Sebastiano
is a stickler for the pretty and spectacular features
of jousting, and looks to the ladies for the applause.
I have heard it said he is a 'lady-killer,' as much
as he is a man-killer, the very things to overawe
and make slow his quaking opponents. Confront
him with something unusual and abnormal and his
confusion will offset his skill, giving a less experienced but cool headed man an opportuniuty to take
quick advantage of his uncertainty. It requires but
a single false move, on his part, to give the opening
I would desire.

"He feels secure in his popularity, and I warn
you, it is the fear of this very overwhelming popularity, that has prevented your finding an opponent
to meet him—not the fear of the man. He who de-
feats the public idol must flee the wrath of the mob.
A popular idol falls hard and begets a mob quickly.
It is popular equality that makes it safe for men
to meet each other in contests of skill. Favoritism
is a tremendous weapon for the man who receives
it in a contest—"

Again both the Duke and the Count were on their
feet, and now stood admiringly before Don Alvard.

"My dear Count Berrasta, you have truly worn
your disguise well, to conceal your real identity. You
are a student of men, and a philosopher, as well as
a giant man-at-arms. You invoke our highest admiration."

"And I will humble your proud Sebastiano,"
modestly said the Don.

"We respectfully solicit your views as to the best way to accomplish this, we must make no mistakes," said the Duke.

"It is simple," replied the Don, feeling himself on equal terms with them in the enterprise. "I must be treated as the fool I now appear to be, before the whole committee. I must be bantered and teased, making myself a sacrifice to the ravenous Sebastiano through my own perverse anger. I will become boastful. I will point to the great stick upon the *museo* wall, naming it the 'jousting stick of Jove,' and declare, that, if I am permitted to use this staff, I will appear in the arena naked to my waist, and riding a jack-ass, and I will conquer the pretty hero. I will cast upon the table all the money I have, a hundred pieces of silver, and offer to wager it that I will do all this. You will quickly take the cue that a great farce can be made of the joust, whisper it about and then call my proposition. Then quickly adjourn your committee meeting and scatter broadcast the huge joke to be perpetrated. Prevail upon Sebastiano to accede to your plans, especially to enter the arena in the manner I have suggested."

"And if you fail?" softly asked the Duke.

"You will have provided a show for your king, and won sufficient money to give me a decent burial," doggedly replied the Don, and the Duke looked at him with sympathy—it was his own proposition.

"But, if I succeed, provision must be made to meet that contingency. How much money am I guaranteed should I succeed?"

"More than you can carry away with you," whispered the Duke, and the Count acquiesced. "When you offer your wager, I will make the proposition that the committee cover each piece of your money with one hundred similar pieces; the count will place this money in suitable form for you to take your quick departure, for I fully agree with your opinion that your grotesque defeat of Sebastiano would be taken as an affront; a mob does not reason."

They now returned to the outer room where the committee had been impatiently awaiting them.

With a sly, insinuating smirk, the Duke glanced at the sullen, half angry Don and carelessly remarked, as he examined some papers lying upon a table:

"We have found a worthy opponent for the admirable Don Sebastiano, but he has no suitable accoutrement; in fact he has never even witnessed a joust-at-arms," and, with a shrug of seeming contempt, he seated himself at the table as though through with the matter.

Suddenly, like a roaring lion, Don Alvard flung out his arm, and pointing to the great staff on the wall, exclaimed:

"Allow me to take that jousting staff of Jove, and I will go into the arena naked to my waist, and on the back of a jack-ass, and humble your pretty hero. Here! all the money I possess, one hundred pieces, will I wager on this challenge," and he cast the silver upon the table.

Uproarous laughter was checked by the Duke,

who, with seemingly injured pride, confronted the Don, and leaning forward he said:

"Stranger, ordinarily, it would be unbecoming Spanish gentlemen to bandy words with a man of your uncouth appearance, but you have made a gesture intimating that we are weaklings. This we cannot permit to pass unnoticed. Your intimation that our grand Sebastiano can be humbled by a common swashbuckler is an insult which only Sebastiano himself may punish, therefore, this committee accepts your challenge, exactly as you have made it, and it places on every coin you have cast upon this table, one hundred similar pieces. This is our wager against yours, that you cannot make good your loud boasts, and that you cannot meet Sebastiano in the arena and come out alive. The money you here wager will be sufficient to bury you.

"We, as a committee, with full authority, waive all rules which this extraordinary transaction contravenes. It remains for us to pursuade the proud and noble Sebastiano to forgive the insult which we put upon him by resenting it in the arena. It will be amazing if he submits himself to such unheard of ridicule.

The universal approval of this arrangement was voiced by the committee, as the money rattled upon the table to cover the Don's wager. The Count Sclassa acting as treasurer.

A broad smile extended the lines in Don Alvard's face as he watched the angry, excited committee count out their money.

"And when shall I know that my terms are acceptable to Señor Don Sebastiano?" he calmly inquired.

"Before you leave this room," sharply replied the Duke.

"And in the name of what fair lady do I enter the arena?

A roar of laughter was the first response, but Count Carpendo exclaimed:

"Why not the Countess Charlotte de Gabriella? If this farce is to be, let's make it complete."

Don Alvard recognized this name as one anciently applied to a character selected to figure the common people, in a contest in which the nobles usually lost—a mere sop to the mob. The selection for the character usually was an aged and homely charwoman. She was painted and dressed according to the social custom.

Here was a new situation. The Duke and Count Sclassa looked covertly at each other. There was such a thing as carrying a joke too far. The cunning Charles had not abandoned the common people, neither had he openly embraced the nobles. Should this uncouth stranger conquer Sebastiano in the name of the commoners, it would be most offensive to the official class, including many sycophant nobles, and these could convert the unthinking rabble into a vengeful mob, on the excuse, that, the laboring class had been borrowed as a cloak under which to smuggle into the arena this disguised

giant, to humiliate Sebastiano and his strong political following.

All of this had to be quickly considered.

"When may I have the pleasure of meeting the
charming countess, that I may give her assurance
that I shall lay my laurels at her feet?" asked Don
Alvard.

After a hearty laugh, there was whispered con-
sultations, and, then, the Don, alias the Count Berrasta, was informed that the countess, with several
other distinguished ladies, would hold a reception
for his especial benefit at high noon on the following day, in the committee room. Two hours later
he must be in readiness for the joust.

A comfortable room was assigned to the distinguished Count de Berrasta, and instructions issued to give him all the food and drink and other
personal comforts he required.

The Don, true to his habits, went to where Belial
was stabled and made quite certain that his comrade
was well provided for. St. Belial was equally profuse in greeting his master, almost telling him that
he had the key to the oats bin, the Don's money having established this favor. This was not, however,
the principal object of his visit to the hostler. He
desired a large, strong ass to be ready for his service
and he liberally provided the hostler with money
with which to procure such an animal. Moreover,
he arranged to have Belial fully accoutred and ready
for travel, immediately following the encounter with
Sebastiano. Having made this precautionary ar-

rangement, the Don returned to his own quarters, had his head tonsored and his face shaved, then took a refreshing plunge in a pool of water. He ate a hearty meal, with little wine, retired to his comfortable couch and slept for twelve hours. Partaking of a light breakfast, he again made a secret visit to his hostler, patted Belial upon the cheek and asked for his pack, from which he selected all that he required for the show. First he laid out his dress of a gentleman, the friendly hostler taking the garments to his own wife to have them put in order. Then he laid out the toggery which he was to don for his encounter with Sebastiano, his tin breeches, his tattered buskins, his battered bonnet, with its pathetic plume, and his tremendous saddle. These he placed in order, with full instructions to the deeply interested hostler, handing him a handful of coins with instructions to wager them on the fall of Sebastiano.

It had been discretely whispered about, that, a great comedy was to be enacted in the arena, because of the unfortunate circumstance that no worthy man-at-arms, with the temerity to meet the great Sebastiano in combat, had been found. The whole city was in a hubbub of excited expectation, and was laughing in advance, at the huge joke.

At noon a committee of gentlemen, with suppressed merriment, waited upon the doughty Count de Barrasta to inform him that a committee of distinguished Spanish Duchesses and Countesses awaited him, constituting the ladies committee on entertainment.

To their utter undoing a Spanish gentleman of distinguished personality greeted them with the assurance that it was a part of his life's mission to please the ladies, bidding them lead the way to where they awaited him.

He was conducted to the committee room where some dozen giggly Spanish noble-women had been "let in on the secret."

The tittering ceased immediately upon the introduction of the distinguished man, who exhibited all the poise and polish of a gentleman.

Upon being introduced to the Countess de Gabriello, he readily observed, by her discomposure, and the antics and conduct of the other ladies, that she, as well as himself, were mere victims of a great hoax.

She was a woman of perhaps sixty years of age, and, undoubtedly, the homliest woman in Spain. The Don treated her with the greatest courtesy and defference, assuring her that her cause would be well defended, and, that, she should not blush to sit in her box, for she should witness the humiliating defeat of his adversary.

Stepping to the wall, he lifted from its resting place the huge "Staff of Jove," of unknown origin, and weighing one hundred pounds, wielding it as a riding master might play with his whip, he gracefully bowed himself from the presence of the ladies.

Every person in that room realized that tragedy

had displaced comedy in this tournament, and they went forth in a state of wonderment, to see the fatal denouement.

Had Jove, himself, stepped down from heaven and thus carried away his ponderous staff, it would have created no greater consternation.

The Duke Arraza and Count Sclassa expressed equal surprise as they looked knowingly at each other and caught an intelligent glance from the cool and collected cavalier as he strode away with the great weapon.

"Something startling is going to happen," whispered the Duke, as the party dispersed to meet in the arena.

CHAPTER XXI

THE FIGHTING CLOWN

HE WHO DISSEMBLES CONFUSES HIS OPPONENT

MADRID, like a painted vampire, was smirking and smiling at Europe. Feeling the secret slurs aimed at Spain, because an indifferent Hapsburg had impudently crept upon her throne, she was straining every point to make it appear that she was again in the full swing of her joyous life. Music was being drilled into all Spain. Athletics were being revived, and the greatest emphasis was being put upon her exploitations in the new world. She was determined to rise above political criticism.

Never before had the annual tournament at Madrid been so elaborately advertised.

Never before had the arena been so elaborately decorated for the great popular entertainment, now coupled with a graver cause for joy.

Such throngs had never before besieged her gates. It seemed like a siege, with all Europe clamoring for admittance. Yes, Madrid was at her best, in full gala dress, and breathing excitement and expectation; the very air was full of suppressed mystery; everybody was softly inquiring of everybody else what it was. The propaganda had been so adroitly broadcasted, the whole populace was on the tiptoe of expectation.

This tense situation had a tendency to soften the usual ribauld swagger and boisterous arguments which had previously been noticeable. Cheerful good nature prevailed during the early morning hours while throngs awaited the opening of the arena gates.

At nine o'clock all that could be jammed into the great show place had been admitted, with angry thousands left standing without.

The contests were on, the uproar and applause could be heard for miles, old heroes fell, and new ones were welcomed by the throngs, in mighty salvos of applause. When the old idols successfully defended their titles, they received the greater applause and their defeated opponents were correspondingly jeered—there is small pity in a mob.

The Royal box of King Charles was surrounded by the boxes of the nobility of all Spain and Portugal, who entertained the royal and noble visitors from the other nations. This was the most elaborate entertainment of its kind ever attempted by any nation of people.

Visiting strangers, from throughout Europe, were thoughtfully provided for—Madrid was flaunting her glory.

As hour pressed upon hour, with each minute making new gladitorial history, the maddening throng howled itself hoarse, and perspired itself into an exhaustive lather. From sheer fatigue, excessive enthusiasm began to lag. Manifest impatience for the main event began to possess the crowds. Great interest was now centered upon a commotion about the royal box on which all eyes were at once riveted. Rich draperies were drawn aside displaying a splendidly decorated box. A royal parade was passing the king. All the nobles and even the king himself arose and saluted a distinguished personage being conducted to her box.

An arch was raised above the box with an inscription wrought in roses.

"Countess Charlotte de Gabriello
whose lover has challenged the great Sebastiano to mortal combat."

The secret was out. So, this was the cause of all the suppressed excitement?

When this fabulous name appeared it meant a farce. Politically, it was a sop to the laboring masses.

As the countess was conducted into her box, by a retinue of Grandees, with all the pomp and rigor due a queen, the throngs were convulsed with uproarous laughter.

The farce was always good naturedly tolerated as a compliment to the common people, taking much of the stiffness out of the entertainment usually evident when the king was present. Not infrequently, too, the laurels were placed at the feet of the chosen countess, who, as a rule, was a very aged and homely woman.

It had been reported, that, no suitable opponent had been found to face Sebastiano, therefore, to make him a part of this farce was an extraordinary thing, for he was a pompous and proud character. Little did the light hearted people dream, that, an overshadowing tragedy hovered back of the scenes of their mirth inspiring farce that day—the most astonishing reversal of the Spanish arena ever recorded.

From nowhere a Jove was to step into the arena and bid their idol dismount and lick the dust.

Up to the last moment the conqueror was treated with derision and contempt.

A trumpet blast announced the arrival of the mighty moment when the fun would begin, and the audience was on the *qui vive*.

At the first trumpet sound a richly appointed esquire rode into the arena and took his position as standard bearer for the noble Sebastiano. He wore the chain armor of the twelfth century, to distinguish between that period and the up-to-date man-at-arms, which Sebastiano portrayed.

Then, a curious thing occurred. A common man, in the clothes of an ordinary workman of Madrid, strode into the arena, paused and saluted the king's box, then approached the box occupied by the Countess de Gabriello, bowed lowly, touching one knee to the ground, and spread upon the railing of the box the ragged and faded royal robe of Don Alvard de Ricalde, who was masquerading as Count Berrasta.

As the eyes of the great throng viewed this ancient purple, now drab with age, and pathetic in its tattered gold lace, a strange silence fell. It resembled too much the draping of a bier. This solemnity smelled of the unexpected, with no adequate forecast of the nature of the surprise. An ominous quiet prevailed; the whole act was too pathetic and real to be a joke. Even the nobles temporarily ceased their chatter and their gorgeous fans ceased to flutter, as they craned their necks in anticipation.

The trumpet sounded the call for the gladiators to enter the arena and take their positions.

Sebastiano! The magnificent Sebastiano; favorite of the king! idol of the people!

Like a tidal wave the vast assembly arose *en masse*, and its welcome was like a roar of thunder.

Like death ahorseback, the haughty hero proudly entered, the epitome of all that was powerful and impressive in the mighty game of jousting—a grim glittering glory—yet a deadly thing.

A blanket of black but shimmering mail encompassed his black palfrey, whose every motion was a well trained pose. From his alert ears to his silver-shod hoofs he was protected.

His was the up-to-date accoutrement; saddle with high pommel and cantle, new for the occasion, and silver mounted trappings. As the master sat in this saddle, with *guarde-cuisse* almost covering his thigh and leg, he was practically glued to his steed. To lift him out of his seat was to tear him limb from limb, and also to rend his hauberk of plate with its plate sleeves and gauntlets—the last word in armor, the ground work being black to match the trappings of his palfrey.

His polished bonnet was provided with a solid visor of steel, and a jaunty tuft of yellow cock-feather decorated its crown prettily nodding with every motion of the head. The lance was of beautifully carved, flexible wood, inlaid and embellished with silver, gold and mother of pearl. It was heavy and long, with the semi-blunted point in vogue at that period.

He looked proud and handsome as he slowly rode to the front of the king's box and gravely bowed, his every attitude meeting with loud acclaim.

Suddenly he stood high in his stirrups, raised his visor and looked long and interestedly at the ragged *manto* draped across the box of the Countess de Gabriello. Whirling his charger, he galloped, at full tilt, toward his esquire; snatched his banner from his hand, and dashed back to the king's box where he planted the staff in the ground. This was all full of grace and tragic effect. The audience rent the air with shouts of approval.

As he now slowly returned to his position, master and horse seemed cast as one. An awed hush fell upon the assembly. Pity, seldom expressed by an excited mass of people, seemed to manifest itself in this silence. It was like wanton murder to pit any human being against this invincible machine of death. This did not last for long however, for the Spaniards were lovers of blood.

The trumpet again sounded, reminding the audience that Sebastiano's challenger was keeping the

king waiting. Why had he not obeyed the first call
—this was next to treason.

No bold and defiant knight, with glittering armor and gaudy plume, had brazenly made his appearance. Why?

The Assembly was on edge and was beginning
to exhibit impatience.

Without warning, and from an unexpected quarter, there burst upon the scene the most uncanny,
and at the same time the most comical, thing that
had ever before been seen in the Spanish arena.
So great was the surprise and consternation, the
whole assembly was agape, the nobles rising in their
boxes in actual alarm, excitedly jostling and whispering, seeking to understand this uncouth spectre.

Then the reaction came; pity was cast to the
winds, and a mighty roar rent the air. This was
a clown. Why, of course, it was all a joke, so clev-
erly arranged, it came as a tremendous surprise.
Only a big, funny play. Ha! Ha! No one was to
be slain.

Don Alvard dashed into the arena astride a big,
black jack-ass. He was naked to the waist, his
nether limbs being clad in his warped and twisted
tin breeches. Cocked on one side of his head was
his battered bonnet with its broken plume fantastically dancing in the air. His ugly stirrup cuffs,
with their huge rosettes, seemed likely to fall off
at any moment, while his flapping sandals swept
up the dust about him. Ye Gods! what a sight he
was to that fastidious gathering. Satan himself

could not have created greater consternation had
he appeared in person.

A new sensation was aroused upon realizing that
this grotesque figure was a man seven feet tall, and,
that, he was belaboring his mule with the butt end
of a hundred pound shaft as a riding master would
use an ordinary riding whip.

The audience was crazy with delight at these
thrills, until it had observed this phenomenon. This
feature was no joke. A murmur of amazement was
heard, but that did not trouble Don Alvard, he was
having too much trouble with his mule to care what
the mob thought, and he lathered the animal's ribs
with his giant slap-stick.

After much maneuvering he succeeded in bringing his mount to the king's box where he made a
profound salute. In mock courtesy the nobles arose
and acknowledged his salute to encourage the farce.

The Don forced his mule to the box of the Countess de Gabriello, bowed and then rode to his position.

A trumpet call brought the combatants to arms.

It was afterwards reported that the unfortunate
Sebastiano had remarked, upon observing these
strange things, that he had not engaged to fight the
devil. This caused the Duke de Arraza to recall
the remarks of Don Alvard, that, the unusual made
the glorified hero hesitate.

The audience could not believe otherwise than,
that, this intrepid man was making a willing sacrifice of his life, and, that, he was doomed to die at

the hands of the skilled and trained fighting machine. It was little prepared for what happened a moment later.

The charge was sounded; the fateful moment had come, and the audience ceased breathing till the impact was heard and felt, a groan of horror following.

At the bid of his master, Sebastiano's eager palfrey half arose in the air, to give greater impetus to the charge; the master leaned gracefully forward, poised his weapon, and came like an avalanche toward the pitiful Don Alvard, whose stubborn mount was trying to turn tail and go in the opposite direction. But, by sheer force of legs and staff, he brought him about, and he took an unexpected notion to run forward, spurting toward Sebastiano, whose charger now towered above them like a smothering cloud. The mule decided to sit down upon his haunches. It was a thousand to one, that, Don Alvard's fate was sealed, when, like a streak of lightning, the twenty foot staff of Jove shot upward into the air, before the black palfrey could bring his master down to the level to give the stroke. Catching Sebastiano beneath the right arm, it literally ripped him loose from the saddle, impaling him dangling in mid air. The impact was so terrific it forced the beautiful steed back upon his haunches, and then sprawling upon the earth, and rolling over on his side in the dust, where he lay groaning, as though he, too, had received a mortal wound.

The assembly, now, standing, was stunned for a

brief moment, then burst into an uproar—but it was not ended. The encounter had occurred directly in the front of the box occupied by Duke de Arraza and his friends. As in the days of yore, when he pitched great fork-fulls of hay onto the stack, the Don kept his word with the Duke, and, much to his consternation, and danger to those in his box, the Don gave a dexterous turn to his staff and tossed this human husk into their midst, setting them scrambling and dodging for safety.

The tuft of cock feathers had dropped from Sebastiano's proud bonnet and now lay in the dust. The Don picked it up, flicked off the dust, strode to the box of the Countess de Gabriello, and, with a ponderous bow, presented the plume to her. She extended her hand to him; he kissed it, cast his purple *manto* over his naked shoulders and started to leave the arena, when someone leaped over the railing and placed a laurel wreath about his scrawny neck. He acknowleded this token with a profound bow, as he recognized his loyal hostler.

The entrance of Don Alvard into the arena was comical in its absurdity, but the strangest sight that Madrid had ever beheld, was to see this mediaeval giant striding away, leading his jack-ass and trailing the staff of Jove, with his scrawny neck encircled by the laurel badge of a conquering hero, with thousands of voices shouting and screaming in a veritable bedlam.

Don Alvard had a mind as big as his body; he was as much a philosopher as a warrior. He had warned Duke Arraza, that, the defeat of Sebastiano would be resented. He had quickly caught the discordant note of the fanatical Spanish mob, above the loud applause, the inspired mob of cultivated fanaticism, the fruits of the fiendish policy of Isabella. The Spanish blood was saturated with it. It had developed from the burning in public of ten thousand innocent people, and the driving out of Spain of, perhaps, a million more.

Being wise to this, the new champion was not going to remain and argue with the mob, but headed for the shortest way out of Madrid. He had not forgotten, however, that he had committeed himself to another important mission, and it was his desire to discharge this duty before leaving the city, but, just how he was now to accomplish this, with safety to himself, in the extraordinary circumstances, puzzled him.

The Duke de Arraza was a gentleman of his word. He, too, knew what was likely to happen should the Don defeat Sebastiano, therefore, he had selected two trusted servants to have Belial properly accoutred, doubled the amount of the Don's winnings and presented him with a splendidly equipped palfrey to enable him to travel more rapidly.

The Duke and the count were gleefully awaiting the Don to bid him adieu.

"You have done me a great favor, my good Count Berrasta. I cannot tell you now, but, I hope I may have the honor of meeting you again when the people forget. It is urgent for you to hasten."

Drawing the Duke aside the Don whispered:

"I regret my time is so limited, for I had a most urgent matter about which I desired to consult with you, and beg your advice."

The Duke hesitated for a moment, then said:

"Ride away with my servants who will safely conduct you out of the city. I will instruct them and follow after you, overtaking you as soon as I am free to do so."

The Don was soon away, accompanied by two armed escorts. When nightfall overtook them, they rode into a splendid hunting lodge where they were snugly ensconced for the night.

A fine old Spaniard and his wife prepared an excellent meal for the tired men, and they went over the events of the tournament. The Don was a hero with these people, because they belonged to the Duke de Arraza.

About midnight horsemen were heard to arrive at the place, and the Don quickly recognized the Duke's voice and waited patiently for him to announce himself.

With a flagon of good wine before them, they went into immediate conference.

"This is my hunting lodge," said the Duke, "and I heartily welcome you to its comforts, but, my good Don, it will greatly oblige me if you can permit me to take my departure from here tonight, that I may ride back to Madrid at once. I have come at your urgent solicitation."

"I cannot thank you too much for this favor," replied the Don. "I shall be brief."

He related to the Duke the story of Rizzi. I want to restore this property to the Rizzi family," he said.

"Have you formulated any plan of procedure?" asked the Duke, looking keenly at the Don.

"Yes, providing I may arrange matters so I may deal directly with the usurpers without state interference," replied the Don.

"And, in the event of such protection, what action would you take?" asked the Duke.

"I should go there in person, if need be, taking Rizzi with me, and we would take possession without permitting this fact to become known," was the reply.

"I understood you to say you were from Savoe," said the Duke.

The Don then frankly identified himself.

The Duke listened with silent interest, gravely nodding his head and staring intently, first at the floor, then at the ceiling.

"And you found my er-er. You found Don Carlos Rizzi a prisoner there and brought him away?" mused the Duke.

"Yes."

"And, now, without making any inquiry, you propose to seize this property in the name and interest of Rizzi. Is this a logical procedure?"

"On the contrary, I was advised to hasten away from Madrid, by yourself, before I could make such inquiry. I am now seeking advice from you, whom I know to be a responsible and honorable man. This is the first advice I have sought. I have not committed myself to any personal action in the matter, not even to Rizzi. Moreover, my good Duke, I desire you to know me as a man of broad, worldly experience, and not as a poverty stricken swashbuckler, as you playfully suggested. I am accustomed to using due discretion, having an accurate knowledge of myself, I seldom err in my judgment. I feel convinced that I may place inmplicit confidence in you, and I assure you that my future plans will be wholly governed by the advice I receive from you," and the Don paused.

"My good friend, Don Alvard de Ricalde, I am informed by high authority, that, you are the most dangerous character in all Europe. You do not seem surprised that I mention this report."

The Don's face was overspread with his big smile as he boldly looked directly into the Duke's sober and serious face, saying:

"You have some evidence of the truth of this rumor."

"I do not refer to your physical prowess or achievements," said the Duke.

"Let us not finesse, either we must be friends or enemies. You have called me friend, therefore, I shall assume that you prefer this attitude. Neither, I am sure, will do the other a wilful injustice, if we continue to deal as man to man. I have reasons for preferring that you be my friend, since you have already been my benefactor," and the Don's earnestness greatly moved the Duke, who quickly responded.

"You speak well. Don Alvard, I shall have to have extraordinary reasons for doubting your honor. Nevertheless, if your true character must be gauged by the reports of your powerful enemies, you must be a very evil man. Do you know one Francis Borgia?"

"A grim and sinister smile gave a new aspect to the Don's face. The seam across his cheek slowly assumed a livid hue. The Duke was startled at the effect of his own words upon the giant. Where he had been suave and pleasing in his manners, he now fairly bristled with exuding venom.

"Permit me to answer your question by asking one of you, Duke Arraza. Is Borgia listed as your friend?"

The Duke quickly replied:

"I am not aware that Francis Borgia is listed as anyones friend, and I hasten to assure you that I do not choose my friends of Satan's followers. Borgia is not on my calling list."

"Well said," responded the Don. "Beware of the man who pretends to be neutral. I class as enemies all men whom I cannot openly announce as my friends."

"But you do not say whether you consider Borgia a friend or foe," urged the Duke.

"I have no scruples to prevent my frankly acknowledging that I have never come in personal contact with Borgia, but I have encountered his agents and I judge the man by his company. I do not class them as among my friends."

"We may now speak without reserve," replied the Duke. "If for no other reason than, that, you are opposed to Borgia, I prefer to name you my friend, for Borgia and I are open enemies. We may be useful to each other."

"But you are a Catholic," said the Don.

"Yes, as a matter of form. All Spaniards are Catholics. But I have no respect for the religious pretensions of the church of Rome. I am not a fanatic."

"That is quite sufficient," responded the Don.

"And, now, I have something amazing to tell you, Don Alvard. Don Carlos Rizzi is my nephew. It was I who suggested sending him to the nitrate mine, and I have been much provoked that he has made no reports to me, or returned to tell the condition of the mine, which had ceased to pay profits. Whereas, it had long previously been a source of large income to the Rizzi estate. In few words you have explained it all to me. I shall reciprocate your friendly interest by relieving you of further trouble in the matter, unless, of course, you have a personal desire to participate. I am in a position to assist my nephew in the restoration of his rights in this property. You may suggest such compensation as you think due you for the good services

which you have rendered in his behalf.   I shall
gladly recompense you without question."

Don Alvard thanked him for thus relieving him
of an irksome obligation, assuring him that no compensation was due him.   He requested of the Duke
that he express his compliments to Rizzi, urging
also quick action to prevent Don Miguel's leaving
the mine.

"And now, my friend, let us speak a little more
of Borgia," said the Don.   "What is he doing in
Spain?"

"He is attempting to establish the Spanish inquisitorial system in a wide spread secret espionage,
to destroy all opposition to the church," said the
Duke.

"He is not wholly meeting with success because
of the suspicion, that, his contemplated organization seeks to seize upon the new world as a separate
organization," suggested the Don.

"Ah! tell me this.   I have heard such rumors,"
eagerly exclaimed the Duke.

"It may be easily explained," said the Don.
"Leo being a Medici naturally refused to lend his
approval.   Clement being a Medici naturally follows Leo's precedents, hence he does not recognize
the new order.

"Does the Medici group hold so strong a grip
upon the sacred college and Italy?" asked the Duke.

"Yes, it is quite true, that, a Medici or one representing the Medici faction will long hold the pon-

tifical throne, which is wholly controlled by church politics."

"Should I send to Rome a strong representation against Francis Borgia, would it have the friendly attention of the Pope?" asked the Duke.

"Clement is not given to enthusiastic support of private quarrels, but readily listens to any complaint against persons who threaten encroachment upon his prerogatives. The church is playing for control of Borgia's enterprise because it has to do with the secret acquisition of vast territories in America. Hence, openly, Borgia is supposed to be very close to the Pope, but enmity secretly stands between them.

"Clement is of an extremely jealous nature; his weakest point being his own family. His chief ambition is to restore to his own house the ascendency over Italy through the power of the church. Leo designed for his nephew the sovereignty of Tuscany, and for his brother the kingdom of Naples. Through his master stroke of absolving Louis XII from the anathemas of a vicious Julius II, Louis at once began to favor the Medicis, who, in turn, agreed to sustain Louis in his pretentions to Milan. Clement has fretted under the conditions which have prevented his doing similar things. More than once he has been tempted to openly espouse the Borgia enterprise, but Borgia in turn is equally suspicious of the Medici."

"This is serious talk, Don Alvard. These matters are not known here; is your information authentic?"

"Absolutely, my informant has been for many years attached to the papal household as secret advisor to the popes, and is in direct contact with vatican secrets," replied the Don. "For your private information, I warn you, that, only recently, Clement issued to every inquisitorial agent instructions to confound those who openly advocate this new order, because the church has not been able to wholly control it. Therefore, Duke Arraza, you have before you a strange situation. I know that Borgia has designs upon the political situation at Madrid. If you should oppose him, you will bring yourself under the ban of his secret organization, the power of which is unkown, but should you advocate Borgia and his order, you will bring down upon you the satanic inquisition, for they are not wholly united."

"Don Alvard, you have opened my eyes to a strange condition throughout Europe. One dare not make an open move in important matters lest he bring disaster to himself and friends. I am puzzled to know how to overcome such impositions— tell me."

"They are all political, selfish and without legal or moral justification. They are wholly sustained by superstitious fear on the part of the ignorant people. There is but one remedy; adopt their own methods, challenge wit with wit, and meet force with strategy. Secrecy is the boog-a-boo of all such powers. Nature gave to all animal kind the power of secret thought, and the night in which to conceal ones acts in defense of ones life against strong and vindictive enemies. It is wholly a battle of wit. Above all things, go to the heads of predatory organizations and boldly declare that their lives must pay the penalty, when they abuse the common laws of men established by nature, the first law being the law of self-defense and self-preservation. They have so wrought upon the common masses that martyrdom is sought to demonstrate a false and fanatical loyalty born of secret fear, therefore, it is essential to place the leaders under the same spell of fear. They are arrant cowards when confronted by real danger. Hence they surround themselves with their murderous gangs who know neither conscience nor legal restraints. I know whereof I speak. Let it be known that you are always well armed and will kill on the slightest provocation, and you will find that every road has two directions and your enemies do not take the same direction with you."

"You speak like one who knows, Don Alvard, but you are a veteran."

"Tell me what progress Borgia has made in Spain, if you know," said the Don.

"Very great success, I am informed," replied the Duke. "But not with the nobility,"

"Good, I understand that Borgia is to visit Madrid. I will tell you how to make him leave your city as promtly as I left it. I told you to use

their methods.   Select a few trusted men to can-
vass Madrid night and day, circulating a story that
a strange band is coming to establish an anti-Chris-
tian order to destroy the Catholic church.   Diligently
work up a fanatical resentment against Borgia.   On
the day that he arrives meet him with a surprise
welcome, leaving it to the well organized Spanish
mob to hoot him out of the city.   I will guarantee
that, should the pope himself be with him, they
will turn tail and run from the inspired mob, its own
greatest force.   Am I a coward?   Yet I took my
departure quickly in the same circumstances.   If
you can secretly convey to Borgia that his life will
pay the forfeit, he will not come."

"Don Alvard, you are a genius.   You have placed
in my hands a deadly weapon which I shall use.   I
understand what you mean by meeting wit with
wit.   I shall adopt your suggestion.   I thank you
for your confidence and your frankness.   Yours
has been a lesson in courage I shall not forget.

"Now, my horses await me.   I must leave you.
I trust it may be my pleasure to meet you again."

Cordially grasping hands, they bade each other
adieu.

As the Duke raised the latch the Don whispered:
"Clement and Borgia are not lovers of each
other."

The Don's mind had been so preoccupied that
he had almost lost his bearings.   The relief it gave
him to know that the Rizzi affair was well off his
hands enabled him to sleep soundly.   But, the mo-

ment he awoke it came to him with a shock, that, he must keep faith with Count Berrasta. He was informed that the Duke's faithful servants had returned to Madrid with him, but that the splendid palfrey he was to retain as a gift from the Duke.

St. Belial smiled upon being informed that another horse would bear the bulky cavalier, even though he blushed at the prospect of becoming a mere beast of burden to eat their dust, carry his rival's oats, and have his sides lathered with the Don's toggery.

The cavalier made haste to carry the good tidings to the Count Barrasta. Imagine, therefore, his surprise and pleasure, upon his arrival at the house of the peasant farmer, upon being informed that the Count had quickly recovered, and had become so infatuated with the daughter, that he had married her and had carried her away to his castle in Savoe, a very grateful and happy man.

CHAPTER XXII

THE CRUCIFIXION OF GONSALVO

A GUILTY CONSCIENCE RETURNS THE MURDERER TO THE SCENE OF HIS CRIME

A STRANGE, hypnotic influence impels men who commit crimes against nature and humanity, to revisit the scenes of their unnatural acts. Experience justifies the belief, that, they are returned there for punishment, for, in a large proportion of cases, justice or calamity overtakes the criminal on such occasions.

It is a fact, too, that the alleged agents of the Christian God are no exception to such laws; at least Don Alvard thought so. Something which he had learned while at Madrid had caused him to start for Sebastian, the trip fulfilling his promise to Count Barrasta taking him somewhat out of his way.

Being now well supplied with money, he decided to keep the horse presented to him by the Duke de Arraza as a riding horse, and to use Belial as a pack horse, which provided him greater comforts in travel.

Some irresistable impulse impelled him to pay a visit to Pampero, on his way north. It involved additional hardship, and he knew of no particular reason for this side issue. Nevertheless, some prodding influence urged him on. He smiled grimly as

the admonition of Monetho came back to him to
heed such impulses. Asking no questions he headed
his caravan toward Pampero.

As he plodded the tedious miles, and his mind
grew weary of thinking, he began to grow impatient at the thought that he was going back to the
original scene of his life's sorrow with no apology
that he had not, by one stroke of his blade, avenged
the crime. The vision of his mother and sister rose
up before him; he could see their questioning eyes,
and, despite his hardened nature, he alternately
groaned and cursed.

Another face confronted his conscience, that of
a pale, haggard face, half concealed in filth and
matted hair, creeping from the dark recesses of
a sodden cell in the Castle St. Angelo. Then it
smiled and the sweet face of his beloved countess
cheered him, and encouraged him to proceed on
his way. Yes, it was a pilgrimage of love; he would
fulfill the mission. It would rekindle in his heart
the smoldering flame of revenge; his time would
come.

As he put day after day behind him, and checked
off the weary miles, he alternately brooded over
the early days of his youth, and reveled in his more
recent experiences, frequently jingling his heavy
pouch of coins and chuckling at the ease with which
he had obtained it; he had never found it necessary to draw upon Bambo or Count Brabon.

He now recognized occasional familiar landscape features, indicating that he was approaching

the vicinity of Pampero, finally arriving at a prominence overlooking the valley.

Pausing, he viewed the land of his happy, early boyhood, noting, here and there, new features, indicating changes since that time. It was now thickly populated by devout Catholics, as fanatical as the former people were peace abiding. This was the system of Catholic colonization.

There, where the cedars were still growing, he saw the spot where was located his home. He pondered the strange fact that, the land was barren, and no structures were upon it. His heart was sore and sad as he contemplated all these things. Why had not these lands been confiscated? Was it left as a bait for his return?

The memory of his good father, and his dear mother and sister brought no tears, but aroused bitter anger, and deep and savage oaths escaped him; he was not a man to weep, pray, forget or forgive.

Like a narrow, brown ribbon, the public highway could be seen worming its way from Pampero, passing directly by the Don's old homestead.

Suddenly he sat erect in his saddle; he plainly saw approaching, a score of mounted soldiers. Craning his long neck, he watched them as they drew nearer. The glint of arms, and their scarlet coats at once identified them as crusaders of the Holy See.

Don Alvard was electrified again into the avenger, the very sight of these soldiers bringing back the recollection of that other day, when a similar band of cut-throats had outraged and murdered his loved ones, and burned his home. Ah, Monetho's was a wonderful mind; he had guided him hither to fulfill prophecy.

Rage almost smothered him as he pictured Gonsalvo leading that other band. He hoped and prayed that this same villain, cloaked by a hypocritical priestly smock, might also be with this band of brigands.

Leading Belial into a bunch of scrub cedars, he left him standing. He then rode cautiously along the ridge until he recognized the old road descending into the valley, and intersecting the highway directly in the front of his old home.

Taking a concealed position, he waited. The soldiers came dashing along until they arrived at the ruins.

Above Don Alvard, and upon the edge of a high cliff, overlooking the whole valley, was a large, wood cross, erected there by some shepherds while he was yet a boy. He caught a vision of this cross, standing in bold relief against the clear, blue sky. It seemed like a live thing beckoning to him, almost forcefully taking his attention from the soldiers. A grim smile wreathed his face; he had conceived an idea; the voice of Monetho was whispering to him.

His heart began to pound like the hoofs of a galloping horse, as he saw the troop stop at the ruins, and the leader point, as though explaining some matter of interest. He was dressed in the manner of a legate, traveling by horse and escorted by soldiers.

Riding slightly away from his soldiers, the leader waved his hand and dismounted. The troop rode slowly forward upon the public highway, leaving him standing alone. For a while he stood quite still, then he began prowling about the ruins.

Don Alvard waited until the troop was well out of sight, and beyond a bend in the road, then, he slowly rode to a point near to the ruins and dismounted.

He was almost crazed with joy as he approached and recognized his enemy, Gonsalvo. His hour of vengeance had come, and some strange power had planned that this villain should expiate his crime at the place where he had committed it.

So intent was Gonsalvo in his study of the ground he did not observe the approach of his nemesis.

The Don folded his arms across his big, heaving chest and stood contemplating his prey.

Gonsalvo was moving a piece of metal upon the ground with his boot, finally spurning it with a contemptuous toss of his head—it was a remnant of that same hay-fork with which Don Alvard, on a previous occasion, had vanquished his body guard. Strange thoughts must have stirred the heart of Gonsalvo, for he mechanically brushed his hand over his face, doubtless remembering that his terrible disfigurement was a constant reminder of his crime.

A sinister grin was upon the cavalier's face, enhancing the ugly scar which had been left upon his cheek by the treacherous hand of Santillo in the bout at Rome. It was a Satanic face to unexpectedly confront.

The priest turned towards his horse, and beheld with horror, the giant form of the terrible Don, the man of all men whom he most feared. He had found that for which he was seeking, but well did he know, at the cost of his own life. He knew his time had come. The whole vatican army could not save him. He was face to face with the futility of prayers to the saints. The long scar on Gonsalvo's face seemed to open up, giving his ashen face a dual aspect.

Don Alvard said not a word, but drawing his great sword he pointed to the priest's horse. Gonsalvo mounted and the Don led the horse by the reins to where his own animal was concealed.

Mounting he handed the reins to the priest and pushed him towards the ascending road.

Not until they had ridden well beyond the possibility of surprise by Gonsalvo's soldiers, was a word spoken.

Gonsalvo, turning in his saddle, asked: "Whither are we going?"

The cross was now in full view. Don Alvard pointed to it. A great fear entered Gonsalvo's heart. He seemed inclined to pause, but Don Alvard urged him forward on the steep and rugged trail. It was useless for him to attempt to escape, the Don having displayed his pistol.

Reaching the summit, they came upon a level plateau overlooking the valley below.

"Look!" said Don Alvard, "the spirits of my blessed mother and sister have brought us both here this day.

Gonsalvo had been wondering why the Don had carried with him a strong pole, some six feet in length, which he now cast upon the ground, bidding Gonsalvo dismount.

To his horror they approached the great wood cross, the Don dragging the pole after him. This cross had long been a land mark, no traveler ever passing along the high-way without saluting it.

Stopping, Don Alvard moved by deep emotion, said:

"I am the avenger; do you wish to pray to your fictitious Saints? Your hour is come."

"Is it useless to plead for my life?" whined Gonsalvo.

"Did you give heed to the pleas for mercy from my innocent mother and sister?" demanded Don Alvard.

"Soldiers cannot be restrained in the excitement of action," replied Gonsalvo.

"Then it is criminal to turn soldiers loose upon innocent communities, if they may ravage with impunity and go unpunished," growled the Don.

"Communities must obey the edicts of the church," whined the priest.

"What legal authority had the church of Rome to issue an edict to the innocent people of Pampero, who in no manner were connected with the church? I observed that you had full control over your soldiers in the face of danger to themselves; is that the cowardly character of your holy soldiery?" demanded Don Alvard.

"I cannot argue with you against your misconception of the purpose of the soldiers of the Holy See," haughtily replied Gonsalvo.

"Yet you shall expiate on yonder cross the crimes for which I know you are responsible," said the Don. "If your confiscated Christ could, unsolicited, force himself upon humanity as a sacrifice for sins, you surely cannot complain that you must suffer the penalty of your own sins."

"God alone can judge and punish," whimpered Gonsalvo.

"And you, posing as God's agent, judge and murder the innocent? Then why may I not assume the same authority and judge and execute the guilty?" asked Don Alvard.

Gonsolva shuddered but made no reply. The Don took him by the neck and forced him down flat upon the earth. Placing his huge knee in his back he forced him to extend his arms, placed the pole across his back, and bound the wrists securely to its ends and then bound it to his neck.

He stuffed a gag of grass into the priest's mouth and bound his ankles. Dragging him to the cross, he cast a strong cord over its arms and lifted the body upward till the pole corresponded with the bar, and there he fastened it.

For a moment he viewed the hanging body, then drawing his sword he said:

"In the name of my innocent mother, and virgin sister, whom you caused to be tortured to death, I pronounce upon you the death penalty by your own method, cricifixion. I shall wound you to near death and leave your vile carcass to the tender mercies of yon waiting vultures." With this he ran the body through in a manner to insure a lingering death.

He now placed about himself Gonsalvo's cloak, in the capacious pockets of which he found all the identifying credentials of the Holy See, together with instructions for the execution of inquisitional crusades against alleged heretics in many places. He laughed as he added the cardinal's sapphire ring to his collection of official rings.

Many travelers, observing the strange aspect of the cross, devoutly crossed themselves, paused to wonder, then hurried on.

Two days later a terrified shepherd reported that the form of a priest was hanging upon the cross and the vultures were fighting over it.

The troop of soldiers now searching for Gonsalvo, hearing of the shepherd's story, went to investigate, and were amazed to find it the body of their leader.

Gonsalvo had expiated his crimes, but who was his executioner?

Some of the men of the company were comrades
in the raid which had desolated Pampero, and little
doubted this was the work of some vengeful heretic.
Yet, there was not one in the present Catholic community who could be accused of this deed, therefore, the people escaped the usual policy of the inquisitors of *destroying the whole community rather
than permit one guilty to escape*—a Christian theory
which has subsequently been adopted by civil government.

Leaving behind him the spot of his first joys, and
his first grief, the Don, in a mood of deep and grinding anger, took his way toward Sebastian.

In his recent experiences the cavalier had uncovered much evidence of a secret, though limited
knowledge of Gnosticism concealed beneath the
cloaks of traveling priests and monks, who, like
himself, doubtless were searching in their own way
for some tangible clue of a wider knowledge of the
same mystery.

At a wayside inn, he encountered a traveling
priest and his servant. While he was not in a mood
for seeking new acquaintances, or listening to conversation, he was by habit ever on the alert for agents
of the Holy See or the inquisition, therefore, he listened patiently to an abstruse talk on the authenticity of the gospels and the Christian doctrines.

"While we of the inner priesthood give some
latitude to our own conceptions of these matters, it
becomes all good Catholics to rigidly maintain the

external safeguards of the church mysteries," said
the priest. "Paul said—."

The Don interrupted:

"You quoting Paul? Why Paul was a Gnostic.
He knew nothing about saints; he never heard of the
four gospels; he never even heard of his alleged
epistles to Timothy, Titus, or the Hebrews. Paul
never dreamed of such an absurdity as applying
the theory of the immaculate conception to the
christ character, nevertheless, being a Gnostic, he
knew the significance of the idea. He did no preach
the resurrection of the material body of Christ; he
never claimed that Christ performed miracles; he
was an impatient, intolerant savage, who cursed and
swore like other good Christian men; he particularly
is made to consign the fabulous Peter to a hotter
place than Rome. Both Paul and Peter are the
apocryphal characters conjured out of the romantic
minds of the *'church fathers,'* to represent the ecclesiastical powers at Rome, hence his alleged clash
with Paul was figurative. The church was warning Paul, meaning the *church worker,* that he was
not acting square in his preachings. He was
openly accusing certain learned men of stealing the
keys to knowledge, meaning the keys to the Gnostic
wisdom. He was not in favor of suppressing the
Gnostic wisdom and plunging humanity into the
total darkness of ignorance; that was the church
policy. The church placed in Peter's mouth words
condemning the Gnostic philosophy as 'vain conversation received from forefathers by tradition,'

hence he whose *nom de plume* was Paul, was being lectured from Rome.

"Paul was not saving souls, he was searching out Gnostics who were dangerous to the great secret priesthood, but, in his zeal he was revealing too much, hence he was scolded. He symbolized the last of the true Gnostics to desert the ancient brotherhood and ally themselves with the Roman priesthood, which they believed would absorb and submerge Gnosticism. Therefore, it would be interesting to identify Paul as an individual.

"The name merely signifies the church worker, but his alleged writings were from the pens of Gnostics.

"The alleged Paul was a learned man and a savage gentleman who didn't like to be interrupted. Peter was a pathetic picture of ignorance, and was posed as a naked fisherman, symbolizing the masses, without which the priesthood could not be maintained, hence, he became the rock upon which the church was built—the symbol of church nourishment and maintenance.

"The word *rock* is derived from *clud*, the term *'dull clod'* often being used to describe a dull, ignorant person, hence, Peter symbolizes the church element, of the earth earthy, the *cloud* of people, the ignorant masses.

"Paul, in all common respects, symbolized an ordinary man, leaving his wife at home while he traveled, falling in love with other women, and writing them love letters."

"Stop!" exclaimed the priest. "Let me catch up with you. What is your authority for declaring that Paul signifies a character, and knew nothing of the doctrine of the immaculate conception?"

"It is well established that Paul never preached such a doctrine. Christ himself is not credited with having preached it. It is not mentioned in heathen, Jewish nor Christian history until more than a hundred years after the alleged birth of Christ. Ignatius, of Antioch, who first mentioned the idea, was versed in the Persian mythology from which it is deliberately confiscated, and adapted to the fake Christian purposes. Zoroaster, the Persian Christ, was said to have been born of an 'immaculate conception' by a ray from the divine reason, centuries before the Christian era. He also was crucified.

"Paul knew nothing of the doctrine. It was actually necessary to give divinity to the Christ character—to deify a person born in the usual way was inconsistent, and opened the way for all men to proclaim themselves Christs.

"Perhaps the first mention of the idea was by Ignatius, more than a hundred years after Christ, in these cautious and palpably deceitful words:

" 'There was concealed from the rulers of this world the virginity of Mary, and the birth of our Lord.'

"Now the word Mary is derived from *mer*, or *mere*, signifying the sea. This was the mythological origin of the Persian virgin. The divine ray was the sun's ray impinging upon the waters and begetting living matter."

"You astound me," said the priest. "But about the material resurrection?"

"Paul was a spiritualist, he disputed the resurrection of the material body. He preached that the resurrection and ascension were one and the same. In view of his Gnostic training he could not have believed otherwise. He preached Jesus as a Gnostic, putting words in his mouth.

"The ecclesiastical power at Rome had first conceived the idea of a universal church, and greatly feared Paul, who was strengthening a secret priesthood based upon the Gnostic wisdom. It was essential to smother and submerge Gnositcism or absorb it into the priesthood, therefore, Paul's work was diverging from this purpose, and the alleged Peter was sent to Jerusalem to caution Paul, and they quarreled, because Paul was running amuck with the Jews, and quarreling with them. It reached the condition where the Gnostic teachings of Paul could not be eliminated without eliminating the Christ character, which had been deliberately appropriated from the *Hindoo mythology—the Christ is the Hindoo Krishna*, (1156 B. C.). The whole story is a romantic play and these are the characters.

"Gnosticism was the treasury of all worldly knowledge, including these facts, therefore, the necessity for putting it out of existence—it threatened to expose the false pretenses of the church of Rome.

"There is no serious doubt regarding the fiction of such a character as Paul, but some one assuming this character, nailed down his work in a manner to necessitate reams of fiction to mend and patch the rents he tore in the original Christian fabric. This work was entrusted to the late lamented Christian fathers who found it impossible to eliminate Gnosticism from their fictitious gospels because they, too were Gnostics.

"Those cheerful old liars, Eusebius, Origen, Irenaeus and others, had little scruples in preparing their patch quilts of mythology. They frescoed the new Christian church with romantic screeds for humanity to gape at, while the founders of this astonishing secret priesthood began preaching to the vulgar masses these fictitious gospels literally, and the fabulous *'Jesus Christ and him crucified.'* *But, to the initiated, burning with desire for the divine mysteries and celestial widom, they communicated the Logos.*

" 'It is given unto you to know the mysteries of the kingdom of heaven but to them (the ignorant masses it is not given.' (Matt. 13:11.)

" 'Therefore speak I to them in parables; because they seeing see not; and hearing they hear not, neither do they understand.' (Matt. 13:13.)

"The vail of mystery in which the Christian priesthood masked its assemblies fostered the suspicion of indulging in a criminal secret worship."

"I am not going to dispute with you regarding the early questions of the church," said the priest, "but I now must charge you, who apparently are not of the priesthood, of being in possession of vatican secrets denied to all priests but the bishops and cardinals, for which the pope would draw the nails from your fingers and toes.   I, myself, have sought in vain, for many years, for the opportunity to delve into the inner mysteries.   You have declared against papacy; hence, with your knowledge you cannot be other than a Gnostic.   Permit me to ask of you one question; your answer will bind us in a life friendship, or cast us asunder.   Is there a living God?"

"Yes, but not the God of Christianity," promptly replied Don Alvard.   "The living God of nature is a tangible and intimate state of being—the word God simply means good."

"I can accept that doctrine.   I am a Gnostic," said the priest.   "There are few who have the courage to speak this aloud."

Both solemnly arose and made the ancient sign of the Gnostic adept, pointing the right index finger upward and placing the left upon the lips.

"What you have said convinces me that you know the truth; have you a friend connected with the vatican?" asked Don Alvard.

"My friend for many years was Cardinal Bambo, a good and true Gnostic," replied the priest.

Don Alvard thought it not wise to divulge to a stranger his acquaintance with Bambo.   He had listened intently to the priest, realizing that secretly

the whole church world was more or less interested
in the future of Gnosticism.

Originally, it had been the secret purpose of the
priesthood to promise to reveal to mankind the great
Gnostic mysteries as a temptation to come into the
church, and, in time, cast over the world a parental
glow of a paternal institution. The first word the
masses were taught to speak was *papa,* the origin of
the name Peter and Pope. The pope was to be
enthroned as the living God reigning upon earth.
All civil power was to be brought under his control. This was to be the establishment of the Kingdom of God upon earth.

"All power is given unto me in earth." (Matt.
28:18.)

"Then cometh the end, when he shall have delivered up the Kingdom to God, when he shall have
put down all rule, and all authority and all power."
(I Cor. 15:24.)

"And hast made us kings and priests and we
shall reign on earth." (Rev. 5:10.)

Is any one fool enough to say that this means
that God's rule and power are to cease? It necessarily signifies that, all civil rule and power is to
be surrendered to the church—supreme church control.

Bambo had made this plain to Don Alvard. Leo's
attempt to manufacture an artificial glow, to take
the place of the lost Gnostic wisdom, was puny and
worldly, therefore, it was of short duration, reflecting more credit to Leo than glory to the church.

The eternal fear that, the original Gnostic records might sometime fall into the hands of the heretics as a deadly weapon against the church at Rome, was the nightmare of papacy.

Knowing this, Don Alvard did not entertain a fear of the Holy See as something invincible. Why harbor a fear for a thing which was consciously its own enemy? Time would eliminate it by self disintegration. All organizations must sooner or later disintegrate.

Hypocrisy is a deadly disease which produces cumulative inoculation to break out in greed, selfishness, hatred and kindred ills. It is incurable, progressive and destructive.

To support a wide spread priesthood the contributing congregation is necessary, that is the church, which provides *Peter's pence.*

When the sheep are herded into the corral it requires but a single shepherd to mind the gate and keep them from straying from the fold.

Leo X knew the necessity for enlarging the congregation, and he did not hesitate to smirch his own reputation, and blacken the name of the church, by establishing a bargain counter in sin, and advertising broad-cast the sale of indulgences. The whole decent world condemned this act which could not be recalled without a papal acknowledgment of fallibility.

It was the immediate cause of the so-called Reformation—a more befitting name would have been the Secession for no real reform occurred.

Don Alvard was not easily deceived. He knew that every public highway in Spain had been policed to apprehend him, but he was always abreast of the warning. The captain at Salamanca, and Gonsalvo, had paid the penalty.

CHAPTER XXIII

THE ENCOUNTER WITH CARDINAL SALVISO

THAT WHICH THRIVES ON EVIL IS EVIL BY NATURE

D ON ALVARD had kept his engagement; he again confronted the sinister Cardinal Salviso. In all appearances it was an accidental meeting, but the wily cavalier was not easily deceived. In a few minutes after the contact, he began to look for some form of treachery which he had perceived lurking in the shifting eyes of the dissembling priest.

Notwithstanding the Don's aversion to discussion, he was forced into conversation, assuming a polite attitude toward his adversary.

His was a strikingly impressive figure, clothed in the outer garment of a messenger of Rome, which concealed his chain cloth hauberk. Formerly his bristling aspect struck terror into the hearts of those with whom he came in contact.

The cardinal could not conceal his surprise at the startling change in the Don's manners and appearance. He was plainly puzzled regarding his status.

Don Alvard, himself, had realized the advantages of this better approach to people. He observed the expressions of respectful awe and admiration as compared with the fear he had formerly inspired. He had learned fast to couple together the deeper sentiments.   He was quick to see that respect begets love, and fear begets hatred.

Contact with higher minds had broadened his perception, and taught him the true meaning of discretion and diplomacy; consequently, he had long assumed a more conservative attitude towards those with whom he expected a clash, until he had measured their argumentative strength, whether physical or intellectual.

He was not deceived by the suave manners of the crafty Salviso. He knew that he had acquainted himself regarding his attitude towards the church of Rome, therefore, he considered him an enemy. But the cardinal did not know the tremendous resources of this cavalier of mystery, else he would not have sought an encounter with him. The man who measured wits with the Don usually nursed a sore head, as well as a mutilated conscience.

Upon discovering the presence of Salviso, the Don pretended to evade him, thereby creating in the cardinal's mind the impression that he feared an encounter.

Bambo was right, here was one "defender of the faith" to be handled without gloves when the time was ripe.

Don Alvard knew, that, to save his own neck from the axe of the inquisition butchers, it might become necessary for him to administer to the cardinal a couple of feet of raw steel to purge his body of an evil soul. He had already classed him with the despicable Gonsalvo and Santillo. It was this type of soulless conscienceless men that made the inquisition possible.

At last the encounter occurred, in the beautiful gardens of the *hote del Marius*—by "premeditated accident" on Salviso's part. More than once the Don had secretly observed the cardinal hovering about, seemingly maneuvering for the right spot and conditions. Now he had met him, face to face, with mock surprise; he knew Salviso was ready.

Nevertheless, he treated the cardinal with great respect and courtesy, which did give him real surprise, in fact, it threw him wholly off his guard.

"You will not take offense if I remark, that, your manners toward me show a marked improvement, cavalier?" smilingly said the cardinal.

Don Alvard winced under this challenge of his former treatment of him, and he retorted in like:

"A cavalier sometimes finds it profitable to be civil to the devil himself," and he bent upon the priest a look intended to settle, for once and all, any suggestion of fear on his part; but it did much more, it sent a chill to the very marrow of the conceited prelate, as he saw the seam across Don Alvard's face broaden and turn livid, recalling to the cardinal's mind the admonition of Gonsalvo, who had warned him concerning the dangerous man. Among other things Gonsalvo had said: "Across his left cheek is a deep scar, due to a slash that I gave him in our last encounter. When this scar turns a livid hue don't press him."

The scar was now glaring out from the bronzed

cheek like a bright streak of paint. The cardinal felt a shiver trickle down his spine, for he knew this man was no respecter of priests when in anger.

Nevertheless, he had made up his mind to fathom this mysterious being and he stood manfully to his task.

The man who stood in the open and challenged the highest church authorities, and fearlessly hurled defiance at the inquisition, was no ordinary person, and some understanding of his future purposes was urgent.

Throughout Christendom this order had been heralded:

"Find him and hand him over to the nearest inquisitors."

It was a notable fact, that, no inquisitor, or any other agent of Rome, traveled at night in his zeal to capture the courageous cavalier who knew not fear.

Ignoring the Don's jesting retort, Salviso said:

"We may speak frankly here, as man to man, Don Alvard. I am anxious to know something regarding your adventurous life, which has been intimated to me by the gossip which drifts into my diocese; we must take the good, bad and indifferent stories we hear and sift them for the truth. It will be interesting to have at first-hand the strange things you doubtless can relate."

The bold and fearless gaze of the Don did not give him comfort; he knew that his patronizing airs had fallen upon irresponsive soil.

"What would you have me tell you, cardinal," asked the Don.

"You are, of course, a good Catholic?" asked the cardinal.

"I am not," bluntly replied the Don.

"Why, surely, you are not a protestant," piously exclaimed the prelate, rolling his eyes.

"I am not," replied the Don.

"Ah! You are then not a Christian at all?"

"No."

"Then you must be an atheist," groaned Salviso, with uplifted eyes.

"That does not follow," retorted the Don.

"What! You believe in a God and you are not a Christian? Impossible!" sputtered the prelate, with a false pretense of brave, pious indignation.

Don Alvard smiled grimly as he replied to the prelate.

"Cardinal, if the world knew all priests as I know them, thousands of able bodied men, licking their fat jowls about plentiful church tables, would be aiding overburdened humanity, by themselves engaging in useful occupation and producing something.

"The most impudent and selfish pose assumed by you priests is, that, you are right, and no argument to disprove this must doubt or go back of your canonized law, and question and dispute the origin of your assumed and wholly impossible doctrines, or deny your Christ character, confiscated from generations upon generations of antiquity.

"You know that your Christian God is an impossible thing, which you dare not attempt to demonstrate. That which cannot be demonstrated to the human senses is not revealed truth. You cannot logically demonstrate his existence by any doctrine you profess, hence, you beg the question, and deny all debate involving the origin and authenticity of your alleged divine authority, and your absurd and foolish doctrines.

"Nevertheless, I have a God that may be logically and scientifically demonstrated; he is not to be taken on faith or blind superstition; he is known by personal understanding—"

"Stop! You shock me!" excalimed the cardinal, with uplifted hands. This is worse than heresy; it is blasphemy. Do you not know that such utterances will forfeit you your life?"

Don Alvard folded his great arms across his chest; the scar on his face was now livid. Looking the cardinal boldly in the face, he said:

"Cardinal, I detest vain conceit and hypocrisy. Your assumed indignation is an insult to a person with the common intelligence necessary to see your deceit. If you were not the low born coward that you are, you would not hold the psition that you do. If I did not know that your whole exterior is a false-pretense, and that you are merely measuring my strength and courage, I would instantly run you through, for what you have just said, for I have as much divine right to resent an insult to my God, as you have for yours. I spare you, that I may tell you some things, that, perhaps, you do not know about your own church."

"I will not listen to such blasphemy," angrily exclaimed the cardinal.

"O, I think you will," mildly said the Don, pressing him back upon the seat.

"You sought me out to measure me for your inquisitors. You first suggested a conversation, as 'man to man,' and you are going to remain here and listen to what I have to say. Moreover, I shall require you to answer some of my questions."

"You would dare use force to detain me, a cardinal of the Holy See, against my will?" sputtered Salviso.

"I know of nothing to prevent my doing so. Your foolish formula means nothing to me. If you decline to remain at your own will, I shall certainly detain you," blandly replied the Don.

"I shall call for assistance," said Salviso.

"I will run you through at your first utterance," declared the Don and he placed his hand upon the hilt of his sword.

"Well, what would you have with me?" asked the prelate, exhibiting great fear.

"I would have you act the part of a man and carry out your first purpose of sitting here and calmly discussing with me matters directly or indirectly concerning your church. You yourself suggested that we could speak as man to man, and without interruption, and you first brought up questions of God. I feel that I have the right to complete the conversation. As you are in no humor to ask questions of me, I shall quiz you," and Don Alvard seated himself upon the bench occupied by the cardinal.

"Talking unofficially and as man to man, cardinal, if you could convert me to the doctrines of your church you would do so, would you not?"

"I certainly would," eagerly replied the prelate.

"Then you cannot justly deny me the right to convert you to my truths, if I can do so. I know of no law giving you a monopoly on religious discussion."

"Why do you say truths?" asked Salviso.

"Because it does not require a blind and superstitious faith in something not experienced by the common senses to understand the true God of nature. My experience with the priesthood is, that, the priest will tell or act a lie as quickly as he will tell the truth, to gain his end," retorted Don Alvard.

"Of course. I cannot resent your offensive assertions," growled the prelate.

"Yet you do not deny the imputation," smiled the Don.

"That which is for the good of the church cannot be evil," declared the prelate.

"That which thrives on, or in any manner depends upon evil, is evil by nature," replied the Don. "Your reply is so manifestly evil on its face, I will not dispute with you. Moreover, it is so well authenticated that your church is based upon evil, and maintained by corruption, it is not necessary for us to debate that phase, either."

"And that, I must dispute," said Salivso.

"Which brings that question into the realm of legitimate debate," responded Don Alvard. "But I shall make my argument brief and unanswerable —the gregorian reform is church history. There could be no defense for the moral decline of the priesthood of the tenth century, and natural laws dispute any claim that an institution could erect a substantial, moral structure upon so rotten a foundation.

"From the end of the Carolingian dynasty in 887, to the tenth century, the known evils of the church threatened its very existence; all pretense of religion had given place to a vast political machine, bent upon submerging all civil governments as it had smothered Gnosticism, to give to the ecclesiastical autocracy at Rome complete temporal power to enable it to compel every living human being to come under the rule of the church by law, and hand over substance for the support of a vast parasitical priesthood.

"The process is so palpable it cannot be concealed.

"1—The ecclesiastical power at Rome completely eradicated the Gnostic brotherhood and appropriated its recorded wisdom, falsifying it as its own.

"2—It compelled the many Christian associations to come under the direct control of the bishop of Rome to establish its claim to universal authority, preparatory to making the same claim regarding civil governments.

"3—It prepared the way for a papal empire by repeated attempts at territorial confiscation.

"4—It long contemplated enfranchising the Italian people under papal control.

"5—It has never ceased its trend toward temporal power over sovereigns.

"6—Its final goal is to rule governments to enable it to dictate compulsory laws to compel all people to contribute toward the support of the church.

"7—No crime has been too vicious to advance its ends. Your bishops are openly recognized as political chieftains.

"8—So radical were the departures from the original Christian purposes, that, your doctrines had to be sustained by coercive councils, and enforced by the most drastic instruments of black-mail ever invented by men—the excommunication, a system of social boycott unparalled in history.

"9—During the ninth and early part of the tenth century, the Christian churches were wholly neglected because of the evil and dissolute lives led by the priests.

"Now, Cardinal, I still have much in reserve, but I ask what answer you have to make to this indictment?"

"All nonsense! culled from the slanders circulated by heretics. Of course, no one disputes that there are always some black sheep in every flock," impatiently replied the prelate.

"But this is not chargeable against your so-called flocks. It especially refers to your ordained shepherds, the alleged keepers of your flocks. Moreover, if what you say is true, your sainted Gregory was a heretic, for he is the unquestioned authority for all that I have said," laughingly replied the Don.

"It was the greatest constructive period of the church," declared the prelate.

"Then the greatest destructive period of human rights, for it is demonstrable that, as the church gains power, the people lose their individual and personal rights," was the Don's answer.

"Do you mean to advance the theory that the masses of people should have freedom of speech and action not first censored by church or state?" asked the prelate.

"Do you mean to advance a theory that God would create free men, giving to them the powers to think and reason, and then place a censorship of evil men over these inherited rights?" retorted the Don.

"But the leading spirits of the church are not evil men," declared the prelate.

"What matters it whether the leading spirits are good or evil, if the execution of their rule is entrusted to evil subordinates? It has long been a trick of the priesthood to pluck a goat upon whom to cast blame for manifestly evil deeds. Nevertheless the church benefits—this is not saying your leaders are not evil.

"I repeat that, the church cannot refute the facts of previous great evils of its sustaining priesthood, and I hold that, it is contrary to natural laws to bind a sound beam to a rotten one and not set up decay in the sound one.

"It is a fact established by records of the vatican archives, that, when Hildebrand was appointed to the Monastery of St. Paul at Rome, he found offices of devotion neglected; sheep and cattle defiling the house of prayer, and monks associated with women. Was this debased state not also due in Germany and France?

"The offices were sold openly to the highest bidder. An arch-bishop of France, forty-five bishops and twenty-seven other church dignitaries confessed to the criminal processes by which they had come into their offices.

"It was necessary to issue a decree against pawning, by the clergy, of the rich vestments and communion plate. Marriage of the clergy was almost universal, contrary to the church law prohibiting the association of priests with women.

"The churches had become scenes of wild nocturnal revelry; clerical immorality was universal—."

"Stop!" exclaimed the cardinal. "This is an unpardonable slander against the present day church!"

"Now, Cardinal, you have practically admitted the truth of what I have said concerning your same

institution in earlier periods. I am willing to leave
to the people of today whether or not your church
has improved in manners or morals. If murder,
rapine and arson are evidences of moral grace, instead of turpitude, then I am wrong in my opinion
of your present day church. But I know of no period
in history when these were classed as virtues under
the civil law," was the Don's sarcastic reply.

"I prefer not to discuss with one not of my church
rank, questions of such vital importance," whined
the prelate.

"Do you deny that church evils do exist?" asked
the Don.

The cardinal remained silent.

"Very well, Cardinal, I shall accept your silence
as admission, that, what I have said is true. Now,
I shall bring my persecution to a climax. I do not
expect you to make further reply. These statements are unanswerable, in the face of unimpeach-
able vatican records.

"During that period of crime and corruption, one
of two things must have been true; either your
Christian God abandoned your church, because he
was powerless to control and prevent this evil, or
else he condoned it, therefore was responsible for
it.

"I am quite sure, Cardinal, that you are not
prepared to admit that your priesthood abandoned
the Christian God at that time, and no priest or
pope has ever been able to name the time when
your alleged God returned to your church, therefore,

you must admit that, not even your divine scriptures
can vouch for the truth that any God is now associated with your ecclesiastical autocracy, excepting,
perhaps, the remnant of temporal authority to which
the Holy See clings with vicious intent to rule or ruin
humanity.

"I am in a position to know that the priesthood
is as corrupt today, as when Gregory and others
attempted to enforce their ineffectual reforms.

"You see what I am getting at. There is no de-
finable God back of your institution, and there never
has been. There is no true moral code governing
your priesthood, nor has there ever been.

"It is a man-conceived, man-made and man-con-
ducted aggregation of greed, selfishness, hypocrisy
and duplicity, engaged in building a secret super-
government for self-gain and self-aggrandizement,
at the expense of the producing masses of humanity.
It has strewn the earth with ignorance and consequent imbecility; poverty and consequent crime;
fanaticism and consequent hysteria. Its evil work
is progressive, cumulative in power, and unending.

"That is all, Cardinal," and Don Alvard arose
as though the conversation was ended.

The prelate sat looking thoughtfully up at the
grand figure for a moment, then humbly begged the
Don to again be seated.

"I am deeply shocked, Don Alvard; you speak
with a broad and convincing knowledge of your
subject. I am more deeply impressed than you
think. The secrets of the church of Rome of course

are not for the vulgar. I admit that, you know what I know, that the church was originally founded on fanaticism, and nourished on selfishness and political corruption. Human authority and power constitute the God of Christianity, fluctuating in importance with the vicissitudes of the ecclesiastical forces at Rome.

"The struggle for temporal power has been essential to neutralize the civil governments, and sustain the fictitious claims of divine authority.

"I am compelled to admit this to you—as man to man—because I am curious to know the source of your information. What you have said is only accessible to the exclusive few. Not many are permitted to forage in the *Archivio Secreto* of the Vatican, where only such knowledge may be found. You must have had a friend at court.

"Inasmuch as you admit you are not of the priesthood, how did you obtain these matters?" and the prelate looked earnestly into Don Alvard's face.

It was not a kindly face the Don turned upon the prelate. A baleful light gleamed in his eyes as though some sinister thought was in his mind, as he addressed Salviso.

"Cardinal, I have an ugly record of church men whom I have trusted. I have found few who were true to their manhood and conscience as against the unscrupulous practices of the church. I can read you to the marrow. I know you are mentally consigning me to your damnable inquisitors, while you attempt to deceive me by fair speech into the belief that you are interested in me.

"I know that, within a few rods of us, you have concealed your agents to pounce upon me at a motion of your hand, therefore, I shall require you to cordially take my arm and walk with me along yonder path. You shall have the pleasure of seeing me despatch your two skulking agents."

The Don arose and stuck out his huge arm akimbo and the cardinal, quaking with fear, hooked his hand into the extended arm and was guided along the path leading to a clump of shrubbery.

Directly back of the shrubbery was a six-foot stone wall.

Suddenly the Don stopped, looked sharply into the bushes and exclaimed:

"Come out of that! Come out, I say! or I'll run you through!" and he whipped out his sword.

Two ugly, brutal-faced men emerged, both grinning savagely and betraying little fear. Each had his hand upon the hilt of a short sword.

"Take your hands off your irons," roared Don Alvard.

The command was so emphatic and so unexpected they mechanically obeyed.

"Why do you spy upon his Eminence Cardinal Salviso?" he demanded as he approached them.

Before they could surmise what his intentions were, he had cuffed them apart and tossed them over the stone wall, each dropping with a thud, indicating anything but a gentle drop.

The cardinal turned chalk white at this display of courage and strength.

"Come, we will pay our respects to your local agents of the inquisition," was the Don's amazing suggestion.

The cardinal threw up his hands, exclaiming, "What next!"

The Don pointed his long finger in the face of Salviso, saying:

"Your life will pay the forfeit if you even wink an eye to betray me. I am going to demonstrate the cowardly character of your inquisitorial agents."

CHAPTER XXIV

DON ALVARD CALLS UPON THE INQUISITORS

Mystery Is the Meanest and the Mightiest Weapon of Men

UPON his insistence, the cardinal reluctantly accompanied Don Alvard to the office of the local inquisitional court, much puzzled to know the purpose of so foolhardy a venture. The wily Don was using the church methods.

As they entered the inquisitors arose and saluted the cardinal, looking askance at the giant with him. Dressed as he was, in the garb of a traveling agent of Rome, yet carrying his tremendous sword, they were unable to determine his official character.

"Proceed, gentlmen, we will wait," said the Don, in a tone of authority, showing the cardinal scant courtesy—this had its effect.

A man, heavily chained, was before the court, and well guarded by two well armed brutes, a farce on its face, for the prisoner could scarcely stand erect.

The guards, believing they were pleasing the visitors, began to exhibit extreme cruelty toward the helpless prisoner.

One of the inquisitors began to ask questions.

"Are you ready to inform us of the hiding place of your mother?"

Don Alvard's anger began to rise. Looking at

the cardinal, who, also, had winced at this question, he whispered in his ear and placed his hand upon the hilt of his sword.

The cardinal hesitated, then asked of the inquisitors:

"What is the charge against this man?"

" 'Compounding heresy.' His mother is charged with having in her possession a protestant prayer book which she will not surrender to this office. This, her son, has wilfully aided her in concealing herself, and impiously refuses to reveal her hiding place," was the answer from one of the pompous inquisitors.

A startling turn came in the trial at this point. Don Alvard demonstrated the power of mystery and a bold demeanor.

Arising, he held up his mighty hand, exclaiming: "Stop!" Striding to the table at which the inquisitors were seated, he said: "Arise!" More in alarm than respect the three men arose and stood at attention.

Upon leaving the Gnostic retreat, Monetho had given to the Don a large copper talisman, saying:

"When you are confronted with real danger, or desire to impress others with the power of mystery, use their own methods. Produce and exhibit this talisman, and make your demand in its name, and you will be amazed at the result. Mystery is the power back of practically all usurped authority."

"Is this the only charge against this man?"

The astonished inquisitors shrank back from the towering, commanding figure.

The spokesman recovered his courage sufficiently to reply, with an impudent stare of assumed incredulity.

"Is that not sufficient?"

Suddenly Don Alvard whirled about and roared at one of the soldiers who was stealthily stealing from the room.

"Stand here!" and he pointed to a position near him.

Again turning to the inquisitors, he said:

"Answer my question."

The inquisitor sullenly replied:

"That is the only charge."

Don Alvard drew himself up to his full height and glared savagely at the three alarmed inquisitors, then at the cardinal, and, in tones of undeniable authority, he said:

"I am not privileged to reveal my personal identity. It is sufficient that I demand the immediate release of this man, upon this symbol of authority. If you do not understand its significance, you have no right to be sitting in judgment of men, and he dashed the strange smybol down upon the table.

After a partial recovery from their surprise, the chief officer picked up the medallion, inspected it on both sides, passed it to the others, then looked inquiringly at the Don.

"That you may know that I speak with authority I ask that you examine this," and he exhibited the ring of a traveling legate with which Bambo had armed him, which he held in reserve for just such emergencies. It was quickly recognized as the authoritative code ring of a traveling plenipotentiary officer of the Holy See. This brought both, the inquisitors and the cardinal to full attention.

Don Alvard pointed to the prisoner, standing, more dead than alive, from long imprisonment and horrible torture, his naked back being one mass of festering sores from the frequent application of the lash, and peremptorily ordered the guards to strike off the galling chains.

The miserable man dropped upon his knees before Don Alvard, and, with clasped hands and streaming eyes, blessed him for his deliverance.

Turning now to the really perturbed inquisitors, the angry Don demanded that every prisoner they had confined be immediately brought forth for his inspection.

"Give your orders to these two guards," said Don Alvard, then turning savagely toward the two soldiers, he exclaimed:

"Strike off every iron, miss not one, and speak to no one, if you value your lives."

Nevertheless, as the guards passed into the prison court, two other guards came running to them and excitedly told of their own experience with the stranger in the garden.

"The cardinal is in the office with him and dare not open his mouth. He is an agent of the Holy See, inspecting prisons," said one of the guards, and they proceeded to release some sixty persons from the vile prison dungeons, some of whom had to be supported, being unable to walk.

It was indeed a wretched lot that filed into the inquisitorial room and stood in shame, with bowed heads, believing they were to be sent to the wheel or stake.

"Curse of Christendom!" exclaimed Don Alvard.

Turning upon the cardinal, he demanded:

"Is this your method of carrying your Christian faith to these people? Can you look upon this and claim to be a man of God? Sign their release at once," demanding of the inquisitors to draw a blanket release.

Consternation prevailed. The cardinal alone knew that this intrepid imposter was playing a rank trick. But he, himself, was in a panic and dared not even intimate the deception, because the Don never left his side, and he was in authority.

Turning to the amazed inquisitors, Don Alvard gave even greater evidence of authority.

"Summons twelve well armed soldiers and instruct them to obey my orders," he demanded.

In a short time the soldiers came clanking in, the pompous captain being almost as large as the Don.

"Take these prisoners to the court of the cardinal's palace. Those who cannot walk must be carefully conveyed in stretchers. I will hold you personally responsible, captain, for any discomfort they may experience."

The captain hesitated, looked inquiringly at the inquisitors, then at the cardinal, at whose nod he marched the procession out.

"Come with us to the palace," said the Don to the three inquisitors.

Keeping the trio well under his eye, he took the cardinal by the arm and they walked to his palace which stood nearby, and passed through an arch to a large patio and garden, in which the prisoners and their guards awaited them.

With a sweep of his hand he commanded the cardinal to find suitable clothing for the scared and uncertain prisoners, that he might conduct them to a higher tribunal.

The cardinal raised his hands in amazement, exclaiming:

"Where am I to find clothing for so many?"

"You must solve that problem and quickly," replied the Don.

The cardinal in a great state of confusion, motioned for the captain to come to him.

The Don smiled, grimly, and stepped into the conference to prevent the wily cardinal from issuing some secret order.

"Take men and go to the old monastery and bring cassocks," said the cardinal to the captain of guards.

Cassocks and sandals were brought and placed upon fifty of the prisoners. The cardinal again threw out his hands in utter dismay. This was the limit of impudence, taking inquisitional prisoners away in the garb of monks. He looked appealingly at Don Alvard, but that unperturbed savage gave him no sympathy.

"How many soldiers have you left at the barracks, captain?"

"Thirty able bodied men," replied the captain.

"That is sufficient. I will return these to you soon. Have my mounts brought here. I will entertain the good cardinal, and the inquisitors," and he turned to them holding brief conversation while awaiting his horses, thus preventing any contact with the guards until the procession was on the march.

Belial and his riding horse were soon sniffing the extraordinary atmosphere. The Don mounted and then put his company in order to march away from the place so horrible to them. For the final effect the Don lectured them.

"Men, your fate depends upon your good behavior while on this journey.

"Guards, the first hand of cruelty raised against one of these men will be cut off.

"You, whom we leave behind, because of your inability to travel, I leave in the tender and merciful care of the good cardinal who has promised to nurse you back to health. God will punish him should harm befall you during my absence. March!"

The soldiers marched in advance, followed by the fifty monkish figures, and the Don, bidding adieu to the dejected cardinal, and the puzzled inquisitors, followed in the rear.

Well did this master of the minds of men know that pride would prevent the cardinal from betraying him to the inquisitors. Such was the power of the doctrine of infallibility. He would immediately report what had occurred, shut himself up in gloom, and await instructions. But, little did they know the extent of this raid.

The Don laughed heartily at the cardinal's discomfiture, knowing that, to confess weakness or error to a subordinate was contrary to the church rules. Confession must always be made to the superior.

A short distance from the town a halt was called, and the Don selected a number of the stronger and more intelligent men for a conference, confiding to them the truth, that, his play was but a wholesale prison delivery, and, that, it was his purpose to thus deliver all the inquisitional prisoners he could reach.

This confidence was received with expressions of deep gratitude, they declaring that they would prove this appreciation by their loyalty.

The Don instructed them to dissemble sleep, when nightfall came, and to secretly increase their number sufficiently to surround and disarm the accompanying soldiers.

The plot worked out beautifully, and, almost before darkness had covered the camp, the soldiers had been stripped of their arms and uniforms and placed under guard. Twelve strong men had exchanged their cassocks for the uniforms, proving that the uniform and arms make the soldier, and the garb makes the monk. The ex-soldiers took their plight with better humor than was expected, some begging to remain with them.

This was the beginning of a great army, which long mystified Europe, and terrorized those to whom the Holy See had entrusted the cruel execution of the inquisition, a definite step in the ecclesiastical enterprise, as previously had been the plundering crusades.

These twelve recruits, led by Don Alvard, and marching at the head of the other rescued prisoners, retraced their steps, and, before the sleepy captain was aware of their presence, they had taken possession of the barracks. Here another exchange was made. Each man donned a soldier's uniform and appropriated the arms with it. More, they lined up a packtrain with ample rations. The cardinal was left behind, but the captain was made prisoner. Every horse found in the town was confiscated, all being well mounted.

Thus did a new crusade, launched in the name of suffering humanity, ride out of Bayonne as an avenging force. Don Alvard filled them with confidence and enthusiasm.

From point to point they traveled, releasing and arming prisoners, until the army had developed into a force to be reckoned with, more than a thousand strong.

That which vexed and puzzled the inquisitional forces was, they could not distinguish between friend and enemy, because the uniforms were identical. Therefore, when an open clash occurred Don Alvards' forces had all the best of it, he having provided a secret mark for his own soldiers, who frequently had a hearty laugh to see the enemy forces fighting among themselves.

This phantom crusade swept over Northern Spain and Southern France, terrorizing anything smelling of the inquisition.

To every officer of the inquisition captured, forty lashes were given, and they were chased out of the towns. Thus a reaction to the damnable Romanish policy was gradually brought into the open. A new courage was put into the frightened people, and a new era was promised for all Europe. It was a fact, too, that, the towns visited by this independent crew of liberators were not again molested by the dreaded inquisition.

What a pity it was, that, humanity did not arise in its might and smite Romanism, before fifty millions of innocent people had been sacrificed to the fiendish cruelties of its so-called inquisition—the burning of the tares.

A dozen Don Alvards would have turned the tide, and the peoples of Eurpoe would have been spared untold miseries and suffering. Threatened with the loss of all temporal power, the church turned to wholesale murder, and Europe wept blood.

CHAPTER XXV

HELEN De BALDE

WEDLOCK AND LOVE SOFTEN THE SORROWS OF
SEPARATION

DON ALVARD, more than ever, became the nemesis of ecclesiastic Christianity, and the terror of priests. His strange campaign bid fair to break down the world system of the ecclesiastic exploitation.

Bambo, the hunchback, the despised, was right, mystery and ridicule were doing their deadly work. It was to destroy all possibility of concealed intrigue against the church, that, a new secret organization of espionage, to be known as Jesuitry, was being formed. Don Alvard was on the alert for this slimy, creeping thing, and more than once found it reaching out a tentacle for his crusade, which was now in full swing. Rising indignation against the fiendish cruelties of the inquisition was rapidly manifesting throughout Europe. Don Alvard's new and mysterious vigilance army was tearing holes in the church organizations, and was gaining strength daily. It was now an open challenge to the inquisition, and was perceptibly checking its atrocities. Had kings been men instead of puppets, this campaign would have redeemed Europe.

In the midst of Don Alvard's campaign, another German army invaded Rome, chiefly composed of

Lutherans, who took the city, sacked it, and compelled Pope Clement to retire to St. Angelo, and he
was not allowed to come out of it except upon a
promise to put this fortress into the hands of the
emperor and to pay him three hundred and fifty
thousand ducats of gold, with other promises of
surrender of papal provinces.   This gave the *papal
temporal power*, and infallibility, a hard set-back.

Clement could not make good.   God's vicar on
earth had to escape from his prison like a sneak-
thief, disguised as a merchant to take refuge in a
distant land.

The Don had suddenly crossed the trail of his
old colleague, Cardinal Bambo, the circumstances
rendering it almost imperative that he should immediately go to him.

He had not for a moment neglected his special
mission.   Every step he had taken had helped to
clear the way for his future work.   Nevertheless,
he was much annoyed by the constant reminder,
also, that his own successes had more deeply determined the ecclesiatsts to counter his open defiance
with that silent espionage which prowls like a thief
in the night.   He foresaw the future possibilities
of Jesuitism as a militant branch of Catholicism,
and working in the dark, doing those things for the
church which it dare not do itself in the open.

It would be a great pleasure to again exchange
adventures with Bambo.   It was a curious fact, too,
that a conference was almost vital at this time.   He
had practically organized a standing army without

any other authority than self-reliant judgment and undaunted courage. He foresaw that this, sooner or later, must lead to a clash with some civil power, and he desired to consult with Bambo as to what was best to do.

It was evident, from his information, that Bambo was on his way to Rome, in which event he would doubtless go first to visit Count Brabon. Something of an extraordinary nature had occurred in Rome, for Bambo had virtually burned his bridges behind him, at the time of his flight with the Countess Milliette.

The Don called his strong men about him and made known the fact that he was called away on most urgent business, instructing them to pursue the same course as heretofore, choosing from among themselves an executive leader.

Belial was growing old and feeble. The Don had retained the splendid animal which had been given him by the Duke de Arraza, becoming much attached to him. He had abandoned practically all of his former junk, retaining only such portion as was necessary for his work. This had reduced Belial's burdens to a degree to enable him to travel under his pack without groaning.

The Don turned their heads toward Barcelona, arriving there after several days hard travel. Finding a comfortable home for his horses, he took ship for Italy. He was amply supplied with money, and traveled in good comfort.

Before leaving Barcelona he had renewed his

wardrobe, with an unusual attention to the style of the modern gentleman. The motive for this was probably his own secret.

In due time he arrived at the castle of the Count de Brabon and was shocked to learn that Bambo had been recalled to Rome. Francis I had practically forced Charles V to reinstate Clement upon the papal throne. Bambo had gone to Rome, and received from Clement, in confidence, that, it was his purpose to strengthen the Medici family and he was an agent in this reconstructive work. Bambo had returned to the castle of the count and confided to him that he had rejected the solicitations of Clement, on the ground, that, he was deeply involved in other matters. Clement pressed him to the point that he confessed that he was investigating the organization of Jesuitry, and he warned the pope that, this new order, if sanctioned by the church, would, in due time, rule the Holy See.

Clement was so impressed that he agreed to forego the assistance of Bambo and gave him information which sent him hurriedly to Avignon.

He expressly requested that, should any word be received of the whereabouts of Don Alvard, to send him forthwith to Avignon, if a messenger could reach him.

After this important interview, the Don whispered to the count, that, if it met with his approval he should like to spend a little time in the garden with the countess. The count smiled, good-naturedly, and gave his most cordial consent. The Don had already made a rendezvous with the willing and now happy, Helen.

The wonderful moon, that holy lantern of love, almost laughed aloud upon seeing the huge cavalier come striding down the flower scented path looking eagerly for his lady love. She was there; it was a true lover's tryst. The countess held wide her arms, and the Don enfolded her in one tremendous embrace, which must have recalled his amorous stories told to the women at San Peste.

There was no foolish reserve; this ecstatic reunion had long been anticipated, and they made no pretense of concealing their joy. It was their hour, and they did not restrain themselves. They indulged in the sweet confidences of ardent lovers, renewing all their former vows.

In a general way, the Don related his adventures since they had last met, much to the amazement of the happy lady. Time rapidly passed, and, with reluctance they agreed that they should join the count.

Upon again taking up the conversation with the count, the Don found that usually conservative gentleman quite emphatic.

"I cannot blame Bambo for refusing to again subject himself to the insults of that clique of saintly hypocrits," he said vehemently. "The leaky old Christian hulk of state needs a pilot who knows the channel. Bambo is that pilot, but there is no good reason why he should take the helm if God's vicar is unable to keep her off the rocks."

"The recent experiences of Clement must have shaken his faith in the infallibility of popes," suggested the Don.

"All politics! All politics!" exclaimed the count. "God is in politics, if we may judge by the actions of the court of Rome. If you are familiar with the crusades, Don Alvard, you may readily trace the political course of the church, step by step, from the very beginning of the Christian era. It was a premeditated conspiracy from its first inception to cover political intrigue as long as governments endure, with always in sight the temporal power by which the church, by creating rulers, may control all governments and dictate all legislation."

"Mind you, Don Alvard, evil is to be legislated into all humanity, to vindicate the doctrine of 'original sin.'"

"History substantiates all that you say Count Brabon, but there is a better, and more certain evidence which proves, beyond dispute, the ulterior motives of ecclesiasticism."

"And that is?" inquired the count.

"Their own secret code," replied the Don.

"Ah, I have not been idle during the absence of you and Cardinal Bambo. Thanks to the excellent beginning of my education by you. I, too, am a student in this tremendous subject and, if it is not taxing your good nature, and valuable time, I beg that you will read, at your leisure, the results of my research. I have written a brief essay upon the wicked crusades, and to some extent, I have

made use of the code which Bambo left with me.
If you are not already familiar with this history,
you will be amazed to recognize a well defined continuity linking all these murderous enterprises into
one vast system. Millions of human lives have been
the food and fuel of this monstrosity," and the
count opened a cabinet and took therefrom a neatly
bound manuscript which he placed in Don Alvard's
hands.

Don Alvard smiled broadly as he accepted the
brief, saying:

"My good host, it will be pleasing for you to
learn that, your work reflects the results of the
propaganda which the Cardinal Bambo and I have
spread out over Spain, France and Italy, and to
some extent, in Germany. We have an excellent list
of interested, conscientious, thinking men, doing
exactly what you have done. In time we hope to
reveal to the world that this ecclesiastical enterprise seeks to possess and devour the world and
enslave greater mankind. I shall, with your kind
indulgence, retire at once and read your essay, in
order that I may, to that extent, add to my knowledge of the subject before I start on my journey
to Avignon. For Bambo to have undertaken that
arduous trip there is some important matter involved, therefore, I shall be on my way at the earliest
possible time.

"And, now, my friend, I have a subject to broach
which causes me some trepidation. I scarcely know
how to proceed."

"Speak, Don Alvard. You must not hesitate to ask for anything I possess," earnestly said the count.

"Your generosity gives me courage. Your advice will modify my request. But, may I ask that you permit your niece to become my wife under all the peculiar circumstances surrounding us at this time. We both have confessed our love, and I feel that life would be more bearable for both of us did we wed."

The count looked long and earnestly at the Don, then said gently:

"Don Alvard, you honor me by this confidence, and you have given me great mental relief. Helen is grieving her heart out. I should have broached this subject had you not anticipated me. I am delighted to have you link your good name to mine. In this, my province, I have the sole authority to unite in wedlock members of my own household. May I have the honor of immediately performing that ceremony?"

"I am happier already at your acquiescence," eagerly replied the Don.

The count quietly arose and left the room, soon returning with a huge volume, and leading the countess by the hand.

"Helen," he said. "Don Alvard de Balde has done me the honor of asking me for your hand in marriage. Would you be happier were you wedded to our dear friend, although you will be much separated thereafter?'

"My dear uncle, if I may wed Don Alvard with your consent, I will be most happy indeed. We have long loved each other and I know we would be more contented with our lot," and she went to the now almost bashful cavelier's side and gently leaned her head against him. He placed his arm about her and the count smiled.

"You will both inscribe your names in this volume and I will make you man and wife," and the count spread the volume upon the table.

It was done and the countess became Helen de Balde.

CHAPTER XXVI

AVIGNON

EVEN GOD MUST FLEE FROM THE WRATH OF MEN

UPON proceeding toward Avignon, Don Alvard was in no pleasant state of mind. After having read of the ridiculous crusades, he was more than ever puzzled that humanity was so dumb and credulous.

If the Christian God possessed all the powers attributed to him, why were his earthly representatives so wholly at the mercy of ordinary human events?

When the Roman Catholic church was first established, it was definitely declared that Rome was the permanent seat of St. Peter's. This was emphasized by the erection of the great church structures to symbolize this fact. However, he was now on his way to Avignon, to which place St. Peter had fled in 1309, with his porter, Clement V, lugging the moth-eaten papal ward-robe; sundry rosaries, breviaries and a head-ache, to place himself under the protection of Philip of France, a strange situation for God.

But that had been a long time ago. Nevertheless it was something to think about.

It was a long and tedious journey, with little to relieve the monotony. At times he was hard pressed for provender for himself and animals.

Money was absolutely useless and worthless, in fact
was a burden, where there was nothing to buy and
no one to sell it.   At last he was approaching the
end of his journey.

Ah! there before him lay a wonderful picture.
He could see the juncture of the river Rhone with
the Durance, and there, a few miles above, on the
Rhone, nestled the beautiful gardens of Avignon.
A little above the city could be seen the ruins of
the Pont Saint-Bénézet, a bridge of the 12th century.

The parks and gardens seemed endless, the clean
cut roads and boulevards resembling ribbons strewn
about through the green.

The walls and towers of the powerful ramparts,
built by the popes in the 14th century, seemed as
unbroken as when first constructed.   At the north
arose the *Rocher des Doms* stretching into a plateau toward the south.   Its gardens could plainly
be seen to the cathedral of *Notre Dame des Doms,*
and the palace of the popes, with its gilded statue
of the virgin surmounting the western tower.   The
cathedral itself is dwarfed by the grander edifice,
the palace of the popes.

Don Alvard studied the picture long and earnestly.   Feeling the breath of the hated mistral whip
his face, he remembered the proverb, because of
the violent winds which torment Avignon:

"Windy Avignon, pest-ridden when there is no
wind, wind-pestered when there is."

"What a strange thing this Catholicism is, with
its pestiferous priesthood.   Not one iota has it alle-

viated the suffering of humanity, and pestilence
seems to be ever present where it is most active.

"How many lives, and how much treasure coined
out of human energy, suffering and blood had been
expended on this spot, to appease the insatiable
vanity and pomp of heartless, conscienceless, and,
only too often, brainless popes. There, lying dormant, and non-productive, is untold wealth, while
the portion of humanity at large is slavery to eternal
toil, poverty and ignorance. What blasphemy!"

Thus he had cogitated as he viewed Avignon.

It was not difficult for our cavalier to enter
Avignon, but it was not so easy to locate Bambo.
With an abundance of money, however, this did not
worry him. For two days he wandered about the
narrow, poorly kept streets, finding ample entertainment.

Finally, he located his friend ensconced in quite
comfortable quarters, with sufficient accomodations
for him also. Here they visited and gossiped for a
day before getting down to real business.

"These years have been full of the terrors of
church intrigue, my good Don," said Bambo. "But
they have not wholly been without some compensating events.

"I convinced the Medicis, especially Clement,
that, the company of Jesus would, if it succeeded,
tear the heart out of the Catholic church. It only
desires church recognition to give it a religious aspect that it may make the confessional a part of
its espionage system. I especially impressed them

with the truth that the meanest attitude any institution could assume toward humanity, is one of secret espionage and secret accusation. Nations will not tolerate a system of sneaking spies, and should this Jesuit system become established it would foster secret crimes to accomplish its unlawful ends and purposes, consequently, sooner or later it will be expelled from all countries and will fall back upon the church for support and protection, and it will drag the church down with it. Necessarily, this has created a breach with Borgia which, though concealed, will lead to the weakening of the Medici forces. Sooner or later, I am convinced, there will be a secret union of the church with Jesuitry, then hell will be established on earth, as Julius predicted. I now know what he had in mind.

"Nevertheless, my good Bambo, I assure you that, we have the nucleus of a great Gnostic organization, but what is of the greatest importance, I have inculcated into the minds of all our friends these three powers, ridicule, secret confusion of saints and a secret order of vigilantes. If this system is steadily maintained, in a short time such confusion will reign throughout Europe that Christianity will become a farce."

"And who have you sainted?" laughingly inquired Bambo.

"Why, everything that enters the human stomach. A large part of Spain is secretly praying to St. Pepper, St. Brisket, St. Barley, St. Sal, and a hundred other saints in the belief that these saints will hear and answer their prayers as quickly as any other, and thus they cheat the priest out of his Peter's pence. It is a revival of a semi-totem worship. It is amazing how quickly the fanatical masses will secretly adopt anything which will cheat the church. I tell you, Bambo, the strength of the church does not rest upon the people. The masses are merely a tool to be picked up and used as needed, and a source of maintenance. At one place near Toro, I taught the whole community to cross two sticks and make their confessions to them, proving to them by the French word that this was the cross adopted by the crusaders.

"The old priest threatened to have the whole town excommunicated."

"You have done well, my good Don Alvard. There is more virtue in a prayer to a well skewered brisket of beef, than one to St. Boniface with the alleged reeds thrust under his nails. There is not much difference between St. Sal and St. Peter, they both mean salt petre, the 'rock salt' which seasons the bishop's dinner as well as his sermon, a virtuous economy.

"Let us now discuss some more important matters. It was not upon my own volition that I returned to Rome, and I should not have done so had not an accidental occurrence caused me to realize the danger of remaining with the good count, with Rome ringing her bells for my apprehension. I did not care to jeopardize my friend, therefore I slipped away, and after a tedious journey arrived

in Rome to find His Holiness in great need of my
services. I did not remain long, upon learning the
deplorable plight of the pope. I made my poor
health an excuse for my retirement. You will laugh,
I know, when I tell you that an ample annuity was
settled upon me.

"I undertook a task which ends here at Avignon.
I can now reinforce your own good work by placing
in your hands the whole Jesuit plot. It all is a
Borgia scheme and has been held in abeyance many
years because of the power of the Medici. Clement
has again declined to permit the church to become
identified with it. Borgia's argument caused the
astute Clement to see through his scheme. In his
enthusiasm Borgia overstepped discretion by declaring that the priesthood should stand as the fixed
soldiery of the church, while the militant Jesuits
should represent the flying squadron, to send *here,
there, everywhere,* at a moment's notice. It is to
have no religious significance, and promised to assume responsibility for all the errors of the church.

"Now, my good Don, we not only understand
the dangerous nature of this slimy monstrosity, seeking a hole in the armor of humanity, through which
to creep and inject its poisonous breath, but we may
quickly vision the weak point in Borgia's plan. His
organization is useless without a secret understanding with the church, in order that it may ally its espionage with the confessional. As long as a Medici
is in the pontifical chair, the Jesuit order will not
secure this hold upon the church. It is as dangerous

to the church as it is to the people, because, Jesuitry
is a secret organization for Jesuitry alone; it cares
nothing for the church excepting the advantages
which it may derive from it. I prophesy two very
important consequences, should a Jesuit pope sneak
into power. *Every priest will become a Jesuit,* and
the confessional will become the most colossal and
sinister espionage system in the world."

"Ah! I see a light," said Don Alvard.

Bambo looked questioningly at him.

Continuing, the Don said: "I have learned from
numerous sources that, this Jesuit organization, as
it now exists, consists only of twelve charter members, with innumerable working agents. As you say,
they are moving heaven and earth to monopolize
the confessional. I am convinced that the grand
play will be to install a Jesuit pope and fool the
Catholic world by a pretense, on the part of the
pope, of controlling Jesuitry, by seemingly making
its activities subject to his scrutiny and approval."

"You are correct," said Bambo." They need
only control the majority in the college of cardinals
to accomplish this, and absolutely control the whole
Catholic organization, and direct its future development."

"Which renders our work easy, remarked the
Don.

"Why do you say so?" inquired Bambo.

"It is the age of propaganda," replied the Don.
"It is the age of secret and mysterious controlling
forces. The masses have been rendered impotent

by ignorance and the ruling sovereigns by bribery
and church intrigue. I believe it was you, my good
Bambo, who told me that one of the church for-
mulas is: 'fight the devil with his own fire.' We
should adopt the same method. We should operate
through our own organization a little propaganda
of our own, in anticipation of the emegency of their
getting a Jesuit pope. Let our formulae be:

" 'The Jesuits seek to elect a pope secretly of
their order.'

"That will be something to stir the ire of the
Catholics.

" 'The Jesuits expect to monopolize the confessional by electing a Jesuit pope, in order to spy
upon kings, priests and peasants alike.' "

Bambo softly rubbed his hands, saying:

"You have solved the problem, Don Alvard. I

(NOTE—
1554—Jesuits were condemned by the Sorbonne, Paris.
1594—Expelled from France.
1764—Again totally suppressed in France and their property confiscated.
1579, 1581, 1586, 1602, 1829—Expelled from England.
1607—Expelled from Venice.
1708—Expelled from Holland.
1759—Expelled from Portugal
1767—Expelled from Spain.
1769—*Suppressed by Pope Clement XIV.* (May 19.)
1814—Restored by Pius (Aug. 4.)
1818—Expelled from Belgium.
1820—Expelled from Russia.
1820—Expelled from Spain.
1835—Expelled from Spain.
1831, 1845—Expelled from France.
1834—Expelled from Portugal.
1848—Expelled from Sardinia, Austria and other states.
1860—Expelled from Italy and Sicily.
In consequence of the activity of the order on behalf of the papal
supremacy, a bill for its expulsion from Germany passed by the
parliament at Berlin, July 19, 1872.
In view of this appalling record, is America safe as the protector
of Jesuit Catholicism? A curious feature of Jesuitism is, notwithstanding it calls itself the "Company of Jesus," there is practically
no mention of the new testament in its own literature, and originally
it was not a religious organization.)

will make another prophecy. Jesuitry will be per-
emtorily ejected from every country in Europe as
soon as it raises its head, and thus it will be the
means of breaking the papal ambition for temporal
power. The approval of Jesuitry by the pope will
mean the downfall of the power of the court of
Rome, Don Alvard, therefore, we may calmly
watch the encroachments of Borgia and his clique.
Nevertheless, not one move must escape us, and our
own organization must be strengthened."

"And, now," said Bambo, "let us compare notes
regarding what we have learned of this movement.
I am informed that these conspirators have a rendezvous in Paris, where the leading spirits meet
and indulge in wild revelries and live the lives of
profligates. Borgia has selected the crippled Iñigo,
your cousin, to be exploited as the founder of the order. I have learned that, since we were at Montserrat, Iñigo did make a pilgrimage there. It is
said it required three days for him to confess his
sins. Borgia has concealed Iñigo's identity by the
high sounding title, Ignatius Loyola, whatever that
signifies. It sounds too much like *Ignis fatuus*, or
fool's fire, but let me read to you:

" 'As a young and handsome Spanish gentleman,
clad in sumptuous attire, his copious locks fashion-
ably arranged, and himself well mounted, and accompanied by two servants, was seen ascending the
heights of Montserrat; this was Don Iñigo Lopez
de Recalde.

" 'From Montserrat came one Ignatius Loyola,

clad as a mendicant and begging from door to door. He was to make his first appearance at Barcelona, but at her gates, he was informed that a pestilence was ravaging the city, and, instead of emulating the Christ under whose name he traveled, he ignominiously fled to the town of Manresa, nine miles away, where he continued as a beggar.'

"You may expect to find all the apocryphal rot about this character that usually embellishes every saint. His close associates are Francisco Rienzi, Peter Faber, a low born Savoyard. You know enough of Savoe to know what this signifies. Francis Xavier—I believe this is none other than Francis Borgia himself, for he is described as being of a noble Austrian family, handsome, accomplished, learned and covered with academic honors. He is put down as the actual founder of Jesuitry, not being subordinated to the Loyola. A careful explanation is made that he had little more to do with Jesuitry than to lend it his name. I find no explanation however of the inconsistency of a highly educated, noble gentleman lending his name to and associating himself with an ignorant beggar, for Loyola has practically no education. There is a strange attempt to prevent Xavier's identification as a Jesuit by exempting him from all the regulations and rules of the order. He aspires to become its general.

"The next one is James Laynez, a native of New Castile. To him will be assigned the astute work of forming the constitution of the order, a lad only twenty-two years of age. He has associated with him, one Alphonso Salmeron. What a puny foundation is beneath all these sinister, Christian organizations.

"There is a young Spaniard, named Nicholas Alphonso, whom they also call Babadilla. He comes from Valladolid, where he was rejected as a teacher. And there is a young Portugese, named Simon Rodrigues d'Arevedo, handsome, and of a good family. A mystery concerning him is in, that, he was maintained at college by the King of Portugal. He has not fully identified himself with the movement.

"It is intimated, but I have not authentically established it as a fact, the following names are on the Jesuit roll:

"Claude le Jay, a Savoyard, John Coduse and Pasquier Brouet, of Picardy.

"Now, my good Don Alvard, you and I, who know so much of the working code of the vatican, may draw deductions which would escape the notice of those not so much interested. The history of this early order is, that, they were assembled wholly by accident of casual meetings. An analysis, however, reveals that, Jesuitry originally was intended as a counter movement to Christianity; the coming of a second Christ with his apostles—read these names.

John, who praises the Lord.

Peter, the rock.

James, the supplanter.

Simon, obedience.

Nicholas, victory.

Claudius, lame.

"Ignatius Loyola perhaps signifies 'the loyal un-known,' from the Latin Ignotius, meaning unknown.

"Francis Loyola was said also to be a Franciscan monk. Xavier means saviour, and you have a story too palpable to be chargeable to accident. Do you grasp the full meaning of this, Don Alvard?"

"I cannot say that I do," replied the Don.

"It means the organzation of a great propaganda to exploit the dark wilderness of America. I foresee a rush of Jesuitry to the wilderness of the new world, as soon as it can procure a papal endorse-ment," said Bambo.

"I am inspired to join you in your work, there-fore, I suggest that we hasten to Paris; install our-selves and become thoroughly familiar with the haunts, habits and plottings of these men."

"You have so occupied my mind with your sur-prises, I have almost forgotten to tell you of equally important matters," said the Don, and he proceeded to explain to Cardinal Bambo his own experiences. The cardinal was silent for a while in deep thought, then he said:

"I am glad you have withdrawn from this move-ment. We have no direct conflict with rulers or na-tions and your connection with so radical and inde-pendent a campaign would have brought you into conflict with civil powers. I cannot believe that your again attaching yourself to this force can ma-terially advance the impulse more than it will progress under the present leaders. This other matter is of very much graver importance. This is my candid opinion."

"With which I emphatically agree," replied the Don.

Shortly thereafter these two counter-plotters were snugly ensconced in Paris, the political city of Europe, and the rendezvous of all the villainous intrigues having to do with the court of Rome. Here they remained a sufficient time to thoroughly inform themselves regarding the Jesuit order.

Their next move was for Bambo to return to the castle of Count de Brabon until Don Alvard had completed a secret mission to the province of Gipuscoa.

"And, now, good Bambo, I make you my confessor," said the Don, betraying some confusion.

"Eh! What great crime have you committed?" demanded Bambo.

"When you arrive at the castle of our mutual friend, kindly deliver to Helen, my beloved wife, this letter," and he handed to Bambo a letter.

The cardinal set quite silent for a few moments, then raising his smiling face, he extended his hand to the cavalier with the simple words:

"I gladly extend to you my congratulations, and blessing."

These two men knew each the others heart.

CHAPTER XXVII

THE SPOILERS

WHEN ROGUES QUARREL, HONEST MEN HAVE A CHANCE

T HE school of necessity, of that strenuous period, between the ascension of Ferdinand and Isabella, and the reign of Elizabeth, produced few men who could rise above the spawn of inspired fanaticism. A murderous desire to excel in cruelty seemed to possess the heart of every ruler directly under the influence of the court of Rome. Sad to say, before she had the courage to break away from the clutches of Rome, England had become so saturated with the virus of cruelty, and vindictive hatred, she treated her own people with shameful disregard for justice and human sympathy. This was the policy of whipping the people under control by fear.

No sooner was Isabella, who wholly dominated Ferdinand, seated upon her throne, than she was brought under the hypnotic spell of the priesthood, and Spain began to weep blood. This murderous woman was so infatuated by the Roman cruelties, she turned her hand and heart against her own people. No less than ten thousand of her own subjects were publicly burned at the stake, with the king, queen and nobles being entertained by this horrible spectacle on gala or festival days.

Isabella's virtues fell far short of her faults.

Misguided historians, fascinated by the romance of that bloody period, have deceived subsequent generations by an ignorant glorification of virtues which she did not possess. If bloodshed and terrorism were virtues, she possessed an overflowing heart.

Few writers have attempted to enlighten the world as to where she developed this vicious disposition.

She was educated in everything Catholic, in a narrow country cloister, under the tutelage of bloody minded men hiding beneath the Catholic cloth, and peering out upon the suffering world with saturnalian glee.

Upon becoming queen, she began raising a vast army for her own wicked purposes.

To fight, forage and pillage, without license or restraint of government, had been the rule in Spain, this having been inherited from the papal freedom to plunder, given to the crusaders. Much of the great wealth of the nobles had been thus acquired.

It was Isabella's purpose to deny this freedom to the nobles, and she raised her army to enforce her edict, placing Ferdinand at its head. This army began to forage for the state on a tremendous scale.

In her insane Catholic zeal she began to burn her own people at the stake, and drive others out of the country, a million being deported.

During this bloody period, a sturdy lad was developing brain and brawn in a quiet and peaceful part of Spain. Very early he had begun to take notice of the crimes against innocent, ignorant humanity at large. Even before he was prepared for college, he knew the fictitious nature of the "divine authority," which had inspired these unnatural outbreaks of fanaticism. While he was yet a boy his father, recognizing his precocious development, began to teach him the truth, telling him that all the ills of Europe were due to a clique of ecclesiasts at Rome, drunk with power and evil living. There was no God back of this power, except the God of selfish greed, vanity, and cruel hypocrisy.

Subsequently, as he grew to sober and thoughtful manhood, and developed his career out in the world, Don Alvard de Balde had stored in his great heart the fire which was to avenge the wrongs of humanity. He now felt that he had postponed too long the reaping of his harvest of tares.

Cruel wounds in his own heart were yet unhealed, and unavenged. He had struggled, night and day, for a light which would put into his soul the power to bring to an accounting the savage hordes who bid fair to desolate Europe. His strenuous life had not softened his sorrows nor brought peace to his mind, the work seemed too farfetched. He wanted to avenge the ungodly wrongs of the people by more direct and drastic action. He judged the sorrows of all others by his own. Some freak of nature had endowed him with great mental and physical strength, and he desired to exercise these; he would deny this impulse no longer. Blood atonement was an invention of ecclesiasticism, the same forces had done him wrong; they must swallow their own nostrum. He would find them, try and execute them, killing until his guiding conscience bid him cease, or adopt some other method of ridding the world of the cannibalistic parasites.

As the pope, with no legal authority, had proclaimed himself the vicegerent of God upon earth, and assumed the right to kill with his own hands those who opposed him, Don Alvard proclaimed, by the same identical theory of divine inspiration, that, he was God's avenger for wrongs which he could rightfully judge and justly punish.

Bambo had bidden him a last farewell, so he believed. Monetho's voice seemed small and far away, but there was one call ever strong and persistent, the voice of his Helen, urging him forward.

Uppermost in his mind, now, was the restoration to mankind of the records of Gnosticism. He had laid the foundation for a powerful organization which could assimilate, teach and defend the system.

For some time, he had felt himself drawing closer to an understanding with some invisible and imponderable mind, urging him toward a great duty, and it had to do with Gnosticism. Could it be possible, that, Monetho was in distress, and was attempting to establish a telepathic contact with his mind? He was convinced of the truth of the Gnostic theory of a universal mental medium.

He resolved, now to put himself in order to return to the Gnostic retreat and delve further into the great mystery while indulging in a substantial rest.

Again he assumed the role of Don Alvard, the wandering soldier of fortune; in outward appearance a pilgrim on the road to nowhere. He had not surrendered Belial, although he had dispensed with practically all of the former junk with which he had burdened him. A long rest had put much wholesome horse-flesh on the battered ribs, rounding up his barrel in a manner to give him quite a respectable appearance—he was ashamed to mention his age.

From this time the Don decided to be himself, therefore he laid aside his cardinal's disguise, and all his former toggery, and donned the respectable garb of an up-to-date man-at-arms. He would abandon his former ribaldry, and attend strictly to his own business. Now having an ample pension, Bambo had provided the Don with a large sum of money with which to continue his work.

The old horse seemed to realize that he was in for some of their strenuous stuff, and he did not relish the prospect, nevertheless, he almost expressed aloud his utter surprise that he was not loaded up with the old junk, swelling out his chest in imitation of his master, that he was no longer a common pack-horse but the steed of a cavalier.

The Don had taken into consideration that Belial was no longer a frisky colt, and he had lightened his load to the last dispensable ounce for a long and tiresome journey.

It seemed like a decade since they had ridden out of Paris, when, tired and dusty, they drew up at an old Spanish, wayside tavern on the river Ebro.

After having seen to the comforts of Belial, the tired cavalier prepared for an evening of quiet pleasure, including a substantial repast of mountain-goat, black-bread, cheese and wine. It was his intention to attempt a long and tedious mountain trip on the following day, in order to avoid the deadly desert.

Notwithstanding his cumbersome, hearty nature, from long practice the Don slept like a cat, with one eye and one ear open for danger and surprises. His subconscious senses seemed ever awake, and he could analyze sounds even in his sleep. He was to learn again this night, that, fate knows neither time nor distance, when man starts on a speculative journey, but she is ever ready to guide and guard those whom she takes under her care.

He never occupied a room in which other persons were sleeping, therefore, upon this occasion he had requested such accommodations. He was informed, with profuse apologies, that, the only small room in the house had been previously engaged, by courier, for two Catholic dignitaries who were traveling to Pampeluna. But, it was also intimated, that, perhaps the landlord's daughter might be persuaded to surrender her room for the night; it was small but the only hope.

The Don very promptly negotiated with the

buxom young woman, and, for a liberal bribe, he was consigned to a room so small he could hardly stretch his ponderous limbs without pushing out the walls. He was informed that the expected guests would occupy the adjoining room.

Hurriedly devouring his meal, he cautioned the landlord that he was traveling on a confidential official mission, and he desired to remain in seclusion, therefore, he would retire for the night. Taking his candle he ascended the narrow stair to the upper floor and made a close inspection of his room and surroundings.

He was pleased to find that the boards of which the partition was constructed, also the floor, were so loosely joined, and so shrunken with age, by extinguishing his light he had a plain view into the adjoining room, and the reception room below, by applying his eye to the cracks—his chuckle, at this discovery, nearly shook down the house. Something told him this was to be a fortunate accident. He had cautioned the landlord that he would arise early and be on his way, and, that, his presence was not to be mentioned.

Yes, he was about to write a new page in his book of adventures.

Preparing himself for sleep in the rough manner of a soldier of that period, which consisted of removing of little more than bonnet and buskins, he extinguished his light. Selecting the widest crack in the creaky floor, he sprawled his big body in as comfortable a position as possible, and went on guard.

He had scarcely taken his position, when the confusion at the entrance of the tavern, indicated the arrival of the dignitaries. He was scarcely prepared for the surprise that greeted him.

A garrulous, quarrelsome man was giving pompous instructions to the hostler and the landlord in the same breath. A curious bundle came rolling itself into the reception room. A pair of plump hands, covered with sparkling gems, crept from under a great traveling *manto* and were extended toward the cheerful fire which was glowing on the hearth. Then, a hood was cast back, but the man's face was not plainly visible. The second man now entered with great bluster and noise.

"Curse of Christendom!" softly exclaimed Don Alvard, and his big heart began to pound against the floor.

Removing his own outer garment, the large man assisted the smaller, who seemed to be a cripple.

The now excited Don could scarcely believe his own eyes upon recognizing his beloved friend, Santillo and his cousin, Don Iñigo, now traveling under the name, Ignatius Loyola, which had no connection whatever with his family name. This hard-boiled, untutored, cripple was being openly exploited as the founder of an organized body called the "Society of Jesus," which had been cautiously approved as a secret agent of the Roman Catholic church, by Pope Paul III.

Don Alvard now understood the significance of the "loyal unknown." He and Bambo had examined the name, finding that it was derived from *ignotus, unknown.* Especially unknown to fame, which was a polite way of putting, uneducated, ignorant, all of which fitted the case of Iñigo.

With difficulty did the Don restrain his eager desire to learn the purpose of this visit to Pempeluna. Nevertheless, he was well entertained by their antics for an hour as they reveled in a banquet of roast goose, sundry other luxuries and copious indulgence in the excellent wine of the tavern, all of which made the big Don hungry and savage.

Santillo came near to precipitating a disaster by impudently chucking under the chin the tavernkeeper's buxom daughter, with the insinuating remark that the night would be cold, which insult, neither she nor her father dared resent. But, Don Alvard stored up an extra one for the unworthy priest.

At last, they came thumping up the stair to their room. As the keeper entered, long streaks of light flashed into the Don's room. As they had prepared to retire, the watcher had readjusted his position, and now had a full view of their room.

"Jesuitry," the name which John Calvin had given to the "Society of Jesus," was getting a dose of its own medicine—and an overdose.

"Ugh!" shiveringly exclaimed Iñigo. "This cannot be near to hell."

"A day's ride from here, if you attempt to execute your purpose," replied Santillo.

"Are you weakening, Santillo?"

"I have not been strong on acting too hastily in putting into execution this new method of plunder. I do not share your excessive zeal," replied the priest.

"You do not grasp the extent of my authority. The church does not appear at this stage of the conversion at all. The estates remain as they are until the present incumbents have died or have been convicted of opposition to the church, which justifies confiscation. I have in my possession full authority, signed and sealed, of the legal heirs to these estates, who have allied themselves with the Society of Jesus. They have, of their own free will and accord, assumed the position of mendicants, and gratuitously willed to the church their prospective inheritances. I have only to examine the titles of these estates and place this on record, in order to prevent a transfer which may jeopardize the interests of the church. Can you see anything illegal or improper in a person's abandoning his future prospects to the church?"

"I must confess that, I cannot approve of a system which so plainly discriminates between persons associated primarily for gain. The church, by your process, surrounds itself with possible wealth resulting from this indirect confiscation of large estates. Borgia declines to surrender his fortune, and desert his family for the cause of the Society of

Jesus. Yet these sacrifices are being forced upon
the other members of your order," said Santillo,
doggedly.

"Is that your chief reason for declining to become a member of the society?" asked Iñigo.

"Not the principal reason," replied the priest.
"I am convinced that a deep seated espionage system, so closely identified with the church, will undermine it and finally bring suspicion and disgrace
upon it. The very fact, that, Borgia would not trust
Clement, a Medici, with super-control, and so
promptly adds the disputed 'fourth vow' and offers
to His Holiness, Paul III, this vital distinction, in exchange for recognition, lays both the church and the
society open to the suspicion of connivance in a
desperate intrigue which will not bear the light of
public opinion. This brings the sacred college under the same ban. Paul had previously been a superior of the college."

"Since when was the Holy See influenced by
public opinion?" calmly inquired Iñigo.

"It is very rapidly coming under the scrutiny of
public opinion, and because of the growing determination on the part of the church to shirk responsibility for acts manifestly done in its interests by
secret agents. I warn you, it is no delicate matter
to surreptitiously take possession of these ancient
estates, especially in the province of Guipuscoa.
Your own father, I believe, will rise up and resent
this as an encroachment upon his ancient rights,
which not even the Holy See has deemed it wise

to molest. Moreover, you are not the eldest son, why should not your elder brother resent your meddling?"

Don Iñigo listened patiently to Santillo, then replied: "You do me injustice, Santillo. Do you think me so foolish as to attempt to do these things without taking into consideration opposition of my powerful father? It is my duty to approach him with caution, and warn him of the church policy, and that he must take a friendly attitude toward it. Under its present powers it is suicidal for the feudal nobility to oppose the church. If my father takes a friendly view of the inevitable, he will not be molested during his life; excepting, of course, the possibility of his being declared mentally incapable of properly conducting his estate in the best future interests of the church. I will fall heir to his estate at his death, at which time, according to my oath, I shall transfer to the Holy see, all my right, title and interest, in exchange for rights in America given to the society and in which its members directly participate. Thus we shall reap publically the reward of praise for a great donation to the church, and privately a rich compensating reward in a new land, which, in due time, will enhance into tremendous wealth and power, under the Jesuit-Catholic government."

Santillo stood over Iñigo as he listened to this diabolical scheme, as though uncertain as to the action he should take. Suddenly he exclaimed:

"Iñigo, I cannot longer restrain what is uppermost in my mind. I am no Saint, and it would be as blasphemous to saint me as it was to have sainted many of the popes, but there is a limit to every man's depravity, and mine halts at this new scheme to confiscate the estates of the nobility of Europe. Poverty levels all men to crime. I am deeply opposed to this deceitful order which is being forced upon the church through intrigue which is debasing the sacred college to a mere political machine. Especially am I opposed to this arch plotter, Alexander Farnese, who has forced his way to the papal throne, and whom I detest above all men. I say, emphatically, that, either you are dishonest at heart, or you are simple minded, to thus be led into the plundering of your own blood kin. Your father will be deeply offended should you even suggest your scheme. He was the close confidential friend of the family of de Medici, throwing his whole strength toward the election to the pontifical throne of both Leo X and Clement VII. You cannot believe that he will sanction what you propose in such circumstances.

"Moreover, on what authority, do you make the assertion that you will inherit your father's estate and fortune? You have several elder brothers, and Christobal, your eldest brother, and the natural heir, is now practically in control of the estate. What provision have you made to overcome this logical opposition. I am asking this to learn the truth, whether or not you are sure of your ground, for you will surely be held responsible for your errors as well as your successes.   There is no soft sentiment in church diplomacy."

"The formal ecclesiastical recognition of our society, in the form of a bull from His Holiness, Paul III, has not been published, therefore, I cannot reveal the secrets of the society to you, not a member, but I can assure you that the will of the Society of Jesus must be executed, if not by suasion, then by force," coldly replied Iñigo, unmoved by Santillo's plain talk.

"Do you mean that a few irresponsible men can band themselves together, and bind each other by an oath which supercedes the vows of the church, or their allegiance to their king, and secretly commit acts prohibited by either or both?   By what legal authority have you brought this Society of Jesus together and given it an equal moral standing with long established institutions which may be disarranged by its unlawful operations?" demanded Santillo.

Iñigo raised to his feet, by the aid of his heavy cane, and glaring into the face of the priest, snapped out his words:

"This Society of Jesus purposely has been organized as a secret order.   It owes no allegiance to any super-power, religious or civil.   It is a law unto itself.   Its will is as potent to itself, as God's will inspires the church.   It is to the church and state, as the human imagination is to the body.   No law can reach it.   No law can accuse, judge or punish it.   Each member is sworn to disavow responsi-

bility for the order, and the order disavows responsibility for the acts of its members. These vows
and our oath are not written codes, but they are
obligations deep cut upon the fleshy tablets of every
Jesuit heart, and self-execution is the penalty of
disloyalty. Neither pope nor king, prayer nor law,
can alter the mind of the Jesuit after he has received
his instructions from his superior. This order must
not be identified with the orders of Benedictines,
Augustinians, Franciscans or Dominicans. They are
allegedly religious bodies, the Jesuits are not religious, but wholly militant. They conceal their
persons and express their thoughts in enigmas. The
Jesuits expose their persons and secrete their purposes and acts. Do you now have a better understanding of the Society of Jesus?" and Iñigo looked
defiantly at Santillo.

"That is mere talk, meaning nothing more than a
wilful defiance of all law, and might apply to a
band of criminals. In view of your statement your
hypocrisy is profane. You boast of your piety, your
charity and your reverence for 'Mary,' the 'Mother of
Christ,' naming her the 'queen of all virgins.' I
myself have seen you weep in pretended ecstatic
hysteria. While, at this very hour your associates,
Peter Faber, Alphonso Salmeran, Nicholas Alphonso, or Babadilla, who like you, has disguised himself under a more sanctimonious name, and others,
are reveling in wine, women and song in Paris. It
was to learn your explanation of these undignified
things that I attached myself to you. Are these all

a disguising play to conceal your ulterior significance?"

Don Iñigo attempted to calm the excited Santillo,
saying, in a subdued voice:

"It is not necessary for you to preach these matters from the housetop. Even the clod below can
understand some words you are saying. Your loud
voice and angry tones, intimate that you are scolding me. I have anticipated this criticism. I am prepared to meet any obstacle the Holy See may care
to cast in our way. If it will relieve your mind I
will answer your last question. Yes, it is all play."

"I warn you, then, this defiant attitude will win
nothing for you at Rome," doggedly said Santillo.

Iñigo looked sharply at the priest and replied:

"Santillo, you are not a cardinal. You are too
shallow. Why did you not ask me in the beginning
if Paul was elected pope by the Jesuit control of the
sacred college? Why has not Borgia adivsed you?
When the time comes that we get nothing from
Rome, Rome will get nothing from us, and she will
starve to death. You will have to return to San
Peste and preach for cabbages, onions and carrots,
for you would never choke to death on what you
got from Rome," and Iñigo laughed.

"And now I see the light," grimly said Santillo.
"Why are you, the supposed leader of this clan sent
here to close and take over these estates?"

"For a very simple reason; the first body we
gathered together deserted the cause, the moment
freedom to attend to their own affairs was granted

them. When it came to breaking up family ties, they had to speak for others, and they were not interested. This time I am not taking chances of our followers coming again under home influences. I have taken from each a legal process, and authority to turn over to the church their property under such conditions as may arise."

"Iñigo, I readily grasp that this Jesuit movement is one of the progressive steps in a process of confiscation, of which the crusades was the first. It is a damnable conspiracy against established civil conditions. There is another rumor being whispered about. It is to the effect that you seek to take upon yourselves the office of confessors, in order to broaden your inquisitional scope."

"Ah, have you heard that? Yes, but for an entirely different purpose. I do not hesitate to say that the Jesuit connection with the church does permit us to confess only women of high rank and wealth, especially widows needing consolation and advice," smilingly said Iñigo.

"What is this? It is something new," exclaimed Santillo.

"To further the secret objects of the pact between the church and our order," calmly replied Iñigo.

"We will not quarrel, but listen to this," said Santillo earnestly. "You are now sowing the seeds of your own destruction. The world is short sighted, but not so blind as you believe. In due time the people will rise in their might and force their governments to repudiate you. The church will be held responsible, and will be forced to the false-pretense of repudiating you. You will be expelled from Europe. You have borrowed your ideas from that human skunk, Peter the Hermit, and the German monk Godeschel, and declared your first crusade against the German Lutherans. You accuse Luther of being the seducer of youths, a vulgar term applied to a legitimate winning away from the church of Rome the German younger generation, while you have been filling the heads of your maudlin mob of young and unsophisticated men in Paris with the romance of Jesuitry while steeping them in dissipation and dabauchery to deaden their conscience and half formed judgment.

"You have tampered with the loyalty of subjects of Savoe, Newcastle, Toledo, Picardy and Portugal, and now you confess that you prevent the return of these youths to their native countries and the counsel of their parents, because you fear they may be persuaded to abandon your admittedly lawless cause. Do you suppose that your admissions to me will forward your interests at Rome?" and Santillo stood looking down upon Iñigo.

Looking up into the gloomy face of the priest, Iñigo laughingly said:

"Something you said to me caused a brain commotion. I care nothing for your preachings, for I know you are trying to get from me information for your own satisfaction, but you have suggested, that, possibly, it would be unwise for me to identify myself as Ignatius Loyola, therefore, I shall go into the provinces under my usual name, Iñigo. No one will know me as the former gallant Don Iñigo Lopez de Recalde, with this war battered form."

"I happen to know that your limbs were broken in a cowardly attempt to escape from the citadel of Pampeluna, but let that rest; how are you going to disguise that beak of a Recalde?" said Santillo.

"Ha! ha!" laughed Iñigo. "That at once becomes my identification, and my disguise. Every member of my clan is blessed with a big nose. Everybody will believe anything that is told them by a Recalde, and many will not know from which branch I spring. I shall only announce that I am the duly authorized agent of these gentlemen who have placed in my hands the disposal of their fortunes."

"But you cannot long deceive the world regarding these moral derelicts whom you have chosen as your associates," said Santillo.

"We shall be safely tucked beneath the protecting apron of the mother church of Rome before the world can learn the truth. Besides, my imbecilic associates will soon depart this world by their own dissipations. We shall keep them amply supplied with means for bringing about this martyrdom. Paris would corrupt God himself."

"It is unfortunate that St. Peter's and the Vatican were not established in Paris, the popes surely would have had a hell of a time there," said Santillo. "Now, about your father; do you propose going to his castle at this time?"

This question seemed to thoroughly arouse Iñigo. Arising he hobbled across the floor, then pausing he faced Santillo, saying:

"Santillo, if I had not been duly warned by Francis Xavier, judging from your talk tonight I would be compelled to believe you a rank enemy of our cause. I know you do not stand well at Rome because of your irritating and garrulous disposition, and I do know that Borgia trusts you. Now tell me; is it jealousy of me that causes you to assume this abusive and inquisitional attitude toward me? If this is true eliminate it from your mind, for Francis Borgia—in our ranks Francis Xavier, is the organizer of the Jesuit order, not I. I am the pathetic figure on the cross, the Christ, required to dissemble and play the leading role assigned to me. Now, do you wish to be with me, or shall I report to Borgia that you are our secret enemy?"

Santillo looked cautiously at Iñigo, shrugged his beefy shoulders and replied:

"You are stronger than I believed. Of course, I am with you," and he placed his hand upon Iñigo's shoulder.

"I will, then, briefly make known to you my plans," quickly said Iñigo.

"My eldest brother, Christobal, is at Pampeluna awaiting my arrival. I propose that you go to him and announce that I cannot arrive there in less time than a week, because of weariness requiring my resting on the way. In the meantime I will hasten directly to Ognez, where my father's estate is located.

I have had serious correspondence with my other
brothers, giving me assurance of their support.
They are eager to seek adventure in the new world,
the promise being held out to them of great wealth
in the Americas. Francis Xavier contemplates an
early voyage to the new world, and I shall make
it my business to ship them over there with his
cargo of troublesome persons.

"I am convinced that my father is incompetent
to control and care for his great estate, therefore,
my first move, after the departure of my other
brothers, will be to charge Christobal with opposition to the best interests of the church in the matter, and have myself appointed as custodian of my
father's estate and guardian over him."

"And your reward?" inquired Santillo.

"Borgia, as trustee for our order, has made
ample provision for rewarding our original group
with grants and rich concessions in America, which
transactions, are to receive the sanction of the
church for the purpose of giving substantial, diplomatic recognition to our order."

Santillo looked in astonishment at Iñigo, as he
made this frank confession, sat thoughtfully staring at the floor for a moment, then arising, he said:

"Very well, I shall leave here tomorrow at noon,
going direct to your brother at Pampeluna."

Soon thereafter the rafters were ringing with a
duet of sonorous snores.

CHAPTER XXVIII

THE GATHERING STORM

Only Fools Plot Between Four Walls

"NOW I have a new cause," softly whispered Don Alvard. "Again this vile thing has turned its poisonous breath toward my blood kin. This viper Iñigo is the son of him who helped to betray me to the inquisitors. It seems like retribution, that, the father should now be threatened in the plotting of his own son; but, if they are innocent, the brothers of Iñigo shall not be seduced, or fall victim to this dishonest scheme to confiscate their properties."

With these thoughts forming in his mind, the tired Don lay down and slept soundly till the early dawn, when he was awakened by the crowing of a number of cocks, warning him it was time to arise and be on his way. The rafter shaking duet in the adjoining room was in full swing, as he quietly arose and passed down the rickety stairway.

He held a brief conference with the inn-keeper, passing him some silver, cautioning him that the life of his whole family would be forfeited, did one word of his presence reach the ears of the other two men.

Then he took the shortest course to Pampeluna.

He found there his cousin, Christobal, and quickly made himself known to him, frankly relating the despicable plot against him. He also related the

sad story of his own loss at Pampero, which seemed
greatly to arouse Christobal. He did not withhold
the fact that Christobal's father had connived with
Sanatos to betray him to the inquisitors.

"No matter what your Catholic zeal, my cousin,
you are not immune against destruction, should these
agents of hell desire to confiscate your property.
After all his devotion to the church, Count Bertram
is doomed, and I fear that your own brothers have
been guilty of indiscretions which commit them to
this dreadful betrayal. Your own brother, Iñigo,
is the master plotter." Thus did Don Alvard convince Christobal that a conspiracy threatened his
whole family. His cousin greatly impressed Don
Alvard by his calm and dignified self-control.

"What measure for our protection have you in
mind?" he quietly asked.

"You must permit Santillo to come here and see
you. He was to have left the inn at noon which
would bring him here only a few hours after my
arrival, therefore, we must rapidly formulate our
course of action. Let him start for Ognez in the
belief, that, you will remain here for a week to await
the arrival of your brother. I shall advise you when
he is actually on his way to Ognez. He will doubtless inform you that he is journeying to some other
point. We may then take the shortest way and
anticipate their arrival, remain in seclusion until we
know their exact mission, and, at the proper time,
confront them."

"That seems to be a wise course," said Christobal. I heartily endorse it."

"Permit me to ask you," continued Don Alvard. "Have you one brother in whom you have implicit confidence?"

"Yes, my brother, Bertold. I can trust him."

"Good. We must devise some means by which we may consult with him unknown to your father and your other brothers, previous to the arrival of Iñigo and Santillo," said the Don.

"That, we can arrange. I have a hunting lodge on the estate, only a short distance from the castle I have permitted Bertold to occupy this lodge, he being given to study and research. We may arrive there at night, and go direct to the lodge."

"I would suggest that you fortify yourself with the truth by asking of Santillo questions which no doubt he will refute when he arrives at the castle," said the earnest Don, and he suggested a number of vital questions for Christobal to put to Santillo.

Christobal assured Don Alvard, that, he placed full confidence in all that he had told him, and in as much as he had at his disposal a comfortable *cocheo* and trusted servants, he would arrange, at once, relays of horses for rapid travel, which would be quite certain to anticipate the arrival of Iñigo at the castle.

With all arrangements complete the Don left Christobal and went to where he had left Belial to arrange for his indefinite care.

Almost within the hour, Santillo called upon

Christobal, seeming to be in great haste to discharge his message.

Christobal received him cordially, and upon his delivering Iñigo's message, thanked him profusely, expressing deep concern that his crippled brother should have attempted so long and arduous a journey.

"Are you traveling with my brother?" he asked of Santillo.

"No, I only casually met him on the way. In order to give him comfort, I spent the better part of a day with him, which makes me late on my own itinerary. I am traveling to St. Sebastian with important messages for the bishop."

This oily tongued ambassador of Satan was calculating upon leaving Count Bertram's castle with Iñigo, before the week had expired, and be safely away before Christobal could learn the truth.

"You are traveling ahorse?" inquired Christobal.

"Yes."

"Then you, too, have a fatiguing journey before you. In view of your thoughtful kindness toward my brother, you will permit me to extend to you the courtesy of my *cocheo* and servants to speed you on your way with better comfort," smilingly suggested Christobal.

This generous proposal seemed to greatly disturb Santillo who hastily explained, that, he was well mounted and could not accept so excellent an offer.

"You will at least remain here for a day or two

and permit me to entertain you while you take a much needed rest?" urged Christobal.

Santillo thanked him, but insisted that it was imperative that he should leave that very day.

Thus they parted, with Christobal fully convinced of the importance of all that Don Alvard had told him.

A few hours later he and the Don were dashing toward Ognez behind four strong palfreys, which would be exchanged before nightfall for others to enable them to continue their journey through the night.

In due time they arrived at an isolated tavern, off the regular highway, where they refreshed themselves, then continued their journey by horse.

It was in the evening dusk that they arrived at the lodge, where a single servant was in charge, the faithful caretaker.

Christobal confided to him that their presence must be kept secret from all but his brother, Bertold, whom he must find and send secretly to the lodge.

Shortly thereafter Bertold came to the lodge, filled with wonderment that his brother should thus surreptitiously visit his own home, he being master of the castle.

The brothers affectionately embraced, Don Alvard was introduced, and they promptly went into conference.

Bertold admitted he had been approached by his brothers, in fact, they anticipated the coming of Iñigo, who would be accompanied by one Cardinal Santillo, from Rome, to discuss their becoming identified in some great work of propaganda in the new world.

Don Alvard explained that Santillo had never been a cardinal, or even a bishop, because of his tricky, unworthy nature. Until Gonsalvo's death, Santillo had been his swashbuckler, and had long snooped about the vatican as a spy of Spain. At such times, under the protection of Gonsalvo, he would strut about among the cardinals, posing as a very pious and promising priest.

"Is it possible, my good cousin, that, after all these years that my father has shown his faith in the integrity and good intent of the court of Rome, raising his sons to manhood in that belief, that he should now be selected as a victim of a dastardly plot of this kind?" asked Christobal.

"You will find that it is not only possible, but it is a cold-blooded fact," replied the Don.

"Explain to us your particular motive for having rendered to us this great service in giving us timely warning," said Christobal.

"You may explain later what I have already related to you regarding the massacre of my own pure and good mother and sister. I frankly admit to you that this warning is only incidental to motives of revenge on my part. My discovery of this conspiracy against you is wholly accidental, and, no matter what the outcome, it cannot in any manner profit me other than to add to my systematic punishment of those who have wronged me.

"I have a natural abhorance for your father for having willingly sacrificed one of his own blood, in his willingness that I should be turned over to the inquisitors, therefore, my having come to you and given you these facts for your own protection demonstrates that, I do not hold blood relations responsible for your father's wholly unpardonable betrayal of one of his own blood. It is a strange coincidence that one of his own sons is now plotting with these same powers for his destruction. As between the two I prefer to take up your cause.

"However, it is a truth which you must keep ever in mind, when a name has once been engrossed upon the tablets of the court of Rome as a name for vengeance or exploitation, it is there forever. If this great estate is marked for reprisal, for some imaginary indiscretion on the part of its master, it will remain so until it is converted into the treasury of the church. The blood of Recalde is checked for elimination from the Catholic body, because of the friendship it betrayed for the Medici family. If you would know another reason, you will find locked in the strong-room of this castle certain chests of records which reveal the distribution of the proceeds of the plundering crusades, inspired by the popes.

"This plot against your father is a trivial incident. The baser scheme is to establish this treacherous band of church spies, rape Europe, and flee into the wilderness of America, there to erect a permanent secret government to govern and control all nations gathered there under a state of mixture and confusion, the actual Babylon of its system, where it can rule without direct governing responsibility.

"In our life time, my cousins, you will see this monstrosity expelled from every country in Europe, even from Spain.

"From sheer necessity, to avoid public censure, the church at Rome will find it necessary to publicly repudiate it or accept responsibility for its detestable acts. Later, the church will surreptitiously take this bastard offspring back into its arms and mother it."

Don Alvard was now excitedly walking the floor, and his cousins sat in deep and moody thought.

Arising, Christobal placed his hand upon Alvard's arm, saying:

"My cousin, in so far as any other knowledge on our part is concerned, these may be mere accusations growing out of your bitter resentment toward those who have done you great injury. Nevertheless, we have confidence in you, and shall accept all that you say as truth until urgent reasons cause us to think otherwise. We now accept you as our ally as against a common enemy."

"That puts us on a fighting basis. We shall fight the devil with his own fire," exclaimed the Don. "I believe Iñigo will be intercepted by Santillo, and they will arrive here together tomorrow morning. It will be necessary for my cousin Bertold to participate in their reception, and, especially in the conferences which will take place. He can report to us all that transpires. Therefore, I desire to clear the way for him to do this with a clear conscience. This is purely a Jesuit enterprise, and we may apply Jesuit rules to our own conduct.

"Bertold, the Jesuit code requires members to take an oath to become a member of any other order to betray that order. This includes the sacred councils of the member's own household if needs be. A Jesuit is bound by oath to betray father, mother, wife or child. This, Bertold, will enable you to read these men as open books. I have already observed your reason for occupying this lodge. You are a student of literature which would consign you to the fires of the inquisition, were it known. For a single incautious utterance you may be put upon the rack, giving excuse for raiding this place."

Careful instructions were given to Bertold and all was now in readiness to receive Iñigo and Santillo.

They planned till far into the night the action for the morrow.

Calling his faithful old servant, Christobal gave him instructions to go out and secretly assemble the heads of the Ognez clans at a given point, where they were to remain armed and ready for quick action if called upon by Christobal, their recognized chieftain.

CHAPTER XXIX

THE EXPOSE

Unjust Men Often Fall Victims to Their Own Wiles

"THE living evidences that the God of Christianity is not the God of nature, are observed in the well known facts, that, the sun smiles alike upon joy and tragedy; the lightning strikes the church steeple, and kills a godly priest and his congregation and burns his church, more often than it does the home of the impious heathen; the rain falls as heavily upon the prelate as it does upon the man whom he calls an evil doer, and men of the Christian faith, including prelates, die with the same diseases as those which take off the common, sinful herd caring nothing for the Christian teaching. Moreover, in proportion to their numbers, the clergy commit more real, secret crime than is committed by the common run of men.

"And, yet, there is a living God, knowable to all who will recognize him by his living manifestations, the great creative being, invisible as a whole, because of his vastness, but visible in his parts which function about us, giving us life and freedom of thought, and reason to guide us along the path of a well defined and understandable evolution.

"Why cumber mens' minds with fear of that

which they can neither see nor avoid. Nature has provided for every physical act it performs.

"In one breath the scriptures tell you to fear its God, and in the next breath tells you he is no respecter of persons, exactly as I have previously said. (II Chron. 19:7.)

"All the prayers, pious confessions and penances on earth could not divert the bolt of lightning when once directed toward the church steeple. Moreover, when disaster strikes the church it overcomes a multitude who would have escaped had they not been assembled there, proving conclusively, the futility of worshiping a fabulous and fictitious God who has not the power to protect his own against natural forces.

"Nowhere else in the scriptures is it more plainly confessed that this Christian God is a mere egotistical, pompous human being, than in Moses' speech to his appointed judges.

" 'Judgment is God's; and the cause that is too hard for you, bring it unto me, and I will hear it.' (Deut. 1:17.)

"The high priest is the Christian God."

Don Alvard had arisen early, as was his custom, and found neither Christobal nor Bertold was abroad. Observing some curious hand-made sheets of paper upon the table, he examined them, finding written in excellent Spanish characters that which we have just written.

"Huh!" he grunted. "Here is philosophy."

Hearing some one approaching, he turned and was cordially greeted by Bertold.

Placing his hand upon the sheets, he said:

"May I ask who is the author of this?"

Bertold looked confused and confessed, that, he had recently thus given some expression to his own thoughts.

Don Alvard placed his huge hands upon Bertold's shoulders and earnestly said:

"My cousin, you are a philosopher. I have the greatest admiration for your intellectual attainments; I approve of every word you have here written, but conceal this quickly. With two Jesuits upon the ground you may be betrayed by one of your own brothers, turned over to the inquisitors, and be broken on the wheel or burned at the stake for this."

Bertold quickly acted upon the Don's advice, then left the lodge to take up his duties at the castle in the reception of the anticipated visitors.

It was a glorious morning that dawned upon the ancient and rugged castle of the very Catholic Lord of Ognez, "defender of the faith," but a cloud, not larger than two men on horseback, was seen slowly creeping toward it. They were recognized as the fakir, Iñigo, and the son of Satan, Santillo. The sons of Bertram rode in a body to greet them and escort them in pomp to the castle.

Count Bertram himself greeted them at the portal of his palace, embracing Iñigo and welcoming his companion.

To Bertold's utter astonishment, the first question Iñigo asked was:

"Where is my brother, Christobal, that he does not welcome me home?"

The treachery revealed by this question at once corroborated in Bertold's mind all that Don Alvard had said, but he was hardly prepared for the answer which one of his brothers made:

"Oh, Christobal has gone on a pilgrimage to Montserrat, and will not soon return."

Here was a mystery developing at once. He previously had not been advised of Christobal's intention of going elsewhere than to Pampeluna, and his now having returned proved this announcement to be a falsehood.

There were visible evidences of collusion between the brothers and these visitors—wise looks, cautious whisperings and eagerness for some anticipated activity.

This announcement concerning Christobal was clearly intended to deceive the aged father.

The day was spent in entertainment, neither Iñigo nor Santillo being accustomed to hunting. Toward evening a brief conference was held to arrange for a night council between the six brothers, and Iñigo and Santillo, whom he had introduced as a cardinal, and a special messenger from the Holy See.

A splendid banquet was laid for the visitors early that evening.

Bertold was so thoroughly convinced of pending

evil, he jeopardized himself by smuggling into a small ante-chamber, Christobal and Don Alvard, that they might have at first hand all that was said and done.

After some hours of feasting and wit, the aged count arose and begged to be excused, saying:

"My age no longer permits me to participate in strenuous discussions. My sons may well represent me in the absence of their elder brother, Christobal, which I deeply regret. I think he should have been present in the discussion of matters which must be of vital interest to him as well as to all of us."

Bertold had quickly passed to his side and now offered his arm and led him out of the room.

The great doors were tightly drawn, that no listener might hear. This gave Bertold his opportunity. Conducting Count Bertram to another room, he cautioned him not to express surprise or alarm, but it was urgent that he hear the conversation which would ensue between his sons and the emissaries of Rome.

"Do you mean to intimate that my own sons would do evil against me?" demanded Count Bertram.

"Christobal and I, also, are your sons, father, and we both believe so. It is urgent to know if it is true, is it not?" said Bertold.

"But Christobal is not here," replied the count.

Placing his fingers upon his lips to enjoin silence, he whispered:

522   THE LAST OF THE GNOSTIC MASTERS

"Christobal is here, with one who has come to warn you of grave dangers; they are concealed in your secret cabinet off the banquet room. I am to conduct you there that you may be judge of what transpires between your sons and these visitors, if it is your pleasure. It would be fatal, however, for this to be known in advance. Do you want to join them?"

"Christobal here?" Why, that is strange. They told me he had gone to Montserrat. I am being deceived. Yes, I will join them," said the count.

"Come, quickly and quietly, they will miss me," said Bertold, as he conducted his father through a secret entrance to the ante-chamber where were Christobal and Don Alvard.

All conversation in the banquet hall could be plainly heard here.

Bertold softly opened the door and Christobal received his father in a silent embrace. Don Alvard also silently pressed his hand.

Bertold reentered the banquet room, the doors were closed, and he seated himself at the council table.

Iñigo apologized for remaining seated while addressing them but his affliction necessitated it.

"I regret that our brother, Christobal has shown his disapproval of this important family conference. I advised him that it was for the good of our father, and his house-hold, that he be present and I take it as a direct affront that he has chosen to absent himself at this time. I shall be generous, however, and

attribute his clumsy mistake to a lack of worldly
experience. He, perhaps, does not know, that, the
feudal system is fast being eradicated from Europe
as a disturber of moral equilibrium, and interna-
tional quietude. The quarrels and wars between
the feudal chieftains, which were so frequent in
the eleventh and twelfth centures, were interrupted
by the edicts of state and church, issued during the
great religious movements called the crusades, rendering all civil wars practically impossible, because
of the call for volunteers to the holy cause. This
breaking up of the feudal system brought about a
far reaching desire on the part of princes to directly
ally themselves with the church, which laudable
sentiment the Holy See accepted with gratitude that
the trend of human progress was toward God and
his divine government.

"Those princes who gracefully yield to the inevitable march of human progress, under the glorious banner of the church, have been well provided
for in compensation for having placed their worldly
possessions under the holy administrations of the
church, for the better charity and benefit of mankind. This is a trust which none may judge or mis-
interpret, without reflection upon the church.

"Being in direct communication with the church
policies, which policies are uniformly endorsed and
praised by all the Christian sovereigns of Europe,
I am aware that the province of Guipuscoa has been
scheduled for reconstruction. Necessarily, I knew
this would, sooner or later, involve our father's great

estate.   Therefore, I cautiously went about inter-
ceding on my father's behalf, on the just and proper
grounds, that, he had been of great service to the
church, and, that to bring about exciting changes
at his present feeble age would hasten his death.

"His Holiness graciously granted me the con-
cession I asked, that, no direct action be taken at
this time, or during the life of our father, but, that,
a preliminary understanding be entered into with
his sons and heirs, in anticipation of the time when
the church would deem it necessary to administer
his estate, because of incapacity of old age, or death,
in a manner to best comply with the demands of the
times, and to the best credit of the church, which
aspires to become the custodian of all earthly things,
and mother of all the oppressed of the world.   This
policy necessarily works hardship upon the few for
the good of the whole, a policy which must in the
future rule the world.

"Just consideration of the vested rights of the
sons in our father's ancient estate has been given,
and, again we may feel grateful toward the gracious
attitude assumed by the Holy See regarding this
question.

"I hold here, evidence that this is a special dispensation, and due reward for our father's previous
services to the church.   This is legal authority
whereby I take over all right, title and interest, in
the name of the Holy See, in several of our great
neighboring, feudal estates, in this province.

"In our case we are to be privately compensated, in a manner which could only be suggested by such a prince of the church as Francis Borgia. He personally solicited of me the right to, himself, intervene in our behalf, and as a personal favor, he engages himself to help administer our father's estate in a manner to determine the property right of each son, then he will take these sons into his confidence, concerning his great colonizing enterprise and propaganda in that new paradise in the new world, under the protection of the church, establish them in grants of valuable properties in his colonies, and place them in the forefront of practically unlimited future possibilities of wealth and power in America.

"I have been privately informed that our brother, Christobal, has expressed his disapproval of the policy of the Holy See concerning these great estates, which should be under the control and administration of the church, and, that, he has, in some degree, influenced our father, thereby bringing them both under suspicion at Rome. I shudder to think, that, possibly, one self-interested son might, by some froward act, or slur upon the good intentions of the Holy See, bring upon our ancient house the correcting influences of the inquisitional court, with the outstanding obedience, on the part of our neighbors, accusing us of stubbornness toward the church edicts which no one must challenge.

"I have spoken upon our own behalf; our good friend, Cardinal Santillo, who knows the facts even better than myself, being closer to the papal throne, perhaps, than any other prelate in Rome, will now speak to you in the name of the Holy See."

Santillo, now well saturated with Count Bertram's best wine, pompously scrambled to his feet, and, after thanking the brothers for the cordial reception they had extended to him, said further:

"I cannot add much to what your august brother has said to you. I have traveled with him from Rome, not as a bearer of any special message or decree, but merely to give official sanction to your brother's mission. What he has said I corroborate, and, I confess, I feel constrained to congratulate you upon having a pleader at court so eloquent that he elicits the best and most generous sentiments of His Holiness. Frankly, I was opposed to any special dispensations in the execution of the church policy with regard to large properties, in the possession of good Catholics of long standing—it having been unanimously conceded, that, by virtue of the supervision of the church over its people, these properties rightly belonged to the Holy See and should be administered by that body. That which reflects hardships upon the few also becomes a blessing to the many. This is the theory of doing good to the greatest number by an equitable distribution of accumulations of property—a theory not disputed by any good Christian. Personal sacrifice is a cardinal duty of all Christians.

"Unthinking and unchristian persons roundly abuse the church authorities for enforcing discipline on the part of those who oppose policies which, of necessity, work hardships upon the few. But much of this opposition is plain defiance toward the will of the Holy See, in the conduct of its plain temporal duties. It frequently necessitates cruel punishment for those who refuse to obey the mandates of the church authorities, who alone can dispense justice with an even hand, and who alone can escape the charge of selfish motives.

"If I am permitted to act in an advisory capacity, I suggest that you draft a form of oath, or bond of chivalry, which will be a formal pact between you to permit the Holy See to take over the administration of your father's estate at any time it may become apparent to the church authorities that he is no longer capable of conserving it for the best interests of the church. It shall be my painful duty to so report at Rome any serious divergence from this idea."

As Santillo ceased speaking, Iñigo quickly said:

"Your suggestion, my good cardinal is most appropriate and opportune. Such a pact had not occurred to me. I know my brothers feel as I do, that, bound together by a suitable oath, there could be no divergence of opinion. I believe we may immediately put this to a vote, and, if the result is unanimous, which I feel sure it will be, we shall deputize you to draw such an oath as may be acceptable to the Holy See as a suitable test of our loyalty to the church. Let each brother favoring such an oath stand," and Iñigo himself struggled to his feet, as did all his brothers.

A few minutes later a commotion at the castle portal intimated the arrival of some one, and their brother, Christobal, was soon ushered into the banquet room as though just having arrived.

He was greeted by his brothers with deceitful cordiality.

Turning quickly upon Santillo, he exclaimed:

"Why, my dear cardinal! I supposed you were well on your way to San Sebastian; did you change your mind?" He made no pretense of offering his hand to the priest, or wishing him welcome, nor did he pretend to notice the presence of his brother, Iñigo. Much to the surprise and chagrin of his other brothers.

"I met your brother, Iñigo, and by his request accompanied him here," stammered Santillo.

"Ah, I see," said Christobal, looking askance at Iñigo, who sat viciously staring at his elder brother, suspicion written all over his sinister face.

Santillo could only twist his hands and exhibit his confusion.

Looking savagely at Iñigo, Christobal demanded:

"Why did you not keep your engagement with me at Pampeluna?"

Iñigo made no reply.

"And," continued Christobal, "what is the urgent purpose causing you to undertake so arduous a journey here?"

"Have I not the same right here as yourself?" sullenly demanded Iñigo.

"Not according to the records of our family reg-

ister. You have thrice been summoned to this prin-
cipality by your father without response. The purpose of these calls you well knew was to receive
the commands of our father concerning the future
conduct of his estate. You thrice refused to participate. You are aware, that, according to our
family code, you have wilfully disinherited yourself.
After my father, I am master here, and I request
that you make known quickly what your motive is
in purposely drawing me away from here, and de-
ceiving me to keep me away, while you make this
visit. As for this imposter who comes here and poses
as a cardinal of the Catholic church, fortunately
we have the authority to try and execute him without consulting Rome, and as lord and master of this
estate, as proxy of my father, it is my prerogative
to punish him forthwith.

Iñigo arose, and pointing to his brothers, said:

"They will make known the purpose of my visit.
As for your slanderous assault upon the good reputation of this holy man, it is my duty to report your
conduct to the inquisitors at Rome."

Christobal laughed uproarously, and stamped his
foot upon the tiled floor.

Instantly the great folding doors swung wide,
and Don Alvard strode into the room followed by a
clanking troop of armed men, wearing chain armor
and with visors lowered. At a motion of the Don's
hand, guards moved to each avenue of egress.

Consternation prevailed; the brothers being

guilty of treason to their clan, under the feudal laws, the penalty of death was their portion.

Iñigo was thoroughly undone and showed no resistance. In Don Alvard he recognized the man who had helped him to escape from Pampeluna, and he knew he had met up with the nemesis of the Roman priesthood—he looked the part.

Santillo stood gazing in hypnotic terror at his old enemy. He felt there was no avenue of escape; his time had come.

The brothers, including Iñigo, but not Bertold, together with Santillo, were taken to the great dank dungeons beneath the castle, for the night.

The father was prostrated, scarcely knowing what it was all about.

At the break of day a company of troops placed the five traitors upon horses, and bound them in their saddles, to be conducted to the Pyrenees mountains, where it was known that Christobal possessed a private prison institution—history does not record that any one of these traitorous brothers ever again returned to the world.

As the prisoners were being brought forth, Santillo was not in sight. The keeper humbly acknowledged that the priest had in some mysterious manner escaped.

"Where is Don Alvard?" demanded Christobal.

The keeper declared that, upon being told of Santillo's escape, the Don had uttered a savage oath, sprung upon a horse and galloped away.

The Don was not going to permit his prey to escape him thus easily.

There were but two directions by which Santillo could ride away from the castle, the public highway, leading northward in the direction of Pampeluna, and a less traveled road leading southward and toward the desert.

"Ah, my cunning friend, I know your mind like a book. I shall follow you over the less traveled way," mused the Don.

It was not long before he had reasons to believe he had been inspired in selecting the road to the south. He saw before him a large man humped upon a horse, apparently indifferent as to the direction he was traveling.

Overtaking the horseman, he commanded him to halt; it was Santillo. Seeing a narrow divurgent road, the Don pointed saying: "Ride there."

This took them directly into the smothering desert, where, for three long, heart breaking hours, thy trudged the red-hot sands.

Again halting the now exhausted prelate, he talked with him without dismounting.

"Your time is come, Santillo," he calmly said.

"I should think my having escaped from prison would convince you that it is not God's will that I should die at your hands," rejoined the priest.

"You are not going to die at my hands. Do you mean to say your own conscience does not condemn you to death?" demanded Don Alvard.

"Not for anything I have done to you," answered Santillo.

"Not for the attempt you made upon my life, leaving this scar? Not for your attempt to have me mobbed at San Peste? Not for your diabolical connivance with Iñigo to plunder his own father and brothers? Then what character of crime would condemn you?"

"All of which you yourself would have done in the same circumstances," growled Santillo.

"Very well, then, I shall forgive you all these crimes and condemn you only for being a priest. I am God's avenger. I will forego the pleasure of sitting in judgment at your trial. I will go further, I shall leave you in the presence of your God and we shall see if he will rescue you. I have brought you face to face with your God. He will try you with no Catholic priest to prejudice your case. If he sees fit to spare you I will no longer hold a grudge against you. If you are guilty of these crimes charged against you, you can spend the balance of your hours praying to your saints in vain. God will surely rid patient humanity of your vile presence, that you may not commit greater crimes at the behest of your murderous inquisition. Ride on!"

They again trudged the scorching sand, the avenger constantly watching the sky; he was estimating the long and constantly augmenting streams of vultures trailing behind them.

"Stop!" he commanded, and pointing above them he said:

"These are your inquisitors. They represent the tribunal which will try, convict and execute you. That great judge whose scorching rays have seared your brain, these last few hours, will sit in judgment upon you, ere he sinks behind the horizon to try priests in other lands. Dismount!"

Like an accusing eye the red-hot sun glared at them, seeming so close they could feel its breath. In long, ribbon like rays it cast a violet reflection upon the shimmering hot plain, seeming to twist themselves about the scant scrubby, desert brush, in search of life to torment. It literally smelled of death.

Had Don Alvard not once previously been spared by it, he would have had a fear that it was also about to deliver him to the stench of this desert inquisition.

"I will give you a chance. You may start from here to escape from this desert, but you shall go naked," and he literally tore the clothing from the priest and threw him upon his face in the sand.

"Now taste the terrors of the roasting pan. These hungry inquisitors will draw the nails from your fingers and pluck out your eyes."

A vulture, then another, and another swooped near them to inspect their anticipated feast, their stinking odor sickening them. Well did Santillo know that death stood by.

Throwing Santillo's clothing across the saddle of the priest's horse, he mounted his own. Then

looking down upon the condemned man, who made
no effort to arise, he said:

"Santillo, I know you have personally conducted
so-called crusades against innocent, peace loving
communities; you have witnessed the outraging of
helpless women and children, and the cold-blooded
murder of men.   Did your heart soften in those
hours of torture?   When young women lay pleading
before your hellish soldiers, did you raise a staying
hand?   No!   You raised your foolish cross, rolled
your hypocritical eyes and uttered your poisonous
effusion, 'God wills it.'   Now your time is come, Santillo; try your formula upon yourself; there is the
true Christ looking at you.   He is going to kill you,"
and he pointed again to the sun, and rode away.
Santillo, making no plea for mercy, lay exhausted
in the blistering sand.

After a ride for an hour he paused and looked
back.   The sky was literally blackened with vultures
fighting over their prey, a funnel-shaped mass spiral-
ling about the spot where he knew the torn body
of Santillo lay.

It was a hard drive, but he felt duty bound to
ride back to Ognez and explain his hasty departure.

CHAPTER XXX

THE AVENGER

When the Serpent Swallows His Tail the Cycle Is Ended

WORN and weary, sick at heart, and thoroughly disgusted that all mankind was fighting for the mere right to live in peace, comfort and happiness, Don Alvard struggled out of the desert before he paused for a much needed rest. Upon reaching the forest he searched about until he found a clear little stream of water which renewed the waning energy of himself and his tired horses. Scattered bunches of grass gave his animals a mouthful of new life, but he remained hungry.

It was early dawn when he rode into sight of the portals of the castle of Ognez. Some great commotion was visible and loud shouts could be heard.

The intrepid cavalier never hesitated, but abandoning his extra horse he rode forward at full tilt.

A body of soldiers were cutting and slashing at the castle guards, when a tremendous horseman, with a gleaming fighting iron, so long it resembled a jousting stick, plunged into their midst and brought the conflict to an early end, but Don Alvard was too late. Christobal lay upon the ground with life flowing from many saber wounds. The Count Bertram lay not far away quite dead. A wounded servant was lying by his side, having saved his own

life by simulating death. As the Don kicked his
way through the fallen soldiers, the servant raised
his hand and pointed toward the highway, saying
with his last breath:

"Bertold! Priest!" and then he rolled over on
his back and expired.

That was sufficient. Don Alvard mounted his
horse and dashed wildly away. Taking the circuit-
ous route by which he and Christobal had previously
come to the castle, he came out upon the main highway. Hearing the pounding hoofs of horses in
the near distance, he awaited their approach.

Little did he expect what now confronted him.
Sanatos! A grim smile wreathed Don Alvard's
face, as he beheld the arch enemy of his dear friend,
Bambo. Riding with the *Legate* were two huge
soldiers, between whom rode Bertold, bound.

"Halt!" commanded the Don, and he held his
ponderous sword in fighting position.

Sanatos drew to one side of the road.

One of the soldiers pointed forward on the highway, doubtless hoping to draw the Don's attention
away from them, for he immediately made a mad
assault upon the cavalier.

Poor fool, little did he know with whom he
sought to cross swords. A deft parry, a single thrust
and he was unhorsed to die in the dust.

The Don took no chances but disposed of the
second guard with equal dispatch. Then turning
upon the terrified Legate, he pointed his sword toward the castle and shouted:

"March!"   And Sanatos shivered as he realized that he must return and face the evidence of his crime.

Releasing Bertold, he said, that, urgent duty would prevent his returning with him to the castle, but for him to hasten there himself.

At the guard-house, at the junction of the two roads, the Don called, and a very much frightened old woman appeared.

"What have you in the house to eat?" he inquired. "Bring it quickly."

In a few minutes the woman returned bearing a large metal platter upon which were a huge portion of roast mutton, and an "elephant's-foot" of black bread.

"Have you some wine?" asked the famished Don.

The woman hurriedly produced a gourd bottle of wine. Don Alvard dropped some silver into her hand, greatly to her surprise, for she held it in her palm and stared at it as they rode away.

Again that terrible grind toward the flaming desert was begun. Little did Sanatos know what horrors lay before him.

The same fierce heat pounded them, and the prelate visibly wilted, but his terrible master gruffly bade him keep moving, prodding his animal sharply to keep up his spirit.

At last they were approaching the spot where the Don had left Santillo to the tender mercies of his inquisitors.

Sanatos, having reached the limit of physical

endurance, viciously pulled his horse about and demanded, in as strong a voice as he could command:

"Where is this to end?   Where are you taking
me?"

"I am taking you before my inquisitorial court.
There is your judge," pointing to the sun.   "And
there are your inquisititors," pointing to a vast number of vultures still screaming and fighting over
the bones of Santillo.

A look of horror came upon Sanatos' face and
he was about to plunge off his horse, when Don
Alvard seized him and held him in his place till
they reached the bones of Santillo, now picked to
a glistening whiteness.   Not two bones were left
attached.

Quickly alighting, he dragged the prelate off
his horse, more dead than alive.   Roughly standing
him up he pointed to the scattered bones, saying:

"Allow me to present to you His Eminence, Cardinal Santillo."

"Santillo!" exclaimed Sanatos, with a shudder.

"Yes, he was found guilty by the same judges
that will try you," and the Don pointed at the grinning sun and the impudent vultures, whose stench
sickened them.

Tearing the clothing off Sanatos' body, he viciously slammed him upon the sand, exclaiming:

"Bambo is avenged.   I shall whiten this desert
with the bones of priests.   I have honored your rotting carcass by giving it a place in this "grave-yard
of priests.""

Sanatos was too utterly exhausted and overcome to offer the slightest word of protest. Don Alvard left him lying and rode away, taking his old course toward the lost monastery. It was his purpose to again pay a visit to Monetho.

Ten years passed by. The nemesis of priests seemed to have left the highways, but each year added to the pile of whitened bones in his desert grave-yard.

Bambo passed peacefully away at the home of his friend, the Count Brabon, as also did their friend, the count.

Don Alvard had paid several visits there to enjoy the greetings which were his only pleasure in life. In addition to Helen he now had two lovely boys to make his life more satisfying.

One bright spring morning a little caravan left the castle Bonelle, consisting of the giant Don Alvard, his excitedly happy Helen, two boys, and some staid old servants. They were well mounted, and extra pack horses carried ample comforts for an extensive journey.

Monetho had died, and Don Alvard was to take his place to guard the Gnostic treasure house. He had prepared a perfect home there for himself and his beloved family, surrounded by every comfort nature could provide.

He and Monetho had buried the bodies which were in the outer cells, but had left the masters as they were.

Two years after their departure from Castle

Bonelle, a great earthquake occurred in the Pyrenees mountains, rendering passage into the regions, where legends said was located the lost Gnostic Monastery, impossible.

This doubtless engulfed all that remained of the last of the Gnostic masters, with their precious records. Ecclesiasticism breathed easier as the years passed with no word of the intrepid Don Alvard de Balde. But, the Gnostic seeds had been well distributed, and the Christian false-pretense was compelled to shun its impossible God, and its fictitious Christ into the junk pile of ancient religions and build up a political power to maintain itself by intrigue.

Today it stands as the wealthiest institution in all the world, every dollar of which was coined out of human energy and eternal toil.

CHAPTER XXXI
GNOSTICISM AND CHRISTIANITY

"THE WISDOM OF THIS WORLD IS FOOLISHNESS WITH
GOD." I COR. 3:19.

SOME men are born fools.

Some men make fools of themselves.

Some men permit others to make fools of them.

According to the best, modern authority, all men are, in some degree, mentally or physically, abnormal.

This is quite raw stuff, eh?

Well, you read this little story through to the end, and you will be amazed to find yourself chasing yourself around a circle to see just how you stand in this category of foolishness.

Are you aware of the fact that, all authorities on the subject are agreed, that, based upon present increase statistics, the time may be closely estimated when the whole human race will be hopelessly insane, if the same conditions prevail?

Of course, you are not. Why waste your time worrying about future generations of crazy people?

If this fits your case, it places you. Selfish indifference towards the welfare of future humanity, for which every man is, in some degree, responsible, is a species of social insanity.

Nature never intended that human kind should evolve into insanity. That is easily proven by an examination of the organic and physiological structure of man, and his special sense organs and their functions.

Insanity, then, is an acquired and abnormal condition—a mental disease.

Of course, there must be a cause for such abnormality. If this cause may be found in the false training of the human mind, we may at once trace it to its source by examining the systems and methods of educating and enlightening the human race. If men are responusible for defective methods, they must have a motive. If many men band together, to exploit a common system, that is an institution, whose influences may be responsible for human dereliction.

Therefore, if we find the masses of unthinking people believing in, and supporting, an institution which teaches untruths, and misleading doctrines, we may suspect that this institution has a sinister motive in fooling the people—the innocent, believing dupes, made fools by others.

The greatest influence upon the intellectual development of humanity has been exercised by the so-called Christian system, during the past two thousand years.

Are you a Christian? Why? The answer evidently is: because you believe what you have been taught by the agents of this institution.

Suppose you were convinced that not one word of truth has been preached to you in the churches, would you still be a Christian?

Yes? That classifies you.

No? Then we are going to convince you that your prayers to fictitious saints, and gods, avail you noth-

ing; and that the time and money which you have contributed toward the upkeep and support of the church
represent the valuable waste which would have largely
added to the mental strength to prevent your being
made a blind, believing fool.

Let us eliminate all the hypnotic mystery, and hysteria, which have cast the world into semi-idiocy, and
bring the whole problem under the search light.

Just stand back in line there, clergymen, we do not
need your assistance. Make your explanations to the
people in language which they may understand, not in
parables, which your bible confesses they do not understand. Your fabulous Christ secretly confided to his
apostles:

"Unto you it is given to know the mystery of the
kingdom of God: but unto them that are without, all
these things are done in parables.

"That seeing they may see and not perceive; and
hearing they may hear, and not understand." (Mark
4:11, 12.)

Do you grasp the full significance of this? This is
what we call fooling the people. We have said there
must be a motive, and we are easily vindicated here
by a direct motive:

"Lest at any time they should be converted, and
their sins should be forgiven them." (Mark 4:12.)

It was never intended that common humanity
should enjoy immortality.

"Now, lest he put forth his hand and take also of
the tree of life, and eat and live forever." (Gen. 3:22.)

Can you get that?

Did it ever occur to you that, were there no sin or

evil in the world, there would be no necessity for a saving Christ or the church?

Of course not, or you would have asked your priest
or preacher some embarrassing questions and been
reprimanded.

Remove the doctrine of "original sin" from the
Bible, and you would have no original reason for the
church.

There was a tremendous motive in the doctrine of
"original sin." Just keep this in mind, we shall take
up this motive in a startling way a little further along.
We first desire to reveal some superficial evidences of
a premeditated exploitation of humanity by a designing organization of wise and learned men.

Preceding Christianity, there was a school of science and philosophy which had accumulated practically
all the wisdom and knowledge understandable to mankind. The object was to broadly educate the masses
of people by a unit system which would give to humanity a wisdom in common. This was the most
potential period in human intellectual advancement the
world has known.

This school was called *Gnosticism*. *Gnosis* means
to know—knowledge. *Christianity* means to *believe*—
ignorance.

These are the two schools; the one advocating the
universal education of men, and the other, the *universal ignorance* of men. The one desired to develop the
unit man, the other desired to suppress the unit and
level all mankind to a *common plastic mass.*

To accomplish this necessitated the suppression of
all extant knowledge; the closing of all the avenues

through which the people might acquire the independent learning, education, and intellectual training, and the debasement of humanity in abject ignorance.

This was the first broadcast sowing of the seeds of insanity in the world. Ignorance is closely akin to insanity; crime is insanity.

Now, reader, you are gasping at this suggestion of a wilful and premeditated degradation of humanity.

You, of course, want to know what evidences proves these assertions. You should not be disappointed.

If you desire to verify what we say, you will find it an excellent part of your education, but, we assure you, that we have ample authority for the truth of all we write. You need not trouble your mind about its authenticity.

True history is no respecter of persons. Fake history, sooner or later, betrays itself.

The school which pitted itself against Gnosticism assumed the name *Ecclesia*. This name at once identified the purpose for which the organization was created—to seize control of governments, that it might exploit mankind for profit, and for its own glorification. Temporal power was the church goal.

The name *Ecclesia* was derived from the Greek, and signified the legislative body which governed ancient Athens, long before Christianity was invented.

The first essential act of the Ecclesiasts was to suppress Gnosticism, and confiscate its vast accumulation of wisdom and knowledge, in order to control the education of future generations in a manner to adjust mankind to its purposes. Therefore, the Gnostic wisdom was not wholly lost to the world, but its great, universal educational system was *supplanted*.

It is a well-established, historical fact, not denied by the church, that it required about five hundred years to accomplish this submersion of Gnosticism, and to degrade the new generations in ignorance equal to a state of imbecility.

History again points its accusing finger at the living evidence. The horrible results of such a crime against nature and mankind are pictured in the "dark ages" (486 to 1495), a thousand years of semi-imbecility. Not even princes or prelates were permitted to learn to read or write. Even bishops could barely spell out their Latin. During this period of mental darkness, the ignorant masses were trained in intolerence, bigotry, fanaticism, and superstitious fear of an invisible power secretly controlled by the church; all of which begat a state of hysteria and imbecility.

Through this terrorism the popes seized control of the *temporal power*, retaining this control for nearly five hundred years. They appointed and deposed kings at will, hence they dictated legislation to their ends and purposes—the very essence of government.

This brings us back to the doctrine of "original sin," and its secret purpose.

First, if there were no sin in the world there would be no necessity for the church, hence the church introduced sin.

If there were no laws there would be no sin.

"Because the law worketh wrath: for where no law is, there is no transgression." (Romans 4:15.)

Transgression is sin, and sin is disobedience to the law.

Does it begin to dawn upon you now, reader, that "original sin" was legislated into mankind for a specific purpose?

Did it ever occur to you that our modern, so-called, appalling increase in crime is contingent upon this same principle? We are literally smothered in statutory, criminal laws, and the legislative mills are grinding out an endless grist of new laws. It is clear, that, if present laws are inadequate to check crime, crime is not controlled by law. On the other hand, new laws must of necessity create new criminal classes.

Can't you see that, every new law placed upon the statute books creates a new class of criminals, and to that extent increases the general volume of crime?

That is why crime seems to be increasing more rapidly in proportion to the increase in population, and the irritations of such conditions naturally produce insanity; therefore, insanity is being legislated into humanity along with crime.

Do you believe there is no underlying motive back of this? Well, you may guess again. This process of legislating evil into mankind is to vindicate that damnable doctrine of "original sin," which slanders nature and insults all mankind.

The church confesses its purpose to involve all men.

"Now we know that what things soever the law saith, it saith to them who are under the law: that every mouth may be stopped, and all the world may become guilty." (Rom. 3:19.)

The purpose here plainly is to bring all mankind

under the law, and suppress free speech, that resentment of the unit man may be choked in his throat.

No law but superstitious fear can prevent a man's thinking. It is in this dark cell that hatred is born.

We feel certain you have not yet grasped the great purpose concealed in this scheme.

St. Peters in Rome was constructed with the money raised by the open advertisement of the sale of criminal indulgences by Pope Leo X in 1513. This was recognized as a cleancut trafficking in crime. It caused the so-called Reformation. Did that stop the sale of indulgences? Not that any one can see!

If there had been no transgressions, there could not have been an excuse or reason for the sale of indulgences. But this is not the greatest evil in this vicious church policy. In order to avoid the criticism of governments, it insidiously instilled into the civil legislative powers the great possibilities in this process as a source of profit.

Did you ever think of the similarity between the sale of indulgences and the fines collected because of the violation of laws?

They are identically the same. "For where no law is there is no transgression." Do you see the great temptation to bring every act of mankind under this form of compulsory tribute? Every joy, every pleasure, every comfort, every necessity, must pay a tax, and the legislatures of governments devote more attention to the profit in crime than to any other form of legislation. There is no intimation whatever that crime is decreasing because of new laws.

No matter what the manner and method of levying and collecting taxes, the motive and purpose are the same, to live off the energy of humanity. Mankind, to live, must pay tribute to both, the ravenous church, to support a parasitical organization and priesthood, and to support insanely extravagant governments.

If this is not double taxation, name it. The churches do not perform one function that may not be performed by the logical civil government.

Do you know that Matthew, the alleged author of the first gospel in the new testament, was originally Levi the *tax collector?* He was called the Publican, "the people's servant," and was hated as much as modern tax collectors—the naming of public officials the "people's servants" is a palpable hypocrisy. The word *levy* comes from the same source, meaning *to seize property.*

We speak of the *tax-levy* in the same bitter sense. The name originates back in the scriptures, Levi being one of the sons of Jacob.

Jacob means *to usurp* or *supplant.*

Levi means *associated*—the tax collector.

Only too often do we feel that the *tax-levy* smacks of usurpation or confiscation.

Now let us step back to Ecclesiasticism. Originally the motive was to confiscate the intellects of man, but the modern policy is much more concerned in confiscating their personal rights and property.

Here is the other aspect of the suppression of Gnosticism. Its method of teaching was an understandable symbolism. It specifically recognized nature as the great teacher, and visible things as the traditional

records of past events in a progressive evolution, from
the lowest state to the highest, with thinking, reasoning man as the highest evoluted being. Man did not
fall, he was raised up by a natural promotion.

Hence, every man was a Gnostic to the extent of
his accumulated knowledge and understanding. Thus
each unit man became a teacher, and all men were
given equal rights in the acquirement of knowledge.
It was wholly an educational system, and a natural
sequence in evolution.

The Ecclesiasts, being thoroughly familiar with the
Gnostic wisdom concerning *astronomy, chemistry* and
mathematics, as demonstrated by the splendid systems
of Babylon, Egypt and Assyria, conceived the idea of
developing a Religio-political form of universal government, to control and exploit the future generations
of people upon the earth through living, personified
agents of the imaginary heavenly powers.

This necessitated the development of an invisible,
unapproachable, divine power to delegate supreme
authority to a vicegerent on earth who was to be "King
of Kings, and Lord of Lords." (Rev. 19:16.)

"God is a spirit." (Jno. 4:24.)

"A spirit hath not flesh and bones." (Luke 24:39.)

"No man hath seen God at any time." (I Jno.
4:12.)

Did it ever occur to you, that, according to the legal
codes of nations, such a God could not establish a legal
standing on earth? Let some wise lawyer explain
how he could.

To monopolize such a divine power as that contemplated made it necessary to personify nature, using

the Gnostic system of symbolisms, and to give to these
wholly imaginary beings names and functions. The
Gnostic system had to be confiscated, and Gnosticism
suppressed to prevent exposure.

*This is why Christianity is so viciously antagonistic
towards science and philosophy,* these belong to the
original Gnosticism, to destroy which necessitated that
the Christian day begin with the darkness of the
night.

The "dark-ages" was this night.

Darkness, in the Ecclesiastical code, symbolizes
ignorance, adversity, affliction.

"And the *evening* and the morning were the first
day." (Gen. 1:5.)

The rising sun was to be the new era of intelligence
with which Ecclesiasticism was to flood the world—the
figurative Christ.

"I am the light of the world." (Jno. 8:12.)

It is in the brazen plagiarism of the Gnostic simili-
tudes that Ecclesiasticism betrays itself. By the code
which it worked out for the use of its inner circle, a
rank fraud upon humanity is revealed. Moreover, the
truth that it deliberately confiscated the Gnostic symbolisms is made plain beyond dispute. It has attempted
to monopolize the whole universe, in order to destroy
all previous forms of worship of the heavenly bodies,
and the planetary phenomena. And, by this process,
it demonstrates its own God as a clearly-defined product of evolution, descending from:

Sun-worship,

"He set a tabernacle for the sun." (Ps. 19:4.)

Fire-worship,

"For our god is a consuming fire." (Heb. 12:29.)

Light-worship,

"God is light, and in him is no darkness." (I Jno.
1:5.)

Man-worship,

"The son of man."

"I am the light of the world." (Jno. 8:12.) Jesus
Christ, the son of man, a human being, is worshiped
as God on earth.

It was necessary to figuratively crucify the original
Christ character, in order that he might will to a living
vicegerent, the head of the church, his alleged divine
powers.

*Do you see, now, why Christianity antagonizes nat-
ural animal evolution up to and including man?* Here
is an example of men making fools of themselves.

Again, let us ask you questions.

If you were convinced that such a character as
Adam never lived, would you still confess yourself a
Christian, and go on handing your hard-earned money
to the church, for it to add to the *billions of untaxed
property* which it has amassed by cultivating human
credulity?

Don't you feel a little foolish upon reading this?

"If we have sown unto you spiritual things, it is a
great thing if we shall reap your carnal things?" (I
Cor. 9:11.)

Did you ever pause to think that this spiritual stuff
costs absolutely nothing; can do you no possible good
in this world, and, that you know nothing of the alleged

next world, and, that, your carnal stuff means *bread, meat and good wine on the lees for the fat-paunched prelates?* Try to figure out where God gets any of the vast church wealth.

Well, let us continue about Adam. He is the alleged forefather of Christ, but no possible connection can be traced, because both are bald fakes.

Now, if you had it demonstrated to you that no such human being as Jesus Christ ever lived, would you go on being a worshiper of a fable?

This is your affair, but it is a mighty important matter to humanity.

We shall go further and say, that, when you hear the next leather-faced evangelist yowl that he believes every word of the Bible is true, exactly as written, you are morally safe in putting him down as a wilful liar —or maybe he belongs to the born fools, for not one page in the Bible is truth—and the preachers know this.

We shall now give you a whole mouthfull of surprise, revealing the manner by which the Ecclesiasts attempted to personify the Gnostic symbolisms and make up a code system to fool humanity.

Remember, the Bible is taught literally, and the code significance reveals the truth which disputes the Bible teachings.

The first ten words in the Bible reveal a clean-cut deception, and a purpose to class the greater part of humanity as merely a producing force, while favored classes pose as ruling gods.

"In the beginning God created the *heaven* and the *earth*." (Gen. 1:1.)

Interpreted by the secret Ecclesiastical codes, *Heaven* means the *Ecclesiastical government*. *Earth* means the producing masses of mankind.

The ancient scientists adjusted their scientific research to the formula: *air, earth, fire* and *water*.

The Ecclesiasts changed this to,

> *Earth, water, air* and *fire,*
> *Adam, Noah, Abram* and *Moses.*

Adam heads the Earth period.

Noah heads the Water period.

Abram heads the Air period.

Moses heads the Fire period.

Let us examine the Ecclesiastical beginning. It seeks to establish an earthly empire, which it calls *heaven*, signifying an *Ecclesiastical government*, with supreme power over civil rulers.

The same power personifies the productive earth as *Adam*, symbolizing *productive mankind* — Earth means *producer*. *Adam* is from the sanscrit *Adim*, meaning *the first;* hence, Adam signifies the *first ancestor of humanity*.

It was first necessary to establish a people to justify and support the governments.

Adam's offspring represent the essentials for producing and maintaining this people.

	Ecclesiastical	*Gnostic*
Cain		
	Possession	Vegetation
Abel		
	Breath	Atmosphere

Seth

Compensation   Animals

Cain is in *possession* of the earth by contact.

Abel is *Ab* = father + el = god, signifying the breath or vital element which binds the respiratory animals to the earth.

God is from the sanscrit word *good*:

Seth, compensation, signifies the respiratory exchange between the animals and vegetation. The vegetation inhales carbon dioxide and exhales oxygen; the respiratory animals inhale oxygen and exhale carbon dioxide, the leaves of the trees, as also symbolized by Abel, acting as the breathing apparatus of the vegetation, become the medium, as the atmosphere is the medium between heaven and earth.

Right here, we are going to remove all doubt as to whether or not man is naturally evolved out of the lower animal life.

"And to Seth, to him also, there was born a son; and he called his name *Enos.*" (Gen. 4:26.)

Enos means *mortal man subject to fall.* This clearly differentiates between the previous creations and mortal man.

We also have positive proof that it was the intent and purpose of this scheme to make mankind good or evil as occasion required.

Right in the early part of the new testament we find this command:

"Either make the tree good, and his fruit good; or else make the tree corrupt, and his fruit corrupt: for the tree is known by his fruit." (Matt. 12:33.)

THE TREE OF GOOD AND EVIL.

"Adam (the earth), begat a son in his own likeness after his image." (Gen. 5:3.) The earth and fruit are globes.

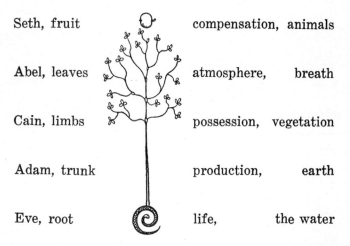

Seth, fruit		compensation, animals
Abel, leaves		atmosphere, breath
Cain, limbs		possession, vegetation
Adam, trunk		production, earth
Eve, root		life, the water

The Gnostic significance of this is important. There is a clearly defined evolution up to the compensating fruit of the system as personified in *Seth,* but no intimation of man having been born.

This fruit, to reproduce, must be surrendered by the tree and fall back to the corrupt earth.

"So also is the resurrection of the dead. It is sown in corruption; it raised in incorruption." (I Cor. 15:42.)

This explains the figurative *fall,* and the *resurrection.* It is a physical act of nature. But it yet has not revealed man.

It is self-evident that, if Seth is the fruit, he must drop back to earth and pass through the chemical processes of nature (the fires of hell, meaning the grave), to be resurrected as a new tree. Naturally, this is the point where Ecclesiasticism attempts to create man as a special dispensation.

"And to Seth, to him also there was born a son; and he called his name Enos." (Gen. 4:26.)

Enos, meaning *mortal man subject to fall*, gives us a pre-vision of the future Christ as *symbolizing humanity at large*.

This gives a reason for debasing and crucifying mankind as the first great act of Christianity.

"Except a man be born of *water* and of the *spirit*, he cannot enter into the kingdom of God." (Jno. 3:5.) That is the process by which the new tree is raised up.

Man is a living soul, soul is spirit, and spirit is breath, or *wind*.

Water means *ordinances* and *afflictions*.

In many languages *spirit* was synonymous with *wind*, meaning *judgments* and *destructive war* and *conflict*.

Mankind surely has experienced all this.

This brings us to the water period personified in *Noah*.

Noah means *consolation*, rest. Here the physical creations cease.

Water means *afflictions, ordinances*.

HIS OFFSPRING

	Ecclesiastic	*Gnostic*
Shem	Renown	Flesh
Japheth	Expansion	Muscle
Ham	Zeal	Bone

This is the new man to be servant to the church.

The air period, personified in *Abram,* means the *high father.* As $Ab + ra + ham$ he means the *high-hot-father,* meaning the *heat of the sun,* the father of a multitude, which is symbolized by the rain drops. Rain means doctrines.

"My doctrine shall drop as the rain." (Deut. 32:2.)

Abram (heat) comes out of *Ur* (fire). (Gen. 11:28, 32.) This is the patriarch of the new generation:

HIS OFFSPRING

	Ecclesiastical	*Gnostic*
Isaac	Laughter	Sunlight
Jacob	Supplanter	Absorption

Jacob becomes *Israel, the church of God.*

This plainly conceals another intimation of encroachment upon civil institutions. The bargain made with Abraham gave Canaan to the Jews. *Canaan* means *merchandising* and *trading.* The bargain made with Jacob also provided for a ten per cent tax. (Gen. 28:22), to come to the high priest.

The fire period is personified in *Moses* the *law giver,* and *Aaron* the *teacher. Fire* means *judgments* —legislation. *Aaron* means *enlightener*—the schools. *Joshua* is the third element in the trio.

Jo is an abbreviation of *Joseph.*

Joseph means *increase.*

Shua means *wealth.*

Jo + *shua* is *increased wealth.*

The savior of the Ecclesiastic exploitation:

Jesus is the Greek form of Joshua, and is the savior of the Christian enterprise.

Are you Jew or Gentile? Both are worshiping the same God.

Now let us finish off this lesson in Christian intrigue, and give you final cause for questioning yourself as to whether you are being made a fool of by others.

The word Christ may be eliminated from further consideration. It is not a proper name, but merely a modifying word signifying a thing anointed with oil to give it a shining or conspicuous aspect. Moses anointed everything in the tabernacle, including the pots and pans.

The word Christ is a form of the Hindoo *Christna,* known hundreds of years before the equally fabulous Jesus the Christ was invented.

This brings the word Jesus to the front. This name is merely the translation of the Hebrew *Joshua* into the Greek *Jesus.* We have already revealed what the name signifies—*increased wealth* as the savior and salvation of the Ecclesiastic—Christian exploitation.

In the Christian period *Joseph* signifies *increasing humanity,* the basis of the increased wealth.

He espouses *Mary,* the alleged mother of Jesus by the *holy ghost.* This is a very sinister suggestion.

Mary means *rebellion.*

The *holy ghost* means the *breath*. In practically all the ancient languages *breath* means *wind*.

In the Ecclesiastical code *wind* means *desolating wars*.

"And ye shall hear of wars and rumors of wars: see that ye be not troubled, for all these things must come to pass.

"For nation *shall* rise against nation, and kingdom against kingdom." (Matt. 24:6, 7.)

Jesus, symbolizing the multiplying humanity, is carried by *increase,* his adopted father, and *rebellion,* his mother, into Egypt, meaning *oppression* and *trouble,* later to take refuge in *Galilee,* meaning *revolution.*

We may now read with understanding the words placed in the mouth of the fictitious Christ:

"Think not that I am come to send peace on earth: I come not to send peace, but a sword." (Matt. 10:34.)

"For I am come to set a man at variance against his father, and the daughter against her mother." (Matt. 10:35.)

This is a brutal acknowledgment that the most sacred, natural human ties are to be torn asunder to foster an abnormal and wholly unlawful cause.

Now, reader, the next time your pompous preacher mentions your Christ as the prince of peace, pull this on him, and demand an explanation—and get a scolding.

All the good found in the new testament may be found in the teachings of all good men in all ages. The so-called scriptures of the old testament are too vile, vulgar and suggestive to be permitted to remain in circulation, and should be suppressed.

Practically every leading character in the Bible is a drunkard, a murderer, a hypocrite, or a degenerate of some kind.

All the blather about their teaching morality is pure bunk. Who would dare to suggest patterning our school books after the obscenities found throughout the old testament? Then why permit the churches to teach this vile stuff?

Are you still a Christian?

If you are, you are in some degree responsible for the following: Twenty per cent of the people of the United States may be classed as absolutely ignorant.

The increase in crime and imbecility is devouring the nation.

The people are being smothered under a blanket of imbecilic statutory laws, to that extent adding new criminal classes.

Taxation, in every conceivable form, is confiscating the energy of the masses to such an extent that eternal drudgery and hardship are debasing human intellect, and suppressing the higher national aspirations as this was done in the "dark ages." A new night is being brought down upon mankind.

So-called physical-culture has superceded mental development, solely to increase productive human energy, to support the parasitical, non-productive classes, and fight their senseless, murderous wars.

The churches have been permitted to amass billions of property, coined by struggling humanity.

Hundreds of millions of this usurped wealth is snugly tucked away in the form of interest-bearing, non-taxable securities.

Upon all this wealth no taxes are paid. Why should the poor pay taxes and the wealthy churches pay none?

Hundreds of thousands of idle, so-called clergymen are supported by the poor boobs who believe in the fabulous Christian hypocrisy.

Thousands of sycophant organizations, hangers-on of the Christian enterprise, take their cue and reap a harvest in the name of fake charities.

One of these boasts of having amassed a surplus of hundreds of millions.

Truly that formula, "If we have sown unto you spiritual things, is it a great thing that we shall reap your carnal things?" (I Cor. 9:11), is a "go-getter."

While the people are being gutted by these ravenous vultures, the nation is being smothered in crime, ignorance, imbecility and taxation.

Eighty per cent of the people are in some degree defective.

Wherein is Christianity a benefit to this or any other nation, in view of these horrible conditions found throughout the world?

Here is one example of church charity: When the late war was on us, with all its harrowing demands upon the people for all they could give up, the churches brazenly made a drive for one billion of dollars upon the United States, bringing to bear every form of secret coercion they knew how to wield—especially emphasizing patriotism.

Stop and think of this: ten dollars for every man, woman and child in the United States. For what?

Isn't this sufficient?

Are you still a Christian?

We invite the churches to resent this. It is mild compared with what we hold in reserve.

It is high time that our government appoint a commission to investigate to what extent the churches have abused the limited privileges granted them under our constitution. Shall they be permitted to usurp the legislative powers through political intrigues? Every thinking man knows this is the church aspiration.

"For the time is come that judgment must begin at the house of God: and if it first begin at us, what shall the end be of them that obey not the gospel of God?" (I Peter 4:17.)

Thus is exposed the final purpose of church legislation—near the end of the Bible.

All the people are to be legislated into crime to vindicate the doctrine of "original sin."

The sales of indulgences are to be disguised under penalties for law violations, and the church is to be supported out of the public treasury.

And, lastly, all the people are to be legislated into the church through the control of legal judgments.

Moreover, it practically may be determined at approximately what period the church may control the intrinsic wealth of the nation, by the cumulative powers of non-taxation. Their present wealth exceeds that of any other institution in the world. Instead of this adding to the wealth of the world, it places upon the back of humanity the golden casket and the mummified burden of a non-productive corpse. This is the modern ark of the covenant with the Jews.

How long will the people continue to be the fools

and unconscious tools of designing forces concealed in
a lamb's skin? How long will the so-called Christians
be deceived into worshiping the *Hebrew Joshua* in the
disguise of the *Greek Jesus?*

Can it be possible that, at this time, all men are
born fools?

If not, why do they not assert their natural common sense and reason, and cast off this heart-breaking
burden which is sapping the very life-blood, sanity,
and morality of the nation, as well as absorbing its
material wealth? Under the concealing cloak of the
church of God, Israel is making good the usurpation of
Jacob.

In view of the political activities of the churches in
the United States, we call attention to the fact that:

Four original documents form the legal foundation of this nation:

1.—The Declaration of Independence.....1776
2.—The Articles of Confederation.......1778
3.—The Jeffersonian Ordinance 1784
4.—The Constitution of the United States
        of America....................1787

Only once in all these tremendously important instruments of human government does the word *God*
appear, and that is the "God of nature," and acting
under the "laws of nature," found in the Declaration
of Independence.—

The name of Jesus Christ does not appear at all.

The word church does not appear.

No intimation of religion is found in the oath
taken by the president upon entering upon the duties
of that office.

Article VI of the Constitution distinctly eliminates religion as a factor of government.

On the other hand, the makers of these documents especially acknowledge that they act solely:

"In the name and by the authority of the people."

"Governments derive their just powers from the consent of the governed," to the extent that:

"For cause, the people shall have the right to alter or abolish the government."

Here God and religion are wholly eliminated from direct participation, both in the forming and dissolving of the government.

The Constitution provides for the "promotion of science."

The Christian churches openly denounce the promotion of science.

The cost of building and maintaining the churches, and the support of the clergy, in the United States, is more than sufficient to establish and maintain the whole national school system, with a tremendous surplus towards other national expenses, if properly applied and expended.

Let this suffice.

CHAPTER XXXII
WHAT OF THE FUTURE?

IT IS NOT DIFFICULT TO JUDGE THE FUTURE BY THE PRESENT.

IT is every man's privilege to be imposed upon, if it affords him satisfaction, pleasure or profit; providing, however, that he is not aiding, abetting and fostering some system, or institution, which lives, thrives and fattens at the expense of human credulity. Only such a sycophant fool would permit himself to be hum-bugged upon learning the truth.

We shall exhibit a limited vocabulary of Biblical names and words to demonstrate conclusively that Ecclesiasticism is a clean-cut hypocrisy. This will open up the way for interested persons to delve deeper into the subject of Biblical interpretation, for their own edification.

Of course, it is essential to have the proper Bible dictionaries and vocabularies, to reveal the Ecclesiastic code. It is difficult, at this time, to procure the more ancient vocabularies, they having been carefully gathered up in order to suppress them. The dictionaries do not always reveal the true meanings.

The first ten words in the Bible reveal the secret purpose of the Christian exploitation of humanity:

"In the beginning God created the *heaven* and the *earth*."   (Gen. 1:1.)

Heaven means the *Ecclesiastical government*.

Earth means *productive humanity*.

The word *ecclesia* is derived from the Greek, and signifies the legislative body which ruled ancient Athen.

It is also definitely known that the original manuscripts read "the gods"; hence, there is even dishonesty in translation charged against the Ecclesiasts.

Adam—earth.
Eve—life.
Cain—possession.
Abel—vanity, breath.
Seth—compensation.
Enos—mortal man subject to fall.
Cainan—lamentation.
Jared—empire.
Enoch—discipline.
Lamech—poverty.
Noah—consolation.
Shem—fame.
Ham—zeal.
Japheth—extension.

Who can be so absolutely bigoted that they cannot see a consecutive and progressive scheme concealed in these names?   Not one of these alleged characters ever lived.

Upon these the church is founded.

Abraham, the *high priest or father*.

Ab = father, ra = high, ham = hot.

The high, hot father—the heat of the *sun*.
  Abraham came from *Ur*, meaning *fire*.
Isaac, joy and laughter—the *sunshine*.
Jacob, the supplanter, usurpation.
  As *Israel* he is the *church of God*.
Rebekah, snare, trap—mother of Jacob.
Rachel, a sheep, disciple.
Esau, the hairy man.
Hori, the cave-dweller.
Edom, the red-man.

In the whole imaginary family of Jacob, we have
the original scheme of organizing the priesthood.
Israel, the church of God, combines with the disciples
to establish the system.   *Ishmael*, the brother of Isaac,
furnishes the suppliant people.

Ishmael means *whom God hears, supplicant*.   He is
progenitor of the *Arabians*. *Ambush*. *Arabia* means
a mixture of peoples or tribes.

In the confiscation of the Gnostic idea of simili-
tudes the Ecclesiasts attempted to personify natural
forces, and put under control the visible things of
nature.

The arched sky, the heaven, Ecclesiastical govern-
ment.   The sun, moon and stars, governors and priests.
Rain means *doctrine*.
"My doctrine shall drop as the rain."   (Deut. 32:2.)
Dew means *conversions*.
Thunder means *to preach*.
Lightning means *vengeance*.
Fire means *judgment*.
Day means *a gospel period*.
Light means *intellect*.

Night means *adversity, affliction, ignorance.*
Darkness means *misery, ignorance.*
Earthquakes mean *revolution.*
Grass means *lower classes.*
Trees mean *great nobles.*
Mountains mean *Christ's church.*
Hills mean the *schools.*
Earth means the *producers.*
Sea means the *army.*
Waters mean *afflictions, multitudes, ordinances.*
Wind means *destructive war.*
And thus every visible thing is used as a symbol.

THE TWELVE SONS OF JACOB

Agents of the usurpation of temporal power over governments, and the super-control over humanity, by the Ecclesiasts.

Jacob means to supplant, *usurp by trickery.*
Jacob is disguised as *Israel.*
Israel is the *church of God.*
Rebekah, the mother of Jacob, means *snare, trap.*
The twelve sons are symbols concealing the priestly system.

Ecclesia means a *legislative body.* The word is derived from the ancient Greek name of the legislative body ruling Athens.

Reuben means *prophecy, dream, vision.*

"Your sons and your daughters shall prophesy, your old men shall dream dreams, your young men shall see visions." (Joel 2:28.)
Denounced as criminal. (Gen. 35.)

Simeon means *obedience.*

Denounced as criminal. (Gen. 34.)

Levi means *associated, restraint.*

Denounced as criminal with Simeon. (Gen. 34.)

Christ's ancester (Luke 3), Levites, the priesthood.

Judah means *praise, approval, exaltation, glory.*

Received part of merchandising and trading. (Josh. 15.)

Issachar means *reward, price, compensation.*

See bargain with Jacob. (Gen. 28:20-22.) "Servant unto tribute; burden bearer." (Gen. 49.)

Zebulun means *dwelling, habitation, abode.*

Begets fear, strength, and hope. (Gen. 46:14.)

Dan means *judge, judgment.*

Formerly called Laish, Lion, meaning *seeing.* (Gen. 19:49.) A place in *Arabia, mixture of peoples. Ar* means to *awaken. Abia* means *God is my father.*

Joseph means *increase, addition.*

Name of three of Christ's ancestors. (Luke 3.) Son of *usurpation and the flock.* (Gen. 37:3.) Increase is sent into oppression and trouble to preserve a posterity to Israel the Church of God. (Gen. 45:7.) Husband of *Mary, rebellion,* mother of Jesus. *Increase* and *rebellion* carry *Jesus, humanity at large,* into Egypt, *oppression and trouble,* to later take refuge in *Galilee, revolution,* and to *Capernaum* for *repentance* and *comfort.*

Benjamin means *right-hand, protection.*

First called *son of grief and sorrow.* "Benjamin shall devour the prey in the *morning* and at *night* divide the spoils." (Gen. 49:27.)

Day means a *Gospel period.*

Night means *adversity, affliction, ignorance.*

Naphtali means *comparison, likeness, that fights.* Associated with *enmity* and *empire.*

Gad means *troop, armed and prepared,* captivated by miracles.

The God of Israel stirred up the spirit of two kings of Assyria, *Pul, destruction, hurtful, baneful. Tiglath-pilneser, captivity, miraculous,* and carried them, together with the *Reubenites, visionaries* and *prophets,* and the *Gadites, armed* and *warlike,* and the *Manassehites, forgetfulness,* unto *Habor, fertility. Hara, hill, the school,* and *Gozan, fleece, pasture, nourishing of the body. Assyria* means *happiness.*

Asher, felicitation, blessedness.

He built *Ninevah, an agreeable dwelling place.* Associated with *Manasseh, forgetfulness.*

Thus we find the most vital elements of the ecclesiastical enterprise concealed in a fictitious list of names, allegedly the members of one Jewish family.

The same false-pretense applies to the whole system, as it leads up to the Christian scheme to deceive humanity, and conceal the underlying political intrigue, and the ulterior purposes to seize temporal control over sovereigns and their peoples.

Moses is the law giver.

Mo means *water*.

Waters mean *ordinances*.

Aaron, the enlightener, the school.

Levites, priestly descendants of Aaron.

Midian, strife.

Moses committed murder and fled to Midian.

Strife is the son of Abraham the high priest.

Jethro is *high priest of Midian*.

Jethro means *posterity*.

Jethro suggests the appointment of usurpative judges.

Jethro is also *Raguel, the friend of God, a prince* of Midian.   Father-in-law to Moses.

Joshua, Savior.

Jo+shua means *increased wealth*.

Joseph means *increase*.

Jo is an abbreviation of Joseph.

Shua means *wealth*.

Shua is also the father-in-law of

Judah, praise, exaltation.   Wealth exalts.

Shua is extended to Shuah, a son of

Abraham, the high father, the *high priest*.

Shuah means *a pit* or *pitfall, humiliation.*   Thus wealth is made a snare, or pitfall.

Shuah is the brother of *Chebub,* the *basket.*   *Caleb* was the *basket* for *Joshua.*

In Deut. 26, we have a startling explanation of the significance of *the basket*.

Jesus is the Greek form of *Joshua*.   The *Jews* worship their *Joshua* in the field of *merchandising and trading*, allotted to them by the bargain between them and the ecclesiasts, as Canaan. *Canaan* means *merchandizing and trading*.

The *Christians* worship their *Joshua* in the Greek form of *Jesus*, and seek their *increased wealth* in the church field, trafficking in indulgences in evil.

The *Gentiles* serve the God *Mammon*, meaning *worldly riches*.

Christ declares in Matt. 6:24, "Ye cannot serve God and mammon."

Now, as the Jews and the Christians both worship the same God, *increased wealth*, under the disguise of *Joshua* and *Jesus*, it is clear that Christ is not discrediting *mammon*, but he is merely pointing out the truth, that, men cannot worship riches under two names and do justice to both—all are worshiping *wealth*. Increasing commerce is the wealth of the Jews. Increasing humanity is the wealth of the church. Increasing prosperity is the wealth of humanity. In each case human energy provides.

Saul means *the destroyer, the sepulchre*.

King of Edom—the *red-man*.

Isaiah 34 declares that the destruction of the redmen was premeditated, he not belonging to any of the civilized races of Europe.

Saul becomes *Paul*, meaning the *church worker*.

This is a sinister thing. Saul is Hebrew for Paul, hence the grave becomes an agent of the church in two ways. In one instance it removes objectionable opponents, and, in the other, provides an income for the church through the dispensation of condolence.

Grief, sorrow and pain are church commodities for which it has a ready sale.

David the beloved, symbolizes *love*. This most sinister character in the Bible is named as the father of Jesus Christ. (Matt. 1:1.)

David was a *drunkard*, a confessed *brigand*, a *murderer*, and a *profligate*. Read (II Sam. 11.)

Solomon, recompense, symbolizes *wisdom*. He is the son of David by his concubine, *Bathsheba*, the wife of Uriah, whom David had murdered in order to take his wife to himself.

"Thou hast killed Uriah the Hittite with the sword, and hast taken his wife." (II Sam. 12:9.)

Uriah means *light*, symbolizing *intellect*.

Bathsheba means an *oath*.

Hittites mean *those broken by fear*.

Solomon, the offspring, symbolizes *wisdom*, this being the *recompense* for an oath-bound alliance with the church.

Sol-om-on, all have reference to the *sun*, and *sunlight*, as the dispenser of all visible things contributing wisdom and knowledge to human understanding and intellect.

Sol means the *burning sun*.

Om means the feminine sun, the *moon*, the generative power of the mother.

On means *pain, force*, and *iniquity*.

That *on* means the vision made possible by the sun, is evidenced by the fact that *On* is the grandson of *Reuben*, meaning *vision*, and son of *Peleth, freedom*.

In the Greek, *On* means *Heliopolis*, the *"City of the*

Sun," noted for its learning, temples, shrines, monuments, and religious schools.

So much for the *love* and *wisdom* of this freak institution.

Love is vulgar animalism.

Wisdom is a monopoly.

But prophecy is a more far-reaching thing, and preconceives human conditions which may be brought about by force, by religious and political powers. Prophecy as prediction of mysterious fulfillments is a bald fake.

"Wherefore, behold, I send unto you prophets and wise men." (Matt. 23:34.)

Let us analyze the prophets of the Bible. To begin with, prophecy is a coercive thing. See Deut. 18:20. Death is the penalty for uttering words not put in the prophet's mouth.

"When a prophet speaketh in the name of the Lord, if the thing follow not, nor come to pass, that is the thing which the Lord hath not spoken, but the prophet hath spoken it presumptuously: thou shalt not be afraid of him." (Deut. 18:22.) Fulfillment also is a coercive thing. (Matt. 1:22.)

The Major Prophets—Passive

Isaiah, salvation of the Lord.
Jeremiah, grandeur of the Lord.
Ezekiel, strength of the Lord.
Daniel, judgment of the Lord.
Hosea, help of the Lord.
Joel, will of the Lord.
Obediah, servant of the Lord.

The Minor Prophets—Active

Jonah, he that oppresses.

Micah, he that humbles.

Nahum, he that comforts.

Habakkuk, he that persuades.

Zaphaniah, he that discovers secrets.

Haggi, he who impresses.

Zechariah, he who remembers.

Malachi, God's messenger.

Here we have a set of passive prophets, and a set of active prophets, suggesting anything but religion. The writers of these books of the Bible knew this.

We may now pass into the New Testament, expecting to find a continuance of this humbuggery.

The Twelve Apostles

Simon, hearing, obedience.

Called *Peter,* from *pater,* the enduring father or *high priest.* Called also the *rock,* meaning an *eagle,* the Egyptian *Roc.* St. Patrick is *St. Pet-rock.* Peter allegedly founded the Christian church among the Jews. (Acts 2.) Not the Gentiles. Spokesman of the apostles. (Acts 10.)

Andrew, Peter's brother, meaning *manly.*

James, son of Zebedee.

James merely brings forward into the new administration, *Jacob,* meaning to *supplant,* or *usurp* by trickery. *Zebedee* means *God's abundant portion.* He is a fisherman of *Galilee,* meaning *revolution.* Husband of *Salome, Salmon, reward.*

John, brother to James, son of Zebedee.

> *John* means *God's gift.* He is Johanan, *God's mercy.* Contraction of *Jehoh-anan. Anan* means *cloud, prophecy.*

Philip, warlike. He comes from the *house of fruits.*

Bartholomew, a *son that suspends the waters.*

> *Waters* mean *multitude of people. Suspend* means to *render innocuous.* The massacre of St. Bartholomew, in Paris, Aug. 24th, 1572, was one of the most henious crimes charged to the Christian church. Seventy thousand men, women and children were wantonly murdered by the mob led by priests.

Thomas, a twin, found.

> Greek name Didymas.

Mathew, gift, given, reward.

> Contraction of Mattathias, father of the *Maccabees,* meaning *the hammer.* The original name is *Levi,* the *tax-collector of Capernaum. Levi* means *associated, restraint. Capernaum* means a *place of repentance.*

James, same as *Jacob, usurpation.*

Lebbaeus, a *man of heart.*

> Also called *Thaddaeus, wise, that praises.*

Simon, the Canaanite.

> *Simon* means *obedience. Canaan* means *merchandising* and *trading.*

Judas Iscariot, betrayer.

> *Judas* means *praise. Iscariot* means the *cities, the callings, man of the bag, hire, or murder.* A man of Damascus, meaning *a sack full of blood.*

Why should they select this grewsome character as the last of Christ's apostles? Merely to make the betrayer a horrible example.

There is absolutely no intimation of religious sentiment in this sordid aggregation. Not one of these characters ever lived, and there exists not one iota of evidence to justify their recognition as a part of the Christian forces other than indicating a secret scheme concealed in this code system.

This is Christianity. If you are a Christian it is your religion. By it you may classify yourself, and, if you so desire, continue to foot the bill.

We may well close this book by a brief review.

When the darkness of night settles over the earth like a sombre and sickening pall, ghouls prowl in search of their prey, and slimy things creep forth from secret places to spawn, and to exhale their fetid breaths into the pure atmosphere to humiliate nature and confound her greater creations.

Back there in antiquity, mankind, covered with hair, eager eyed, in like manner peered forth from their caves to wonder at the glories of the rising sun of civilization. Seeing that the light was something to reveal to them new, and hitherto unknown, wonders, and feeling the friendly and soothing influence upon their own conscious ignorance, they stood in the open and marveled at the phenomena about them. Constructive thought seized upon the virgin mind and reason was born. Vision had become the master passion of the world; to see was to know and to understand; demonstration was the hall-mark of all true knowledge. Men climbed rapidly from the dark cavern life to the glorious balconies of science, philosophy and the knowledge and wisdom of nature. The sun of human intellect had risen above the horizon of the lower creations, and man stepped forth as the flower and fruit of natural evolution, and reached out to grasp the blessings of the tree of knowledge.

The heavenly bodies, suns, moons and stars, drew near to the earth, and men studied them, learned their habits, and became familiar with their influences upon the living things upon their own planet, and astronomy became an understandable subject of thought.

Men searched out the marvelous correlations between the elements of which ponderable, material things are composed, and chemistry became an exact science.

The physical and organic beings upon the earth were subjected to the scrutiny and examination of learned men, and physiology and anatomy became a part of the essential studies of mankind to determine the line of least resistance to a higher state of being.

This natural progression in the enlightenment of men was as definitely defined as was the course of the sun across the clear and unclouded sky. Its purpose was equally apparent. Nature had originally intended to endow man, as the highest type of living evolution, with a subjective mental intelligence to light him through periods of clouded skies, and the darkness of night. Reason was to be the sun of the night, to enable men to plan for the new day while resting and recuperating their physical bodies. Knowledge was to be the fuel of this mental fire, and potential wisdom was the storehouse of this fuel.

All mankind was to participate in a common understanding of all that was knowable, in order to fulfill the original purposes of a preconceived, natural evolution from the first spark of life in physical being to the highest type of the mentation in matter.

Thus was man lifted out of the lower forms of creation. It was never intended that he should involute or be debased into evil conditions, or remain in a state of helpless ignorance. Every facility was provided by nature to promote him to the higher state, as is clearly evidenced by his external sense organs. If these agencies are not supplied with stimulating food they remain dormant, and will not execute their natural, educational functions.

It was intended, from the first respiration of living being, that the parent should teach the offspring, setting the child free upon its becoming self-sustaining. The mother bird feeds her young, and teaches them the use of their wings, then pushes them out of the nest. Even the tree sustains its fruit, from the period of blossom till it ripens, then it releases it to the earth to reproduce its kind.

Thus the traditional story of nature is recorded in the visible life upon the earth, and the minds of living creatures are cultivated by mother earth until abstractive reasoning and constructive thought set them free.

The adolescent period is the speculative period, when experience and new contacts teach the most enduring lessons. The child touches the glowing fire to learn that nature forbids this contact, and begins to wonder why.

Thus the mental powers of all animated nature

were progressively brought forward, each generation being wiser than the past, until natural education culminated in the super-mind of man.

This natural process of traditional understanding drew man forth from the protection of the trees, caves and flight, and placed in his hands wit and cunning with which to protect himself from surrounding dangers, and thus was the law of the survival of the fittest vindicated, and evolution perfected.

It is criminal to say that nature intended that man should apply these laws against his own kind. The survival of the fittest is based upon conflict, while the goal of evolution is peace and harmony, which may only exist between units of like species.

Freedom of action gives license to speculate beyond the speculative period, and evil conditions arise from involution in individual thought. Such diversions from the normal purpose of evolution break the natural trend towards perfection. Confusion and mixture take the place of continuity and progression. If we break the course of a placid stream following a definitely established channel, it becomes turbid, and quarrelsome, as it spreads out, or piles up, to overcome the obstruction and re-establish its peaceful course —this is primitive rebellion.

The course of civilization is identical with this simple law. Nature originally gave to the animals vision to see the examples she sets; hearing, to take the place of vision in darkness, and other senses to, in like manner, serve the physical body. Like the foolish child who touches the fire the second time, the being who refuses to follow the dictates of reason must suffer the consequences of indiscretions.

He who diverts the stream from its natural course is responsible for its meanderings. Again the same law applies to the diversion from its natural course of human progression.

The evidences are multiple, that the world had progressed to a high state of learning, with natural laws and lessons the basis of profound understanding and knowledge, when an abnormal interruption in its natural course broke the continuity and cast the whole world into a state of mixture, confusion, oppression, trouble, affliction, adversity, ignorance, and destructive warfare.

Who will say that nature purposely brought about this desolating condition? Wherein is the sense, reason or logic of such inconsistency?

Those who declare that these conditions do not exist are not worthy of a thought. History is made of authentic records of its truth, and authentic and true history traces it all back to its origin, and to a perverse system which premeditated the identical evils which beset the world. It had a specific object and purpose. It openly challenged nature; cursed her science and philosophy, deliberately confiscated its vast accumulation of wisdom and knowledge, and destroyed men and institutions daring to oppose it by attempting to re-establish the natural avenues of universal education.

This horrible debauch was indulged in by abnormal and sinister forces—men soured against the world and balked in their desire to classify men in a manner to place over the common producing masses super-lords.

These men were fanatics but not fools. They deliberately conspired to insult nature, and deceive men, by a violation of the confidence placed in mankind by nature, that they would not abuse the liberty which accompanied their emancipation from the lower animal kinds by virtue of a super-mentation, of which reason was the fruit.

The origin of this break in the natural continuity may easily be traced to sulking, filthy, unsentimental, selfish, so-called monks, who, not being satisfied to follow the dictates of nature, in her forward impulse, chose to physically involute, returning to the caves and crevices which were the former abodes of cowardly beasts and slimy monsters, there to rot in seclusion while recording their vituperations against the natural progression of humanity towards a higher and better state of being.

Well did they know that mimicry is a law of nature, and that example is the most potent teacher of unthinking ignorance; hence, they set the example of going back to the cave to start all over again in darkness. Their goal was the ruling of the masses by super-men-gods.

The invention of gods was a curse to humanity.

Two things were absolutely essential to prosper the exploitation.

The accumulated wisdom of the age had to be destroyed, and established educational systems broken up.

The submersion of mankind in darkest ignorance,

symbolizing the night of human intellect, was a basic necessity.

Of necessity, this involved some deep and sinister motive. Moreover, it had to be concealed in secrecy and mystery to make it correspond with the cave and the night. It was a figurative romancing from its earliest conception. The ecclesiastical days in Genesis begin with the night, nature manifests with the sunrise.

The motive is immediately revealed in the name it selected for the mother organization—*Ecclesia.*

The *Ecclesia* was the legislative body which ruled ancient Athens.

It needs no abnormal mentality to grasp this; human control was the prime asperation.

It is important to observe that the ecclesiasts boldly plagiarized every important theory and doctrine they advocated.

It required about five hundred years for ecclesiasticism to suppress gnosticism and confiscate its wisdom, which was the accumulated knowledge of the world at that period.

That empire was its goal is equally well recorded by authentic history, the *temporal power* of the church over civil rulers enduring for nearly five hundred years.

The secondary motive was to amass wealth and acquire worldly grandeur. This requires no especial elucidation; the church at large is the wealthiest institution in the world. Untold billions have been turned into its coffers without public accounting.

This is the natural result of control over the peo-

ple. Every dollar of this wealth has been coined out
of human energy, causing poverty and slavery to become established human institutions.

So much for the motives; let us examine the means.

History definitely defines a period of abject ignorance when education was forbidden under penalty
of death.

It is interesting to review the course of this monster in the early history of the Christian period.

The night time of the beginning comprises about
one thousand years, beginning about 486 A. D., and
lasting till 1495. Despite the fact that at the beginning of the Chrisian period the most brilliant scientific and philosophical wisdom prevailed, during this
dark age all humanity groveled in abject ignorance,
not even princes and prelates were permitted to learn
to read or write. All scientific research was forbidden, and a drastic censorship was placed over all literature. Only that which was prescribed by the
church was even permitted to be in the possession of
the people.

The power of the popes was an insult to nature
and decency, making cowards of men.

708. The custom of kissing the pope's toe was introduced. It inspires a sense of disgust and
contempt to realize that the rulers and nobles
of the earth indulged in this filthy practice.
But it was through fear more than venera-
tion. It is a contemptible god who requires
such debasement of manhood.

780. Vanity is a cardinal element with popes. Adrian
I caused money to be coined with his name.

And it became a fad to adopt some fictitious name upon being elected pope.

800. Traffic in sin by the sale of indulgences in crime began under Leo III.

1054. Pope Leo IX kept a standing army.

1077. Pope Gregory VII obliged Henry IV, Emperor of Germany, to stand three days in the depth of winter, and barefooted, to kiss his foot and implore his pardon.

1079. The pope's authority was fixed in England.

1161. Henry II of England held saddle stirrup for Pope Alexander III to mount his horse.

1191. Pope Celestine III kicked the Emperor Henry VI's crown off his head while kneeling, to show his prerogative of making and unmaking kings.

1226. The pope collected the tenths of the whole kingdom of England.

1493. After the discovery of America, Pope Alexander VI granted to the Portuguese all the countries to the east, and to the Spanish all the countries to the west of Cape Non, Africa, which they might conquer.

1517. Pope Leo X went into partnership with the devil by publishing the sale of general indulgences throughout Europe, thereby bringing about the reformation. And so on down the line.

Reader, do you realize that this was only four hundred years ago, and that the United States is now about 150 years old? This is well worth thinking about. A hundred years is a small thing to ecclesi-

asticism struggling for universal control. It is absolutely devoid of honor and conscience. As long as
the ignorant mob sustains it, it will cling to the original determination to rule or ruin, therefore ignorance
is as essential to this invisible power today as when
the exploitation was first conceived.

Let us go back to that beginning to see if we may
take a closer view of the originators of this tremendous
scheme to supplant normal human governments.

Who were the monks, the alleged authors of Christianity?

From the Greek we have *monachos,* meaning *soli-
tary.* They originally hibernated in concealed caverns.

Monk, one of a male community inhabiting a monastery, and bound by vows to a life of celibacy and
religious exercise; a religious recluse or hermit. To
this definition add, mean, hatred and fanaticism.

Insofar as this explanation is concerned it means
nothing to society.

To whom does the monk make his vows? To a
superior. From whom does the superior derive his
authority to make such vows binding? From no one
but his own god, created in his own freak imagination. Most of these vows are treasonable to established governments.

Religious means one who has taken monastic vows,
and it is a significant fact that ecclesiasticism found
it essential to absorb the monastic orders before it
could safely launch its Christian scheme. Moreover,
it is amazing that the so-called Christians and Gentiles
have been so gullible as to kneel to the god of the
Jews, fictitious Jews at that. The Jewish history in

the Old Testament is bald-faced false-pretense. Not one Hebrew character ever existed.

We have seen that ecclesiasticism is the plagiarized Ecclesia, or legislative body of ancient Athens.

We have seen that *Jesus* is but the Greek form of *Joshua*, the Jew Savior.

We have seen that Christ is not a proper name at all.

What, then, are the Christians worshiping?

What are they paying money into the church for? Why do they maintain this freak thing?

The answer is simple.

It is an hysterical disease which has taken permanent hold upon certain types of people. They are intolerant, bigoted and fanatical hypocrites. They are so terrorized they dare not withdraw from the church. That threat of the damnable excommunication has assumed a multitude of forms, and the followers of the fabulous Christ, while cringing under the whip of the church, become embittered against those who are not so enthralled, and they bend their greatest efforts towards surrounding free humanity with absurd and senseless restraints. Mean and selfish themselves, they cannot bear to see others enjoy life.

The churches stand as the greatest menace to the best interests of humanity, and good human government and enlightenment.

This is our indictment. Let the world choose its future course.